# Life Skills Activities for Secondary Students with Special Needs

## DARLENE MANNIX

### Illustrations by Tim Mannix

**THE CENTER FOR APPLIED
RESEARCH IN EDUCATION**
West Nyack, New York 10994

**Library of Congress Cataloging-in-Publication Data**

Mannix, Darlene.
    Life skills activities for secondary students with special needs /
Darlene Mannix ; illustrations by Tim Mannix.
      p.  cm.
    ISBN 0-87628-541-8
    1. Handicapped teenagers—United States—Life skills guides.  2. Life
skills—Study and teaching (Secondary)—United States.  3. Life skills—
United States—Problems, exercises, etc.
I. Mannix, Tim.  II. Center for Applied Research in Education.  III. Title.
HV1569.3.Y68M363  1995                           95-12270
371.91—dc20                                   CIP

Printed in the United States of America

10   9   8   7   6

ISBN 0-87628-541-8

**THE CENTER FOR APPLIED RESEARCH
IN EDUCATION**
West Nyack, NY 10994

On the World Wide Web at http://www.phdirect.com

# ABOUT THE AUTHOR

Darlene Mannix has been a teacher in public and private schools for the past sixteen years where she has worked with students of all ages who are at-risk, language disordered, and emotionally, mentally and learning disabled. Prior to completing this book, she taught alternative education classes for middle school students.

Ms. Mannix holds a Bachelor of Science degree from Taylor University and a Master's in Learning Disabilities from Indiana University. She is an active member of the Council for Exceptional Children.

Ms. Mannix is the author of several books published by The Center for Applied Research in Education: *Oral Language Activities for Special Children* (1987), *Be a Better Student: Lessons and Worksheets for Teaching Behavior Management in Grades 4-9* (1989), *Life Skills Activities for Special Children* (1991), and *Social Skills Activities for Special Children* (1993). She is also the author of several workbooks published with other companies that deal with reading, behavior management, and forms for teachers.

This book is affectionately dedicated to

**Adventure Road**

the horse that a little girl dreamed of many years ago, and to

**Terry Stephenson**

teacher, trainer, coach, philosopher, magician, and friend.
Thanks for putting it all together for me!

# ABOUT THIS BOOK

*Life Skills Activities for Secondary Students with Special Needs* is a resource for teachers, counselors, parents, and others involved with instructing adolescents with special needs. You will find a unique collection of illustrated activity sheets, discussion questions, applied exercises, and evaluation suggestions for focusing on a particular life-skill objective. The book is divided into seven sections with a total of 190 specific activities, each of which can be taught to a group of students or modified to meet individual needs. Extension activities are presented as optional lessons for class use, depending on time, needs, interests, and students' abilities.

## Why Teach Life Skills?

As children mature, their life needs change. Adolescents need to develop a variety of skills as they prepare to complete their formal education and look forward to entering life beyond school. They must be prepared to possibly face the world of work, take on responsibility for a family, and make decisions ranging from what to wear that day to solving problems on the job. At the same time, they must come to terms with living with themselves – figuring out who they are, what they are capable of achieving, devising their own value system, and enjoying their uniqueness as a person.

Schools have become so much more than institutions for learning to read, write, and do calculations. It is at school that many children learn to operate in a cooperative group, bargain collectively, struggle with peer pressure, ask questions, solve problems, and think about life beyond the next ten minutes. While the primary objective of schools is to educate children, the concept of "education" has broadened to include social skills, vocational skills, and other skills formerly outside the realm of traditional education.

## Who Will Benefit from This Book?

The activities in this resource are directed towards students with special needs in grades 7 to 12. Some activities may be too juvenile or not applicable to any given grade; however, there are alternative activities and ideas suggested for you to consider for use with your students. Modifications can easily be made on the activities for adapting them for individual/classroom use, emphasizing oral discussion rather than requiring written responses, allowing the student to use his or her creative abilities to demonstrate mastery of the objective, and involving all students in some aspect of experiencing the life skill.

## What Will You Find in This Book?

*Life Skills Activities for Secondary Students with Special Needs* is divided into the following seven sections:

**Interpersonal Skills** – 30 lessons covering the areas of considering one's uniqueness and the uniqueness of others, friendship skills, and being part of a family

**Communication Skills** – 15 lessons to teach understanding others, expressing oneself, and resolving conflicts

**Academic and School Skills** – 32 activities in the subjects of reading, writing, math, and study skills

**Practical Living Skills** – 39 activities for getting information, managing money, traveling, driving, and managing a home

**Vocational Skills** – 22 lessons that introduce students to recognizing present skills and interests, using school records to plan, and entering the world of work

**Lifestyle Choices** – 27 activities for forming values, inventorying one's personal habits, considering sexual issues, having a good reputation, and recognizing and dealing with stress

**Problem-Solving Skills** – 25 lessons that involve handling problem situations, making decisions, using resources, setting goals, and taking risks

Each activity contains the following components: (1) an objective that specifies the focus of the lesson; (2) brief comments about the importance of the objective; (3) one or two introductory activities that can "ready" the class to pay attention to the primary activity; (4) a ready-to-use worksheet (with accompanying answers, materials list, and discussion questions); (5) several extension activities that can be assigned on an "as needed" basis and may require additional class time; and (6) evaluation activities that can be assigned as a quiz, objective check-up, or simply for a quick review of the material.

A list of parent activities and suggestions is included in this introduction. These activities can be reproduced and given to parents to use in conjunction with the activities being worked on in class. You may also wish to add activities of your own to the list as well as include some of the reproducible activity sheets to provide extra reinforcement of newly learned skills.

## Summing Up

*Life Skills Activities for Secondary Students with Special Needs* is a resource for educators, counselors, parents, and others who are interested and involved in helping adolescents with special needs. Life skills for this age group include not only school skills, but vocational skills, problem-solving skills, interpersonal skills, and communication skills. All of the lessons you find in this book can be tailored for many age and interest groups, and include several types of activities. Good luck to you and your students!

*Darlene Mannix*

# CONTENTS

## Section I
## INTERPERSONAL SKILLS                              1

### Uniqueness of Myself and Others

### Friendship Skills

### Being Part of a Family

## Section II
## COMMUNICATION SKILLS                             75

### Understanding Others

## Section III
# ACADEMIC AND SCHOOL SKILLS     117

## Section IV
# PRACTICAL LIVING SKILLS     201

# Section VI
# LIFESTYLE CHOICES 369

## Section VII
# PROBLEM-SOLVING SKILLS     449

# PARENT ACTIVITIES AND SUGGESTIONS

## Section I – Interpersonal Skills

### Uniqueness of Myself and Others

1. Ask your child to tell you why he or she is unique.

2. Make sure you introduce your child to adults. Use that opportunity to add a positive comment about your child. Make your child feel important, worthy of being introduced to someone.

3. Praise your child when you catch him or her doing something thoughtful or kind to others.

4. Model "acts of kindness" by plotting to do something nice for someone else. Involve your child even if it is just to inform him or her that you are planning something.

5. Make it a family project to go to the library to get books to research something that is of interest to your particular background – an important leader of your ethnic group, a cultural tradition, a recipe, etc.

### Friendship Skills

1. Encourage your child to host a party. Include invitations, a "theme," decorations, and whatever else will make this a memorable event.

2. Talk to your child about gangs in your community. Keep communication lines open. Is this a real threat?

3. Find out who your child's best friends are. Invite them over and get to know them.

4. When friendships change, encourage your child to view this as growth. Go over names of people who were good friends with your child as he or she was growing up.

### Being Part of a Family

1. Attend or plan a family reunion.

2. Get a family photograph taken. Frame it and display it.

3. Give your child a sense of family "history" by going through old family photo albums, videotapes, anecdotes, and any other pieces of memorabilia that will make the extended family more real to your child.

4. Have family "meetings" on a regular basis. Make this a time for family members to share their feelings and concerns. This may be a good time to revise the list of who does what chores around the house, bedtimes and curfews, and attitudes about being part of the family.

5. Make sure your child has someone he or she can talk to, whether it is a distant relative, neighbor, older friend, pastor, or someone who is a good listener and model for your child. It may be hard for a child to discuss family problems within the family, but make sure that there is someone whom the child knows is available when he or she needs to talk, and let him or her know that this is okay.

6. Don't hesitate to attend parenting workshops, family groups, or other community resources if your family is involved in a divorce or unhappy stepfamily relationship.

7. Make it a point to DO something as a family. Perhaps you could set aside one night a week for just the family to eat the dinner meal together – no activities, no guests, just the family. It could be something as simple as taking a walk together, playing a game, going to a movie – whatever works for your family.

## Section II. Communication Skills

### Understanding Others

1. After watching a television show, ask your child to summarize the basic plot. Did he or she tend to focus on one detail or was the child able to get to the "heart" of the show? Talk about what happened.

2. When events come up in the community or at school involving other people, ask your child, "How do you feel about that?" or "How do you think he or she feels?" Encourage your child to take the viewpoint of another person.

### Expressing Yourself

1. Have your child give you directions for how to get to specific destinations. Be patient – let him or her correct the mistakes.

2. When your child seems quiet or moody, ask him or her if he or she can put the feelings into words. Try to pull out what is on his or her mind and help make it into words or phrases that will help express the feelings.

3. If your child rushes when speaking or doesn't enunciate words, don't nag the child but use his or her words to repeat back what was said. When you repeat them back, however, speak clearly so the child will hear them spoken appropriately.

### Conflict Resolution

1. As conflicts come up, help your child (and family) by trying to draw on past successes to solve the problem. "This problem has come up before. What did we do last time that took care of it? Should we try it again?"

2. If you use strategies such as compromising, be sure to identify them as such to your child. Put labels with the techniques you are using so your child will be able to identify what you are doing.

3. Don't solve conflicts for your child, but help him or her think of alternatives.

## **Section III. Academic and School Skills**

### **Reading**

1. Make weekly trips to the library or bookstore. Second-hand bookstores sell recycled books very cheaply. Make it easy for your child to have access to good reading material.

2. If your child is interested, join summer reading programs at the library.

3. Hand your child parts of the newspaper that may have articles interesting to him or her – even if it is just the comics. Your child may also look up what's on television that night and read the synopsis of movies.

4. If your child is having problems with reading, look for a peer tutor who may be interested in helping out. Depending on the age of your child and difficulties, you may want to contact your child's school or teacher to get some ideas.

5. Older students who are soon going to be drivers might find the state driver's manual very interesting and important!

6. Order your child a subscription to a magazine that he or she chooses.

7. Be a good example of a reader by taking the time to read every day – demonstrate that this is a pleasurable activity (if it is for you).

### **Writing**

1. Insist that your child take phone messages for you and write down the information accurately.

2. Have your child add items to a weekly grocery list that may be held by a magnet on your refrigerator. As the milk gets low or the cereal box is emptied, have your child write the items on the list. He or she can probably figure out how to spell the words by looking at the empty packages.

3. Encourage your child to send away for free information. Provide envelopes and stamps, but let him or her address the envelope and fill out the information. Look for items in magazines, newspapers, or books that request a letter or form.

4. Your child may be interested in writing to a pen-pal from a different part of the United States or from a foreign country. Your local librarian can help you find information on pen-pals.

5. Keep a family journal or diary if you take a trip or attend a special event. Record the family members' impressions of the place visited, predictions about what might happen, anecdotes about the trip or event, and don't forget to include postcards or photos! This could become an heirloom!

### **Math**

1. Spend some time reviewing the day and thinking through the various tasks performed that required math skills. Have your child help you make a list.

2. If there is a particular area of difficulty in math, resolve to spend 10 or 15 minutes, twice a day, specifically working on that skill. You may need to get a set of flash cards, help from a friend, a special computer program, a math game, or whatever. Make it a fun and profitable time.

3. Check your child's math homework from time to time. Have him or her explain the steps involved in solving each type of problem.

4. Have your child take a calculator along on a shopping trip. Use it to figure out sales tax, amount saved on sale items, the total of purchases on that trip, or even just the amount that would be needed to buy some things you wish you could afford.

5. Make and refer to graphs and charts for all kinds of tasks – time spent each day viewing television, comparison of miles ridden on a bike each day of the week, whose day it is to clean out the cat litter box, etc. Show how these aids can be used to record information and make some tasks more efficient.

## Study Skills

1. Find a calendar that introduces and uses one vocabulary word a day. Have every member of the family learn the definition and use the word in conversation several times that day.

2. Know what your child's classes are in school and ask about them. Find out specifically what topics are being discussed. Look for interesting, related articles on television or in the newspaper.

3. To help organize a study room or office, have your child go with you to the office supply store to purchase items for his or her desk – a large calendar, a stapler, perhaps an in-and-out box, colored markers, a good desk lamp, and a bulletin board. Help make this an attractive, comfortable area.

4. Begin keeping a lookout for a good science fair project at the beginning of the year.

5. If television is a problem in competing for your child's time, make viewing time contingent on the report card that is brought home. Perhaps each "A" could correspond to 15-20 minutes of time each weeknight.

6. If possible, volunteer to help out in your child's school on an occasional basis. Let your child know that school is important to you.

7. If you go over your child's homework with him or her, highlight a question or two that your child may have about the material. Encourage him or her to ask questions in school. It is okay to raise a hand in class to ask questions as well as to answer them.

8. If you have a problem or disagreement with your child's teacher or principal, reserve judgment until you have heard both sides. Sometimes children do not bring home the entire story of a given incident. If you model disrespect for your child's teachers to him or her, how can you expect him or her to be respectful? Instead, remind them of the conflict resolution ideas that have already been discussed.

## Section IV. Practical Living Skills

### Getting Information

1. Invest in a set of encyclopedias. Use them for school projects, but also as interesting topics come up. Find out about lifestyles in other countries, information about interesting individuals, and all sorts of fun facts.

2. Encourage your child to watch at least a half hour of the news with you. Ask for his or her opinions about what is going on locally and nationally.

3. Buy your child a good dictionary and make sure that he or she can use it. There are lots of dictionaries available; search for one that is not too overwhelming, but is still useful.

### Money Management

1. Promise your child a 12% increase in his or her allowance if he or she can correctly calculate how much that would be.

2. Encourage your child to save up for a special project or desired item. Outline a savings plan: How much can be saved each week? Are there ways to earn extra money?

3. If your child is ready, open up a savings and/or a checking account. Go over the monthly statements with him or her and then have him or her give you a monthly report on the status of each.

4. Share (within reason) your bills and other household operating expenses with your child. Is a $390 electric bill high? How could you hold down the phone bill? By making a direct link between lifestyle and expenses required to live that lifestyle, the child may come to realize that everyday activities do affect those bills at the end of the month.

5. If you provide money for your child's lunches, food, gas, and clothing, have him or her become accountable to you. Ask for a weekly total of how much was spent in each category.

### Travel

1. Before taking a family vacation, map out the plan using an atlas. Locate interesting side trips that your family may want to take. Use your encyclopedias to get some background information on the destination.

2. Select several community destinations and have your child figure out how public transportation could be used to get there. Obtain a copy of time schedules for whatever system your community uses.

3. Keep a log book of expenses related to transportation. For example, could the same local trip be made by using public transportation systems (or riding a bike) rather than using a car? How much does a bus (or subway) pass cost?

### Driving

1. Let your child know how much your insurance rates will increase after he or she becomes a driver.

2. Become a good example of a driver in front of your child by wearing your seat belt, staying within the legal speed limit, and driving more carefully than you may normally tend to drive!

3. Make a plan for how you and your child will handle situations in which he or she may need a ride home from a party or other event in which drinking may be a part of the festivities.

4. Go over your personal rules for using your family car carefully and clearly with your child before handing over the keys. Is smoking allowed in the car? What about food? Who will pay for the next fill-up?

**Home Management**

1. Assign your child the task of changing all light bulbs when they have burned out.

2. Monitor your family's heat, electric, and phone bills for a period of several months. Analyze what factors may have influenced the total. What can be done to keep costs down?

3. Set aside one evening a week for your child to host and prepare a meal. Help in whatever way is appropriate, but let your child plan, prepare, and serve the meal. No unfavorable criticism allowed!

4. Collect favorite recipes (perhaps for nutritious meals) and save them in a special book for your child.

5. Have all family members take turns with doing washing, ironing, and sorting clothes.

6. If you use the classifieds to do some shopping, have your child make a few preliminary calls to find out: (a) cost, (b) condition of the item, (c) location of the seller, and (d) any other pertinent details. Let him or her become involved in tracking down that needed purchase.

## Section V. Vocational Skills

### Present Skills and Interests

1. If possible, take your son or daughter to work with you for a day.

2. Encourage your child to dabble in lots of hobbies, especially if they are not too expensive. Sometimes there are classes in music, dance, art, pet care, and other topics through a community agency. Encourage them to use this time of their lives to explore their interests.

3. Help your child analyze his or her likes and dislikes about certain occupations. Is there any common thread?

4. Praise your child for his or her accomplishments. He or she may not receive a trophy or blue ribbon for writing a short story or teaching a Sunday School class, but these are accomplishments that are noteworthy.

### School Records and Planning

1. Save school records. Sometimes there are patterns that can be seen when viewed over the course of several years. Do teachers keep making the same comments about your child's strengths, weaknesses, and general characteristics? What does this tell you?

2. Find out about after-school tutoring if your child needs some extra help in a certain subject. Often, an older student is willing to give some one-on-one assistance just for the experience.

3. Attend parent conferences. Bring a list of questions with you (if you have concerns) and make sure they are answered.

4. Encourage your child to finish high school, even if you did not. The job market is competitive; any edge will be a plus!

5. Encourage your child to become involved in extracurricular activities – sports, clubs, service organizations, etc. This is another way for him or her to find out what kinds of skills are important in reaching a vocational goal.

### Working

1. If your child is not old enough to have a work permit, you may be his or her first employer. Be businesslike – "hire" your son or daughter for specific tasks, evaluate the work, give feedback, and give a bonus for an exceptional job.

2. If summer jobs are hard to come by, keep an eye out for volunteer experiences. Students are often welcome to volunteer at hospitals, nursing homes, and even some child-care centers. Although the work is not being reimbursed, the time put in translates to work experience.

3. Be a model of responsibility for your child by having a good attitude. If your job is distasteful, it is certainly fine to explain your feelings, but if your job is necessary for your survival, explain to your child that work is part of life, you have a responsibility to arrive on time, work well, and so on.

4. Have your child practice filling out job applications.

5. Find out how your child views your relationship with your boss. What comments have you made that have contributed to this picture?

## Section VI. Lifestyle Choices

### Values

1. Think about your own value system and how you have arrived at that place. What shaped your life to this point? Are you passing your values down to your child?

2. When people in the news express strong statements, discuss the situations with your child. What would make someone donate all of his or her money to the poor/kill a doctor who performs abortions/protest the wearing of animals' furs/have seventeen plastic surgeries?

### Personal Habits and Choices

1. If you do not wish to have your child smoke cigarettes, this might be a good time to quit yourself.

2. Make sure your child takes a shower daily before school and at least leaves the house looking presentable. Students can be quite cruel to other students, especially where matters of hygiene are concerned.

3. Express your views on drinking, drug use, and cigarettes. Your child should know where you stand on these issues.

4. Involve the entire family in some sort of exercise program. Perhaps tennis lessons, jogging, bicycling, or walking through a park with the dog could be incorporated into a daily exercise routine.

### Sexual Issues

1. An unexpected, unwanted pregnancy is a situation that no one wants to face. If you suspect your child is contemplating becoming or is already sexually active, don't pretend it is not happening. If possible, have your child make an appointment with your family doctor for a frank discussion of consequences.

2. Make sure your child is familiar with the "facts of life," whether it is taught in Biology class or a booklet from the Girl Scouts. Know what your child is being taught, and be aware that your values may or may not be expressed.

3. Have your child spend some time babysitting an infant. Children may not realize that little babies are not the same as cute little dolls.

4. HIV and AIDS are real. Have your child separate the facts from the rumors and be able to explain what he or she knows about these diseases.

### Reputation

1. Ask your child what kind of reputation he or she thinks he or she has among the various social groups that are part of his or her life. Is this reputation deserved? Is it desirable?

2. Page through popular magazines, such as *People*, with your child. Discuss the current reputation of some celebrities. What factors contributed to this reputation?

### Stress

1. Be aware of what events and situations are stressful for your child's age group. What might seem trivial to you could be a major source of concern for your child.

2. Try to provide an outlet for physical energy for your child to relieve stress. This might be as simple as mowing the lawn or walking the dog through the park.

3. Find something funny about each day. Make sure you and your child have laughed about something you saw, did, experienced, or remembered.

4. If your child shows signs of depression, get help. Good mental health professionals can benefit a child who has difficulty coping. Check with your child's teachers, counselor, or pastor.

5. There are choices for everything we do; some just may not jump right out at you. Teach your child to think about alternatives to what may seem like a bleak, dead-end decision.

## Section VII. Problem Solving

### Handling Problem Situations

1. Take time to listen to your child talk about a problem situation. Don't interrupt! Just listen. He or she may solve the problem by hearing him- or herself talk about it.

2. Some problem situations are irreversible. Death, severe illness, transfers, failure in class, etc., are all negative experiences. But attitude toward the problem can be changed. Help your child understand that time can take care of some problems and a change in attitude can be achieved over time as well.

### Making Decisions

1. Allow your child to make many, many decisions throughout the day. What will he or she wear that day? When will that haircut be scheduled? Insist that he or she follow through on the outcome of the decision. By evaluating the outcome, he or she will determine whether or not it was a good decision.

2. You may want to give your child a list of tasks he or she is expected to accomplish in a given amount of time. Be clear on the tasks and the deadline, and then step out of it.

### Resource Management

1. Make sure your child has the necessary equipment or resources to accomplish his or her tasks. If he or she needs something, don't assume it and run out and get it for him or her. Rather, let the child take inventory of the needs for the job and make some decisions about the resources needed.

2. Use daily situations to talk about facts and opinions. The local newspaper and daily television news shows are good sources for sorting through these types of judgments. Letters to the editor often express strong opinions. Discuss these with your child.

### Goal-Setting

1. Set a family goal for each month. Write it down, hang it up, and refer to it often.

2. For fun, set "dream" goals and underneath them list your "realistic" or "probable" goals. It is fun to think big and dreams do come true!

3. Think small, too. Set a daily goal for whatever area you wish – perhaps just getting clothes laid out the night before for school or keeping the kitchen clean for a week. Help each other stick to reaching those goals.

### Risk-Taking

1. Have family members talk about the greatest risk they remember having taken. What made them do it? How do they feel about it now?

2. Have your child identify at least one positive risk he or she would be interested in taking. Maybe tennis lessons in a class in which the child doesn't know anyone else is a scarey task, but it would be worth the risk to learn to play tennis. Then work through that risk. Do it!

3. Spend a dollar a week on a lottery ticket for two months. Keep track of any winnings. Discuss with your child why people take lottery risks. Did you win enough to want to keep playing?

4. Say hello to someone you don't know. Offer to help with a package, open a door, or ask a question of a person whom you have never seen before. Have your child observe the reaction of the person. What type of risk was taken?

5. Everyone makes mistakes. Share some of yours with your child and be prepared to laugh, agonize, be embarrassed all over again, and then summarize the lesson that you learned (valuable, we hope!).

# Section I

---

# Interpersonal Skills

# I-1 Ethnic Groups

**Objective:** The student will identify five to ten major ethnic groups.

**Comments:**

The United States is a "mosaic" of many ethnic groups. Each group brings with it a wealth of characteristics such as language, traditions, stories, and other distinguishing features. It is hoped that each student will come to not only recognize many ethnic groups by name or appearance, but will also be able to identify cultural contributions.

**Introductory Activities:**

    a. Define *ethnic group* for students. (**A group of people with similar characteristics to each other such as ancestry, culture, religion, or having other ties.**)

    b. Have students list as many ethnic groups as they can.

    c. Have students list important or famous people from various ethnic groups.

**Activity:**

Students are to complete the worksheet "Ethnic Groups" by supplying facts about several different ethnic groups. You may wish to assign this as a project to complete over several days. Students may also work on the assignment in small groups if this is appropriate.

    **Materials:** encyclopedias, newspapers, library books

    **Discussion:** Have students or student groups share their findings with others. Encourage input from the entire class.

    1. How did you decide who to select as a person who represented each ethnic group?

    2. Which groups were harder to find information on? Why?

    3. What interesting cultural information did you find?

    4. What ethnic groups are represented in our community?

**Extension Activities:**

    1. Research stories or folklore from a selected ethnic group. How are they representative of this group?

    2. Interview someone from a particular ethnic group. What would you like to know more about? How does this person feel about being a member of this ethnic group?

    3. Make a mini-museum of artifacts or everyday items that certain ethnic groups use. Explain the history and use of each.

**Evaluation:**

    a. Give a simple definition for the term *ethnic group.*

    b. List five to ten different ethnic groups.

    c. Select one ethnic group and write a paragraph describing that group in terms of culture, language, or other characteristics.

# Ethnic Groups

**Directions:** Select five ethnic groups to study. You may wish to use some of the groups listed below, or feel free to use your own. Find out the information requested for each group.

*Examples* – Americans from Asia, Mexico, Ireland, Italy, Poland, France, Germany, Russia, Haiti, Africa, as well as Native Americans.

|  | 1 | 2 | 3 | 4 | 5 |
|---|---|---|---|---|---|
| **a.** Ethnic group | | | | | |
| **b.** Where located in the U.S. | | | | | |
| **c.** Where originally located | | | | | |
| **d.** Language spoken | | | | | |
| **e.** Physical characteristics | | | | | |
| **f.** Famous leader or person from this group | | | | | |
| **g.** Main religion | | | | | |
| **h.** Artistic contributions | | | | | |
| **i.** Interesting cultural facts (weddings, funerals, traditions, clothing, etc.) | | | | | |

# I-2 My Ethnic Background

**Objective:** The student will state and briefly describe his or her ethnic background.

**Comments:**

Many people identify themselves as being part of a particular ethnic group or originally descending from people of a certain country. Part of knowing ourself is being familiar with our ethnic background, particularly if customs and habits are still part of our day-to-day life. This lesson focuses on awareness of our individual backgrounds and taking pride in those origins.

**Introductory Activities:**

a. Have students indicate by raising hands if there are members of their family who recently (in the last generation or two) have come from another country. Discuss this event.

b. Have students volunteer to discuss and describe any traditions their family has celebrated. (Do not force students to participate; some may not wish to emphasize their differences!)

c. Ask students if any of them speak a second language or have family members who do. Have them describe how this is helpful or difficult.

**Activity:**

Students are to complete the survey "My Ethnic Background" by individually writing answers to the questions. They may wish to take the sheet home and have their family members help them fill out the information. Assure students that if they do not wish to reveal their personal lives in class, they will not have to, but encourage them to think about the questions and complete them – at least for their own benefit.

    **Answers:** will vary

    **Discussion:** Have students volunteer to share the information they completed on the worksheet. Emphasize that just because traditions may differ, this does not mean one is right or wrong.

    1. Was this information easy to obtain? Who were your sources?

    2. Are you part of a large ethnic group in your community? Do you feel you are accepted in the community?

    3. Do you feel your ethnic group is stereotyped in any way? How?

**Extension Activities:**

1. Have students compile family photographs or newspaper clippings on a poster or collage. Have students volunteer to explain to the class the significance of the people on the poster.

2. Have students collect newspaper articles featuring their particular ethnic group in the news.

3. Make a class map of the world highlighting the countries where students in the class originated from. They may be surprised to find out the diversity within even one classroom.

**Evaluation:**

    a. What is your primary ethnic background?

    b. How did your family originally come to live in the community where you now reside?

    c. What are some characteristics about your family that reflect your ethnic background?

**Teacher Notes:**

_____

_____

_____

_____

_____

_____

# My Ethnic Background

**Directions:** Complete this activity by focusing on your own family background. Perhaps you have two or more nationalities represented in your family's history. Talk to your parents, grandparents, or other relatives who can help fill you in on your past.

**Find out . . .**

What ethnic groups are in your family?

_____

_____

How did your family come to live where you do now? Did anyone come originally from another country?

_____

_____

What holidays or traditions do you celebrate? Are these different than your neighbor's customs?

_____

_____

Does anyone in your family speak a second language? What? When?

_____

_____

Are your closest friends of the same ethnic group as you? If not, does this present any problems? What?

_____

_____

If someone from another country were to visit your home, what do you think he or she would find most interesting? What object would he or she pick out as being unusual? Would any of your customs seem strange to that person? What?

_____

_____

# I-3 Spotlight on Me

**Objective:** The student will complete a project emphasizing at least three unique or personal characteristics or experiences.

**Comments:**

In this lesson, students can express themselves in whatever medium they feel comfortable. Students should think about ways in which they are unique and about things that have happened to them that may be unusual or different. Be sure that students feel comfortable sharing their projects with the class. Some may not wish to reveal too much of themselves to others too soon.

**Introductory Activities:**

a. Define *unique.* (**one of a kind**)

b. Have students describe ways that an individual could be unique or very different from others. (**physical characteristics, nationality, life experiences, family members, handicaps, intelligence, etc.**)

**Activity:**

**Materials:** arts and crafts materials, posterboard, markers, personal items, etc.

**Projects:** Will vary. Encourage students to be creative!

**Discussion:** Have students share their projects with the class. Encourage questions from others and display the projects around the room. If students do not wish to share extremely personal anecdotes, allow them to share general comments about experiences.

1. What does this project tell about this person?

2. What questions does this project make you want to ask?

3. Do you feel this project helped you think about what is unique about yourself?

4. How do you feel about your project? Proud? Silly? Happy?

**Extension Activities:**

1. Select a particular year – perhaps the year that most of your students turned 13. Research world and national events that occurred during that year. Have students make a timeline of what happened to them during that year. Compare how the same year contained different events and experiences for each person.

2. Put the names of each student in a jar and each day randomly select one. That student is "spotlighted" for that day – look for opportunities to compliment him or her, have the class give that student a round of applause, and give him or her a chance to do something special.

3. Make a description of each student, leaving out the student's name. How long does it take each student to guess who is being described?

**Evaluation:**

a. Define the word *unique.*

b. List three characteristics or events that make you, the student, unique.

# Spotlight on Me

**Directions:** Use your imagination to create a project that emphasizes your unique qualities or interesting things that have happened to you. Below are some examples. What can you tell about these individuals?

JASON

1. _____

_____

_____

_____

2.

_____

_____

_____

_____

JENNIFER
MY AUTOBIOGRAPHY

1980  1982  1985  1986  1992

3.

_____

_____

4.

_____

_____

# I-4 Spotlight on Others

**Objective:** The student will identify at least three positive characteristics of others.

**Comments:**

In this lesson, students are given well-known individuals to think about and describe. While the individuals selected are famous (because it is more likely that everyone will be familiar with them), the process of selecting positive attributes about others can be applied to anyone. Emphasize that you are looking for positive rather than derogatory adjectives. Every individual is capable of both!

**Introductory Activities:**

a. Have students come up with a list of ten to twenty famous people. This can be done individually (and then compare the results) or as an open-class brainstorming session.

b. Have students list ten to twenty adjectives that could describe one of the people on the list. Rate the adjectives as positive, negative, or neutral.

**Activity:**

Students are to compile a list of well-known people. Ideas can be used from the worksheet "Spotlight on Others" or students can use the list made in class as an introductory activity. Students are then to describe each person with three adjectives – and emphasize the positive or neutral.

**Answers:** *(example)* Wayne Gretzky – friendly, athletic, family oriented

**Discussion:** Students should share their adjectives on each of the individuals with the class.

1. Which people were easy to describe? Why?

2. Did you tend to use the same words to describe people? What kinds of words did you use?

3. Did you tend to describe the way the person looked?

4. Would it be easy to change all of the names on the list to people in the class and come up with positive adjectives for them? Would this be easier because you are familiar with each person?

**Extension Activities:**

1. Make a list of ten students who are a part of the student body at your school. List adjectives to describe them.

2. Start with an adjective (beautiful, smart, helpful) and think of someone you know who fits that word. Why?

**Evaluation:**

a. List three positive adjectives for a famous person.

b. List three positive adjectives for a person in your class.

c. List three positive adjectives for someone you admire.

# Spotlight on Others

**Directions:** Compile a list of ten to fifteen well-known people. What characteristics about each of these people makes them interesting or unusual? See if you can come up with three adjectives to describe each person on your list.

**To get you started . . .**

**1.** President Clinton

_____

_____

**2.** Stevie Wonder

_____

**3.** Julia Roberts

_____

**4.** Mother Teresa

_____

**5.** Wayne Gretzky

_____

**6.** Michael Jordan

_____

**7.** Christian Slater

_____

**8.** _____

**9.** _____

**10.** _____

**11.** _____

**12.** _____

**13.** _____

**14.** _____

**15.** _____

## I-5 Encouraging Words

**Objective:** The student will give examples of ways to encourage or praise others in given situations.

**Comments:**

People handle the skill of encouraging and praising others in different ways; some are comfortable with being verbally affectionate, others are not so vocal. But each individual can find a way to demonstrate encouragement to others in a manner that he or she feels comfortable with. In this lesson, students are to use their unique personal qualities to demonstrate how they could show encouragement to others.

**Introductory Activities:**

   a. Define *compassion* for students. (**showing sympathy towards someone else's misfortune or distress**)

   b. Have students give examples of situations in which someone has been distressed or needed encouragement.

**Activity:**

   **Answers:** *(examples)* **1.** We'll still stay in touch; I'm here if you need to talk. **2.** It was hard for me at first too, but let's keep trying, OK? **3.** Would you help me practice for my part? I could really use your help. **4.** May I get you anything? Would you like me to mow the lawn for you?

   **Discussion:** Have students compare their responses. Remember that each student might view the given situations a little differently – perhaps he or she has been through a divorce in the family or been the friend who was disappointed.

   1. Have any of these situations happened to you? Can you tell about how it made you feel?

   2. What if the people in each example really didn't want to talk about the problem? How would you handle that?

   3. Do you think people know if you are just saying something to try to be kind or if you really feel sympathetic toward them?

   4. Are there times when it is better to say nothing than to say something that sounds made up or insincere?

**Extension Activities:**

   1. Have students pair up and create a list of 50 to 100 phrases of encouragement such as: *Good job! Keep trying! You'll get it!* Write the phrase or words on colored posterboard or strips of construction paper and hang them around the room. You'll never be at a loss for something positive to say!

   2. As a writing activity, have students pretend to be a "Dear Abby" character and write their advice to problems that are submitted.

**Evaluation:**

   a. Give a simple definition for the word *compassion*.

   b. Give three examples of words or phrases of encouragement.

Name _____ Date_____

# Encouraging Words

**Directions:** Read and think about the situations given below. What is something that you could say to encourage, support, or praise the person in the example? Write your answers on the lines provided.

**1.** Your best friend just found out that his parents are getting a divorce. There is also talk of him moving to another state to live with one of his parents (who are not speaking to each other). What would you tell him?

_____

_____

_____

**2.** You are supposed to be helping your little sister with her math homework. You try and try to explain division to her, but she just doesn't seem to catch on. She'll listen for a little while, then just throw her paper down and give up, saying it's just too hard. What might you say to her?

_____

_____

_____

**3.** You and a friend both try out for speaking parts in the school play. The results are posted, and you made it! Your friend, however, did not get any part at all. The friend says that it doesn't matter, but you know better. What will you do or say?

_____

_____

_____

**4.** Your father just lost his job – at a company where he has worked for almost 20 years. He always seems to be in a bad mood and doesn't want to talk about it, especially to you. What will you say to your dad?

_____

_____

# I-6 Acts of Kindness

**Objective:** The student will identify an act of kindness that could be shown to someone else in a given situation.

**Comments:**

A popular idea going around is that of doing a "random act of kindness" towards others – usually a surprising and pleasant act, going way beyond what is necessary to show kindness to someone. The act of kindness is not expected, is not necessary, and is not even acknowledged in many instances. Encourage students to be creative in their ways of showing kindness towards others.

**Introductory Activities:**

a. Give students plenty of examples of random acts of kindness. An excellent resource is the small book *Random Acts of Kindness,* second edition, by the Conari Press Staff (Berkeley, CA: Conari Press, 1994). Encourage students to express their responses to some of the incredible deeds done anonymously by ordinary people.

b. Ask students to tell about acts of kindness that have been done to them.

c. Ask students to give examples of any acts of kindness that they have done to others.

**Activity:**

Students are to read each example of a situation in which an act of kindness could be done. Students should use their own unique personalities to come up with their responses. Encourage students to be creative, yet realistic. What would they really do?

**Answers:** *(examples)* **1.** Pay the cashier and don't tell the girl that it was you. **2.** Write Ben an anonymous note telling how much someone liked his work. **3.** Send the girl flowers. **4.** Make sure that Mrs. Miller receives a card from every student in her class.

**Discussion:** There is no single correct answer to these situations. Some students may be able to describe an act of kindness, but would never follow through on it. Ask students to be honest about their responses.

1. Would you want someone to know if you did something kind for somebody? Why would you want to be recognized?

2. How much did each of your deeds cost in terms of time/money/energy?

3. Does doing an act of kindness make the kind doer feel good? Is that why people do these things?

4. After hearing what other people came up with as far as ideas, would it change what you would do? Do you like other ideas better now than your own?

5. Which of these acts of kindness would you ever really do?

**Extension Activities:**

1. Plan to do a wild, exuberant act of kindness. Plot who you will target, what you will do, and then carry it out. What was the reaction of the person you targeted? How did it make you feel? Did you do it secretly or did you want to be discovered?

2. Read the book *Random Acts of Kindness*. Which were your favorite anecdotes? Why?

3. Compile a class book of acts of kindness. What starts happening when people start being outrageously kind to each other?

**Evaluation:**

a. Give a general example of a random act of kindness.

b. Give a very specific example of an act of kindness that you have personally been involved in.

**Teacher Notes:**

_____

_____

_____

_____

_____

_____

# Acts of Kindness

**Directions:** How could the person in each picture below demonstrate an act of kindness? On the back of this sheet, draw or write about a good example.

## I-7 Working in a Group

**Objective:** The student will successfully complete a given task as a member of an assigned group.

**Comments:**

An important life skill that carries through to adulthood is the ability to complete tasks as a member of a group. In this lesson, students are assigned to work as part of a group to complete a given task. After, students will evaluate their own performance and the ability of the group to complete the work.

**Introductory Activities:**

a. Have students list tasks that are easier to complete when they are performed by a group, rather than an individual. **(lawn work, cooking a meal, practicing for basketball, etc.)**

b. Have students think of why some tasks are easier when performed in a group.

c. Have students think of some drawbacks to working in a group.

**Activity:**

Students are to work on an assigned task as a group. Groups should be small, perhaps three to five students. All groups should work on the same task. Many tasks lend themselves to group work, but some ideas are:

- assemble a 100-piece puzzle
- color in a map of the U.S. with all states labeled
- solve a crossword puzzle
- complete a page of math problems (can be coded to reveal a secret message)
- write a poem (must be 20 lines long)

Do not give students any more directions other than to assign the task, help them complete the information on the worksheet "Working in a Group," and tell them the length of the time for this activity. Allow the students to proceed on the task with a minimum of teacher intervention. Just observe!

**Materials:** will vary depending on the task

**Discussion:** After all groups are finished (or time has run out), have students come together to discuss the following questions about working in their group.

1. Did your group select a leader? Who was it and how was he or she selected?

2. How did your group determine who would work on each part of the task?

3. Did anyone NOT participate? Did one person do everything? Was the work divided fairly?

4. What was fun or interesting about working in a group? Was your task completed efficiently because there were many workers?

5. What problems did your group encounter?

6. Which group put the most effort into the assignment? What good ideas did that group come up with?

7. If you had the same task to do over again with the same group, what would be done differently?

**Extension Activities:**

1. Repeat the assignment with another task and with different group members. Have students record or reflect on what was managed better on the second try.

2. Keep the same groups for several tasks, but alternate the students as being a leader of the group. Select one person from each group, take them aside and inform them that they have a special, secret task: to act as a "recorder," to note how many comments of praise or encouragement are given by each leader. When all students (except for the recorders) have been the leaders, have the recorders share their findings.

**Evaluation:**

a. Give an example of a task that is better performed by a group than an individual.

b. Give two reasons why group work can be more efficient than individual work.

c. Give examples of at least two problems that need to be worked out when a task is performed by a group.

**Teacher Notes:**

_____

_____

_____

_____

_____

_____

Name _____ Date_____

# Working in a Group

**Directions:** Each student will be assigned to work on a given task as part of a group. After the activity is completed, you will discuss and answer some questions about the activity. Fill out the information needed below before you begin.

Task:_____

_____

_____

Members of the group: _____

_____

_____

Materials needed: _____

_____

_____

Time allowed for the task:_____

_____

_____

Additional information/comments: _____

_____

_____

# I-8 Working Toward a Common Goal

**Objective:** The student will identify the importance of using strengths of self and others in working on completion of a common goal.

**Comments:**

In this lesson, the entire class is to work on a project. This could be a major project, incorporating a lot of time and energy, or a smaller project, completed in one lesson. Students should be aware of using the strengths of each member of the group to efficiently carry out the project.

**Introductory Activities:**

 a. Have each student list on a piece of paper two or three general strengths or skills they possess. These could be athletic, social, or artistic skills, as well as character strengths – organized, smart, patient, etc.

 b. On the same paper, have students classify themselves as someone who enjoys being in charge (a leader), or carrying out assigned jobs (a good worker), or working alone. Students may have characteristics of more than one group, but try to have them narrow it down.

**Activity:**

Inform students that the entire class is going to be working on one project for which they will all be accountable. The project assigned should be something that is large enough for many students to find an opportunity to participate. Be sure you have administrative and parental support for your activity! *Examples:*

- design a huge poster for the hallway to promote a school event (school fair, football game, library week, etc.)

- organize a schoolwide food drive to collect canned goods for a charitable organization

- design and sell T-shirts, bumper stickers, or pinned buttons with a school motto or logo on it

- challenge another class to a *Jeopardy*-type game dealing with information on a certain subject (history, geography, spelling words, etc.)

- organize an auction in which people donate items to be bid on to raise money for the local animal shelter

Have students complete the worksheet "Working Toward a Common Goal" with information supplied about the project that they will be doing. Encourage them to use the strengths and resources of the members of the class when organizing the project. Also, have them use ideas and lessons learned from the project in Lesson I-6 (working in a group) to include everyone in the project.

**Materials:** will vary depending on the project

**Discussion:** After the project is completed, have students discuss the questions on the worksheet and the following questions.

1. When you first began the project, how did you feel about doing it?
2. Now that you are finished, are you disappointed in the results or happy?
3. How did the class organize this task?
4. Were the individual strengths of the members of the class used to full advantage? How?
5. Was the project successful?
6. Did you choose a leader?
7. What would you change if you did this project again?
8. Did you like having one grade for everyone or did it seem unfair?
9. How did members of the class help each other?
10. What did you learn from this activity?

## Extension Activities:

1. For one week, have students work cooperatively on all assignments, knowing that they will be given one grade. After a week, evaluate the pros and cons of this type of structure.
2. Have students come up with a pool of project ideas and select a second class project to work on. Allow students to design, plan, carry out, and evaluate the project. Look for use of individual strengths and more efficient work.

## Evaluation:

a. Name two projects that can efficiently be completed as a large group.
b. List two personal strengths you can contribute to a large group project.

## Teacher Notes:

_____

_____

_____

_____

_____

_____

# Working Toward a Common Goal

**Directions:** Students will be working on a class project. All students will be expected to participate and all will be given one grade – the SAME grade for everyone. Complete the following information about your class project. After you are done with the project, you will be asked to discuss the activity.

Project: _____

_____

_____

Materials needed: _____

_____

_____

_____

Plan for carrying out the project: _____

_____

_____

_____

Who will do what: _____

_____

_____

_____

Time allowed for project: _____

_____

How will we evaluate the success of our project? _____

_____

_____

_____

# I-9 Serving Others

**Objective:** The student will provide examples of ways to deal with problem situations as a server in a courteous manner.

**Comments:**

Older students may already be part of the work force. They will no doubt encounter situations in which they must play the role of providing a service to customers. A difficult skill to learn is that of being polite to impolite people, patient with impatient people, and thinking clearly when they are not sure how to handle a situation. In this lesson, students are given the opportunity to think through how they would/could/should handle some customer relations problems.

**Introductory Activities:**

    a. Have students list some jobs or careers in which someone provides a service for others.

    b. Have students categorize the jobs on their list as those in which the server is seen as someone with a desirable job or one who commands respect (doctor serving a patient, accountant going over someone's taxes, etc.) as opposed to those in which the server is seen as someone who does not command respect (operating the drive-up window at a fast-food restaurant, perhaps babysitting?).

**Activity:**

Students are to assume the role of a server (a clerk, a waiter, a lawn worker) in the examples on the worksheet "Serving Others." They are presented with some problems from their customers and must think about how they would handle the situations.

    **Answers:** *(examples)* **1-A.** "I don't think that's really using the pencils in the way they were intended to be used. I'll check with the manager, but I don't think I'm allowed to refund your money." **1-B.** "I'll be happy to set this book aside for you if you like. Do you think you'll be back for it by Thursday?" **2-A.** "It's no problem – I can get you another drink and we'll just cook your steak a little longer." **2-B.** "Have a nice day. Good-bye." **3-A.** "I'll go over it again. Sorry." **3-B.** "Please let me know if you're not happy with my work. I'll try harder."

    **Discussion:** Have your students share their responses. Look for creative (yet polite) ideas. Encourage students to use their own unique abilities (sense of humor? patience?) to cope with these situations.

1. Which of these situations do you think would be the hardest for you personally to deal with? Why?

2. Would you tend to have more patience with the older people at their home than with the smart-alec boy at the restaurant? Would you tell either of them exactly what you think?

3. In which situations would you need to check with a manager or supervisor to make a decision?

4. What alternative behaviors did the class come up with instead of showing your anger or being as rude as the customer?

5. What similar situations have you ever been in?

**Extension Activities:**

1. Role-play the situations on the worksheet. Have different groups of students come up with several different endings to each example. Which are most productive?

2. Send students out "on assignment" to observe customers in a bookstore, a restaurant, or other place of business. Are most customers polite or are they demanding? How do the clerks handle themselves?

**Evaluation:**

a. Give three examples of jobs or careers that are based on providing a service for a customer.

b. Give two to three examples of courteous phrases that a server could say to an unhappy customer.

**Teacher Notes:**

_____

_____

_____

_____

_____

_____

# Serving Others

**Directions:** Pretend you are the provider of services in these situations. How would you handle each, remembering that: (a) you are supposed to be polite; (b) you expect people to respect you; and (c) you are being paid for this service. Write or draw your ideas on the back of this sheet.

**Situation 1: You are a clerk in a bookstore.**

A. Hey! These pencils broke when I hit my brother over the head with them. I want my money back!

B. What do you mean you don't take checks? That's really stupid. I don't have enough cash and I'm afraid this book will be gone by the time I can come back!

**Situation 2: You are a server in a restaurant.**

A. I didn't order a cola – I ordered a root beer! And this steak is too rare. I'm not paying for any of this.

B. Here's your tip – it's one penny at the bottom of this bowl of soup. Ha! Ha!

**Situation 3: You are doing lawn work for your elderly neighbor.**

A. You didn't trim those edges very well. See how they're all jagged.

B. When I was a boy, I'd pull weeds for 15 cents an hour. Nowadays kids want money for nothing. They are soooooo lazy!

# I-10 Being Sensitive to Others

**Objective:** The student will demonstrate sensitivity to problems of others by rating (0-5) and explaining the reasoning behind the score.

**Comments:**

It is a good human quality to be sensitive to the problems of others. On the other hand, it is good to be discerning as to the severity of the problem and the amount of sympathy warranted by the problem. Students are to compare the relative severity of the problems given in examples on the worksheet and to evaluate how severe the problem probably seems to the person giving the statement.

**Introductory Activities:**

a. Have students give examples of situations in which they felt unhappy, sad, or concerned about a problem that may have affected how they behaved on a certain day.

b. Have students discuss whether or not it is helpful for them to tell others when they are feeling badly or if they like to keep their problems inside them.

c. Have students offer names of people who they think of as being sensitive to others.

**Activity:**

**Discussion:** After students have completed the activity, compare their ratings on the examples.

1. What evidence did you consider in giving your ratings besides the words the person spoke? **(body language, tears, etc.)**

2. Which situations were you most sympathetic to? Why?

3. Would the teacher giving the test be sympathetic to any of these problems? Which ones?

4. What facial or body cues helped you determine how strongly the person felt about the situation? **(sweat, grimace, shaking, laughing, etc.)**

5. Did you tend to rate higher or lower than the rest of your class? Do you think this means you are a sensitive person *or* lack sensitivity?

**Extension Activities:**

1. Have students write a play or skit in which a character gives every excuse possible to get out of something that then turns out to be pleasant or a lot of fun.

2. Have students make a poster or graffiti board in which they make a "Top 10 List" of excuses to avoid a test (or other task).

**Evaluation:**

a. Rate yourself on a scale of 0-5 as to how sensitive you think you are to the problems of others. Justify your rating.

b. Give an example of a legitimate problem or concern that someone might have to which you would be sympathetic.

c. Give an example of a problem that is simply an excuse to avoid doing something.

Name _____  Date _____

# **Being Sensitive to Others**

**Directions:** All of the students portrayed below are supposed to take a huge final exam very soon. Each is dealing with some sort of problem that may affect how he or she will perform on the test. Give each person a score based on how important you think his or her problem is (from 0 = not important to 5 = very important). Then rate (0-5) how important you think the problem is to THAT PERSON.

|  | | **My Rating (0-5)** | **His/Her Rating (0-5)** |
|---|---|---|---|
| **1.** | My mother just found out she has cancer. How can I concentrate on names and dates for history? | _____ | _____ |
| **2.** | Darn! I broke a nail! I can't hold a pencil, much less do any writing! | _____ | _____ |
| **3.** | No sweat . . . I'll make sure I sit next to "Straight-A Julie" and have a good look at her paper. | _____ | _____ |
| **4.** | I always go blank when I have a test in front of me. I just know I'll mess up. | _____ | _____ |
| **5.** | I can't concentrate. I'm in LOVE with Terry!!!!!!!!!!!!! | _____ | _____ |
| **6.** | We have a test today? I guess I forgot to study again. Well, I hope I get Mr. Elliott again next semester when I have to repeat the class! | _____ | _____ |

## I-11 Being Friendly

**Objective:** The student will identify ways to show friendliness to others given specific situations.

**Comments:**

Not everyone is naturally friendly and outgoing. But even those of us who tend to be withdrawn and shy can learn to appear friendly to others simply by making the first nonthreatening move or just saying "hello." In this lesson, students are given examples of people who are somewhat approachable and would be good targets on which to practice developing this social skill.

**Introductory Activities:**

a. Have students list three to five people whom they think of as being especially outgoing and friendly.

b. Have students indicate by show of hands whether or not they would be the first one to speak if they passed: (a) a complete stranger on the street; (b) passed someone they recognized by sight but didn't know his or her name; and (c) passed someone unknown but who looked grumpy or distressed.

**Activity:**

Students are to draw or write their responses to examples on the worksheet "Being Friendly" in which a person could easily demonstrate initiating friendliness.

**Answers:** *(examples)* **1.** You could ask if the puppy is friendly and remark about how cute it is. **2.** You could smile at the girls and say "Hi." **3.** You could ask the man if he's in a hurry and would like to go in front of you. **4.** You could go up to your teacher and ask if he or she remembers you. **5.** You could offer to take your cousin outside to play catch. **6.** You could just say "hello" if he is busy, or ask for an autograph if it seems he is happy to have the attention!

**Discussion:** Have students compare their ideas to these situations.

1. Do you like it when people who are friendly approach you and begin talking to you *or* are you distrustful?

2. Do you think some people would rather be left alone than talked to? **(for example, the man in the grocery line)** How would you be able to tell whether or not someone would be approachable?

3. If the famous person in situation 6 looked as though he just wanted to go shopping, how could you show friendliness without being annoying?

4. Do you think young children in particular are taught to avoid strangers, especially ones who try to appear overly friendly?

5. Do you think the expression "Have a nice day" is overused and empty of feeling? What friendly expression might you use instead?

**Extension Activities:**

1. Have students make an assignment for themselves: to demonstrate/initiate a friendly behavior toward someone every day for a week. Have them record what they did, how they felt about, and how the person reacted. Does it get easier with practice?

2. Designate one person in your classroom each day to stand outside the classroom and greet every person who enters the class. This greeting could consist of a simple hello, shaking of hands, pat on the back, or whatever seems appropriate. How do students feel when they know they are going to be met with a (hopefully sincere) greeting before class each day? How does it feel to be the greeter?

**Evaluation:**

a. Give two examples of friendly, nonthreatening comments that you could make to anyone in any type of social situation.

b. Give the name of someone who you consider to be a friendly individual and explain why you think this.

**Teacher Notes:**

_____

_____

_____

_____

_____

_____

Name _____ Date_____

# Being Friendly

**Directions:** How might you show friendliness in each of these situations?

1. You are walking along the sidewalk and pass a woman who is walking an unusual little black puppy.

   _____

   _____

2. You are sitting in the park, reading a book, when two little girls go by, laughing, skipping and hopping.

   _____

   _____

3. You are standing in a very long line at the food store ahead of an old man who has two items in his cart.

   _____

   _____

4. You are at a party with people from your neighborhood and see your first-grade teacher.

   _____

   _____

5. You are at a family reunion (borrrrrrring) and notice that your younger cousin looks just as miserable as you are.

   _____

   _____

6. You are at the shopping mall when you notice the quarterback from your favorite professional football team walking around with his wife and children.

   _____

## I-12 Helping Others

**Objective:** The student will identify appropriate ways to assist others in given situations .

**Comments:**

It is a nice idea to think we can always be helpful to others; however, it is important to be cautious as well. Some situations exist in which we are unable to help and indeed, should not even attempt to dabble in something beyond our skills (car accidents, dangerous situations, etc.). In this lesson, students are to evaluate the given situations and decide what type of assistance is needed and who should provide that assistance.

**Introductory Activities:**

    a. Have students raise their hands if they would give a stranger verbal directions for how to get to the post office.

    b. Have students raise their hands if they would draw a map for someone who wanted to get to the post office.

    c. Have students raise their hands if they would allow a stranger to follow them while they were riding a bike to show that person how to get to the post office.

    d. Have students raise their hands if they would get in the car with a stranger who wanted to know how to get to the post office.

**Activity:**

There are different levels of involvement regarding how far someone will go to provide help for another person. On the worksheet "Helping Others," the student is to indicate what level of help he or she thinks is appropriate for the situations given. #1 indicates that the student would directly help the person; #2 indicates that he or she would find someone else to help; and #3 indicates that he or she would not become involved in the activity at all. Inform students that they are to select only *one* of the options. Their choices will be discussed.

    **Answers:** *(examples)* **1.** #2 – call 911. **2.** #2 – call a gas station if it looks like he needs help; he may be fine by himself. **3.** #1 – chase the dog away. **4.** #2 – offer to call someone for him. **5.** #1 – if you know how to do algebra! **6.** #2 – recommend a good French tutor. **7.** #2 – encourage him to talk to the school counselor. **8.** #2 – call a lifeguard if one is close by unless you know water safety. **9.** #3 – your help will probably not be necessary if the door swings open automatically. **10.** #1 – help her out. **11.** #2 – get a salesperson to help. **12.** #2 – encourage him to talk to someone; it sounds like there's trouble involved.

    **Discussion:** Although there is room for individual variety, probably most of the students will agree on the majority of the situations. Ask for their thinking on each.

1. How is situation 1 different from situation 2?

2. How would you handle situation 3 if your parents were home?

3. How would you handle situation 3 if you were home alone and it was night?

4. How are situations 10 and 11 alike and different?

5. Were there many people who used response #3 (avoid the situation entirely) for any of the situations? Do you think most people want to help others, even if it is just by referral?

6. Can you think of examples of #3-type situations that probably should be avoided?

## Extension Activities:

1. Make a directory of agencies, people, and local social services that can be used as a referral resource for several types of problems. What community services are there for helping students who are having financial, social, parental, drug, or school problems?

2. Interview your school counselor. Find out what types of referrals he or she deals with and what kinds of advice he or she would give for situations such as dealing with kids who are experiencing school and home problems.

## Evaluation:

a. Give two examples of situations in which you could provide direct assistance to help someone else.

b. Give two examples of situations in which you could refer a person with a problem to someone else.

c. Give two examples of situations in which you should not become involved.

# Helping Others

**Directions:** Read the following situations. In the space provided, write: **#1** if you would provide direct assistance; **#2** if you would refer the person to someone or something else for help; or **#3** if you would avoid the situation entirely.

1. You pass a car accident at night in which a woman is injured and bleeding. _____

2. You pass a car that is by the side of the road with a flat tire. A man is outside on the highway pulling out the jack from the trunk. _____

3. You and your little sister are walking through the park when a large dog runs up and begins to chase her. _____

4. An unfamiliar man comes to your door and knocks. You open the door and he says he has car trouble and wants to use your phone. _____

5. A friend calls and doesn't know how to do his algebra homework. _____

6. A friend of a friend calls and needs help on translating a paper from English to French. _____

7. A friend is thinking of running away from home because he can't get along with his parents. _____

8. You are swimming in the pool at the neighborhood park and see a little kid who looks like he is drowning. _____

9. A man in a wheelchair is approaching the door to the grocery store. You are several feet behind him. _____

10. In the grocery store, an elderly woman is trying to reach a box of cereal on a high shelf. _____

11. In a sporting goods store, a young boy is trying to reach a bowling ball on a high shelf. _____

12. Your best friend calls and says that he or she needs a lot of money in a hurry and begs you not to ask any questions. _____

# I-13 My Peer Groups

**Objective:** The student will define and give examples of members of a peer group.

**Comments:**

Peers have a tremendous influence over children, particularly as they enter adolescence. It is important for students to recognize that they are part of larger social groups and that these groups can and will affect them. In this lesson, students are to think about what people compose their peer groups.

**Introductory Activities:**

a. Have students list five or six of their closest friends.

b. Have students add to that list by including people with whom they spend a lot of time (because of the activity), though they may not necessarily be "friends" with them.

c. Define *peer* for students. **(someone who is equal to another person, either in social standing or because he or she is in the same age group or has the same status)**

**Activity:**

**Discussion:** Be aware that some students may be perceived as low status or outcasts within the group. You may not want to have students reveal the names they put on their worksheets. What is important is that each student is aware of his or her peer group(s).

1. Did you tend to write names of people who are the same age as you?

2. Except for item 3, did you tend to write names of people who are the same sex as you?

3. Do you consider yourself to be friends with everyone you wrote, or were there people who were part of your groups but not necessarily someone you were close to?

4. What does this phrase mean: "a jury of your peers"?

5. Do you think you would have the same names written if you filled this out ten years from now?

**Extension Activities:**

1. Make a banner or several separate posters of peer groups within the school. Use copies of yearbooks or newspaper photos to get you started (softball team pictures, pep club, etc.).

2. Have students bring in photographs that portray themselves with at least one or two other people. What is the common thread between the people in the photo?

**Evaluation:**

a. Define *peer* or *peer group*.

b. Give two examples of someone in your peer group and state why that person is considered to be a peer.

Name _____ Date_____

# My Peer Groups

**Directions:** Write the name of someone who fits the description of each comment below. Try to pick different people for as many as you can.

**1.** Someone who is the same age as I am:

_____

**2.** Someone who is interested in the same hobbies as I am:

_____

**3.** Someone who is the same sex as I am:

_____

**4.** Someone who gets about the same grades as I do:

_____

**5.** Someone who works with me or does about the same job as I do:

_____

**6.** Someone who comes from a family that is a lot like mine:

_____

**7.** Someone who is on the same team as I am:

_____

**8.** Someone who feels the same way I do about something very important to me:

_____

# I-14 What About Gangs?

**Objective:** The student will define and give examples of membership in an organized gang.

**Comments:**

Students are exposed all too soon to the influence of gangs. Some are part of the "wannabes" and do not realize the danger they are putting themselves in. Though students may view gang membership as powerful or prestigious, there are serious social and criminal consequences linked to gang activity. This lesson is primarily for discussion of students' perceptions, experiences with, and decisions about gangs.

**Introductory Activities:**

    a. Define *gang* for students. **(a group of people associated together whose activities are primarily antisocial and delinquent)**

    b. Have students list characteristics of gangs in general. **(wearing a certain color, special hand signals, signs, etc.)**

**Activity:**

    **Discussion:** Students may have had some exposure to or experience with gangs in your community. Some may act like it is "cool" to be part of a gang and will disagree with the comments on the worksheet. At your discretion, you may want to have students share their anecdotes about gangs. Be prepared to back up your opinion!

    1. What do you think are the good things a gang can offer a member? **(belonging, safety against others, etc.)**

    2. Can these good things be gotten in other ways? How? **(join a different group)**

    3. Do you think most kids who act like they are in a gang are truly gang members or are they "wannabes"? What's the difference?

    4. What consequences are there to committing a crime?

    5. What crimes are organized gang members often guilty of? **(drive-by shootings, knife fights, theft, etc.)**

    6. What would be a way to convince someone to stay out of a gang?

**Extension Activities:**

    1. Collect newspaper articles about gang activity. What type of activity is in your area or close to your community?

    2. If possible, arrange for an interview with someone who was or is somehow involved in a street gang. (Clear this with your administration first!) Has this been a positive experience for the person?

**Evaluation:**

    a. Define *gang*.

    b. Give two examples of positive things that gang membership seems to promise.

    c. Give two examples of negative consequences that can occur because of gang membership.

# What About Gangs?

**Directions:** Read the following comments about gangs. Circle "agree" or "disagree" to show how you feel about the comment.

1. There are gangs in my community.     **Agree**    **Disagree**

2. Organized gangs in the United States are in the business of crime.     **Agree**    **Disagree**

3. Gangs have special ways of showing membership, such as wearing a certain color or having a hand signal.     **Agree**    **Disagree**

4. People who join gangs want to belong to a group.     **Agree**    **Disagree**

5. Older gang members can recruit others by intimidation or by providing a sense of belonging.     **Agree**    **Disagree**

6. New members have to go through initiation to join some gangs.     **Agree**    **Disagree**

7. Once you join a gang, it is difficult to get out.     **Agree**    **Disagree**

8. People who join gangs have experienced some sort of hardship or abuse as a child.     **Agree**    **Disagree**

9. Some people act like they are members of a gang, but they are really not.     **Agree**    **Disagree**

10. Kids join gangs because they want to feel powerful.     **Agree**    **Disagree**

11. Joining a gang can be dangerous.     **Agree**    **Disagree**

12. Once you join a gang, you have lost your power to make choices.     **Agree**    **Disagree**

# I-15 Making Friends

**Objective:** The student will identify three to four ways to initiate a friendship.

**Comments:**

Some students have difficulty making friends. Perhaps they are shy, too loud, or simply try too hard. In this lesson, several ways to initiate a friendship are discussed.

**Introductory Activities:**

a. Have students list two people who have recently become their friends.

b. Have students write the names of two people whom they consider to be friendly.

**Activity:**

Students are to examine the ten cartoon situations on the worksheet "Making Friends" and evaluate how good of a way it is to initiate making friends with someone else. In some cases, "maybe" is an appropriate answer.

**Answers** *(examples)* **1.** No – may be too aggressive. **2.** Yes – acting first. **3.** Yes – go where people are. **4.** No – isolating self. **5.** Yes – acting friendly. **6.** Yes – being helpful. **7.** Yes – acting first. **8.** No – critical comment **or** Maybe – teasing in a friendly way. **9.** Yes – acting first. **10.** Yes – being resourceful.

**Discussion:** Students should be prepared to explain their answers and try to come up with some general ideas for making friends such as: look and act friendly towards others, include others, be available, go where other people are, and make the first move.

1. Which of the ways on the worksheet would you try?

2. Which of the students on the worksheet would you find irritating or offensive?

3. When is the last time you picked out someone whom you would like for a friend? How did you become friends?

4. Is it harder to initiate friendships with someone of the opposite sex?

5. If you are basically a shy person, what are some quiet ways you could initiate talking or contact with someone else?

**Extension Activities:**

1. Have students target someone whom they would like to befriend. Have them practice friendship-making skills to initiate contact with the person. Keep a journal of progress!

2. By secret ballot, have students write the names of three people in the class/school/group who they consider to be good at making friends. Analyze why these people are friendly.

**Evaluation:**

a. List three good ways someone could initiate a friendship with another person.

b. List one way that would probably *not* be a good way to make friends with someone else and explain why.

# Making Friends

**Directions:** Read each situation and decide if it is or is not a good way to approach someone to initiate a friendship. Write **yes**, **no**, or **maybe** on the line next to each item. Be prepared to explain your answers!

1. Hi! Let's be friends.

2. I need a study buddy for the test. Want to work together?

3. I think I'll join the volleyball team. It looks like it might be fun.

4. I'll just eat lunch by myself and work on my homework.

5. May I join you?

6. You look like you could use a hand. Would you like some help?

7. I'm having a party at my house after the game. Want to come?

8. You sure wear weird clothes.

9. Let's include the new kid.

10. Would you introduce me to your cousin? WOW!

## I-16 Qualities of a Good Friend

**Objective:** The student will identify several qualities he or she feels are important in a friendship.

**Comments:**

Many different qualities may draw friends together. Some are based on being thrown together in a time of crisis, having mutual interests, geographical convenience, or simply just enjoying the company of another person. In this lesson, students are to analyze qualities they feel are important in a friendship.

**Introductory Activities:**

a. Have students volunteer to tell about a particularly good experience they had with a friend.

b. Have students volunteer to tell about how a friend helped them through a difficult time.

**Activity:**

Students are to read over the list of suggested qualities on the worksheet "Qualities of a Good Friend" and rank from 1 to 5 (1 is the highest) those they feel are most important. They can add qualities to the list.

**Discussion:** You may want to take a quick class survey to find out which were the top three qualities selected. Be sure to ask which additional qualities were added to the list.

1. Why did you select the qualities that you did? Did you have a particular experience or reason?

2. Which did you think was the single most important quality?

3. Do you think you also possess that single most important quality in being a friend towards others?

4. Are you as good a friend to others as you expect others to be to you?

5. How long do you think someone possesses these qualities (e.g., is really loyal, trustworthy)?

**Extension Activities:**

1. Look for anecdotes of true friendship in books, newspapers, magazine stories, etc. **(e.g., a young man had cancer and lost his hair, so all of his close friends shaved their heads)** What quality does it show as being important?

2. Target a friend and do something special to thank that friend for his or her special quality.

**Evaluation:**

a. List three qualities you think are important in a friendship.

b. Explain which of those qualities is the most important to you. Why?

# Qualities of a Good Friend

**Directions:** Which of these qualities do you think is important in a friendship? Rank each item from 1 to 5 (1 = most important). Feel free to add your own ideas.

_____ is popular

_____ has money

_____ is a good listener

_____ can be trusted with secrets

_____ has creative ideas

_____ doesn't talk behind your back

_____ is usually happy

_____ is a good student

_____ gets lots of attention

_____ is funny

_____ has good ideas for things to do

_____ is interesting

_____ understands how you feel

_____ is respected by other people

_____ is good at sports

_____ comes through in a crisis

_____ loyal, keeps on being your friend even when you're not around

_____ _____

_____ _____

_____ _____

_____ _____

_____ _____

_____ _____

_____ _____

# I-17 Changing Friendships

**Objective:** The student will identify several reasons why friendships change or end.

**Comments:**

It is normal for friendships to change over time. Some reasons include: geographical moves, changing interests, lack of time to maintain the friendship, a crisis, realization that a friend is bad for you, or lack of energy to keep the friendship going. In this lesson, students are directed to think about the friendships that have already changed.

**Introductory Activities:**

a. Have students list four or five people with whom they were friends at least five years ago.

b. Have students circle those on the list whom they still consider to be close friends.

c. Have students suggest reasons why the friendships not circled have ended or diminished.

**Activity:**

Students will consider several examples of friendships that have changed or ended. They are to determine what they think is the reason why the friendship changed and write their answer on the worksheet "Changing Friendships."

> **Discussion:** Answers can be condensed into one or two words, or students may have lengthy explanations for why they think friendships have changed. Students may discuss whether or not they think the friendship could have been maintained and, if so, how.

> **Answers:** *(examples)* **1.** distance; too far to see each other and didn't want to make the effort to stay in touch. **2.** change of interests. **3.** a bad experience. **4.** interests changed; lack of time. **5.** change of interest; unpleasant experience.

> 1. Which of the friendships could have been maintained if both parties wanted to?

> 2. Is it always a bad or negative event to have a friendship change or end? Why or why not?

> 3. In situation 5, would a true friend put another friend in a situation in which he or she could get into trouble?

> 4. What types of crisis situations would bring friends closer together?

> 5. What are some ways people can keep friendships going, even if they are separated by distance and interests?

> 6. Which of your close friends now do you think you will still be close to in five years? Why? What will keep you together?

**Extension Activities:**

1. Write a letter or make a phone call to someone who was once a good friend but with whom you have lost contact. What is he or she doing now? How have you both changed?

2. Make predictions for five years into the future. Which of your friends will you still be close to? What will your friends be doing? Seal them in an envelope and write on the front: "To be opened on _____." Keep it in a safe place!

**Evaluation:**

a. List two reasons why friendships change, end, or diminish.

b. List two ways people can maintain a friendship despite the reasons given in (a).

**Teacher Notes:**

_____

_____

_____

_____

_____

_____

# Changing Friendships

**Directions:** Here are some examples of situations in which friendships have changed or ended. What reason or reasons would explain why?

1. Shannon moved three hours away from her small town _
to Indianapolis. Angie wants to stay in touch with her,
    but neither one likes to write letters and it was just too _
far to travel very often.

_____

_____

2. Tom and Elliot used to play football together all the time. Through the years of high school, _
Tom became interested in swimming instead and dropped football. Now they don't spend
    any time together.

_____

_____

3. Mark and David were friends since grade school. One day during their junior year, Mark
    borrowed David's car to go out on a date. David had spent a lot of time working on the car.
    Mark was drinking and hit a telephone pole. No one was hurt, but the car was dented and
    Mark didn't even bother to offer to pay for damages.

_____

_____

4. Ellen had four close friends throughout high school. When she went off to college, she
    became extremely busy with classes, sports, and working a part-time job. She spent every
    weekend at college instead of going back home. She and her roommate became good friends
    and did a lot of things together.

_____

_____

5. Karen and Marcos were good friends and spent a lot of time together dancing, playing
    volleyball at the beach, and riding bikes. Everything was great until Marcos started getting
    into drugs. Karen still wanted to be friends, but Marcos seemed as though he was changing
    too much. He began asking her to deliver drugs to people she didn't know.

_____

_____

# I-18 Social Situations

**Objective:** The student will identify several social situations that are personally comfortable/uncomfortable for him or her and explain why.

**Comments:**

A way to make (and perfect) friendships is by spending time in social situations. Our comfort level differs, depending on what those situations are. Some students may enjoy dancing, while others fear it as a horrible situation. In this lesson, students are to think about social situations they enjoy and those they may find uncomfortable.

**Introductory Activities:**

   a. Have students volunteer to tell about a situation involving other people in which they felt embarrassed or awkward.

   b. Have students volunteer to tell about a situation involving other people in which they felt comfortable and possibly proud of themselves.

**Activity:**

Students are given examples of ten social situations on the worksheet "Social Situations." They are to indicate which make them comfortable, uncomfortable, or neither. The situations are: smoking, dancing, playing cards, talking about sports, eating, talking about a controversial topic, talking positively about someone else, talking negatively about someone else, drinking, playing sports.

   **Discussion:** Be sure each student understands the context of each picture. There are no "right" or "wrong" answers since each student will respond according to his or her own comfort level.

   1. Which situations would make you feel uncomfortable? Why?

   2. In which situations would you feel quite comfortable or even look forward to participating?

   3. Did you feel "neutral" about many of the situations?

   4. What do your answers reveal about you? **(think of self as a risk-taker, enjoy sports, etc.)**

**Extension Activities:**

   1. Write about your most embarrassing moment. Who was around? How did you handle it? What do you think people thought about you? Does it seem funny now?

   2. The next time you are at a party or social gathering, observe the people around you. Pick out someone who seems to be very social and try to decide what qualities it is about him or her that make the situation fun for him or her. Is the person outgoing? A good listener? Does he or she move around a lot to talk to a lot of different people? Observe!

**Evaluation:**

   a. List two social situations in which you feel very comfortable.

   b. List two social situations that make you feel uneasy, nervous, or bored.

# Social Situations

**Directions:** Here are ten social situations in which people are involved in a lot of different activities. Circle those that show situations in which you would feel comfortable. Put an X on those in which you would feel uncomfortable. Leave alone those in which you would not particularly feel one way or the other.

# I-19 A Positive Role Model

**Objective:** The student will identify a personal positive role model and give at least one reason why this person was selected.

**Comments:**

It is important to have someone to look up to – to admire and to emulate. Part of growing up is modeling oneself after other people. If students can relate to someone who is a positive influence (for whatever reason), this can help them aspire to try to develop the same positive traits in themselves.

**Introductory Activities:**

a. Have students write the name of a peer whom they admire or wish they could be like.

b. Have students write the name of someone else whom they admire, but there are no restrictions – this could be anyone.

c. Have students write the name of an adult whom they admire.

**Activity:**

On the worksheet "A Positive Role Model," students are to pretend they are one of the people they selected as a role model and describe what a typical day would be like for them as this person. Some students may insist on selecting someone who you may not think of as a "positive" person; however, encourage students to pick someone who in some way has a redeeming quality! Allow students to overexaggerate the details in their writing. This may help them use their imagination and have some fun with the project. (You may want to provide parameters on the role model – living/dead, fictional or real-life person, etc.)

**Discussion:** Have students share who they selected as their role model. Ask for volunteers to read their entries if they desire. The bottom line in this activity is for students to identify what it is about their role model that makes that person a positive influence on them.

1. Who did you select for your role model?

2. What positive characteristic about this role model did you focus on?

3. Do you think you could really be like this person in some way? Is the characteristic you like really attainable for you?

4. Do you admire this person because he or she is somewhat like you or because he or she is different in some way from you?

5. Did you pick someone who is the same sex as you?

6. Did you pick someone with the same abilities (**artistic, athletic, etc.**) as you only more pronounced or professional? What does this indicate about you?

**Extension Activities:**

1. Write a letter to a famous role model. What would you like to find out about him or her?

2. Read a book or magazine that contains information about your role model. What has he or she done that you admire? What background information did you find out that interested or surprised you?

3. Conduct an informal survey of your class or other group. Who are popular role models among these groups? Try to predict – movie star? musician? athlete? Why?

**Evaluation:**

a. Identify a person who is a positive role model for you.

b. Give at least one reason why this person is a positive influence.

**Teacher Notes:**

_____

_____

_____

_____

_____

_____

# A Positive Role Model

**Directions:** You have just turned into

_____

(your positive role model). Describe a typical day in your life. *Ideas* – What will you wear? What will you do today? Who will you talk to? How will people respond to you? Will you do anything surprising? (Use the back of this sheet if you need more space to write.)

_____

_____

_____

_____

_____

_____

_____

_____

# I-20 The Death of a Friend or Peer

**Objective:** The student will express feelings or experiences that have occurred from the death of a friend or peer.

**Comments:**

Unfortunately, death is a part of life, and it seems that more and more young people are victims of crime, accidents, or disease. In almost any given school year, there will be several student deaths. This worksheet reflects anecdotes that happened within a year of one school system. They are not written to cause depression or grief, but to mirror the reality that student deaths do occur. Some could have been prevented. Perhaps this will trigger an event or anecdote that means a lot to one of the students.

**Introductory Activities:**

   a. Have students list (collectively or individually) any episodes of student deaths in the community within the past year or two.

   b. Have students collectively make a list of reasons why young people have died untimely deaths.

**Activity:**

   **Discussion:** The names have been changed, but all of the stories are true. Ask students to listen to or read the stories and try to get a sense of how they would feel if they knew the people involved. Tell them you will ask for their opinions after all have been read.

   1. What experiences have you had with a death of a peer, friend, classmate, or member of your family?

   2. The deaths are all tragedies, but did any of them seem particularly more tragic than the others? Why?

   3. How differently would you feel if it were a friend who had died, rather than just someone you knew from school but weren't really close to?

   4. What would you say to the brother or sister of the person who had died?

   5. What would you want people to say to you if it were your close friend who had died?

**Extension Activities:**

   1. Check out your local MADD or SADD groups. Become involved in a group that actively takes steps to prevent teen drinking. Find out what you can do to promote non-drinking activities at and around school.

   2. Find out if there are memorial or scholarship funds for students from your school who have died. Organize a fund-raiser to contribute to this fund.

   3. Find out what student organizations are available to help students who have problems with drug abuse, drinking, family problems, thoughts of suicide, depression, and other problems. Promote awareness of these organizations.

**Evaluation:**

   a. Give three examples (can be from the worksheet or students' own experiences) of untimely student deaths.

   b. Give two examples of safety or common-sense procedures that can be taken to avoid a possibly dangerous or fatal situation.

# The Death of a Friend or Peer

**Directions:** Read each story below. They are all true. All of the victims were in high school and all occurred within one year. Think about how you would feel if you were friends with the victims.

1. Jim was walking home from school one beautiful sunny afternoon. He walked the way he usually walked – along some train tracks. This particular afternoon he was wearing his headphones and did not hear a train coming. Although the engineer tried to stop the train, he couldn't. Jim was killed on the tracks.

2. Alex was driving with a suspended license. He and his girlfriend, Jennifer, were driving along a curvy road through the park one afternoon. The roads were wet from a recent rain. Alex was also driving too fast – 40 in a 20 mph zone. He took a curve too fast and Jennifer, who was not wearing a seat belt, was thrown from the car. She hit her head on some rocks and was killed instantly.

3. Rachel worked at a veterinary clinic after school and on weekends. One evening after she left, she did not return home. Hours passed. Weeks passed. Finally several months later her body was found in a local lake. She had been kidnapped and murdered.

4. Raymond ran around with older kids who tended to get in trouble. One night, after he and two other boys stole a car, they were pursued by the police. During a high-speed chase the car hit a tree. Raymond was killed after he went through the windshield. The other two boys were hospitalized in critical condition.

5. Mindy, a pretty and popular high school student, was walking out of class one afternoon when she suddenly collapsed and became unconscious. Emergency personnel were called, but it was too late – she had died. She had had a heart disorder. There was no indication that anything like this would or could ever happen.

# I-21 My Family Tree

**Objective:** The student will complete a brief family tree, including siblings, parents, and grandparents.

**Comments:**

It is interesting to research one's family tree. Through records, interviews with relatives, and perhaps old diaries, one can reconstruct a brief history of the people who helped create us! In this lesson, students are to attempt to research their own family tree, at least for a generation or two back.

**Introductory Activities:**

   a. Define *genealogy* for students. **(the study of family origins)**

   b. Define *family tree* for students. **(a chart that lists the names of people in a family, showing the different generations)**

   c. Have students list names of their siblings, parents, and as many grandparents as they can.

**Activity:**

Students are to work on drawing and filling in names for an informal family tree on the worksheet "My Family Tree." Students can get information from parents or other relatives to complete the activity. You may wish to have students complete the chart using their natural parents (if they live with a stepparent). Students may wish to include stepsiblings as brothers and sisters. Decide how you want to have them complete the chart. Be sensitive to students who live in foster homes or who may be adopted.

   **Discussion:** Hopefully, students will have learned a little about the people on their charts beyond simply noting their names. Allow time for discussion of what anecdotes they learned about the people in their past.

   1. Who or what were some good sources for you to complete the chart?

   2. What interesting or surprising things did you find out about the people on your chart?

   3. How far back were you able to go (how many generations)?

   4. Were there any common first names among the people in your family tree? Any common characteristics?

**Extension Activities:**

   1. Add to your family tree by locating and including pictures of the people on your chart.

   2. Write a biography about one of your ancestors.

   3. Write a journal for your future grandchildren. Describe to them what your life is like. What is the present technology, food, prices, popular fads, television, etc.?

**Evaluation:**

   a. Define the word *genealogy*.

   b. Define the term *family tree*.

   c. Draw a sample family tree showing an individual, one sister, one brother, parents, and two sets of grandparents.

# My Family Tree

**Directions:** A family tree, or pedigree chart, lists a person's name and the names of his or her parents, grandparents, great-grandparents, etc. On the back of this sheet, try to complete your own family tree, including brothers and sisters. Get information from your parents or other relatives. You can use the sample chart below to get started.

○ indicates a female

△ indicates a male

— indicates people of the same generation (siblings, cousins)

| indicates different generations (parents, grandparents)

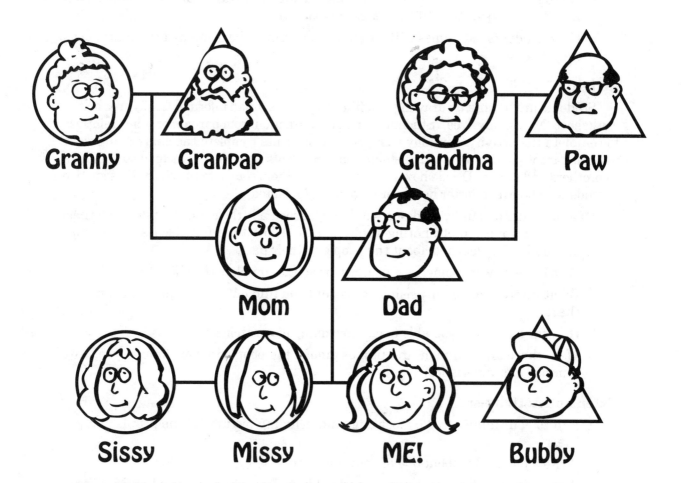

Granny    Granpap    Grandma    Paw

Mom    Dad

Sissy    Missy    ME!    Bubby

# I-22 Members of a Family

**Objective:** The student will describe the members of his or her family and the relationships within that family.

**Comments:**

The people with whom we live have a huge impact on our day-to-day lives. While some of this information may be quite personal or embarrassing for some students to reveal, they should be given the opportunity to reflect or be familiar with their own family structure. This lesson is not intended to "pry" into someone's private life, but rather to acknowledge that there are many types of families.

**Introductory Activities:**

   a. Have students list the members of their family (or the people who live in their home).

   b. Have students add one word after each name to indicate the relationship of that person to him- or herself (e.g., mother, sister).

**Activity:**

   **Discussion:** You may wish to have students complete the worksheet anonymously and then compile the results. Try to draw conclusions that there are many different family types and many different members that comprise a family unit.

   1. What are some advantages to having a large number of people in your family?

   2. What are some disadvantages to having a large number of people?

   3. What are some things that are harder for a single-parent family to do?

   4. What are some reasons that grandparents might live with their children?

   5. What are some problems that merging or blending of two families (remarriage of divorced adults) might run into?

   6. Do you think when you are an adult your family life will be similar or different to the family style you are growing up in?

   7. In what ways do you wish your family life were different?

   8. What are some things you really like about your family?

**Extension Activities:**

   1. Have students look through the greeting cards available at most supermarkets or gift shops. What types of cards can be purchased for specific family members other than the traditional father, mother, sister, brother, or grandparent?

   2. Have students choose a particular member of their family and write about him or her. What makes that person special or particularly important to the student?

**Evaluation:**

   a. Define the following terms: (1) stepbrother, (2) half-sister, (3) traditional family, (4) cousin, and (5) widower.

   b. List members of your family (or household) and describe the relationship of each member to you.

# Members of a Family

**Directions:** Below are some terms or words that describe different members of a family. Circle those that apply to your own family.

traditional family (husband, wife, their children)

single-parent family

grandmother

grandfather

stepfather

stepmother

brother

sister

stepbrother

stepsister

half-brother

half-sister

widow

widower

cousin

uncle

aunt

boyfriend

girlfriend

# I-23 Respecting Authority

**Objective:** The student will state at least two reasons why it is necessary to respect and obey parental authority.

**Comments:**

Older students may find it difficult to follow rules that seem too restrictive or protective. Nevertheless, parents are responsible for the children's actions while they are minors. Rules are necessary for safety, efficiency, and discipline. Rules may change with the age of the child and the amount of responsibility that he or she can handle.

**Introductory Activities:**

  a. Have students raise their hands to indicate who they view as the primary source of parental authority in their house: father, mother, other adult, etc.

  b. Have students list specific rules that apply in their families or households.

**Activity:**

  **Answers: 1.** no; **2.** yes; **3.** no; **4.** no; **5.** yes; **6.** no

  **Discussion:** Have students discuss the examples and decide exactly what rule or request was given and then whether or not it was followed.

  1. At what age should parents begin to give a child more authority? When should it be 50-50?

  2. Are parents responsible to higher authority systems themselves for care of their children?

  3. In which of the examples were parents motivated by concerns for the children's safety?

  4. What things could the people in the examples have done to try to change what they considered to be unfair rules?

**Extension Activities:**

  1. Have students conduct a survey of their class or grade. What is the curfew time for most ninth graders? twelfth graders? girls? boys?

  2. Invite a probation officer or welfare worker to speak to the class about the legal responsibilities of parents for their children.

**Evaluation:**

  a. List two rules that parents or adults in your household expect you to follow.

  b. List two reasons why it is necessary to obey parental authority.

# Respecting Authority

**Directions:** Read each of the situations. Decide whether or not the main person in the story is showing respect for parental authority or not. Write YES or NO on the lines.

1. Tommy is 5 years old. His dad tells him not to play with matches. Tommy puts the matches away and gets his dad's cigarette lighter instead and begins to play with that.

   _____

2. Amy is in high school. She borrows her mother's car to go to work at the local dry cleaning store on weekends. Her mother needs the car at midnight on weekends to go to her job. Amy is supposed to fill up the car with gas each weekend and have it in by 10 P.M. Amy goes out to a party on Friday night with friends and has the car back at the house by 9:30. She then returns to the party by getting a ride with another friend.

   _____

3. Steve is 15. He has a curfew of 11 P.M. on weekends and 10 P.M. on school nights. He has been getting C's and D's on his report card, so his parents change the curfew to 9 P.M. every night until his grades improve. Steve thinks the curfew is too early and unfair so he has been coming in at 10 P.M. on weekends.

   _____

4. There have been several robberies and other crimes in Marla's neighborhood over the past few months. Marla's dad decides he is going to pick her up at school and wants her to stay there to wait for him until he can get her. Marla finds this extremely embarrassing so she tells him that she has a ride with friends and walks home instead.

   _____

5. Sally's older sister just found out she is pregnant. Their parents are extremely upset about this. Now Sally's parents refuse to let Sally even go out on a date at all. Sally is angry at her parents and thinks this is unfair. After all, she doesn't even have a serious boyfriend! She sees her friends at school and talks to them on the phone.

   _____

6. Robert Smith has been skipping school. The probation department is going to prosecute his father if he doesn't make sure that Robert gets to school every day. Mr. Smith leaves for work at 5 A.M. each morning but wants Robert to call him at work right before he leaves for school at 7:30 A.M. Robert calls, then goes to his friend's house to play video games.

   _____

# I-24 Living with Abuse

**Objective:** The student will give examples of child abuse or neglect.

**Comments:**

More and more, children are dying and suffering from child abuse and neglect. It is tragic, not only that parents are not doing their jobs, but that the children of abusive people often live with their trauma for the rest of their lives. In this lesson students will read about situations in which children were abused or neglected by an adult.

**Introductory Activities:**

a. Have students give examples of what they consider to be "child abuse."

b. Have students give examples of what they consider to be "punishment."

**Activity:**

**Discussion:** These cases are based on real situations. Mark's parents divorced and Mark remained with his mother. He recently graduated from high school and is starting college. Ramon was placed in special education classes for the emotionally handicapped. Carla got into trouble throughout middle school and high school. She dropped out, got married, and had a child. Derrick lives in a foster home.

1. How is "abuse" different from "neglect"?

2. If you were Mark, what could you have done to protect yourself? How could you have tried to protect your mother?

3. Do you think there is any connection between Ramon's acts of violence and the way his father disciplined him at home?

4. What mixed feelings do you think Carla felt towards her mother?

5. What could Jackie have done to take better care of her son?

6. When these children grow up to become adults and parents, how do you think these experiences will affect them?

**Extension Activities:**

1. Invite someone from your local welfare agency to talk to your class. Have students prepare a list of questions pertaining to child abuse and neglect. Find out what information is available about these topics and what help is available for abused/neglected children in your community.

2. Have students read newspaper articles about cases of child abuse and neglect. What types of punishments are the courts handing out to the offenders?

3. Assign students to research the topic of child abuse and neglect. Find out why parents abuse their children, what conditions are common to abusive parents, signs that someone is being abused, and agencies to contact.

**Evaluation:**

a. Give two examples of child abuse.

b. Give two examples of child neglect.

c. Give the name of one agency that handles child abuse cases.

# Living with Abuse

**Directions:** Read these situations about students who were in abusive families. What would you have done if you were that student?

1.  Mark's parents were always arguing. Mark's father was an alcoholic. Many times a week he would come home drunk and beat up Mark's mother. When Mark tried to intervene, the father would beat him up. On more than one occasion, Mark came to school with bruises, bumps, and cuts requiring stitches.

    _____

    _____

    _____

2.  Ramon was constantly in trouble at school ever since he was in kindergarten. He was always in the principal's office for bad language, fighting with other children, disobedience to the teachers, and refusals to do his work. Whenever he got in trouble at school, he got in "double trouble" at home. His father, a huge man, would take his belt and whip Ramon for getting into trouble.

    _____

    _____

    _____

3.  Carla, from the time she was six years old, had been taking care of her alcoholic mother. Carla was the one who would go out to find her mother on the streets, bring her home, and make sure she was safe. When she was sober, Carla's mother was affectionate and caring. When she was drunk, however, she would scream at Carla and hit her. She once threw Carla through a window.

    _____

    _____

    _____

4.  Jackie was a single parent. She had to work long hours to make ends meet. Often she would leave her five-year-old son, Derrick, locked alone in the house while she was at work. She said she didn't have the money to pay a babysitter, and anyway, it was only for a couple of hours and nothing would happen. But one day she forgot to lock the door, Derrick wandered out, and was hit by a car. He was taken to the hospital and survived, but Jackie found herself in court for child neglect.

    _____

    _____

    _____

## I-25 Sexual Abuse

**Objective:** The student will identify several sources of help for reporting and dealing with cases of sexual abuse.

**Comments:**

Sexual abuse within families is alarmingly prevalent in almost any community. Many children, particularly those for whom the abuse begins very early, are afraid to speak up or to even recognize that this is not normal, acceptable behavior. Through discussion, students should be made aware of sources of help for themselves or anyone else who may be involved in a case of sexual abuse.

**Introductory Activities:**

Explain that the topic of sexual abuse is sensitive and personal, but that it is important to discuss so that people who are presently victims can try to get help. Within that context, define the following terms:

    a. *sexual abuse* (**touching or non-touching interaction towards another person of a sexual nature; it is unwelcome and/or socially improper**)

    b. *incest* (**sexual intercourse between people who are closely related to each other**)

**Activity:**

    **Discussion:** The story of Maria is true, and is very typical of many abuse cases. Abused children often feel they are to blame, endure low self-esteem, are not believed by other family members, and often do not seek help. In Maria's case, fortunately, she was able to get help and to become a survivor.

    1. Why do you think Maria didn't try to do something when the abuse first started?

    2. Why was she afraid to talk to her mother at first?

    3. Why do you think the mother did not believe or want to believe Maria?

    4. If the mother had not gone to the police, what could Maria have done?

    5. Why do you think Maria wants to become a social worker?

    6. How effective of a social worker do you think Maria might be?

**Extension Activities:**

    1. Research the topic of sexual abuse. Find out the symptoms of abuse, who commits sexual abuse, how many cases are reported annually, and what agencies are available to help this type of situation.

    2. Contact your local welfare agency for pamphlets, videos, and speakers who could provide information about child sexual abuse. What is being done locally for this situation?

**Evaluation:**

    a. Define *sexual abuse*.

    b. Define *incest*.

    c. Give two or three sources of help that a person could go to in cases of sexual abuse.

# Sexual Abuse

**Directions:** Read the story about Maria. As you read, think about the following questions: (1) Could Maria have done anything to prevent this? (2) How do you think Maria felt when she confronted her mother? (3) How did the sexual abuse affect Maria in later life?

Maria had been sexually abused by her grandfather, who lived in the home with Maria's parents and her two brothers, since she was 11 years old. When no one was home, her grandfather would take her into his bedroom and physically and sexually abuse her.

At first, Maria said nothing to anyone. She felt ashamed and bad about herself. She went to school and became quiet, withdrawn and moody. Her teachers noticed that she seemed different, but Maria never said anything.

After several years, Maria confronted her mother about what was happening. Her mother could not believe that the grandfather, who was her father, was doing something like this. She accused Maria of being a liar.

As time went on, Maria's mother began to notice that there were many times when Maria was left alone with the grandfather. One day she came back early from work and discovered that Maria had not been lying to her.

The mother went to the police and to the child welfare department. The grandfather was removed from the home immediately. Months later, his case came to trial and he was sentenced to several years in prison. Maria was now 14 years old and in eighth grade.

The change in Maria was like night and day. She received counseling from the welfare department and spent a lot of time talking to the school counselor. Once her grandfather was in prison, she felt relief and a sense of freedom. She became more animated in school, began to laugh again, and took an interest in schoolwork and friends.

Maria is now in high school. She is active in a local church and wants to eventually become a social worker to help abused children. There is a certain look about her that says, "I'm okay with myself now. Things are under control and I will be just fine."

# I-26 Thoughts About Divorce

**Objective:** The student will express – either in writing or orally – his or her opinion/experience regarding divorce.

**Comments:**

Statistics show that about half of all first marriages end in divorce. Second marriages have a 65 percent divorce rate. With such statistics, it is probable that almost all students have some experience with divorce. In this lesson, students are given the opportunity to collect their thoughts about divorce and to state their opinions.

**Introductory Activities:**

a. Have students raise their hands if they know someone who is divorced.

b. Have students raise their hands if someone in their immediate family (parent, sibling) is divorced.

c. Have students raise their hands if they think they will be divorced at some time in their lives.

**Activity:**

Students are given 20 statements on the worksheet "Thoughts About Divorce." There are really no right or wrong answers to these comments; they are provided to stimulate thought and discussion. Some students may be going through a divorce in their family and have negative or forceful feelings. Be sensitive to this. Students can learn and benefit from the comments of others.

**Discussion:** After students have responded to the statements, go through each and have students volunteer to give their experiences and feelings about them. Students will have a variety of comments, especially those who have come from divorced families. They may be able to see only one side of the situation, so encourage students to listen carefully to the comments of everyone else. Perhaps they will be made aware of other viewpoints and success stories that have come out of divorced situations.

1. What are some reasons why people get divorced?

2. How does having children in a marriage complicate a divorce?

3. What are ways that people can try to save their marriage and avoid a divorce?

4. Do you think it's better for people who don't get along to stay married for the sake of the children?

5. Would children from divorced families answer these questions differently than those from non-divorced families? Why?

6. What problems can arise after a divorce? **(financial problems, custody problems)**

7. Why do children sometimes feel responsible when their parents divorce?

8. What steps might people take to "divorce-proof" a marriage?

**Extension Activities:**

1. Research the topic of divorce using current periodicals (newspapers, magazines). Make a list of 15 to 20 questions about divorce, predict what you will find, and then search for the answers.

2. Check with your local County Recorder's Office to find out the number of marriage licenses applied for in the past year and the number of divorce cases filed during the same period of time. What percentages did you find?

3. If your parents have been divorced, write about your experience. How did you feel? How did you cope? How are things different in your life now? How has this experience affected you? What advice would you give to someone else who is in this position?

**Evaluation:**

a. List two or three reasons why people choose to divorce.

b. List two or three ways that people might try to prevent a divorce.

c. Write a paragraph describing your experience with a divorce and how it has affected you presently and how you think it will affect you in the future.

**Teacher Notes:**

_____

_____

_____

_____

_____

_____

Name _____ Date_____

# Thoughts About Divorce

**Directions:** Read the following comments about divorce. Circle "Agree" or "Disagree" to show how you feel about the comment. If you are undecided, put a question mark next to the comment.

1. Divorce is always wrong.  **Agree  Disagree**

2. I will probably be divorced someday.  **Agree  Disagree**

3. Both people are at fault in a divorce.  **Agree  Disagree**

4. Parents should stay together for the sake of their children.  **Agree  Disagree**

5. Children should get to pick who they want to live with after a divorce.  **Agree  Disagree**

6. Counseling can keep people from getting a divorce.  **Agree  Disagree**

7. The mother should always keep the kids.  **Agree  Disagree**

8. Children can be part of the problem in causing people to get a divorce.  **Agree  Disagree**

9. Many divorces are about money.  **Agree  Disagree**

10. If someone has an affair, they will probably get divorced.  **Agree  Disagree**

11. People who are divorced once will probably get divorced again.  **Agree  Disagree**

12. Divorce is now considered to be socially acceptable.  **Agree  Disagree**

13. If only one person wants to stay married, the marriage will not work.  **Agree  Disagree**

14. Marital problems stem from couples who don't communicate with each other.  **Agree  Disagree**

15. Marital problems stem from couples who don't make commitments to each other.  **Agree  Disagree**

16. Second marriages are always better.  **Agree  Disagree**

17. People should get to know each other very well before they get married.  **Agree  Disagree**

18. It is very easy to get a divorce.  **Agree  Disagree**

19. It is expensive to get a divorce.  **Agree  Disagree**

20. Half of all marriages now end in divorce.  **Agree  Disagree**

# I-27 Living with Stepsiblings

**Objective:** The student will identify at least two problem situations that can arise between stepsiblings and offer an appropriate solution.

**Comments:**

Blended families can include children from two marriages who now are living under one roof as brothers and sisters. Needless to say, this can change living conditions dramatically for everyone. While each family has to work out its own differences, the important thing is that children from both families become a part of the new blended family. In this lesson, problems that may be faced by these children are examined.

**Introductory Activities:**

a. Have students list television shows or familiar stories that are about or include stepparents or stepsiblings. (***Cinderella*, "The Brady Bunch," "Step by Step," etc.**)

b. Have students list tangible and intangible things that must be shared in blended family situations. (**time, space, attention, etc.**)

**Activity:**

**Answers:** *(examples)* **1.** Jamie, stepsisters, father; talk to father alone about the problem. **2.** Art, stepbrother; try to find another room. **3.** Janelle, stepmother; talk to stepmother and explain that she needs time with friends. **4.** Debra, father; talk to father, try to set up regular time to visit. **5.** John, mother, stepmother; talk to a counselor or to father.

**Discussion:** There are probably several students in the class who live with stepsiblings. If they are receptive to the idea, seek out their advice for what has worked for them and what hasn't regarding living with new brothers and sisters.

1. What type of things have to be shared when children from two families start living together as one family? (**time, attention, space**)

2. What are some ways children get to see both parents? (**shared visitation, summer visits, daily – if parents live locally**)

3. What are some good things that can come of having stepsiblings in the same house? (**share interests, have someone to talk to, etc.**)

4. Do you think stepparents would tend to favor their own children over the stepchildren?

5. Who could a child talk to if he or she felt "caught in the middle"?

**Extension Activities:**

1. Interview students who have stepsiblings. What are the good things about their situation? What are the bad things about their situation?

2. Watch and critique some episodes of the TV show "The Brady Bunch." What is realistic about the way the family is portrayed? What is hard to believe?

**Evaluation:**

a. List two situations that can be problems for children and their stepsiblings.

b. Give an appropriate solution for each situation you listed in (a).

# Living with Stepsiblings

**Directions:** There is a problem in each situation below. For this activity, (a) decide who is involved, and (b) suggest a possible solution.

1. Jamie only gets to see her dad two weeks a year in the summer. When she goes out to California to visit him, her stepsisters treat her like she is an intruder. It's *their* house. Jamie wants to spend time with her father, but it seems as though they are always in the way.

   (a) _____

   (b) _____

2. Art had his own room until he acquired a younger stepbrother who touches everything and won't quit talking. Art hates sharing his room!

   (a) _____

   (b) _____

3. Janelle's new stepmother just had a baby. Now it seems as though Janelle is expected to be a built-in babysitter for the new child.

   (a) _____

   (b) _____

4. Of the three girls in her family, Debra was the closest to her father. But ever since he remarried he doesn't seem to have the time to call her or spend time with her. She misses him.

   (a) _____

   (b) _____

5. John's mother and stepmother can't stop fighting with each other. It's obvious they both have hard feelings over the divorce and remarriage. John feels caught in the middle – he can't say anything to either one without upsetting someone.

   (a) _____

   (b) _____

## I-28 Dealing with Stepparents

**Objective:** After interviewing a stepparent, the student will be able to identify two or three problem situations encountered in stepfamilies and offer solutions.

**Comments:**

Students may have to deal not only with stepsiblings, but also with stepparents. Often this is a vaguely defined role that can be uncomfortable for parents and children alike. New roles are thrust upon everyone. Adaptations must be made. New living patterns are established. Discipline must be worked out. Making these adjustments can be difficult. In this lesson, students are to interview a stepparent to find out what difficulties he or she has encountered and what has been helpful.

**Introductory Activities:**

a. Have students compile a list of questions they could ask a stepparent about his or her new role.

b. Have students suggest a list of possible problems that would be common to stepparents.

**Activity:**

Students are to interview an adult who has volunteered to participate in this activity. You may want students to find their own willing participant or you might have one adult speak to the class. Students are to ask questions during the interview and record the answers.

**Discussion:** Be sure to preview any additional questions that students want to add to the list on the worksheet "Dealing with Stepparents." Depending on how well you know the volunteer and how frank you want the discussion to be, you may want to tailor the questions to fit the situation. After the interview(s) are discussed, you may want to go over the following questions:

1. Do you think most stepparents and stepchildren get along?

2. What do you now think is the hardest thing for adults to deal with in a stepfamily?

3. What do you now think is the hardest thing for children to deal with in a stepfamily?

4. Was our list of possible problems accurate?

**Extension Activities:**

1. Write and perform several skits dramatizing a particular problem that might be encountered in a stepfamily. Show various outcomes.

2. Compile and review a list of fairy tales or common stories that have stepparents portrayed as wicked and uncaring. How do you think this got started? Rewrite the stories with a more contemporary character in the stepparent role.

**Evaluation:**

a. List two or three problems commonly encountered in stepfamilies.

b. Give an appropriate suggested course of action for each problem considered in (a).

# Dealing with Stepparents

**Directions:** Conduct an interview with someone who is a stepparent. You may want to add to this list of questions.

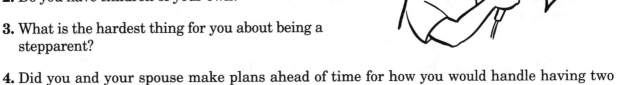

1. How long have you been a stepparent?

2. Do you have children of your own?

3. What is the hardest thing for you about being a stepparent?

4. Did you and your spouse make plans ahead of time for how you would handle having two families living together?

5. Do you feel free to discipline your stepchildren?

6. What do your stepchildren call you?

7. What problems have you encountered with your children and stepchildren living together?

8. How do you and your stepchildren get along in general?

9. What have you found that you really like about your stepchildren?

10. Do you have problems with shared visitation of your stepchildren?

11. Do your children and stepchildren get along with each other?

12. _____

13. _____

14. _____

15. _____

16. _____

17. _____

18. _____

19. _____

20. _____

21. _____

22. _____

# I-29 Chores

**Objective:** The student will identify at least ten chores that are necessary for running a household.

**Comments:**

There is a lot of work involved in running a household. Hopefully, most of the chores are shared by family members! In this lesson, students are to identify common household chores and think about who is primarily responsible for that work in his or her home. Each student should then think about his or her own role in the running of the household.

**Introductory Activities:**

a. Have students volunteer to tell the most-hated chore at their home.

b. Have students tell about common chores they are responsible for in their home.

**Activity:**

Students are to complete the worksheet "Chores," which lists various common household chores, by writing the name or identifying the person usually responsible. Students can make their own key to identify people and can add to the list.

> **Discussion:** After completing the chart, students may have a better idea of the amount of work it takes to effectively run a household. It may be revealing to actually figure out how much or how little certain individuals do.

1. Which chores are more efficiently done if they are usually performed by one person (rather than rotating the job)? Why?

2. Which chores do you personally find appealing? Distasteful?

3. What could/would happen if a particular chore on the list was neglected for two weeks?

4. Do you think children should be responsible for a lot of chores if they are busy with school or sports?

5. Do you think children should be paid for doing chores?

6. Are your family chores distributed equally? How are they selected for each individual?

7. Are chores basically the same for most families in your community?

**Extension Activities:**

1. Add to the chart by figuring out the following information: (a) the frequency with which each chore should be done (e.g., weekly, daily); (b) how much time is involved in completing the chore; and (c) a rating of how much effort or enjoyment is associated with the chore.

2. Figure out how long it actually takes to complete each chore on the list. If someone were paid minimum wage to do each chore, which would be the most expensive? least expensive?

**Evaluation:**

    a. List ten common household chores.

    b. Write a paragraph describing how to efficiently perform your favorite chore; then write a paragraph describing how to perform your least favorite chore. Give reasons for why you like/dislike the tasks you selected.

**Teacher Notes:**

_____

_____

_____

_____

_____

_____

# Chores

**Directions:** Who is responsible for doing these chores in your family? Indicate who does what. Add items to the list that apply to your family.

**1.** mowing the lawn

_____

**2.** washing dishes

_____

**3.** washing clothes

_____

**4.** sorting clothes

**5.** vacuuming

**6.** caring for pet(s)

**7.** preparing meals

**8.** shopping for food

**9.** shopping for other household items

**10.** dropping off dry cleaning

**11.** car maintenance

**12.** washing windows

**13.** waxing/polishing floor

**14.** dusting

**15.** general errands

**16.**

**17.**

**18.**

**19.**

**20.**

**21.**

# I-30 Benefits of a Family

**Objective:** The student will list at least three ways that members of a family can help or benefit each other.

**Comments:**

Ideally, families provide more than shelter and financial security for each other. The members of a family share living space and problems, but they can also share support, encouragement, happiness, and time. Whatever the student's family situation is like, he or she is a member of a very special group that can be a lifelong benefit.

**Introductory Activities:**

a. Ask students to think about what family they wish they could be a part of if they could choose one other than their own.

b. Have students list reasons why they chose that family.

**Activity:**

On the worksheet "Benefits of a Family," students are to read examples of how particular members of families have helped each other. They are to write the specific reason on the lines.

**Answers:** *(examples)* **1.** older brother walked her to school. **2.** the whole family is saving for a vacation. **3.** older brother helped Bobby's football skills. **4.** sister helped Ann get ready for prom. **5.** whole family worked together to make decisions. **6.** whole family spent designated time together.

**Discussion:** No family is ideal; every family has difficulties. But families share bonds of genetics, lifestyle, early experiences, problem-solving, and providing role-models that shape our lives. Not every family will be close-knit, but families whose members look out for each other are precious!

1. When kids get older, why does it become embarrassing to hang around with your family?

2. Do you think siblings of the same sex get along better than opposite-sex siblings?

3. What types of crises might bring a family closer together?

4. What are some activities that families can do together that are fun and enjoyed by all?

5. When you have your own family, do you want it to be similar or very different than the family in which you are growing up?

**Extension Activities:**

1. Find out the origins of Mother's Day and Father's Day. What are some creative ways to celebrate and honor these people?

2. Watch and analyze some family situation-comedy shows on television. How have members of the family helped each other or stuck together through problems?

3. A caricature is a cartoon-like drawing of a person emphasizing outstanding features (like wild hair or pointed ears) or interests. Make a family caricature of the members of your own family.

**Evaluation:**

    a. List three needs a family can provide for its members.

    b. Write a paragraph describing a time when someone in your family helped you out with a problem or really came through for you when you needed support. How did your family help you?

**Teacher Notes:**

_____

_____

_____

_____

_____

_____

# Benefits of a Family

**Directions:** Think about ways family members can help each other. Read each example and write one way the family involved demonstrates how being part of a family can be beneficial.

1. Sally is afraid to go to school because some of the older kids have been teasing her. Her older brother, Frank, has decided to walk to school with her to make sure she gets there safely.

   _____

   _____

   _____

2. The Morgan family wants to travel to Yellowstone National Park for a family vacation. Mr. Morgan is working overtime and the older children are earning money by doing odd jobs. Everyone is putting money into a special account at the bank so they can afford to go.

   _____

   _____

3. Bobby wants to join the middle school football team. His older brother, Tom, played for several years on the local high school team. Tom is spending weekends helping Bobby learn how to throw and catch the ball.

   _____

   _____

4. Ann wants to wear something special for the prom. She went through her sister's closet and found just the right dress. Her sister helped her get ready for the big day.

   _____

   _____

5. When Juan's father died, the entire family grieved for a long time. The family had to make important decisions together and realized that being close was comforting as well as necessary for them.

   _____

   _____

6. One of the favorite activities for the Johnson family is to rent movies on the weekend, make buttered popcorn, and spend an evening together. No one is allowed to have a friend over, and everyone is expected to be there. The Johnsons find that they really enjoy spending family-time together.

   _____

   _____

# Section II

# Communication Skills

# II-1 Being a Careful Listener

**Objective:** The student will demonstrate the ability to listen to a partner for at least two to three minutes without interrupting and to remember at least three main points.

**Comments:**

Listening to what someone is saying is a logical prerequisite to understanding what is on his or her mind. In this lesson, the student is given an exercise in listening to another person.

**Introductory Activities:**

    a. Have students raise their hands if they think of themselves as a good listener.

    b. Have students list ways they can show they are actively listening to someone else who is talking. **(having eye contact, concentrating on what's being said, etc.)**

**Activity:**

Students are to participate in an exercise with a partner in which they take turns listening to each other speak on a designated topic for two to three minutes. The worksheet "Being a Careful Listener" suggests several topics. You may want to tape record both speakers so that they can check for accuracy of what was said. Remind students of the rules: (a) do not interrupt the speaker, and (b) concentrate on what the speaker is saying.

    **Materials:** pen or pencil, tape recorder

    **Discussion:** After students have had a turn being both the speaker and the listener, discuss the following questions:

    1. How well did you listen? How much did you recall?

    2. What helped you remember? Did you use any tricks to help you?

    3. What distractions did you encounter that took your mind off of what the speaker was saying?

    4. Did eye contact help?

    5. Did you find yourself wanting to interrupt?

**Extension Activities:**

    1. Target a person you do not know extremely well and try to engage that person in conversation. Practice being a good listener: use eye contact, ask good questions to keep the conversation going, and don't interrupt.

    2. Practice tape recording short speeches or discussions from the radio or television; then write the main points that you remember. Use these as exercises to work on being a better listener.

**Evaluation:**

    a. List two ways you can improve your ability to be a good listener.

    b. Listen to a tape-recorded message (prepared by the teacher) and write the main points.

# Being a Careful Listener

**Directions:** Perform the following activity with a partner. Listen to your partner talk about one of the following topics for two to three minutes. Tape record the comments.

**Rules:** **1.** Don't interrupt while the other person is talking.

**2.** Concentrate on what the other person is saying.

When your partner has finished, repeat as much as you can remember about what was said. You may want to tape record your comments. Then play back the original tape recording. How much did you remember? How well did you listen?

**Suggested Topics:**

My Most Embarrassing Moment

What I Think About Our School

My Favorite Recent Movie

The Best Place to Eat

If I Had a Million Dollars

Think of some other topics and write them here:

_____

_____

_____

_____

_____

_____

_____

_____

_____

_____

_____

_____

_____

_____

_____

# II-2 Summarizing

**Objective:** The student will accurately summarize a short paragraph.

**Comments:**

Summarizing consists of preserving a message, but in shortened form. In this lesson, students are given short paragraphs to read (or listen to), and then they are to indicate which of the choices is the best summary of the paragraph.

**Introductory Activities:**

a. Have students define the word *summary*. **(a shortened version of a longer passage, covering the main points)**

b. Have students list various types of texts or comments that are often summarized. **(newscasts of speeches, teachers' lectures, etc.)**

**Activity:**

Students are to read the four short paragraphs on the worksheet "Summarizing" and then mark the choice that is the best example of a summary of that paragraph. Remind students that a good summary should include the main point(s) of the paragraph; it does not have to be so long as the original paragraph!

**Answers: 1.** b; **2.** c; **3.** a; **4.** c

**Discussion:** After students have completed the worksheet, discuss why the answer they selected was the most appropriate and why the other answer options were not the best summaries.

1. Does it help to come up with your own summary statement before looking for the choices given?

2. In some of the examples, the choice was true, but was only one small detail – it was not the main idea of the paragraph. Which are examples of this? **(4-a, 4-b)**

3. Some of the choices included information that was partly true, but we don't really know if the rest of the sentence is true. Which choices were examples of this? **(2-a, 3-b)**

4. How can a summary of something be helpful? **(don't have to read the entire text, just gives the main points)**

**Extension Activities:**

1. Have students practice taking summary notes of brief lectures or information presented in short paragraphs. Compare summaries among the students – what is the main idea they should have picked up on?

2. Practice reading paragraphs to a partner and have the partner give a one-sentence summary of what was read. Make sure students include the main idea!

**Evaluation:**

a. Give a one-sentence summary of a paragraph (provided by the teacher). Make sure you include the main point or points and do not include irrelevant details or inferences that are not specifically given.

b. Write a paragraph about a given topic. Then summarize your paragraph in one sentence.

# Summarizing

**Directions:** A summary is a shortened version of what was expressed. Read or listen to the following paragraphs. Put an X in front of the best summary of each.

1. A huge black dog watched the cat cautiously approach a little brown bird. The cat's tail wagged slowly side to side as it focused on its prey. Just before the cat was about to pounce, the dog barked. The little bird flew away, leaving the cat without a target.

   _____ a. A black dog wanted to catch a bird.

   _____ b. A dog scared away a bird before a cat could get it.

   _____ c. A dog chased away a cat who was chasing a bird.

2. Jeremy got an F on his chemistry quiz today because he forgot to study. He now found out he has a test next hour in math class. He also forgot to study for that test.

   _____ a. Jeremy has a bad memory.

   _____ b. Jeremy is not very good at chemistry.

   _____ c. Jeremy was not prepared for his tests today.

3. The tall blonde girl picked up the basketball, dribbled it a few times, and then smiled as she watched it sail through the air and fall through the hoop.

   _____ a. A girl made a basket while playing basketball.

   _____ b. A girl had blonde hair and was very pretty.

   _____ c. A girl was a good athlete.

4. I wanted my best friend to come over this weekend so we could go out for pizza and go to the soccer game, but my mother informed me that my aunt and uncle from Seattle were going to arrive and I would be busy cleaning my room.

   _____ a. My aunt and uncle live in Seattle.

   _____ b. My friend and I wanted to go to a soccer game.

   _____ c. My plans for the weekend changed because we were having guests.

# II-3 Paraphrasing

**Objective:** The student will accurately paraphrase a given sentence or short paragraph.

**Comments:**

Paraphrasing differs from summarizing in that one is looking for different words to convey the same meaning (rather than simply shortening the text). By using different words that mean about the same thing, the student is showing he or she understands the speaker's or writer's intent.

**Introductory Activities:**

a. Define the word *paraphrase.* **(to restate something in different words, keeping the same meaning)**

b. Have students compare and contrast a *summary* and a *paraphrase* of a text. **(both may be shortened forms, a summary could contain the same words, a paraphrase uses different words)**

**Activity:**

Students are to read the sentences on the worksheet "Paraphrasing" and select the answer that best paraphrases the intent of the sentence. Remind students they are looking for the same meaning, but a different form or choice of words that mean about the same thing as the original.

**Answers: 1.** b; **2.** a; **3.** a; **4.** b; **5.** b; **6.** b

**Discussion:** Have students discuss why the selected answer is the best paraphrase and why the answer they did not select was not a good paraphrase. Some reasons may be that it was more of a summary than a paraphrase, too much was implied in the answer, or the answer was too vague.

1. Was this activity harder or easier than summarizing a sentence or paragraph? Were they about the same?

2. In sentence 1, why wasn't (a) a good answer as it was true? **(it didn't address the *meaning* of the sentence; the important fact was that the opponents made excuses for losing)**

3. Why wasn't (b) a good paraphrase for sentence 3? **(it was possibly true, but didn't focus on roller coasters)**

4. How do you know the girl in sentence 5 was angry? **(clues such as her red face, yelling, hitting)**

5. What words in the sentences and the correct paraphrases could you match up as being about the same thing? **(1. excuses/poor sports, 2. 100 degrees/ temperature, 3. thrill/fun, 4. blank/didn't know, 5. yelled and hit/angry, 6. anytime and anyplace/love)**

**Extension Activities:**

1. Practice paraphrasing with a partner. Have a partner give a sentence. Then repeat the sentence but use different forms of the words to keep the meaning.

2. Have several sentences written on the board. Have all students write a paraphrase of the same sentences. Compare the different versions.

3. Practice paraphrasing by taking a nasty or impolite comment and turning it into something appropriate. For example:

    a. I hate your hat. *Paraphrase:* I don't care for that hat.

    b. You are really fat. *Paraphrase:* You're somewhat overweight.

    c. That perm looks horrible. *Paraphrase:* Your hair is different today.

## Evaluation:

    a. Explain the difference between giving a *summary* and giving a *paraphrase* of a sentence or paragraph.

    b. Provide a paraphrase of given sentences (provided by the teacher).

## Teacher Notes:

_____

_____

_____

_____

_____

_____

# Paraphrasing

**Directions:** Paraphrasing is stating something in a way that keeps the meaning, but changes the words. Read each sentence below and put an X in front of the better paraphrase.

1. Our opponents in football made all kinds of excuses when they lost to our team.

   _____ a. We beat the other football team.

   _____ b. The members of the other football team were poor sports.

2. The thermometer nearly hit 100 degrees today.

   _____ a. The temperature was almost 100 degrees.

   _____ b. It was a warm day today.

3. My friend and I loved the thrill of going up and down on the roller coaster.

   _____ a. We thought that riding the roller coaster was fun.

   _____ b. My friend and I like rides.

4. I just gave the baby a blank look when it cried.

   _____ a. I don't like crying babies.

   _____ b. I didn't know what the baby wanted.

5. The red-faced girl yelled at the younger girl and tried to hit her.

   _____ a. A girl had a red face from yelling.

   _____ b. A girl was very angry at another girl.

6. I could eat an entire pizza with three or four toppings all by myself anytime, anyplace.

   _____ a. I am really hungry.

   _____ b. I really love pizza.

# II-4 Body Language

**Objective:** The student will identify several forms of body cues (e.g., posture, mannerisms, facial expressions) and explain how these can affect the meaning of what is expressed orally.

**Comments:**

Messages are conveyed not only through words alone, but through bodily positions and expressions such as facial cues, posture, and nervous mannerisms. In order to understand what someone is trying to explain, one must also take into consideration the clues that are given through other sources as well.

**Introductory Activities:**

   a. Have students list or give examples of cues other than verbal that show how someone feels.

   b. Have students list strong feelings of emotion (e.g., anger, fear, love, boredom, etc.). How are these feelings conveyed other than through words?

**Activity:**

Tape segments of television shows from various sources. With the sound turned off, have students list body cues that express how the character(s) feel. After comments are written on the worksheet "Body Language," replay the tape and have students compare how the voices and words matched with the body cues.

   **Materials:** VCR tape of several types of television programs, pen or pencil

   **Discussion:** Have students discuss how the segments without sound were easy or difficult to figure out. You may want to have part of the discussion before playing it for the second time with sound.

   1. Which segments were easiest to figure out? Why? (**probably strong emotions with many body cues**)

   2. Was the newscast difficult to interpret? (**probably – they are usually unemotional**)

   3. Why would an unemotional facial expression be important for that type of job? (**appear unbiased**)

   4. What are some body positions that showed anger or aggression?

   5. What are some facial expressions that showed specific emotions?

**Extension Activities:**

   1. Play a form of *Charades* in which a specific emotion is given to a group to express. Look for body cues such as: crossing arms, clamping teeth, clenching fists, hands on hips, narrowing eyes, slouching in chair, etc.

   2. Look for pictures or take photographs of different posture positions. What do they convey? Why do you think they demonstrate a certain feeling? (**e.g., hands clenched may be ready to fight, crossed arms may look protective, etc.**)

**Evaluation:**

   a. List at least five examples of body cues that reveal feelings or strong emotions.

   b. Draw a picture or pantomime a given emotion (such as anger, confusion, etc.) using body cues to help express that emotion.

# Body Language

**Directions:** Watch a 5-minute segment of each of the following television programs without sound: (a) a situation comedy, (b) a mystery movie, (c) a newscast, and (d) a soap opera. Look for the body language cues (facial expression, posture, mannerisms, etc.) as you watch to try to determine what emotion is being expressed. Then replay the tape with sound. Were you close?

**Situation Comedy**

cues:_____

_____

_____

_____

_____

**Mystery Movie**

cues:_____

_____

_____

_____

_____

**Newscast**

cues:_____

_____

_____

_____

_____

**Soap Opera**

cues:_____

_____

_____

_____

_____

# II-5 Situational Considerations

**Objective:** The student will give examples of several situations that may affect how a comment or expression is interpreted adversely or unclearly.

**Comments:**

There are times when people may be in a hurry, in pain, running late, or feeling extremely depressed or extremely happy. These are situations that may also affect comments and actions. What is said during that time may not truly be what is meant; these are comments that can be misinterpreted and overreacted to. In this lesson, students are presented with situations in which the characters are in somewhat abnormal positions and their comments do not truly reflect what they would say or do in calmer, more normal situations.

**Introductory Activities:**

   a. Have students give examples of times or situations in which they felt stressed or pressured.

   b. Have students describe situations in which they knew they would get an undesired answer or response from a parent or teacher because of the bad timing or specific situation.

**Activity:**

Students are to read the situations on the worksheet "Situational Considerations" in which characters are placed in stressful or abnormal situations. The responses the characters give are not reflective of what that character would probably normally say or do. The student is to decide what is the unusual or stressful situation affecting the person.

**Answers:** *(examples)* **1.** embarrassment in front of a friend; **2.** in a hurry; **3.** headache; **4.** guilt; **5.** extreme happiness

**Discussion:** Discuss each item on the worksheet and have students conclude what factor(s) might be causing the situation to be abnormal for the characters.

1. How did the character feel in situation l? **(embarrassed by his sister)**

2. What was abnormal about the situation? **(her outfit)**

3. How could the first boy in situation 2 misinterpret what the second boy said and did? **(left in a hurry, left out, rudeness)**

4. What factor in situation 3 could be responsible for the seemingly rude behavior of the girl? **(headache)**

5. In situation 4, what possible other responses could the girl who forgot to wait for her friend have given?

6. Under normal circumstances, how would the girl in situation 5 have reacted? **(probably distressed or angry)**

7. What are some situations that particularly throw you off or make you more irritable than usual?

8. What are some extremely happy situations that might cause someone to act in an unusual way?

9. How can you be sensitive to someone's mood before you approach him or her? What cues are there?

10. What is a more polite way the rude people could have explained that it was a bad time to be approached?

## Extension Activities:

1. Have students find/look for/make/draw pictures of people in obviously stressful situations and then add captions (humorous, if desired!) to accentuate the absurdity of asking for a favor right then. (For example, a kid in three layers of snowsuits asking his mother if he could go to the bathroom.)

2. Have students keep a running classroom list of "Situationally Silly Questions," such as: Taking a spelling test and having someone raise his or her hand to ask, "How do you spell that?" You'll find that there are many silly questions that are asked. Emphasize that it is the *situation* that makes it funny or silly, not that there are bad questions. Look for cartoons that show situationally silly examples also.

## Evaluation:

a. Give three examples of situations that may be stressful or abnormal, causing someone to react in an unusual manner.

b. Write a paragraph of a time when you felt you were misunderstood or treated rudely because the other person involved was in a stressful or unusual situation.

## Teacher Notes:

_____

_____

_____

_____

_____

_____

# Situational Considerations

**Directions:** Sometimes a situation might cause a person to act or react differently than usual. In each example below, what situation is causing the person to act or react in an unusual manner?

1.

2.

3.

4.

5.

# II-6 Clear Directions

**Objective:** The student will provide clear, accurate directions to enable another person to correctly complete a given task.

**Comments:**

Expressing oneself so that others can understand the message is a very important skill. In this lesson, students are given the opportunity to follow verbal directions and then must give directions for another person to follow. The tasks involved are simple drawing of figures. Through trial and error, students will experience how important it is to be very specific and use words the listener will understand.

**Introductory Activities:**

a. Give students the following set of directions as if you really expected them to comply: "Take out a pencil, put it in your left hand, no – make that your right hand, draw two or four concentric circles, shade the middle one in, fold your paper in half or thirds if you want to, and then place it in the upper or right-hand corner of the desk and write your address in Chinese on the top." When students look at you in disbelief, ask them what was difficult about that task. (**too many directions, given too fast, directions were changed, directions were unclear, they were asked to do things they probably didn't know how to do, etc.**)

b. Have students come up with suggestions for how better to give instructions for that type of task.

**Activity:**

Students will be given oral directions (read by the teacher) for the first part of this activity on the worksheet "Clear Directions." They are to draw geometric figures in a specific pattern. On the second part, they are to generate directions for someone else to follow.

**Instructions for Part I:**

1. You will be drawing three squares. Make the first square small. Leave a little space. Then draw a second square to the right of the first one. This square should be medium-sized. The bottom line should be in line with the first square. The third square should be a little bigger than the other two. It too should have the bottom line on the same level as the other two.

2. You will be drawing three circles, in a line. The first circle should be small. Color in the entire circle. The second circle is the same size as the first. Draw it to the right of the first one. Then draw a line in the circle to cut it in half. The line should go from top to bottom. Shade in the left half of the circle. The last circle should be bigger. Draw this circle so that the bottom of it is in line with the other two. Then draw a line going up and down that cuts the big circle in half.

3. Draw a medium-sized square. In the middle of the square, draw a small circle. Make sure the outline of the circle does not touch any part of the square. Cut the circle into four equal parts by drawing two lines, one up and down; the other, sideways. Shade in the bottom right-hand section of the circle.

4. There are three figures in this drawing. First draw a small triangle. Cut the triangle in half by drawing a line from the point at the top to the base. Shade in the right half of the triangle. Now draw a small circle on top of the triangle, so that the point of the triangle touches the bottom of the circle. Divide the circle into four equal parts by drawing two lines: one up and down; the other, sideways. Shade in the upper right-hand section of the circle. Then draw a rectangle on top of the circle so that they touch in only one point. Make sure the long part of the rectangle is going sideways. Cut the rectangle into four equal parts by drawing two lines: one up and down; the other, sideways. Shade in the upper left-hand section.

**Directions for Part II:**

The student should write directions that would enable someone else to draw the figures on the sheet. Examples:

5. There will be three figures in a row. The first one is a small square. Leave a small space to the right and draw the second, a medium-sized triangle with the base on the same line as the bottom of the square. The third is a square, the same size as the first square. Shade it in completely.

6. Draw a rectangle with the long side going across. Then draw another rectangle of the same size, but with the long side going up. The two rectangles should be touching each other like this: the short side of the second rectangle should be on the same line as the bottom of the first rectangle so that the whole short side of the first rectangle touches the second rectangle. Then go to the first rectangle and find the middle of the top long side. Draw a big black dot on that line so that half of the dot is below the line and half is above.

**Discussion:** Students will probably have a lot to say about how hard or fun this task was. Go over the following questions:

1. What helped make the directions clear when you were given things to draw?

2. What directions seemed confusing?

3. How was using shapes an easier task than if you were supposed to draw a dog or a house? **(consistent, all agree on what a shape looks like)**

4. What was hard about writing directions for someone else?

5. What parts were most confusing when you had to direct someone else to draw a picture?

## Extension Activities:

1. Have students draw three or four pictures (using shapes or other agreed-upon items) and write directions for someone else to follow. Trade directions and compare drawings.

2. Have several students go to the board and work on the same set of directions (given orally) at the same time by one person. See how differently people can interpret the same set of directions if the directions are not specific and clear.

3. Try this type of activity with other items. For example, use colored 1-inch blocks and direct students to put them in a certain pattern. Or have two students sit back to back so they cannot see each other and have one proceed to build something. As he or she puts the blocks in place, he or she should tell the second student what to do. The rest of the class can serve as a silent audience to see if the second student is complying with the directions accurately. Try it (a) without allowing the second student to ask any questions, and (b) allowing the second student to inquire of the audience: "Is this correct?" That is the only question that can be asked of the audience. Have fun with this!

## Evaluation:

a. Given a specific geometric drawing, write out clear directions for how someone else could reproduce the drawing without seeing the picture.

b. Given specific written or verbal instructions, draw the pattern or figures described.

Name _____ Date_____

# Clear Directions

**Directions:** For Part I, draw the figures you hear described. For Part II, you will write clear directions for someone else to follow in order to draw the figures you see. Use the back of this sheet for your directions.

**Part I:**

   **1.**

   **2.**

   **3.**

   **4.**

**Part II:**

   **5.**       **6.**

# II-7 Collecting Your Thoughts

**Objective:** The student will state at least one reason why it is important to collect his or her thoughts before speaking or writing.

**Comments:**

Speaking spontaneously is fine in most occasions; however, at times it is beneficial for people to think before talking. Some situations might require a degree of delicacy or diplomacy, and taking a few seconds to think through what you really want to convey is well worth the effort. Students are given situations to think through before stating what they would say to handle the situation.

**Introductory Activities:**

a. Explain that you are going to give students a choice. They must write their choice immediately. State: "Vote A or B. A – we can skip homework for three weeks and you'll have one huge test at the end. B – you will have daily assignments for three weeks and no final exam. Write A or B."

b. Explain that you are going to give students another choice. This time they must think for 30 seconds before they indicate their choice. State: "You notice that a house is on fire. You have time to save one person. Would you save person A – a two-year-old boy who is screaming by a door on the second floor, or person B – a sixty-year-old grandmother who is in a wheelchair by a window on the first floor?"

c. Ask students which activity was more difficult. Did the extra 30 seconds to think about the situation make the choice harder or easier? Why?

**Activity:**

Students will be given several situations to consider on the worksheet "Collecting Your Thoughts." They must take 30 to 60 seconds to plan out what they will say (and do). Then they should write their response on the worksheet.

**Discussion:** The extra time, though short, should give students a chance to think through several alternative responses. After students have completed the activity, compare answers, emphasizing what they did with the "thinking time."

1. What would have been your first response if you didn't take the time to collect your thoughts?

2. Would your response have been the same or did the added time encourage you to change your first response?

3. Why do you think taking time to "think through" a situation would make someone change his or her mind? **(think of more alternatives, new ways to look at a situation)**

4. Why would it be harder to decide which person to save – a baby on the second floor or an older person on the first floor – than deciding when to take a test? **(much more important consideration, more complicated)**

## Extension Activities:

1. Make a list of ten questions other people must answer right away, without giving it any thought. *Examples:* 1. Would you shave your head for $10 right now? 2. Would you shave your head for $100? 3. Are you a happy person? 4. Should all students be given A's? 5. Should school meet on Saturdays? 6. Do you like pizza? 7. Do you like snakes? 8. Would you lie to your best friend to avoid hurting his or her feelings? 9. Would you trade places with the president for a week? 10. Are girls more sensitive than boys?

    Then, pick three or four of the questions, reflect on them for a minute or two, and see if the answers change and why.

2. Begin using the phrase "Collect your thoughts" in class when assigning oral and written work. Encourage students to refrain from even picking up a pen or pencil until they have taken some "think time." Make this a practice so that students learn to expect to think first.

## Evaluation:

a. State one reason why it is important to collect your thoughts before expressing an opinion.

b. Write a paragraph expressing your opinion about whether or not your school should have a dress code. Think first.

# Collecting Your Thoughts

**Directions:** How would you carry out the following tasks? Before you write what you would say, take 30 to 60 seconds to think it through. Collect your thoughts! Now write what you would say.

1. You have to tell your best friend that her very exotic tropical fish just died as a result of your having forgotten to feed it for a week while she was on vacation.

_____

_____

_____

_____

2. Explain to your teacher that your semester research project is not finished and give your reasons.

_____

_____

_____

_____

3. You must give a short talk to the Student Council on your opinion about whether or not you think 14-year-olds should be allowed to drive.

_____

_____

_____

_____

4. Your little sister wants to know if the Tooth Fairy and Santa Claus are real. She trusts you and will believe whatever you tell her.

_____

_____

_____

_____

_____

# II-8 Preparing for Speaking in Public

**Objective:** The student will complete items on a checklist in preparation for making an informal speech.

**Comments:**

Public speaking can be a terrifying experience for many (most?) people, yet it is an excellent way to express an opinion, especially if the comments made are well thought out and the speaker is prepared to deliver the speech. In this lesson, students will take steps to prepare a simple speech that will be given at a later time.

**Introductory Activities:**

a. Have students name or list some people who are good public speakers, or people whom they enjoy listening to. **(perhaps a stand-up comedian, a favorite teacher, etc.)**

b. Have students list reasons why it might be scary to speak in front of people.

c. Have students suggest techniques that make a good speaker seem interesting or easy to listen to. **(humor, interesting topic, interesting voice, etc.)**

**Activity:**

The student is to select a topic he or she finds interesting or might know something about. If the topics on the worksheet "Preparing for Speaking in Public" do not seem appropriate for your class, have students suggest others. Students do not all have to pick the same topic! Students will then go through the checklist, item by item, to prepare themselves for giving a speech. You should specify the length or time involved in giving the actual speech (perhaps 3 to 5 minutes).

**Materials:** Have resources available such as books, encyclopedias, newspapers, or pamphlets. Also, instruct students to obtain note cards (3" x 5") and other materials (posters, markers, rulers, etc.) if they are going to include visual aids.

**Time:** You may want to plan several days or a week to complete this activity. Depending on how much help the students need, this activity might take more time than the usual writing activities. You may want to assign specific due dates to items on the checklist. Have students be available to monitor each other's progress.

**Discussion:** As students progress through the checklist, monitor them carefully to make sure they are not bogged down on certain steps. Some will need help with outlining, writing good introductions and conclusions, and preparing the visual aids. At this point, it is more important that they go through the steps and complete each item even if it is not completely "polished." An outline could be as simple as writing the topic sentence from each paragraph on individual note cards. Go through the following discussion questions to help students focus on the activity:

1. Was it difficult to select a topic?

2. Were your resources readily available? Did you find resources other than printed material? **(such as individuals)**

3. Can you read your rough draft?

4. Do you feel you have outlined your speech adequately? What information should be put on the note cards?

5. How can you keep your note cards organized? **(number them, color-code)**

6. Why is it important to have a good introduction and conclusion?

7. What types of visual aids would be good for your presentation? Why?

8. How many times would you need to practice your speech before you feel comfortable with it?

9. Where are some places or who are some people who could help you feel comfortable with practicing your speech?

10. Why is it important to look at your audience rather than just reading the cards? **(gets audience involved)**

11. Why is it important to speak slowly and to remember to breathe? **(slows you down, makes sure people can understand you)**

## Extension Activities:

1. If students are having particular difficulties with some aspect of this assignment (e.g., outlining, writing a conclusion, practicing), pair students with a buddy who is more competent and allow them to work together.

2. To make interesting visual aids, give students time to work in the computer lab (if available) or use other resources to create charts, graphs, or pictures.

## Evaluation:

a. State the topic of your speech.

b. List at least two important features that will be included in your speech. **(visual aids, interesting statistics, etc.)**

# Preparing for Speaking in Public

**Directions:** Select a topic about which you feel strongly or know a lot about. Go through the following checklist, marking off each item as you have completed or thought through what you plan to do.

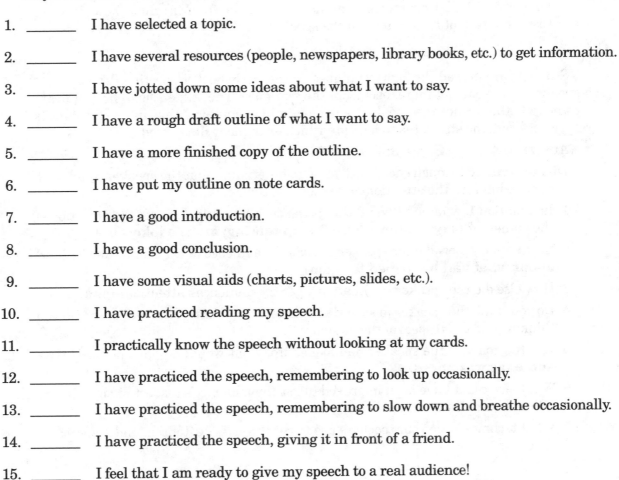

**Suggested Topics:**

- Professional Athletes Make Too Much Money
- Students Should Have More Voice in the Way They Are Graded
- Ways We Can Stop Pollution in Our Community
- Exotic Animals Should Not Be Kept as Pets
- Why We Need a Girls' Football Team

1. _____ I have selected a topic.

2. _____ I have several resources (people, newspapers, library books, etc.) to get information.

3. _____ I have jotted down some ideas about what I want to say.

4. _____ I have a rough draft outline of what I want to say.

5. _____ I have a more finished copy of the outline.

6. _____ I have put my outline on note cards.

7. _____ I have a good introduction.

8. _____ I have a good conclusion.

9. _____ I have some visual aids (charts, pictures, slides, etc.).

10. _____ I have practiced reading my speech.

11. _____ I practically know the speech without looking at my cards.

12. _____ I have practiced the speech, remembering to look up occasionally.

13. _____ I have practiced the speech, remembering to slow down and breathe occasionally.

14. _____ I have practiced the speech, giving it in front of a friend.

15. _____ I feel that I am ready to give my speech to a real audience!

# II-9 Expecting Respect

**Objective:** The student will state at least two techniques to help get the respect of an audience.

**Comments:**

Not everyone is a dynamic public speaker, but there are some techniques that can help shape the audience's expectation towards a speaker. Teachers know that sometimes giving the class the "silent treatment" can be an effective way to gain its attention. Several techniques mentioned in this lesson include waiting for the audience to be quiet, using eye contact, interacting with the audience, and having a sincere, serious demeanor – expect the audience to respect you!

**Introductory Activities:**

    a. Have students give examples of different types of audiences and speakers they have observed during the past week.

    b. Write the words *Respectful* and *Not Respectful* on the board. Underneath each, have students list examples of audience behavior from (a) that showed either respect or lack of respect toward the speaker.

**Activity:**

Students are to read the four techniques on the worksheet "Expecting Respect" that a speaker can use to obtain respect from the audience. The student is to first indicate (yes/no) whether or not the speaker is behaving in such a way that he or she expects respect. Second, the student is to indicate which example is illustrated.

**Answers: A.** no, 1; **B.** yes, 3; **C.** no, 4; **D.** no, 2

**Discussion:** Go through each illustration to determine what the speaker could have done to improve the attention and respect of the audience.

1. In situation 1, what are several things the speaker could do to get the attention of the audience? (**say: "listen, please"; stop talking; make a joke; etc.)**

2. In situation 2, how did the speaker include the audience in her comments? (**talked about what had happened to them)**

3. How else did the speaker in situation 2 get the audience's attention? (**chart)**

4. Do you think the speaker in situation 3 had the attention of the audience? Do you think he had the respect of the audience?

5. In situation 4, if the speaker had looked up, what would he have noticed? (**the audience was bored)**

6. What else could have been improved to get the audience's respect in situation 4? (**shorten the list)**

7. What techniques do your teachers use to get the class's attention and respect?

**Extension Activities:**

1. While students are practicing their speech, tell them to include several checkpoints on their note cards at which point they are to make sure they have eye contact with someone in the audience.

2. Assign students to observe a speech on television (perhaps a TV preacher, politician, special lecture, etc.). Have students jot down audience reactions that show the audience is attentive and respectful to the speaker (or lack thereof). What specific techniques do the students observe the speaker doing to get respect?

**Evaluation:**

a. List two behaviors a speaker can try to get the respect of an audience.

b. Write a paragraph explaining why it is important to have the attention and respect of an audience.

**Teacher Notes:**

_____

_____

_____

_____

_____

_____

# Expecting Respect

**Directions:** You want your audience to respect you while you are giving your speech. Read the examples of ways to get your audience to respect you. Then look at the cartoons below. (a) Write *yes* or *no* to show if the speaker is expecting respect. (b) Then write the number (1,2,3,4) of the suggestion illustrated.

### Examples:

1. Wait for the audience to give you its attention.
2. Use eye contact with your audience.
3. Interact with the audience by including questions or comments about them.
4. Be sincere and serious.

# II-10 Be Convincing

**Objective:** The student will give at least two examples of convincing arguments to back up his or her opinion.

**Comments:**

In some cases, the audience that needs to be convinced of something may be a parent, friend, or stranger. Some techniques that can help strengthen a position include: being enthusiastic, using logic, being interesting, and showing how one's position will benefit the audience or other person.

**Introductory Activities:**

a. Have students list five things of which they wish they could convince their parents, teacher, or a rich relative. This may be an idea, an event, or purchase.

b. Have students list ways they could try to convince the people in (a) to agree with their position.

**Activity:**

On the worksheet "Be Convincing," students are to read the examples of ways to be convincing and then match the example with the situation illustrated.

**Answers: A.** 4; **B.** 2; **C.** 1; **D.** 3

**Discussion:** The audience in these examples consists of a single person, rather than a group. However, the principles can apply to any situation in which one person is trying to convince another.

1. How much of a role does *sincerity* play in trying to convince someone else of something? Is it more convincing if you act as though you truly believe in what you are saying?

2. Do you feel that someone who is very convincing usually believes in what he or she is saying?

3. If you know that someone is trying to sell you something (which is a form of convincing), what might you be cautious about? **(trying to figure out what the salesperson gains from this, be aware that he or she is looking out for his or her own interests too)**

4. What are some occupations that are based on being a good convincer? **(sales, law, etc.)**

**Extension Activities:**

1. Videotape and view ten television commercials. For each, discuss: (a) who is the target audience, (b) what is trying to be sold, and (c) what techniques for convincing are used?

2. Have students write and perform skits in which they demonstrate their ability to be convincing. Skits could include: (a) convince parents to let them stay out past midnight, (b) convince a sister/brother to let them borrow items such as clothes/tapes/magazines, cash, etc., and (c) convince a teacher to put off a huge assignment until the next week.

3. Have students design a product and write a commercial to try to sell it to an audience. Videotape the commercials, if possible. Discuss what techniques were used. Evaluate how convincing is the commercial.

**Evaluation:**

a. List two techniques that can be used to convince someone else to agree with your position.

b. Describe your favorite commercial. Explain how it is convincing and what techniques it has used to convince and appeal to you.

**Teacher Notes:**

_____

_____

_____

_____

_____

_____

# Be Convincing

**Directions:** Read the examples of ways to convince your audience to agree with you. Write the number of the example (1,2,3,4) that is illustrated in each cartoon below.

**Examples:**

1. Be enthusiastic!
2. Use logic or common sense.
3. Be interesting.
4. Show how your ideas will benefit the audience.

## II-11 Giving Your Speech

**Objective:** The student will give a 3- to 5-minute speech on an appropriate topic.

**Comments:**

By the time this lesson is reached, the student should be well prepared to give his or her presentation to an audience. The important points are not only the delivery of the speech, but how well the ideas are expressed to the audience. Since it is assumed that everyone will participate, an evaluation form is provided with space for each student to do a self-evaluation, as well as view comments from a peer and teacher.

**Introductory Activities:**

a. Have students list factors they think are important when evaluating a speech or speaker. **(well prepared, good eye contact, other ideas from previous lessons)**

b. Have students give ideas for how a self-evaluation could be helpful in assessing a speech.

c. Have students give ideas for how having a peer do an evaluation could be helpful.

d. Have students give ideas for how a teacher's input could be helpful in evaluating a speech.

**Activity:**

Since this is quite an involved activity, the following order of events may be helpful:

(a) Give each student a time at which he or she will be expected to present the speech to the class.

(b) Review the items on the checklist from Activity II-8 to make sure everyone is reasonably prepared.

(c) Go over the items on the evaluation form "Giving Your Speech." You may want to pair students to do each other's student evaluations. Make sure students understand what is expected for an "excellent," "good," "fair," and "poor" rating. Students doing the evaluation are to indicate their rating in the appropriate box. Short comments would be appropriate.

(d) If possible, plan to videotape the speeches as this would be helpful when reviewing the ratings and the comments.

(e) After the student has given his or her speech, the student should complete the self-evaluation portion of the worksheet immediately. The selected peer should also complete the evaluation at that time. This may be done on a separate sheet of paper with the results transferred later to the main sheet. Likewise, the teacher evaluation should be completed and transferred so that all information is in one place.

**Materials:** pen or pencil, videotaping equipment, sufficient copies of the evaluation sheet so that students and teacher have copies to complete

**Discussion:** After students have participated in the activity by giving their speeches, distribute the evaluation forms (which now should have all respondents' comments attached and/or transferred to one main sheet). If students feel comfortable with this, play the videotape of their performance while discussing each presentation.

1. Which of your ratings (self-, student, teacher) tended to be the highest? lowest?

2. What would you change about your presentation?

3. What ideas did you get from listening to the speeches of other people about what to do or what not to do?

4. Do you feel you effectively communicated what you wanted to say?

## Extension Activities:

1. Have students work in small groups to prepare a speech or presentation for specific groups – a kindergarten class about drug awareness, a commercial to another class, a short play or skit for parents, etc.

2. Divide students into two groups to take a pro (for) side of an issue and a con (against) side. Have them come up with logical arguments and try to present each side clearly and effectively. Evaluate the effectiveness of the speech using the evaluation sheet from this lesson.

## Evaluation:

a. List two or three things you felt went particularly well with your speech.

b. List two or three things you feel could be improved with your speech. How could you specifically change things to make these improvements?

c. Write a short paragraph explaining the value of having a self-, peer, and teacher evaluation done on the same speech.

Name _____ Date_____

# Giving Your Speech

**Directions:** Read this evaluation form before you give your speech. You will evaluate yourself on the performance, have at least one student evaluate your speech, and have your teacher complete an evaluation.

**Ratings:** excellent/good/fair/poor

| | Self-Evaluation | Student Evaluation | Teacher Evaluation |
|---|---|---|---|
| **1.** Was the speaker prepared? | | | |
| **2.** Did the presentation go smoothly? | | | |
| **3.** Did the speaker use his or her note cards smoothly and efficiently? | | | |
| **4.** Was the speech easy to listen to? | | | |
| **5.** Was the speech interesting? | | | |
| **6.** Did the speaker have the attention and respect of the audience? | | | |
| **7.** Did the speaker have a good, interesting introduction? | | | |
| **8.** Did the speaker have a logical conclusion? | | | |
| **9.** Did the speaker use effective visual aids? | | | |
| **10.** Was the overall performance good? | | | |

# II-12 Identifying a Conflict

**Objective:** Given several examples, the student will identify a conflict in each situation.

**Comments:**

The teenage years are a period in which many types of conflicts are encountered. There are numerous types of conflicts, such as conflicts between school and work; decisions about which classes to take; and personality conflicts between parents, other adults, and peers. In this lesson, the student will have practice learning to identify the conflicting forces in given situations.

**Introductory Activities:**

a. Define *conflict*. **(a struggle between two opposing forces, ideas, or plans of action)**

b. Describe a conflict you have witnessed between people. **(an argument, fight over possessions, etc.)**

c. Describe a conflict you may have had about making a decision when you had two choices.

d. Describe a conflict you have had when both choices were good. **(choice of desserts, spending money)**

**Activity:**

**Answers:** *(examples)* **1.** working vs. studying *or* money vs. grades; **2.** algebra vs. general math *or* studies vs. sports; **3.** demand for trust vs. lack of responsibility; **4.** seeing a mistake vs. told not to interfere; **5.** Terry vs. Dave *or* prior commitment vs. what you really want to do

**Discussion:** After students have completed the worksheet, compare their answers. The conflicts may take several forms (concrete vs. abstract answers), but as long as two opposing ideas are suggested, the student is getting the idea.

1. In which of the examples were the conflicts between people? **(3,4)**

2. In which of the examples were the conflicts within one person; his or her own choices? **(1,2,5)**

3. Were any of the conflicts of an emergency or urgent nature? Which? **(possibly 4; we don't know the time frames on the others)**

4. Would any of the conflicts work out by themselves if the person did nothing? **(possibly 4)**

5. Which of these conflicts do you think is the most important? Why?

**Extension Activities:**

1. Make a balance scale. Demonstrate how conflicts are like two opposing weights. Sometimes conflicts are not always equal in intensity. Go through the examples on the worksheet. What factors could tip the balance of the scale?

2. As you go through the different conflicts on the worksheet, make a list of the different ways the same conflict was perceived. Did most students see situation 1, for example, as work vs. school or was it perceived as money vs. grades?

**Evaluation:**

a. Define *conflict*. Give an example of a conflict between two people.

b. Give an example of a conflict of a decision that must be made by one person.

# Identifying a Conflict

**Directions:** There is a conflict in each situation below. Identify the two parts of the conflict in each by writing the items on the lines.

1.

I want to work at least part time so I'll have some money, but then I'm afraid I'll be too tired to keep my grades up.

_____ vs. _____

2.

If I take algebra next semester, it will help me get into college, but I won't have time to go out for basketball. I'd really like to play! Maybe I should take an easier math course so I'd have time for sports.

_____ vs. _____

3.

Let me go to the party, Dad. Why don't you trust me? You think I'll get into trouble. I promise everything will be fine.

I'd like to think so, but the last two parties you went to weren't so great. The police brought you home. Why should I trust you this time?

_____ vs. _____

4.

Hey – you're putting that together all wrong. You're supposed to put the big piece in first.

Should I tell the supervisor? This could mess up everyone!

You don't know what you're talking about. Leave me alone.

_____ vs. _____

5.

Oh, no – Terry and Dave both asked me out for Friday night. I'd forgotten I promised Terry a long time ago that we'd go out. I'd rather see Dave... What should I do?

_____ vs. _____

# II-13 Compromising

**Objective:** Given examples of conflicts, the student will be able to state how a compromise could be used to resolve it.

**Comments:**

It is not always possible – nor desirable – to completely "win" a situation or force another person to have to back down. Many times a compromise, in which both parties give a little, can serve everyone. In this lesson, students must suggest possible compromises to help resolve conflicts.

**Introductory Activities:**

    a. Define *compromise*. **(an agreement in which two or more sides make adjustments to reach a solution)**

    b. Have students give some examples of situations they have been involved in that required a compromise to resolve.

**Activity:**

Students are to read the situations on the worksheet "Compromising" and suggest (either orally or in writing) a possible compromise. Note that the two sides involved may be between two people or between two choices.

    **Answers:** *(examples)* **1.** Alternate doing the chores – perhaps Samantha could be responsible on the weekends if she has more time then; **2.** Flip a coin and agree to the result; **3.** Spend time with Jennifer, but ask if she would mind if Dana joins them later at the skating rink; **4.** Stick with the group as long as it is doing activities within the law, but state his choice to not get involved in theft at all; **5.** Explain that he will have more money to take her out if she will have the patience to wait for him to go to work.

    **Discussion:** Compare student ideas on what compromises they have come up with. There may be quite a bit of variety and some compromises may not seem to be fair. Discuss these responses and additional questions.

1. How does the use of compromising help both sides? **(it lets both sides win a little bit, seems more fair)**

2. Are there some situations that should be completely decided in favor of one side? In other words, are there some issues on which you should not compromise? **(ethical, moral decisions, etc.)**

3. Do you think it is easier to compromise within yourself – your choices or ideas – rather than trying to work things out with another person?

4. In situation 2, both sides have to agree to live with the result if they can have only one pet. Does this seem unfair to one of the boys? **(yes, since one boy will not have the pet he wants; however, if they compromise on the method of deciding which pet, it would be fair since each has an equal chance of winning)**

5. In situation 4, what conflict is Marcos dealing with? What compromise(s) could he make? **(conflict between having friends who may involve him in legal trouble vs. no friends; only stay with the goup if they are not going to involve him in problem situations or look for new friends)**

6. In situation 5, what is the conflict that Lee faces? **(money vs. girlfriend)** If he didn't want to compromise, what would you suggest he do? **(give up the girlfriend)**

### Extension Activities:

1. Watch the news for examples of compromising in government, between countries (treaties), sports negotiations, and even jury trials. Analyze the procedures. Do they seem fair?

2. Find out how a plea bargain works. Why do lawyers use this procedure in trials? **(saves time and money)** Check out the court reports if reported in the local newspaper. What types of compromises are made?

### Evaluation:

a. Define *compromise*.

b. Give an example of a situation in which a compromise can resolve the problem. (This may be from personal experience or a situation discussed in class.)

### Teacher Notes:

_____

_____

_____

_____

_____

_____

# Compromising

**Directions:** Here are people who are experiencing conflict. For each situation, suggest a possible compromise.

**1.** Deborah and her sister, Samantha, share a room. Deborah thinks the work in keeping it clean is not shared equally – Deborah does the dusting, vacuuming, picking up, and making of beds. Samantha says she is too busy with sports, art club, and babysitting. What is a possible compromise to help this situation?

_____

_____

**2.** Ivan's parents have agreed to a new pet in the family, but, only one. Ivan wants a dog; his brother Jake wants a parrot. Both boys want a pet. What could they do to compromise?

_____

_____

_____

**3.** Kara and Dana are best friends. One weekend Kara wanted to go roller skating with Dana (as they usually did), only Kara's cousin Jennifer was coming to visit. Kara's mother said that Kara had to spend the weekend with Jennifer as she was a relative and didn't come to visit very often. What could Kara do?

_____

_____

_____

**4.** Marcos is part of a group that has started breaking into cars and stealing radios. Some of the members of the group decide they want to steal the entire car. Marcos wants to remain part of the group, but he feels uneasy about being a car thief. What could Marcos do?

_____

_____

**5.** Lee works part-time at a video store. The manager told Lee that as he is such a good worker, he would like Lee to work more hours and even get an hourly raise. However, Lee's girlfriend is already complaining that he is too busy. She's starting to think about going out with someone else who has more time for her. What could Lee do?

_____

_____

# II-14 Finding Alternatives

**Objective:** Given examples of conflicts, the student will state at least one possible alternative to resolve the conflict.

**Comments:**

For any given conflict, there are numerous courses of action that could be pursued. Often just by "brainstorming," a lot of ideas can be generated. Although the unworkable ones can be eliminated, the process of thinking of alternatives can get things started.

**Introductory Activities:**

    a. Have students pretend that a strange person holding what appears to be a gun just stepped up to them and said: "Give me your money." List possible responses.

    b. Have students pretend that they just opened an envelope containing $500 in cash. What possible alternatives do they have for this situation?

**Activity:**

On the worksheet "Finding Alternatives," students are given three examples of situations that require some form of action. They are to add two alternatives to the ones already listed. Specify that the alternatives should be somewhat realistic, but they could be ones that would probably not be in the best interest of the party involved. The important thing is that students begin thinking of new ideas and responses.

    **Discussion:** After students have completed their ideas for alternatives, compare answers. Possibly some of the most "way-out" ideas will be popular and workable.

    1. For each example, select the top two alternatives that you would consider. Then circle the better one. How did you arrive at that decision?

    2. Did you find there were several alternatives that would work for each situation?

    3. What is the conflict in each example?

    4. Is the process of compromising an alternative in some of the situations?

**Extension Activities:**

    1. Practice the skill of brainstorming. Try to come up with eight to ten alternatives for situations. Even if they seem crazy and impossible, include them; you can eliminate them later. Practice thinking!

    2. Have students work through each of the conflicts on the worksheet by thinking through what could or would happen with each alternative.

**Evaluation:**

Given a problem situation, list five to eight possible alternatives for solving the problem. Then select two workable choices. Explain why you chose those alternatives.

# Finding Alternatives

**Directions:** There are usually many alternatives that can be tried to resolve a conflict. For each example below, read the alternatives suggested. Add at least two of your own. Then circle the one you think would be most helpful.

1. You know that someone in your class is planning to cheat on the final exam. In fact, he is even passing around the answer key to other kids in the class. It is important to do well on the test because it will be graded "on the curve" – the best scores will be A's, and so on. What could you do?

a. Do nothing – maybe it won't affect your grade.

b. Tell the teacher.

c. Talk to the other students and get some support.

d. Take a quick look at the answer key and then pass it on.

e. _____

f. _____

2. You have met someone nice, but your best friend is interested in this person too. You want to keep your friendship but you sure would like to get to know this new person better. What are some alternatives?

a. Let your friend have the first chance.

b. Talk to your friend about the situation.

c. Just be yourself and let the new person decide who he or she is interested in.

d. There are other fish in the sea – find someone else.

e. _____

f. _____

3. A friend whom you know fairly well went out drinking but told his parents that he was at your house. He wants his mother to call you to verify the story – that he was with you. If you don't agree to this, your "friend" says he'll tell your parents about an embarrassing little incident you did last week. What could you do?

a. Lie for him.

b. Find someone else to lie for him.

c. Agree to say that you saw him at someone else's house.

d. Tell your parents about your own problem before the friend can blackmail you.

e. _____

f. _____

# II-15 Avoiding Power Struggles

**Objective:** The student will identify ways to avoid a power struggle in a given conflict situation.

**Comments:**

A power struggle usually results when two relatively equal persons experience a conflict. There is no clear leader or authority; rather, both sides see themselves as controlling or in charge. While you don't want to condone completely backing down as a way to reduce a power struggle, there are ways to firmly but politely express your opinion.

**Introductory Activities:**

a. Define *power struggle*. **(when two relatively equal-in-status individuals experience a conflict and each wants to be the one to decide how it is resolved)**

b. Give examples of power struggles from the news, politics, sports, etc. In some cases the parties may be individuals; in others, a group.

**Activity:**

**Discussion:** It is obvious that the second situation resolves the problem while the first story leaves the situation in conflict. Direct students' thinking towards analyzing how the girlfriend handled the situation.

1. What two parties were involved in the power struggle? **(sister, girlfriend)**

2. In what way were the two girls of relatively equal status? **(both had close relationships with Tom)**

3. What issues were conflicts? **(whether to have a surprise party or not; where to have it; who should be invited; etc.)**

4. In situation A, how did the conflict keep growing and get hotter and hotter? **(it polarized very quickly – become "you" vs. "you")**

5. In situation B, how did the girlfriend bring up her points of view and still involve the sister? **(asked questions, made suggestions, kept her cool, etc.)**

**Extension Activities:**

1. Have students role play situations in which they enact two strong parties (a) resolving a conflict, and (b) refusing to resolve a conflict.

2. Follow a current event over the course of several weeks. What is the conflict? Who are the parties involved? What attempts have been or are being made to resolve the conflict? Is compromise involved?

**Evaluation:**

a. Define a *power struggle*.

b. Give an example of a power struggle (specify from what area) and list the parties involved.

c. Give examples of two or three techniques for reducing a power struggle.

# Avoiding Power Struggles

**Directions:** Here are two versions of a story in which two strong-willed people must work out a conflict. Which one avoids a power struggle? How?

**A**

Here's my idea for the surprise party for my brother. We'll get red and black balloons (helium, of course), and send out invitations to go to our house on Friday for the party.

Tom's my boyfriend! I think he'd rather not have a surprise party. Anyway, Friday's not a good time. Everyone will want to go to the game, and then it will be too late. Let's all go out for pizza on Thursday instead.

Well, I think it would be nice if his family got involved in this.

Sure, but you get to see him all the time. I think Tom would rather go out with his friends.

I don't know why you think you know him better than we do.

He's my brother!

He's my boyfriend!

**B**

Here's my idea for Tom's surprise party. We'll decorate our basement and have his friends and our family over on Friday.

That sounds like fun, but do you think Tom would really like to be surprised? Remember how he thought it was really embarrassing when we just sang to him in the restaurant last year?

Yeah, well, maybe we could just tell everyone to come over Friday to our house.

Hey, you know Tom's favorite food is pizza. Do you think we should go to the Pizza Barn? It would be a lot less work for you and your family. I know you're all so busy.

Maybe...but we want to be involved...

Why don't you take care of all the decorations? You're so good at that. We could ask about the private room at the Pizza Barn. Yeah, that sounds good.

# Section III

## Academic and School Skills

## III-1 Reading Skills

**Objective:** The student will identify examples of reading tasks from everyday life, work, pleasure, or school.

**Comments:**

   The ability to read is a skill that permeates virtually all areas of life. The student will use reading skills throughout his or her school, everyday, and work life. In this lesson, students are asked to begin to identify important reading skills.

**Introductory Activities:**

   a. Have students list the last three things they have read. Specify that this does not mean just books, but any piece of paper or item that involved reading.

   b. Have students include on the list at least one item they were good at reading or particularly enjoyed reading.

   c. Have students include on the list one item with which they had difficulty reading.

**Activity:**

   **Answers: 1.** c; **2.** b; **3.** d; **4.** a

   **Discussion:** While there is more or less overlap among the areas, have students determine how or why the illustration is representative of the matching area. For example, reading about history might be considered a pleasurable experience for some, but it matches with "school" for purposes of being an example of a typical school task.

   1. What are some reading skills that are difficult for you? Why do you think this is so?

   2. What are some reading skills that are easy for you? Why are these skills easier?

   3. Which skills represented on the worksheet are those you would probably use throughout your whole life? Which are used mainly just during school years?

   4. Why do you think reading is considered by many to be *the* most important academic subject?

**Extension Activities:**

   1. Divide a poster into the four main sections: work, pleasure, everyday life, and school. Draw or find examples of reading materials that would be typically used in each area.

   2. Keep track for one day of as many types of reading material encountered as you can. The list will become quite lengthy! Then categorize the reading material into the different areas.

**Evaluation:**

   a. Identify four areas of reading (as discussed in this lesson).

   b. Give an example of a typical reading task or item that is representative of each of the four areas.

# Reading Skills

**Directions:** Match the following examples of reading skills with the areas listed below:

a. Work          b. Pleasure          c. Everyday Life          d. School

1. _____

2. _____

3. _____

4. _____

# III-2 Reading for School

**Objective:** The student will give examples of reading tasks in various school subjects.

**Comments:**

Reading is a vital skill (in some respect) in every subject at school. Whether rules to a game, a summary of a class, or textbook information, reading is required in order to fully gain the information available.

**Introductory Activities:**

a. Have students list reading skills involved in their academic classes.

b. Have students list reading skills involved in non-academic classes (e.g., art, music, P.E.).

**Activity:**

**Answers: 1.** d; **2.** a; **3.** c; **4.** b; **5.** h; **6.** g; **7.** e; **8.** f

**Discussion:** Have students discuss the items on the worksheet. They may or may not be typical of reading assignments for their classes, but students should be able to identify with what type of class they would be paired.

1. What alternatives to reading assignments are provided in some classes? **(taped books, oral discussions, making projects, etc.)**

2. How essential of a skill do you think reading is when you consider your classes? **(probably depends on the class and teacher)**

3. Do you think there are any classes in which the skill of reading is not a part or plays a minimal role? **(perhaps music, other arts classes)**

4. What provisions are made for students who have a lot of trouble with reading? **(partner-readers, books of a lower reading level, alternative assignments, etc.)**

5. Do some people learn better from *hearing* material rather than having to read it? Do you think it is still important for these people to be able to read?

**Extension Activities:**

1. Have students make their own matching activity including typical reading assignments from classes they are currently taking. Students can exchange papers.

2. Have students calculate how much time (in minutes) is spent in direct reading activities for selected classes. For example, would you expect that a great percentage of time is spent reading (or on reading tasks) in Literature rather than P.E.? Take one designated day and keep a chart of the results. Any surprises?

**Evaluation:**

a. Give an example of a reading task for several of your school subjects. (Teacher may want to specify how many and which classes.)

b. Write a paragraph stating your opinion about the importance of reading in a particular class.

Name _____ Date_____

# Reading for School

**Directions:** Match the reading activity with the class for which it might be required.

_____ **1.** Read the biography of a famous composer.

_____ **2.** Read the rules for how to play tennis.

_____ **3.** Read the instructions for dissecting a frog.

_____ **4.** Read about weapons used in World War I.

_____ **5.** Read the instructions for playing a game using a certain disk.

_____ **6.** Read a short story.

_____ **7.** Read examples of how to solve a word problem.

_____ **8.** Read rules for which words to capitalize.

| | |
|---|---|
| **a.** Physical Education | **e.** Math |
| **b.** Social Studies | **f.** English |
| **c.** Science | **g.** Reading or Literature |
| **d.** Music | **h.** Computer |

# III-3 Reading for Pleasure

**Objective**: The student will give examples of materials usually read for pleasure.

**Comments:**

Reading can be a source of pleasure for a lifetime. As teachers and parents, we hope to encourage children to find reading material to enjoy. In this lesson, students are given a list of some types of pleasure reading to which hopefully, they will add ideas of their own.

**Introductory Activities:**

a. Have students list two favorite books or stories they have read.

b. Have students list a favorite character from a book.

c. Have students give examples of magazines they enjoy reading.

**Activity:**

The worksheet "Reading for Pleasure" consists of a list of some reading material or types of literature that could be considered primarily "pleasurable." (There is, of course, a lot of overlap between areas – some students may insist they do not enjoy reading anything; others may enjoy reading material that is intended for instruction or school.) Suggest that this is only a partial list and they should add their own ideas to it.

> **Discussion:** Encourage students to check off their favorite types of reading material (as well as to add their own ideas). There will be a lot of difference of opinion, but as long as the material seems to fit the student, and is appropriate, it should be included on the list.

1. What is your favorite type of reading material when you read for pleasure?

2. If you do not enjoy reading, why do you think you feel that way? Do you enjoy listening to stories?

3. How often do you spend time reading for pleasure?

4. Do you read material recommended by friends? teachers?

**Extension Activities:**

1. Find out how books are organized at the library. What are the main categories of the Dewey Decimal System?

2. Make the effort to read one book from each of the categories.

3. Write a short story. Exchange your story with others from the class. Include drawings and/or cartoons if you wish.

4. Write a comic book. Be sure you have a plot and interesting characters. Feel free to add color!

**Evaluation:**

a. List three to five sources of material usually considered to be pleasure reading.

b. Describe one of your favorite stories or books. What did you particularly like about it?

# Reading for Pleasure

**Directions:** The following is a list of some types of reading material often considered for pleasure. Put an X in front of those you read for pleasure. Feel free to add items to the list.

_____ **1.** novels (mystery, romance, etc.)

_____ **2.** comic books

_____ **3.** teen magazines

_____ **4.** crossword puzzles

_____ **5.** movie reviews

_____ **6.** letters from friends

_____ **7.** horoscopes

_____ **8.** sports magazines

_____ **9.** computer games (instructions, playing options)

_____ **10.** poetry

_____ **11.** travel brochures

_____ **12.** joke or riddle books

_____ **13.** television program guides

_____ **14.** craft instruction books

_____ **15.** self-help books

_____ **16.** autobiographies or biographies of famous people

_____

_____

_____

_____

_____

_____

_____

_____

_____

## III-4 Reading on the Job

**Objective:** The student will identify reading tasks necessary or helpful for specific jobs or careers.

**Comments:**

There are tasks involved with almost any type of job that requires reading. True, some people can perform a job once they have learned how to do it without referring to a manual, but at some point reading is a part of acquiring knowledge about the job. Students are to think of ways that reading is a part of either performing a job or of more efficiently performing that job.

**Introductory Activities:**

a. Have students list ten occupations that require reading.

b. Have students list three to five occupations they feel do not require a lot of reading.

**Activity:**

**Answers:** *(examples)* **1.** being able to read the orders; **2.** following instructions for feeding and exercise; **3.** road signs; **4.** alphabetizing names; **5.** reading about the effects of medicine; **6.** reading descriptions of the parts; **7.** reading about the chemicals that are ingredients in some of the products; **8.** following recipes

**Discussion:** Students can discuss the different reading tasks they thought of for each of the jobs listed. Additional discussion questions include:

1. Can you think of any jobs that don't require any reading at all?

2. What type of reading materials would there be that a person could use to improve his or her skills? **(manuals, extra skills training, etc.)**

3. Which of the jobs on the worksheet also involved writing? **(1,2,4,5,6,7,8; possibly 3)**

4. What are some jobs *primarily* based on reading? **(book editor, novelist, jobs for gathering information and research, etc.)**

**Extension Activities:**

1. "Job shadow" a parent or individual you know well. Find out what reading tasks are involved in his or her job. Is the reading task a vital part of the job?

2. Make a game along the lines of *20 Questions*, only using reading tasks as clues. Appropriate questions might include: "Do you read street signs on your job?" "Do you read from a dictionary on your job?" "Do you read papers written by students?" etc.

**Evaluation:**

a. List five jobs performed by someone you know. List two reading tasks involved for each.

b. Write a paragraph describing a job you are interested in doing someday as a career. What reading tasks would be involved?

# Reading on the Job

**Directions:** Below is a list of some jobs. What are some reading tasks that would be required or important in order to do that job well? Write your ideas on the lines.

**1.** Working at a drive-up window at a fast-food restaurant

_____

_____

**2.** Taking care of cats and dogs at a kennel

_____

_____

**3.** Driving a truck across the country

_____

_____

**4.** Being a secretary

_____

_____

**5.** Being a doctor for children

_____

_____

**6.** Placing orders for computer parts ordered by customers

_____

_____

**7.** Running a beauty salon

_____

_____

**8.** Preparing food for a catering service

_____

_____

# III-5 Reading for Information

**Objective:** The student will identify several sources of obtaining information through reading and give examples of the information provided from each source.

**Comments:**

A lot of information can be gained by reading. Students might need to read a textbook for class discussion questions. People who travel to foreign countries would read about the climate, customs, and special information about conditions. Reading (whether from a book or computer) provides a lot of necessary information.

**Introductory Activities:**

a. Have students look around the room to find as many sources of information (dictionary, encyclopedia, map book, etc.) as they can.

b. Ask students which source they would use to (a) find the definition of a word; (b) find the population of a country; (c) trace an outline of Mexico; etc.

**Activity:**

**Answers:** *(examples)* **1.** information about a career; **2.** what's on Thursday at 7:00; **3.** the local weather; **4.** dates of the Civil War; **5.** how to reduce fractions; **6.** how to correct a mistake; **7.** how to make chocolate chip cookies; **8.** fees for a driver's license; **9.** how often to take an aspirin; **10.** how to housebreak a puppy; **11.** how long the machine is warranted for; **12.** what parts are included in the tent; **13.** what jobs at the hospital are available; **14.** when the bus arrives in your town; **15.** how to put batteries in the camera

**Discussion:** Students should share their pieces of information with the class. Some will probably overlap, but there should be quite a bit of variety.

1. How is information organized in an encyclopedia for easy access? **(alphabetically)**

2. How is information organized in a dictionary? **(alphabetically)**

3. Which of these sources do you more frequently use? Why?

4. Why is it important to read warranty information? **(so you know where to send it, what is protected)**

5. Why is it important to follow directions carefully for assembling something or even cooking? **(so it will turn out the way it is intended to)**

6. What are some other sources of information you may use? **(almanac, telephone book, books of lists, etc.)**

7. How is an index, table of contents, or glossary helpful? **(they give an overview of specifically where to find what you're looking for)**

**Extension Activities:**

1. Make a list of 50 to 100 things you want to know. This could be simple facts or pieces of information such as: how many different breeds of dogs are there, who has the best batting average on your favorite team, who wrote *Dracula,* etc. What source would you use to find that information?

2. Form two teams in your class. Divide the questions from (1) and have a race to find the answers. (Make sure resources with the answers are available!)

3. Show off your knowledge or expertise in a certain skill area by creating a manual or documentary about it. Exchange with others. How easy is it to find information in your manual?

4. Conduct a scavenger hunt for information. Have students look at products such as a soda can, candy bar, cereal box, laundry detergent container, etc., to find requested information.

**Evaluation:**

List five sources of information. Then list two pieces of information you could get from each source.

**Teacher Notes:**

_____

_____

_____

_____

_____

_____

Name _____ Date_____

# Reading for Information

**Directions:** Below is a list of many sources of information. On the line write one piece of information you could find from that particular source.

**1.** encyclopedia

_____

**2.** television program guide

_____

**3.** local newspaper

_____

**4.** history book

_____

**5.** math book

_____

**6.** manual for word processing

_____

**7.** cookbook

_____

**8.** driver's manual

_____

**9.** aspirin label

_____

**10.** *How to Care for a New Puppy*

_____

**11.** warranty on a vacuum cleaner

_____

**12.** *How to Set Up a Tent*

_____

**13.** classified ads

_____

**14.** bus schedule

_____

**15.** instructions on how to operate a new camera

_____

# III-6 Improving Reading Skills

**Objective:** The student will identify three to five ways to improve his or her reading skills.

**Comments:**

The best way to improve reading skills is to read, read, read. There are specific skills good readers have acquired, and students who would like to improve their skills can follow the model of good readers and read "smarter." In this lesson, specific reading skills and ways to acquire them are discussed.

**Introductory Activities:**

a. Have students rate themselves on their reading ability, from 0 (poor) to 5 (excellent).

b. Have students list specific things about reading they find difficult, or specific reading tasks they have trouble with (e.g., outlining, answering questions, understanding words, etc.).

c. Have students estimate how much time (in hours or minutes) they think they spend a day on reading activities.

**Activity:**

On the worksheet "Improving Reading Skills," students are to match a given reading skill with an example that shows how that skill might be taught. Be sure students understand the skills before completing the worksheet. *Skills:* sequencing – putting events in order; following directions – completing a task as specified; vocabulary (meanings) – identifying what a word means, synonyms, opposites, etc.; identifying new words – looking up the definition of a highlighted word; word attack – using phonics or decoding skills to pronounce or "take apart" a word; comprehension – understanding what was read, being able to summarize/remember.

**Answers: 1.** e; **2.** a; **3.** d; **4.** b; **5.** f; **6.** c

**Discussion:** There are many specific reading skills. Likewise, there are many ways to acquire these skills. Have students do some thinking to devise ways to become a better reader. After reviewing the worksheet, go over the following questions:

1. What is the purpose of "word attack" skills? **(to help identify unfamiliar words)**

2. Does being able to pronounce a word help you understand the word? **(yes, if you would have known the word when you heard it read aloud)**

3. What are some tasks you perform in school that require following directions? **(cooking, workshop, projects)**

4. What are some problems that could come up if you don't follow the directions carefully?

5. How would knowing synonyms and antonyms help you with reading? **(identify many more words, clarify meaning of what you read)**

6. What are some ways you can figure out the meanings of unfamiliar words without looking them up in the dictionary? **(context, word attack skills to pronounce them, etc.)**

7. What are some tasks that must be performed in a certain sequence? **(building, cooking, driving a car, dressing, etc.)**

8. What are some classes that require reading of material and then responding to comprehension questions? **(science, social studies, etc.)**

9. What are some ways to help remember the core or essence of what you have read, particularly if it was quite lengthy? **(take notes, outline, jot down important details)**

10. Why is it important to know synonyms and antonyms of common words? Why can't everything just be "big" or "good" if that's what you mean? **(makes more interesting reading to use different, more specific words; word choice also reflects more accurately what you mean)**

## Extension Activities:

1. Keep a reading log for a week or two. How much time do you spend on reading? You might wish to have a separate "pleasure reading" journal in which you record the number of minutes spent on a daily basis.

2. Read different types of material. Make a list of at least ten different types – encyclopedia, newspaper, news magazine, directions for a task, etc. Spend 30 minutes a day reading something you normally do not read.

3. Improve your vocabulary. There are self-help workbooks that concentrate on knowing word meanings and how words are used.

4. Tape record yourself reading a passage orally. Practice reading fluently and clearly.

5. Browse through a volume of an encyclopedia. Find some topics that catch your interest and spend some time reading.

6. Get a book of crossword puzzles, word searches, and other word game activities. Work on them daily.

7. Practice skimming textbook material before you read. Look it over, read the headings, and form questions in your mind about what the content will be about. Then as you read, look for answers to your questions.

## Evaluation:

a. Identify five reading skills and briefly explain what is involved in each.

b. For each of the skills you identified in (a), give one example of where or how you would use it in school and everyday life.

c. List two skills in which you feel you could improve and write a possible plan for improving those skills.

# Improving Reading Skills

**Directions:** Here is a list of six important reading skills. Read each example below and match it with the reading skill involved.

a. sequencing
b. following directions
c. vocabulary (meanings)
d. identifying new words
e. word attack
f. comprehension

## Example 1

Circle the consonant blend in each word below:

trap            block            street            friend            thick

Reading skill          _____

## Example 2

Tom wanted to build a doghouse. First he made a list of the materials he would need. He figured out how much it would cost. Then he went to the lumber yard and placed his order. After getting his tools together, he and his father began to work on the project. A few hours later, Rover had a new home. *What were the steps involved in making a doghouse?*

Reading skill          _____

## Example 3

We went to the zoo to take a look at a *marsupial*. It was really cute. *What is a marsupial?*

Reading skill          _____

## Example 4

When you make your map, put a key in one corner that tells what your symbols mean. Use a ✳ to indicate a capital city. Use blue to show water. Be sure to include a compass to show the directions.

Reading skill          _____

## Example 5

Archery is a popular sport that involves shooting with a bow and arrow. In target archery, the archer tries to score points by hitting a target as close to the center as possible. If the archer hits the middle, he or she would score 10 points. That is called a bull's-eye. *What is target archery?*

Reading skill          _____

## Example 6

What is the opposite of:
   direct
   large
   heavy

What is a synonym for:
   tired
   cold
   happy

Reading skill          _____

# III-7 Communicating Through Writing

**Objective:** The student will list and explain common forms of communication using writing.

**Comments:**

Writing is communicating. A simple model of this process is: writer – message – receiver. In this lesson, the student is to identify some types of writing that are directed to a receiver.

**Introductory Activities:**

a. Have students list three things they have written lately.

b. Have students list three people to whom or for whom they have written something in the past week. What were the messages or assignments?

**Activity:**

On the worksheet "Communicating Through Writing," students are given a task involving some form of writing. They are to identify what type of writing (e.g., message, report, application) is required and who is the receiver of the message.

**Answers:** *(examples)* **1.** personal letter/Aunt Edna; **2.** report/teacher; **3.** job application/manager; **4.** short message/mother; **5.** business note/company; **6.** book report/teacher

**Discussion:** There are many ways in which we communicate with each other through writing. Some may be quick and short-lived – a message jotted down, a comment; others are meant to endure – a special letter, a speech, etc. Discuss with students how the type of writing and the message should fit the situation.

1. Which of the forms of communication are you most likely to use?

2. Which types of writing are the most formal? **(business application, report)**

3. What special considerations would you give to a more formal type of writing? **(check for neatness, spelling, etc.)**

4. Does knowing who will receive the message change the way you would write the message? **(probably – if it is someone you know well, you would not have to be as formal)**

**Extension Activities:**

1. Have students collect examples of formal writing such as job applications, business letters, and reports.

2. Have students research guidelines for writing different types of letters – business letters, friendly letters, thank-you notes, etc. Then compile examples of each.

**Evaluation:**

a. List five examples of types of written communication.

b. Identify the examples in (a) as either formal or informal.

c. Specify a likely receiver of the message in each example.

# Communicating Through Writing

**Directions:** Below are some tasks that involve writing. For each task, write an example of what type of writing might be used, such as a message, research paper, etc. Then write who the information is directed to (received by), such as a teacher, parent, friend, etc.

| TASK | TYPE OF WRITING | RECEIVED BY |
|---|---|---|
| **1.** You want to let your Aunt Edna know how you are doing in school | | |
| **2.** You need to write a report about the political history of Haiti | | |
| **3.** You want to apply for a job at a restaurant | | |
| **4.** You should let your mother know you're going out for a few hours | | |
| **5.** You want to receive information from a company about its free offer | | |
| **6.** You want to give your opinion about a book | | |

# III-8 Everyday Writing Tasks

**Objective:** The student will identify five to ten everyday writing tasks.

**Comments:**

Most students will face several types of writing tasks throughout the day. Writing is involved in simple tasks such as taking a phone message or writing yourself a note to remember something. This lesson provides the student with many examples of how writing is part of everyday life.

**Introductory Activities:**

a. Have students list three to five common writing activities they perform at school.

b. Have students list three to five common writing activities they might perform at home or for pleasure.

**Activity:**

**Answers: 1.** history outline; **2.** write poem summary; **3.** note to friend; **4.** shopping list; **5.** office form; **6.** job application; **7.** paragraph about self; **8.** phone message; **9.** letter for information; **10.** science questions; **11.** thank-you note; **12.** journal

**Discussion:** This was probably not a completely "typical day," but there are many common examples of writing in this activity. Have students compare answers.

1. How many of your common writing activities are done with pen or pencil? Do you use a word processor for many of your tasks?

2. What additional "everyday writing tasks" could you add to this list? **(assignment sheet, other notes and assignments)**

3. Do you think writing is more difficult than reading for most people? Why/why not? **(writing may require more effort; it is self-generated, active, etc.)**

4. Which of the examples on the worksheet could be considered more "formal"? Which would be more "informal"?

**Extension Activities:**

1. Have students interview a parent or adult. What typical writing activities are part of their everyday life? How does this differ – or overlap – with a student's writing activities?

2. Have students spend time in the computer lab developing word processing skills. Record improvement in rate and accuracy of typing!

**Evaluation:**

a. List at least five everyday writing tasks that would be performed at home, school, and/or work.

b. Write a paragraph explaining how you feel about one of the following topics:

– Importance of Writing vs. Reading as a School Skill

– Importance of Word Processing vs. Handwriting

– Writing Skills of the 21st Century

# Everyday Writing Tasks

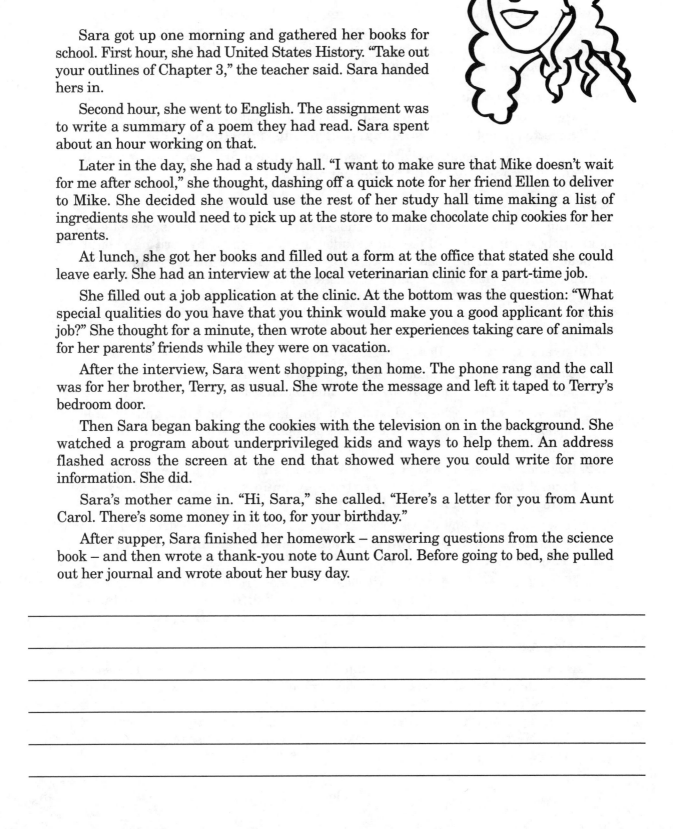

**Directions:** Read the following short story. List as many examples of everyday writing tasks as you can find. Use the back of this sheet if you need more space to write.

Sara got up one morning and gathered her books for school. First hour, she had United States History. "Take out your outlines of Chapter 3," the teacher said. Sara handed hers in.

Second hour, she went to English. The assignment was to write a summary of a poem they had read. Sara spent about an hour working on that.

Later in the day, she had a study hall. "I want to make sure that Mike doesn't wait for me after school," she thought, dashing off a quick note for her friend Ellen to deliver to Mike. She decided she would use the rest of her study hall time making a list of ingredients she would need to pick up at the store to make chocolate chip cookies for her parents.

At lunch, she got her books and filled out a form at the office that stated she could leave early. She had an interview at the local veterinarian clinic for a part-time job.

She filled out a job application at the clinic. At the bottom was the question: "What special qualities do you have that you think would make you a good applicant for this job?" She thought for a minute, then wrote about her experiences taking care of animals for her parents' friends while they were on vacation.

After the interview, Sara went shopping, then home. The phone rang and the call was for her brother, Terry, as usual. She wrote the message and left it taped to Terry's bedroom door.

Then Sara began baking the cookies with the television on in the background. She watched a program about underprivileged kids and ways to help them. An address flashed across the screen at the end that showed where you could write for more information. She did.

Sara's mother came in. "Hi, Sara," she called. "Here's a letter for you from Aunt Carol. There's some money in it too, for your birthday."

After supper, Sara finished her homework – answering questions from the science book – and then wrote a thank-you note to Aunt Carol. Before going to bed, she pulled out her journal and wrote about her busy day.

_____

_____

_____

_____

_____

# III-9 Proofreading

**Objective**: The student will identify several important features to proofread when considering written material.

**Comments:**

When writing, particularly on more formal pieces of writing, students should take care to avoid mistakes. Not only will mistakes result in a poor grade, they can also change the meaning of a message. Proofreading can help the student be aware of common mistakes that should be avoided.

**Introductory Activities:**

    a. Have students volunteer to tell about writing mistakes for which they have been corrected recently. **(e.g., spelling, paragraphs, punctuation, etc.)**

    b. Have students come up with a working definition for proofreading. **(reading something written and making corrections)**

**Activity:**

On the worksheet "Proofreading," students are given several examples of ways to make their writing clear. Make sure students understand why writing should be: (a) neat – so it can be read; (b) well-organized – so the message makes sense; (c) appropriate – the style should be suitable for the receiver; (d) spelled correctly; (e) correct as far as punctuation and capitalization; and (f) written in clear sentences, again so that the message is easy to understand. In this lesson, students are to circle the illustration that demonstrates the example.

    **Answers: 1.** A; **2.** B; **3.** B; **4.** A; **5.** A; **6.** B

**Discussion:** Students should explain why the illustration they chose demonstrates good proofreading and why the other illustration is incorrect.

    1. On what writing tasks should you go through the time and trouble of proofreading? Would you bother with a shopping list? What about a letter to the President of the U.S.?

    2. How important is correct spelling? What does this convey to the receiver? **(on a formal piece of writing, it is extremely important; it conveys accuracy, professionalism, and knowledge!)**

    3. How does a "sloppy copy" (first draft) help when you are expected to write something formal? **(lets you get your ideas out without worrying about being perfect the first time)**

    4. If you know you have trouble with spelling, what are ways you can help yourself avoid these mistakes? **(keep a personal list of difficult words, get familiar with a dictionary, have someone proofread your writing, etc.)**

**Extension Activities:**

    1. Have students find and become familiar with Proofreaders' Marks. (These can be found in most dictionaries. They show symbols that are used to indicate changes in a piece of writing. Some that are appropriate would be indicating a new paragraph, inserting or deleting words, and using capital letters.) Prepare several pieces of writing with obvious mistakes and have students use proofreaders' marks to indicate corrections.

2. Make a classroom list of "Spelling Demons" – words that give students trouble! Post the list in a prominent place in the room. Students may also keep their own personal list of words that give them trouble.

3. Offer students the opportunity to work on spelling skills. Share "tricks" (such as mnemonic devices) for remembering hard words.

4. Have students exchange papers often and search for corrections in each other's writing. You may want to prepare a checklist of items to consider, such as the items on the worksheet. After checking, students should initial each item to show they examined it.

**Evaluation:**

a. Write a paragraph that explains the importance of proofreading something you have written.

b. List at least five items you should consider when proofreading a piece of writing.

**Teacher Notes:**

_____

_____

_____

_____

_____

_____

# Proofreading

**Directions:** Below are examples of ways to make your writing as good as you can make it. For each one, circle the illustration that better demonstrates the example.

---

**1.** Your writing should be <u>neat</u>.

**A.** The history of the old West is quite colorful and interesting.

**B.** The ~~historee~~ of the old ~~west iz~~ west is quite colorful and ~~intirest~~ interesting

---

**2.** The message should be <u>well-organized</u>.

**A.** The tennis club is starting. If you want to join, you'll have to come to a meeting.

**B.** The tennis club will meet this Wednesday after school in the gym

---

**3.** The message should be <u>appropriate</u> for the receiver.

**A.** Hey Teacher — Give me an A! This was a stupid assignment!

**B.** Hey Mom, Can you pick me up after track practice? Thanks! Love, Kathi

---

**4.** Check your <u>spelling</u> for mistakes.

**A.** Go to the store on Friday when everything is on sale.

**B.** The repare man will be hear on Thrusday.

---

**5.** Check the <u>punctuation</u> and <u>capital letters</u>.

**A.** It's important to have a good attitude at work. It makes the day go better.

**B.** many people go to work with a chip on their shoulder they wish every day were Friday

---

**6.** Make sure your sentences <u>make sense</u>.

**A.** In home room our class talked. There are problems. We can think of ways. The parking lot is a big is messy.

**B.** Today we discussed the problem of littering in the school parking lot. There is a lot we can do to make it cleaner.

---

# III-10 Writing Clearly

**Objective:** The student will identify examples of writing that request or provide information clearly.

**Comments:**

In order to be understood, what is written must be clear enough so the receiver can figure out what the intent or message is! Written communication that is messy, vague, or inaccurate is poor communication. In this lesson, students are given examples of pieces of writing that are not clearly written.

**Introductory Activities:**

a. Instruct students to take out a piece of paper. Tell them you will time them for 60 seconds as they write as much as they can.

b. After the 60 seconds are up, ask students if they felt frustrated about the assignment. Why? **(vague, no direction, weren't sure what they were supposed to do)**

c. Tell students they will write for another 60 seconds. This time tell them you want them to describe the plot of the last good movie they saw.

d. After time is up, ask if this assignment was easier. Why? **(more direction, knew what to do)**

e. Ask students to look at both assignments. If someone else were to read the papers, would he or she be able to figure out the purpose of the writing?

**Activity:**

The intent of this lesson is to emphasize clarity in writing. Both the purpose and the presentation should be clear. On the worksheet "Writing Clearly," students are given a purpose for writing and are to examine the piece of writing to determine why it is not clear and what could be done to improve it.

**Answers: 1.** messy; **2.** vague directions; **3.** did not follow directions, poor proofreading done; **4.** did not follow directions; **5.** vague; **6.** vague

**Discussion:** Have students share their opinions as to the problems with the writing on the worksheet. After identifying the problem, ask for suggestions for how to improve the task.

1. What would be "wrong" or inconsiderate about sending a sloppy, messy letter to someone? **(hard to read, shows you didn't spend a lot of time on it)**

2. On which examples did the writer fail to follow directions? **(1, 2)**

3. Why is it important to be specific when giving directions? **(so the receiver can figure out what to do)**

4. How would proofreading (and making changes) have made these examples more clear? **(would have called attention to being neat, more organized, etc.)**

**Extension Activities:**

1. Have students collect examples of poorly written pieces of writing. Critique them and offer suggestions for improving them.

2. Look for humorous examples of proofreading or writing errors. For example, one convenience store/gas station had the sign on the marquee: "Eat Here and Get Gas."

3. Describe the cover of a magazine. Include any print on the cover, colors, arrangement of pictures – everything! Then share your writing with another person and ask how clear your description was.

4. Write about a movie you have recently seen. Leave off the title and see if others can guess the movie.

**Evaluation:**

Rewrite two of the items on the worksheet to make them more clear for another person to read.

**Teacher Notes:**

_____

_____

_____

_____

_____

# Writing Clearly

**Directions:** How could these forms of writing be improved to be more clear? Identify the problem in each.

**1.** a fan letter to a movie star

_____

> Dear Snake,
> I am ~~~~ ~~~~
> your greatest
> ~~~~ fan. Please
> send ~~ me a
> photo!
>         Love,
>         Angela

**2.** directions to a friend's house

> Go up to the big tree —
> turn left — go on a
> ways. Go past a house
> or two. Turn. Back up

**3.** a report on the difference between black bears and grizzly bears

> Bears are an
> interesting group of
> animals big black bears
> are of course dangerous i like them

**4.** an application

> Bob Smith
> LAST NAME   FIRST NAME
> 324-5827
> ADDRESS

**5.** request for information from a company

> Dear Sir,
> Please send
> me the free
> information.
> Tom Reed

**6.** phone message

> Terry —
> somebody
> called
> for
> you

# III-11 Writing and More Writing

**Objective:** The student will complete several writing tasks, showing evidence of proofreading and producing a clearly written product.

**Comments:**

As with reading, the best way to improve writing skills is to practice writing. The student is given a long list of writing activities to work on. He or she should incorporate proofreading skills and demonstrate attempts to write clearly in order to produce a piece of writing that communicates well!

**Introductory Activities:**

a. Have students make a personal list of kinds of writing activities they enjoy. You may have to make suggestions to get them started – plays? riddles? letters? etc.

b. Have students select one item from the list they would really like to spend time working on. Inform them that they will be given this as part of the activity.

**Activity:**

The worksheet "Writing and More Writing" lists 25 writing activities to get students started writing. You may wish to have students select five to ten activities and get a notebook specifically to be kept for these writing assignments. Add other items as students can think of things they would be interested in writing.

**Materials:** writing notebook, pen or pencil – or – computer/printer

**Discussion:** Have students select writing activities and set aside time for students to work on them, on a daily basis if possible. Once students are well into the activities, discuss the following questions:

1. Once you get into the "routine" of writing, does it become easier?

2. What types of writing activities did you choose, and why?

3. Were you surprised to find you enjoyed trying to write something different? Perhaps a poem or play?

4. Are you using a proofreading checklist to help you produce a nice, finished product?

5. What other items did you think of to add to the list?

**Extension Activities:**

1. Have students continue to add writing ideas to a class list. As times come up when students need ideas, refer to the list.

2. Establish a daily writing time for your students, perhaps just for five to eight minutes a day. There are many books available that supply topics, questions to answer, and thought-provoking ideas.

**Evaluation:**

As students complete the various writing activities, have students do a self-evaluation (**Is this the best I can do?**), work on proofreading, exchange papers (if the writing is not personal), and display (with permission) the students' efforts.

# Writing and More Writing

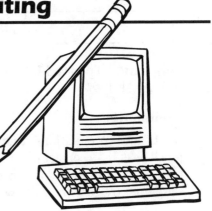

**Directions:** Here is a list of writing tasks. Choose some that sound interesting to you and sharpen your pencil or turn on the computer!

1. Make a list of everything you'd need to take for a week-long vacation in the Bahamas.

2. Write a letter to a local travel agency asking for brochures on biking through France.

3. Choose a favorite sport. Write a paragraph explaining the rules of the game.

4. Pick a position on a hot topic in your community. Write a two-page paper explaining how you feel about it and why.

5. Write a paragraph that you could include on a job application that tells some interesting things about yourself. Include travel, interests, work goals, and educational plans.

6. Write a brief autobiography. What do you want others to know about you?

7. Keep a journal for a month. Keep track of your feelings, events, ups and downs, and any other information you would like to remember.

8. Follow the happenings of one important event in your community. Keep a log of daily changes in that event.

9. Write a news article for your school paper about something that is interesting around your school or community.

10. Interview your favorite teacher or coach.

11. Write a poem.

12. Write a short story.

13. From a book or an encyclopedia, write a one-page biography of a famous person.

14. Do a "Dear Abby" column within your class. Answer the questions and concerns of your classmates (submitted anonymously!).

15. Write an ad explaining why someone from another state would want to visit your town or school.

16. Write a thank-you note to a friend for doing something you appreciated.

17. Write a letter to someone famous asking him or her to visit your school.

18. Write directions for someone unfamiliar with your area for how to get to your house from the downtown area (or other landmark).

19. Copy down three or four of your favorite jokes or riddles. Exchange with friends.

20. Copy the Gettysburg Address.

21. Make an address book/phone book of everyone on your Christmas list.

22. Write your birthday "wish list."

23. Make up an assignment sheet for everything you need to do, get, remember, and complete for a month at school.

24. Send away for free information that you see advertised on television or in a magazine.

25. Make a list of the best things that have ever happened to you or things that make you smile.

# III-12 Writing on the Job

**Objective:** The student will identify ways that people in various careers would use writing skills.

**Comments:**

In most occupations, there are some writing tasks that are a part of carrying out the job. These may consist of writing out orders for someone else to follow, jotting down notes to remind oneself of something, or creating something for others to read. In this lesson, students are to think of how writing is involved in most jobs.

**Introductory Activities:**

    a. Have students list ways that teachers use writing on the job. **(prepare tests, write out worksheets, etc.)**

    b. Have students list ways that their parents use writing skills on their jobs.

**Activity:**

Students are given a list of 10 careers on the worksheet "Writing on the Job." They are to list at least one way in which writing is used on the job.

    **Answers:** *(examples)* **1.** write prescriptions; **2.** write trial notes; **3.** write comments about a photograph; **4.** write an ad to sell a product; **5.** describe a house for sale; **6.** write medical notes for sick animal; **7.** write the conversations between cartoon characters; **8.** describe vacation resort; **9.** write biography of artist; **10.** write directions for caring for lawn

    **Discussion:** Compare students' ideas about how writing is used on the job. Discuss the following questions:

1. Are there any jobs you can think of that do not involve much writing?

2. What are some jobs in which creative thinking or writing is important? **(advertising, writing stories, etc.)**

3. How do jobs that require a lot of writing do these tasks more efficiently? **(form letters, use secretaries, use computers, etc.)**

4. If someone really liked to write, what type of jobs would he or she be interested in as a career? **(novelist, reporter, magazine writer, etc.)**

**Extension Activities:**

1. Invite a writer to visit the class and talk about how writing is part of the job. Have students prepare a list of questions to use to interview the writer.

2. Go through job files or books that describe occupations. Target five to ten unusual occupations. Get ideas for how writing is used on these jobs.

**Evaluation:**

    a. List five occupations and one way in which writing is used on each job.

    b. Write a paragraph describing an occupation you are particularly interested in and how writing is part of that occupation.

# Writing on the Job

**Directions:** How would people in these occupations use writing skills in their jobs? List at least one idea for each.

1. doctor _____

_____

_____

_____

2. lawyer _____

_____

3. photographer _____

_____

4. advertising person _____

_____

5. real estate agent _____

_____

6. person who cares for zoo animals _____

_____

7. cartoonist _____

_____

8. travel agent _____

_____

9. art gallery owner _____

_____

10. lawn care worker _____

_____

# III-13 Math Skills

**Objective:** The student will demonstrate knowledge of common math skills by stating at least one way that a given skill is used in everyday life.

**Comments:**

Math is an academic area with many practical applications. Math and numbers are all around us. Math skills go beyond simple adding and subtracting; it is important to learn how to estimate, problem solve, and apply operations to everyday situations. Students are to think of ways that math skills (e.g., adding, estimating) are used in everyday life.

**Introductory Activities:**

    a. Have students make a list of common skills taught in math class. **(addition and other operations, perhaps some formulas, current topics discussed, etc.)**

    b. Have students list three to five activities they participated in today that involved numbers or math in some way.

**Activity:**

    **Answers:** *(examples)* **1.** figuring out the total on a bill; **2.** figuring out your score from 100 by subtracting the number wrong; **3.** figuring out the number of cookies required if each student wants three; **4.** splitting up money among friends; **5.** calculating the total on the band's fund-raising project; **6.** grouping students into fourths for a project; **7.** getting your height measured by the school nurse; **8.** doing a lab in science; **9.** adding money; **10.** launching a model rocket into the air; **11.** how much decoration you need to put around a bulletin board; **12.** figuring out when school is out for the day

    **Discussion:** Compare students' ideas on the worksheet. Hopefully, students will realize that math concepts are everywhere and apply to many situations.

    1. Do you think math is hard or easy for you? Which parts?

    2. How important is it to know math facts quickly?

    3. How important is it to know how to use a calculator to help solve problems?

    4. Are there any parts of math you think are fun? What?

    5. Do you know of any math "tricks" or ways to do things that help make things easier?

    6. Why is it important to be completely accurate on your math facts? **(foundation for everything else!)**

**Extension Activities:**

    1. Have students skim through their current math text and list the topics contained. Make a glossary of terms that will be important for them to know.

    2. Arrange for tutoring of younger students in math. This could involve making math games, helping students with their work or math activities, going over flash cards, etc.

    3. Have students find and contribute math puzzles, brain teasers, or worksheets they have found fun/interesting/useful. Laminate them and make a class learning center.

**Evaluation:**
   a. List ten common math skills.
   b. List two skill areas that are strengths for you.
   c. List two skill areas that remain challenging for you.

**Teacher Notes:**

_____

_____

_____

_____

_____

_____

# Math Skills

**Directions:** Below are some skills involving math. Next to each one, write one example of how you would use that skill.

**1.** adding _____

_____

**2.** subtracting _____

_____

**3.** multiplying _____

_____

**4.** dividing _____

_____

**5.** counting money _____

_____

**6.** using fractions _____

_____

**7.** measuring in inches _____

_____

**8.** measuring in ounces _____

_____

**9.** using decimals _____

_____

**10.** figuring rate of how fast something is traveling _____

_____

**11.** perimeter _____

_____

**12.** telling time _____

_____

# III-14 Improving Math Skills

**Objective:** The student will identify specific techniques for improving math skills.

**Comments:**

Students are often the best source of knowing how best to learn something that is important to them. Some students learn by memorization, others by thinking things out, some by moving around, others by working with a partner, and so on. In this lesson, specific skills are considered and students are to match examples of ways to help learn those skills.

**Introductory Activities:**

    a. Have students list two or three skills they feel they are good at. Ask for ideas for ways that they learned these skills.

    b. Have students list their own personal preferences for learning math; for example, using notes? working with a partner? using a calculator? etc.

**Activity:**

Students are to match specific skills involving math with a possible technique to help learn that skill on the worksheet "Improving Math Skills." Make sure students understand that these are just examples – there are lots of ways that people learn skills (refer them to the second Introductory Activity).

    **Answers: 1.** d; **2.** b; **3.** f; **4.** e; **5.** h; **6.** g; **7.** a; **8.** c

    **Discussion:** Go over the specific answers with students. Ask students to give reasons for why they selected the answers on the worksheet.

    1. How could you work with a partner to learn math facts? **(quiz each other)**

    2. Why is it important to know common equivalences? **(some problems are given in one set of terms, some in another)**

    3. What are some ways you can solve a "story" problem besides drawing a picture? **(underline key words, look for strategies)**

    4. Why is it important to make sure you are given correct change when dealing with money? **(make sure you are not shorted)**

    5. In what school classes would you use time and money?

    6. Why is it important to be accurate when keeping a checking account? **(so you aren't overdrawn, extra charges)**

    7. Why would it be important to figure out your mileage when driving? **(make sure your car is running efficiently)**

    8. What are some examples of when you would need to know the perimeter of something? **(carpeting, decorating, trimming, etc.)**

**Extension Activities:**

    1. Teach students how to use a calculator to check their work. This will give them extra practice in working on concepts as well as teach them to become familiar with the calculator as a tool.

    2. Have students make their own flash cards for math facts, formulas, key concepts, and so on.

3. Allow students time to use computer games to improve basic math facts as well as thinking skills.

4. Put up a "Brain Teaser of the Day." Encourage students to work together to solve puzzles.

5. Have students be aware of their own strengths and weaknesses in math. If students tend to make the same mistake over and over, analyze the pattern; point out to the student exactly what he or she is doing wrong and give specific techniques for overcoming that particular problem.

**Evaluation:**

a. List two areas of math in which you could improve your skills.

b. Give at least two ways for each of the two areas in (a) that you could try to improve your math skills.

**Teacher Notes:**

_____

_____

_____

_____

_____

_____

# Improving Math Skills

**Directions:** Match the skill with a way you could improve your ability to use that skill.

_____ **1.** learn math facts quickly

_____ **2.** remember equivalences (e.g., 12" = 1 foot)

_____ **3.** figure out a story problem

_____ **4.** give change for a dollar

_____ **5.** figure out the time it will be in five hours

_____ **6.** maintain a checking account

_____ **7.** figure out how far you can drive on a tank of gas

_____ **8.** find the perimeter of a figure

**a.** find out how many gallons your car will hold and how many miles you traveled on the tank of gas

**b.** make a sheet with notes on it such as 3 feet = 1 yard

**c.** make note cards with formulas for figuring out the perimeter of a square, rectangle, etc.

**d.** make flash cards with math facts on them

**e.** watch carefully when a clerk gives you back money

**f.** draw pictures to help "see" the problem

**g.** enter deposits and amounts spent into your account; check for accuracy

**h.** when making appointments for later in the day, figure out how much time will have passed

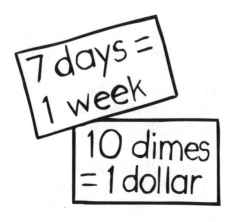
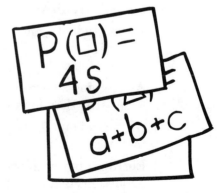

# III-15 Everyday Math Situations

**Objective:** Given an everyday situation, the student will identify several ways that math skills are involved.

**Comments:**

Math is a part of many everyday activities – shopping, eating out, even counting the change in your pocket. In this lesson, students are to think of ways that math skills are involved in some common situations.

**Introductory Activities:**

    a. Have students list five to eight activities they or their parents have done in the past few days that involved numbers.

    b. Have students list two to four activities they or their parents have encountered in the past few days that involved reasoning or problem solving.

**Activity:**

Students are given six examples of common situations on the worksheet "Everyday Math Situations." For each, they are to think of several ways that math skills are involved. One example is given for each.

    **Discussion:** Compare students' responses. There should be a wide variety of ideas for each. The following questions will be helpful for discussion:

1. Why is it important to understand the advertising that often accompanies products that companies want you to buy?

2. Is the "best buy" always the largest can or container?

3. What is "unit pricing"? **(figuring out how much something costs for one unit — one ounce, one pound, etc.)**

4. What is an easy way to figure out a 15% tip? **(take 10% then add half of that to the 10%)**

5. What are some other expenses associated with a car? **(paying for repairs, insurance, etc.)**

6. What units of measuring would probably be involved in cooking?

7. How is the process of reasoning or problem solving involved in everyday math situations? **(estimating how much something will cost, figuring out the likelihood of something happening, etc.)**

**Extension Activities:**

1. Have students make their own worksheets with examples of other everyday activities that are important to them. Show how math skills are also involved in these.

2. After going to a restaurant or fast-food place, have students save the receipts. Compare prices for a hamburger, cheeseburger, fries, etc.

3. Collect menus from restaurants. Have students write math problems using the menus.

4. Borrow a pay stub from someone who is willing to share this. What are all of the deductions taken from the paycheck? What percent is take-home pay?

**Evaluation:**

Choose one of the following everyday situations and list at least three ways that math skills are involved:

a. going to a sports event

b. going to the movies

c. shopping for clothes

d. playing a video game

e. figuring out your report card grades

f. planning a birthday party for a friend

**Teacher Notes:**

_____

_____

_____

_____

_____

_____

# Everyday Math Situations

**Directions:** Fill in the chart with math skills you would use in the following activities. One is given for each activity to help you get started.

**1. SHOPPING**

figuring out the best buy for the money

_____

_____

_____

_____

_____

**2. BANKING**

adding money to a savings account

_____

_____

_____

_____

_____

**3. EATING OUT**

leaving a 15% tip

_____

_____

_____

_____

_____

**4. DRIVING A CAR**

figuring out miles per gallon

_____

_____

_____

_____

_____

**5. COOKING**

doubling a recipe of cookies

_____

_____

_____

_____

_____

**6. TRAVELING**

estimating a motel for two nights

_____

_____

_____

_____

_____

# III-16 Graphs

**Objective:** The student will identify several types of graphs and uses of each.

**Comments:**

A lot of mathematical information is shown clearly by using graphs and charts. In this lesson, four types of commonly used graphs are presented: bar graph, line graph, circle graph, and pictograph or picture graph. Students should be able to identify the type of graph presented and explain how the information is given on that graph.

**Introductory Activities:**

   a. Dictate the following information for students to write: "On Monday, a record store sold 37 CDs and 87 cassettes. On Tuesday, it sold 50 CDs, 28 cassettes, and 9 posters. On Wednesday, it sold 12 CDs, 13 cassettes, and 4 posters." Have students share how they recorded this information.

   b. Have students make three columns on a sheet of paper. Label the columns "Monday, Tuesday, Wednesday" at the bottom of the paper. Have students total the number of items sold on each of the three days in (a). Construct a bar graph that shows the total number of items sold for the three days.

**Activity:**

Explain that you are going to show how to present information by using graphs. There are four graphs that you will be covering: (1) a bar graph – one bar represents one piece of information; (2) a line graph – a continuous line connects pieces of information; (3) a circle graph – shows how much (percentage) of a whole is designated for a given piece of information; and (4) a picture graph – a simple picture as a code to represent how many of a given item are represented.

On the worksheet "Graphs," students are to match the type of graph with the example illustrated.

   **Answers: 1.** picture graph; **2.** line graph; **3.** bar graph; **4.** circle graph

   **Discussion:** Go over the examples with students, paying attention to how each graph clearly depicts the information provided.

   1. Why is it important to have a key when using a picture graph? (**to show what the pictures stand for, how many items are depicted, etc.**)

   2. What would be a good title for the graph in example 1? (**the number of students in class**)

   3. How does the graph show five students? (**half of a person**)

   4. What would be a good title for the graph in example 2? (**amount of snowfall in January**)

   5. Why is a line graph a good way to show this type of information? (**it is continuous**)

   6. What would be a good title for the graph in example 3? (**the number of car sales in a week**)

   7. What other type of graph would clearly show the information in example 3? (**a line graph**)

   8. What would be a good title for the graph in example 4? (**amount of money spent on county projects**)

9. Why is the amount in example 4 shown in cents rather than %? **(it is the portion of a dollar)**

10. Where does most of the money go in example 4? **(juvenile center)**

11. What other type of graph would clearly show the information in example 4? **(bar graph, possibly picture graph)**

## Extension Activities:

1. Have students construct graphs to show information. *Examples:* (a) their height in inches over five years; (b) compare the population of three nearby states; (c) tally the number and kind of pet owned by students in the class; and (d) show the results of a survey asking for the favorite candy bar of students.

2. Look for examples of graphs in the newspaper and magazines. Label the kind of graph and give each a title (if not already provided).

## Evaluation:

Construct one or more of the following graphs (remember labels and titles):

a. Make a bar graph showing the number of televisions serviced by a company in a year: January – 13; February – 11; March – 3; April – 14; May – 10; June – 19; July – 13; August – 20; September – 15; October – 16; November – 11; December – 11.

b. Make a circle graph showing the percent of types of movies students enjoy: horror – 12%; comedy – 50%; romance – 13%; science fiction – 25%.

c. Make a line graph showing Mary's worksheet scores for one week: Monday – 79%; Tuesday – 90%; Wednesday – 85%; Thursday – 81%; Friday – 70%.

d. Make a pictograph with one star representing five CDs. Show the number of CDs owned by each of these students: Jason – 10; Mary – 15; Marcos – 25; Pete – 7.

# Graphs

**Directions:** Write the type of graph (bar graph – line graph – circle graph – picture graph) shown in each example.

**1.**

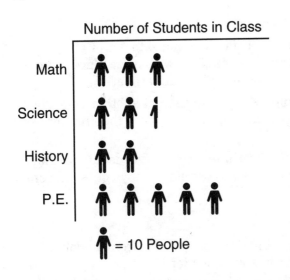

**2.**

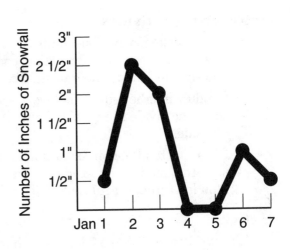

_____

_____

**3.**

_____

**4.**

Amount of each dollar
spent on county projects

_____

# III-17 Charts

**Objective:** The student will construct and be able to interpret information on a chart.

**Comments:**

A chart is another way in which information can be presented. Students should not only be able to read information from a chart, but given information should be able to construct a chart to show this information.

**Introductory Activities:**

a. Do a quick survey of students to find out their favorite place to eat or get pizza. After tabulating the information, construct a simple chart with pizza places across one side and the number of students selecting that place underneath.

b. Conduct another survey of favorite toppings of pizza. Construct another chart, but this time divide the boys and girls into separate columns with the toppings across one side.

c. Obtain attendance information (if possible) for one week and construct a chart showing number of students (divided into grade levels or boys/girls) absent Monday through Friday.

**Activity:**

The worksheet "Charts" depicts a chart showing the sale of items from a bookstore. Students are to use the numbers on the chart to answer questions.

**Answers: 1.** November (totals by month: 186, 153, 220, 241, 202); **2.** October; **3.** pencils; **4.** $8.00; **5.** pencils (226 compared to 193 pens)

**Discussion:** From this activity and the introductory activities, students should have experience on constructing and reading charts. The following questions should be discussed as a class:

1. How does a chart help make information easy to read? **(should be straightforward, uncluttered)**

2. When you construct a chart, why is it important to use labels? **(to make it clear what information you are presenting)**

3. Could you put information on a chart other than numbers? **(yes – any type of description)**

4. What are some types of charts you could make?

**Extension Activities:**

1. Have students construct charts of any applicable information, such as: grades or test scores in a certain class, sports results from teams, amount of money earned from fund-raising activities, favorite movies or books, etc.

2. Collect charts that are in the newspaper and have students write questions using them. Exchange among students and grade for extra credit.

**Evaluation:**

a. Construct a chart using the following information of grades in four subjects for four students:

  – Mary, Kathleen, Todd, and Jamal are the students.

  – The subjects are math, reading, science, and history.

  – Mary's grades (in order) are 79%, 83%, 92%, and 82%. Kathleen's grades are 88%, 86%, 79%, and 94%. Todd's grades are 90%, 82%, 86%, and 77%. Jamal's grades are 79%, 78%, 90%, and 85%.

b. Answer the following questions using your chart:

  – Which student had the highest percentage in math? **(Todd)**

  – Which student had the lowest percentage in history? **(Todd)**

  – What was Kathleen's percentage in reading? **(86%)**

  – In what subject was Mary's highest percentage? **(science)**

**Teacher Notes:**

_____

_____

_____

_____

_____

_____

Name _____ Date_____

# Charts

**Directions:** Use the following chart to answer the questions.

### BOOKSTORE REPORT

|  | Aug. | Sept. | Oct. | Nov. | Dec. |
|---|---|---|---|---|---|
| **# pens sold** | 52 | 37 | 45 | 42 | 17 |
| **# pencils sold** | 36 | 29 | 58 | 70 | 33 |
| **# pads of paper sold** | 53 | 29 | 35 | 63 | 65 |
| **# notebooks sold** | 24 | 27 | 50 | 32 | 64 |
| **# rulers sold** | 8 | 12 | 8 | 18 | 15 |
| **# calculators sold** | 13 | 19 | 24 | 16 | 8 |

**1.** What month had the most sales of all items?

_____

**2.** In which month were the most calculators sold?

_____

**3.** What item sold the most in October?

_____

**4.** If notebooks sold for $.25 each, how much money was made in November from that item?

_____

**5.** Were more pens or more pencils sold over the five months reported?

_____

# III-18 Math Problems

**Objective:** The student will select and complete several types of math activities.

**Comments:**

In this lesson, students are given a variety of activities using math skills. They are to select however many you feel are appropriate and try them out. You may wish to add plenty of activities of your own, depending on what you wish to emphasize in class.

**Introductory Activities:**

a. Have students list three to five types of math activities they enjoy doing.

b. Have students write one math problem they would give someone else to figure out.

**Activity:**

Students are given lots of examples of math problems on the worksheet "Math Problems." Depending on your specific objectives, you may assign them to work on several at their own pace.

> **Discussion:** After students have been given time to work on several of the activities, discuss the procedures and answers.

1. What did you find out about shopping for groceries? Did the amount of money it costs to buy food surprise you?

2. How far can your family's car go on one tank of gas? What factors would change this number? **(type of car, city or highway travel, condition of the car, etc.)**

3. How did your cookies turn out?

4. What is the current interest rate on savings accounts?

5. Which types of soft drinks were the cheapest per ounce? Which were most expensive?

6. What amount did you get on January 31 for problem 13? Were you surprised that it was this great? **($10,737,418.24)**

7. How did you go about estimating the number of beans in problem 17?

**Extension Activities:**

1. Add your own ideas to the math list. Include students' problems/ideas, brain teasers, and current events in math.

2. Post a "problem of the day" in your classroom. Have students work on it in their spare time.

**Evaluation:**

a. List one or two specific skill areas in math in which you would like to improve.

b. Specifically state what you will do or have done to improve your ability to solve math problems in (a).

# Math Problems

**Directions:** Here are some math activities for you to try.

1. Shop for your family's groceries for a week. Estimate the total of the contents of your shopping cart before you find the exact amount.

2. Figure out how far your family's car can go on one tank of gas.

3. Make a batch of chocolate chip cookies. Double the recipe for a larger batch.

4. Calculate how much money you would have if you deposited $100 into a savings account that paid back 4% interest each year and you kept the money in for one year.

5. Figure out your exact age in (a) months and then (b) days.

6. Estimate how far your house is from school. Then (with a car) find out exactly (in tenths of a mile).

7. Make a chart that shows the unit prices of several different kinds of soft drinks.

8. Add the number of calories you consume in one day.

9. Use a calculator to find the average height and weight of the people in your class.

10. Cut out five charts/graphs from newspaper articles. Write three to five questions that can be answered using them.

11. Collect menus from local restaurants. Plan an entire meal, including beverage, appetizer, and dessert. Calculate the cost. Don't forget the tip!

12. Check the classified ads for available jobs. What is the hourly wage of one that interests you? What would your weekly salary be? Monthly salary? Yearly salary?

13. If you are given a penny on January 1 and the amount doubles each day after that (e.g., you would get 2¢ on January 2, 4¢ on January 3, 8¢ on January 4 and so on), how much money would you get on January 31?

14. Estimate (and then figure out) how much everyone in the class weighs if you all stepped on a scale at the same time.

15. If you weigh 1/6 of your normal weight on the moon, how much would you weigh?

16. How far is it around the perimeter of your classroom in feet? yards?

17. Fill a small jar with jelly beans. Estimate how many pieces are in the jar. Then count them.

18. Open a small bag of M&M's®. Make a chart showing how many of each color of candy there are in the bag.

19. Record the temperature at the same time of the day every day for two weeks. What is the range in temperatures? Make a chart showing this information.

20. Read the sports section of the local paper. What is the percentage of completed passes from a football game? What is the hitting percentage (batting average) from a baseball game? What is the won/lost percentage of a favorite team?

## III-19 Keeping a Math Journal

**Objective:** The student will demonstrate ability to keep a math journal, recording important information clearly and accurately.

**Comments:**

Many teachers find it helps students to keep a math journal. The contents of a journal may vary, but would probably include important definitions, concepts, examples of problems, key ideas, formulas, and pictures or diagrams that students would find helpful. In this lesson, students are given an example of a student's notes and are asked to record the information into a journal.

**Introductory Activities:**

a. Ask students to give ideas about what a math journal is and why such a journal would be helpful.

b. Ask students to list ideas of what might be included in a math journal.

**Activity:**

Students are given a sample set of notes presumably taken by a student in math class. They are to redo the notes in a journal (in the right-hand column of the worksheet "Keeping a Math Journal"). You may wish to have students include the following: (1) put the date before each set of comments; (2) underline all definitions; (3) label all drawings clearly; (4) write neatly; (5) clearly indicate what information will be required for a test.

**Materials:** pen or pencil; if the worksheet area is too small, you may have students rewrite the notes on their own notebook paper

**Answers:** will vary – here is one example

**Discussion:** After students have worked on this journal activity, compare styles and ideas. Obviously, each student should record information in a manner that is useful to him- or herself.

1. What words needed definitions on this activity? (**perimeter**)
2. What pictures helped clarify the shapes? (**square, triangle, circle, rectangle**)
3. What formulas were in these notes? (**formula for the perimeter of a square, rectangle, and triangle**)
4. When is the test on this material? (**Monday**)
5. What information will be required to know for the test? (**how to figure out the perimeter of the three shapes**)
6. How did you highlight the important information? (**with colored marker, underlining, etc.**)

**Extension Activities:**

1. Have students keep a math journal in class for several weeks. Go over the information collectively. What tips did students find to help organize the material?
2. If students are having difficulty keeping up with a math journal, keep a section of your chalkboard specifically for math notes. Allow students to copy these notes into their journals. Check periodically to make sure students are copying them correctly.

**Evaluation:**

a. What information is important to include in a math journal?
b. How can you highlight important information?
c. How can a math journal help you review math skills?

Name _____ Date_____

# Keeping a Math Journal

**Directions:** Below are some math notes taken by Fred for a week. Help organize them into a journal.

**Math Journal**

Monday 9/19
  Perimeter – the distance
  around a flat object.
    □ square  ○ circle
    △ triangle  □
            rectangle

Tues.
  P. of a square is
  4 times the side
        ↑
      KNOW        Hi! 🐷

Wed.
  P. of a rectangle =
  l + w + l + w
      (or) 2(l + w)

Thurs
Triangle – ~~6 sides~~ 3 sides
  Perim. = a + b + c   a △ c
                        b

Friday – (Study for
         test on Monday)
  * Know how to figure
    Perim. of □ △ and □

# III-20 School Tasks for Success

**Objective:** The student will identify 10 to 15 skills that are important for success in school.

**Comments:**

Most teachers and students would agree that there are certain skills that separate the "good" students from those who have problems in school. In this lesson, students are to consider a list of student skills and rate themselves according to how well they think they are doing on each.

**Introductory Activities:**

a. Have students list three skills they think are important to doing well in school.

b. Have students list three skills they think their teachers would say are important to doing well in school.

c. Have students list three skills they think their parents would say are important to doing well in school.

**Activity:**

**Discussion:** Since this is a personal survey, students may or may not want to share their responses. You may inform them that you won't even look at them, but hope that it will be helpful to them to improve their skills.

1. Which of the skills on the list would you pick as your biggest problem area?

2. Which would your teachers select?

3. Which would your parents select?

4. Which skills do you think are the most important for any student to do well at?

5. Do different teachers have different ideas or expectations of what they feel is important to do well in school or in their classes?

6. Are there any skills on the list you feel are not important?

**Extension Activities:**

1. Conduct a class survey. Which skills are the hardest for most students to follow? Why? Which are considered the most important?

2. Add skills to the list. You may want to list different sets of skills for different classes.

3. Write a handbook for younger students explaining what skills are important for your grade level and how they can begin developing good student skills now. Illustrate the handbook with humorous drawings.

**Evaluation:**

a. List eight to ten important student skills.

b. Explain why five of the skills you selected are important to do well in school.

c. Write a paragraph selecting one student skill you would like to work on and outline a brief plan for how you could improve in that area.

# School Tasks for Success

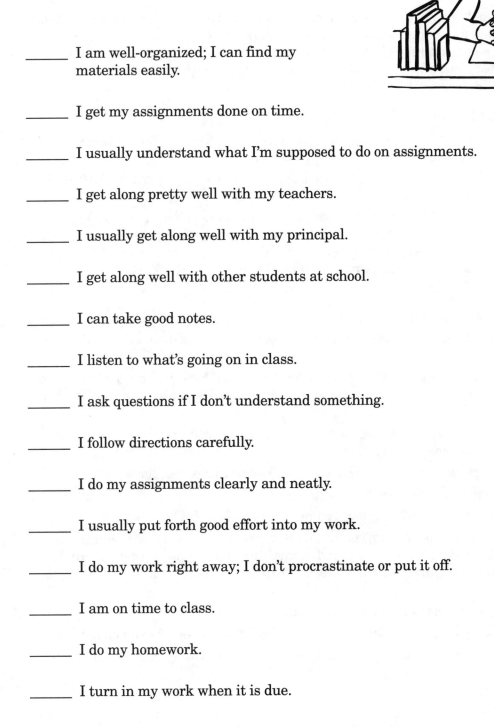

**Directions:** Below is a list of skills or tasks that help someone do well in school. Rate yourself from 1 to 5 (1 = poor, 5 = excellent) according to how well you see yourself performing each skill.

_____ I am well-organized; I can find my materials easily.

_____ I get my assignments done on time.

_____ I usually understand what I'm supposed to do on assignments.

_____ I get along pretty well with my teachers.

_____ I usually get along well with my principal.

_____ I get along well with other students at school.

_____ I can take good notes.

_____ I listen to what's going on in class.

_____ I ask questions if I don't understand something.

_____ I follow directions carefully.

_____ I do my assignments clearly and neatly.

_____ I usually put forth good effort into my work.

_____ I do my work right away; I don't procrastinate or put it off.

_____ I am on time to class.

_____ I do my homework.

_____ I turn in my work when it is due.

## III-21 Getting Organized

**Objective:** Given a task, the student will identify what steps are necessary to complete the task in an organized efficient manner.

**Comments:**

Often students have no idea how to approach a task involving more than one step. Being organized is more than simply knowing where one's materials are; it involves having a good understanding of the task itself, sequencing what needs to be done, obtaining necessary materials, and then actually doing it! In this lesson, students are given tasks to organize.

**Introductory Activities:**

a. What do you need to do to get yourself organized in the morning before school? **(take shower, find clothes, have breakfast, etc.)**

b. What are some "school tools" you need to have almost any given day? **(pencil, paper, calculator, etc.)**

c. If you were given a list of five things you had to do – such as: clean your room, make cookies, mow the grass, do your homework, pick up milk at the store – how would you begin to organize what to do first? **(take a look at your time, where everything is located, what needs to be done before dark, etc.)**

**Activity:**

Students are given six typical school tasks. On the worksheet "Getting Organized," they are to figure out what materials are needed to complete the task and then list where they would obtain the materials.

**Discussion:** Compare students' responses on the items. Most will probably involve obtaining common materials, such as index cards, encyclopedias, markers, and so on.

1. When you have a special project to work on at school, what materials are usually involved? What type of equipment is needed?

2. What are some ways you organize your material or equipment for school?

3. What are some ways you organize your time?

4. Do you consider yourself an organized person in general? Why or why not?

5. What are some simple things you can do to make a task easier for the next time you have to make something or find something? **(put books back in order, replace broken parts, put markers away in the same place every time, etc.)**

6. Where do you normally do your work when you take it home?

7. How do you organize materials needed for a hobby or something you do for fun?

8. Do you have a desk or particular place at home where you can put your schoolwork?

**Extension Activities:**

1. Have students add column D to the worksheet with the heading "What to Do First." Then complete the first step for each of the tasks.

2. Have students draw a map of their workplace at home (or at school) and show where they keep their pens, paper, other work materials, etc.

3. Make a list of 15 tasks that students do routinely. Time each one to get an idea of how long it takes. Then make a list of the steps involved in completing the task. Try to find ways to "streamline" the task. Have students time themselves now!

**Evaluation:**

Select one of the following tasks. For each, list the materials needed, where to obtain the materials, and steps involved in completing the task.

a. Write a brief report about ten presidents of the United States. Include important dates in their lives, a picture, events that happened during their presidency, and information about their personal lives.

b. Cook a typical meal from a European country.

c. Describe an invention of the future that will make the average person's life easier in some way. Include a diagram, advertisement describing the benefits of this invention, and a name.

**Teacher Notes:**

_____

_____

_____

_____

_____

_____

# Getting Organized

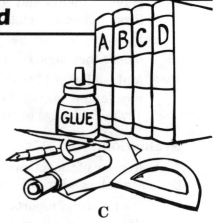

**Directions:** Complete the following chart. A task is given in A. Under B, list what is needed for the task. Under C, list where you can get what is needed.

| A<br>What's the Task? | B<br>What Is Needed? | C<br>Where Do I Get It? |
|---|---|---|
| **1.** Outline a report using 3" x 5" cards. | | |
| **2.** Make a poster of some endangered species of animals. | | |
| **3.** Make a circle graph showing how much time is spent on daily activities at school. | | |
| **4.** List each 50 states, its capital, state bird, state flower, population, and motto. | | |
| **5.** Color in a map of your state showing the average rainfall in each area. | | |
| **6.** Make 30 practice flash cards of math formulas or facts. | | |

# III-22 Taking Notes

**Objective:** The student will demonstrate ability to read (or listen to) a short passage and take summary notes.

**Comments:**

The ability to listen to or read information and then understand it well enough to summarize it is a skill that is helpful throughout an entire school career. Much information is presented orally, especially in the upper grades. While some teachers use notes and chalkboards to list important information for students to know, others expect students to listen, analyze, and write information quickly and accurately. In this lesson, students are given an opportunity to write notes as if they were listening to a brief lecture.

**Introductory Activities:**

    a. Have students list classes in which note-taking is a frequent activity.

    b. Ask students how they know what information presented in a class is important to know. **(written on board, teacher says "Know this!," etc.)**

**Activity:**

The students are to "pretend" they are listening to a brief lecture given by a science teacher. You may want to read this to students or have them participate by reading it orally. The students are to jot down notes on the material at the bottom of the worksheet "Taking Notes."

    **Discussion:** Students will probably record the information in different ways. Some may use pictures with labels to help remember; others may use words. Compare the ways in which students selected what they thought was important.

    1. How did you know what was important to write down?

    2. What clues did the teacher give that something was important? **(definition on the board, comment "Remember that.")**

    3. How did the pictures on the board help? **(something visual to go with the labels)**

    4. What information about this material do you think might be on a test?

    5. How do you organize your notes?

    6. Is it easier for you to take notes from oral or written material? Why?

    7. Is it important to be a good listener for oral information and a good reader for written information?

**Extension Activities:**

    1. Have students pay attention in each class for clues or techniques that his or her teachers use to highlight important information. Make a list.

    2. Prepare mini-lectures (or have students participate in this) with a quiz at the end. Practice emphasizing what notes should be taken and studied in preparation for the test.

    3. Jot down an incomplete outline on the board before you give a lecture. As you talk, have students complete the outline on their own paper. Compare notes at the end.

**Evaluation:**

Have students use the notes they took on the worksheet to complete the following "quiz":

    a. What is digestion?

    b. How do the teeth and tongue help with digestion?

    c. Where does food go after you swallow it?

    d. What is the esophagus?

    e. What is the stomach shaped like?

    f. Where does food pass to after the stomach?

    g. When does food go to the large intestine?

    h. What is waste?

    i. How does waste leave the body?

(*Answers:* **a.** breaking down food; **b.** moisten and crush it; **c.** into the esophagus; **d.** short tube that connects the throat and stomach; **e.** letter J; **f.** small intestine; **g.** after small intestine; **h.** what the body does not use; **i.** through colon)

**Teacher Notes:**

_____

_____

_____

_____

_____

_____

# Taking Notes

**Directions:** Mr. Knowitall is giving a science lecture. What notes would you take if you were a student in his class? Use the lines at the bottom to take your notes.

_____

_____

_____

_____

_____

_____

---

## III-23 Studying Smarter

---

**Objective:** The student will identify reasons why characters in examples are not studying effectively.

**Comments:**

On any given assignment, students in a class probably have about the same amount of time and length of work involved. However, some students use that time much more constructively – they study "smarter." This lesson highlights some problems that get in the way of being a good student.

**Introductory Activities:**

a. Ask students the following question: If you had 15 minutes to learn the capital cities of ten European countries, how would you go about using that time to work on this task?

b. Ask students to list their ideas or techniques for "good studying." What are some ways they use their time wisely?

**Activity:**

On the worksheet "Studying Smarter," students are to examine the examples of students who are not studying in an effective manner. They are to pick out the problem in each.

**Answers: 1.** disorganized; **2.** procrastinating; **3.** didn't keep quizzes or notes; **4.** didn't plan ahead; **5.** using time to socialize instead of studying; **6.** not finding out instructions; **7.** listening to music instead of concentrating; **8.** joking around

**Discussion:** Have students go over their ideas for each. Have them offer suggestions for a better use of the time.

1. How could each student on the worksheet study smarter?

2. Which are examples of problems of (a) time? (b) organization? (c) attitude?

3. How could you go about making changes if this were your situation?

4 Do you think some students study better with background music or TV? **(emphasize word "background!")**

**Extension Activities:**

1. Have students role play these and other situations. Have them come up with alternative endings that show good use of time.

2. Have students come up with a specific plan of attack for each student on the worksheet. What would they suggest for each?

**Evaluation:**

a. List two ways students can effectively use time to study efficiently.

b. List two ways students can effectively organize materials to study efficiently.

c. List two ways students can effectively use a good attitude to study efficiently.

# Studying Smarter

**Directions:** Each student below could be a little smarter in the way he or she is studying. What is the problem in each?

# III-24 Following Directions

**Objective:** The student will identify common school directions and possible consequences of not following them.

**Comments:**

The ability to follow directions is very basic to survival in school. Assuming the student understands the directions given, the next step is careful compliance with them. Students are given examples of common directions heard in school and are to think of what could happen if they were not followed correctly.

**Introductory Activities:**

a. Have students give examples of directions they have been given at home in the past few days (or hours).

b. Have students give examples of directions they have been given at school recently.

c. Have students give examples of directions that might be given by someone in position of authority such as principal, mayor, president, etc.

**Activity:**

Students are given examples of directions on the worksheet "Following Directions" that might be given in school. They are to write a possible scenario of the circumstances in which they might be given the direction and to decide on a possible consequence of what might happen if the direction were not followed correctly.

**Answers:** *(examples)* **1.** math; may do the wrong problems; **2.** taking a history test; answers may not be read correctly by the computer; **3.** reading; reading more than you have to; **4.** math; getting some problems wrong; **5.** English; may get filed with the wrong class; **6.** computer lab; lose all of your work; **7.** social studies; may look like a country instead of water; **8.** cooking; chips won't be mixed in equally; **9.** business class; names will be out of order; **10.** math; the teacher may be busy and you would waste time when you could probably figure it out yourself

**Discussion:** Have students share their responses to the items on the worksheet. Be sure to praise creative answers!

1. Why would it be important to follow the directions given?

2. If you think you had a better idea, how could you suggest it in some of the situations?

3. What are some occupations for which it is extremely important to follow directions? **(life and death situations!)**

4. If you did not understand the directions, what could you do to make sure you complete the task correctly? **(ask, watch someone else, etc.)**

**Extension Activities:**

1. Have students collect items that have extensive (and important) directions on them, such as assembling a model, playing a video game, driving a foreign car, mixing hair color, etc. Have them present humorous scenarios that demonstrate what could happen if the directions were not followed.

2. Invite a guest speaker – perhaps a doctor, military person, pilot, etc. – to talk about how important following directions is to his or her career.

3. Have students make puzzles in which sets of directions that must be followed sequentially are mixed up (cooking something, assembling something, etc.). Have students put them in the correct order.

**Evaluation:**

a. Give an example of types of directions given in the following classes: math, science, P.E., etc.

b. Write a paragraph describing what could go wrong if the following directions were not followed:

– a surgeon performing open heart surgery

– a chef in a fancy restaurant trying out a new recipe

– a mechanic working on a car

– a lab technician testing evidence for fingerprints

**Teacher Notes:**

_____

_____

_____

_____

_____

_____

# Following Directions

**Directions:** When might you hear these directions being given? What is a possible consequence of *not* following the directions?

**1.** Do the odd-numbered problems only. Show your work.

_____

_____

**2.** Use a No. 2 pencil on the scantron sheet.

_____

_____

**3.** Read the passage first, *then* answer the questions.

_____

_____

**4.** Check your answers by randomly re-doing some of the problems.

_____

_____

**5.** Put your name, date, and the subject in the upper right-hand corner of your paper.

_____

_____

**6.** Save your work on your disk.

_____

_____

**7.** Use the color blue to represent water on the map.

_____

_____

**8.** Put the chocolate chips in *last*.

_____

_____

**9.** Alphabetize the names by the last name.

_____

_____

**10.** If you're stuck, re-read the chart in the book before asking the teacher for help.

_____

_____

# III-25 Doing Homework

**Objective:** The student will list several ideas that help with the task of completing homework.

**Comments:**

The downfall of many students is their failure to understand, complete, and return homework. Homework can be a time to reinforce concepts already taught at school, extra time allotted for completing tasks that weren't done at school, or a time to explore something new and related to activities introduced at school. In this lesson, students are asked to think about different ways to help make doing homework easier.

**Introductory Activities:**

a. Have students discuss how often they have homework.

b. Have students mention which classes most often assign homework.

c. Have students list several purposes of assigned homework.

**Activity:**

**Answers: 1.** b; **2.** c; **3.** f; **4.** a; **5.** e; **6.** d

**Discussion:** Go over answers with students. Discuss how the tip would be helpful in completing homework.

1. Is completing homework a problem for you? Why?

2. What specific problem areas do you have in doing homework?

3. What are some ways you could set things up before doing your homework to ensure that you know what to do and have all needed materials?

4. What are some safeguards you could have available to you in case you have trouble with understanding the homework?

5. How could you make sure you turn it in correctly and on time?

6. What type of atmosphere is best for you to study in?

7. How can homework assignments help you get better grades or get a better understanding of the work?

**Extension Activities:**

1. Have students chart their homework for a month. They should record the class, assignment, completion percentage, and any other relevant information, including any problems encountered.

2. Have students record the number of minutes spent in homework (defined as any time spent working on or studying concepts for a class) for each class. Is there any connection between time spent studying and the grades achieved?

**Evaluation:**

a. Write three to five helpful ideas for doing homework.

b. Write a paragraph explaining how homework can be helpful to achieve learning in a particular class of your choice.

# Doing Homework

**Directions:** Here are some tips to doing homework successfully. Match the tip with the picture that shows a student following the idea.

**a.** Know what to do.　　**d.** Ask if you have questions.

**b.** Have all materials.　　**e.** Do everything you are supposed to do.

**c.** Find a place to work.　　**f.** Put the work in a safe place where you'll have it to turn in.

# III-26 Managing Daily Assignments

**Objective:** The student will monitor his or her daily assignments for a specified length of time.

**Comments:**

Many students do not take the time to write their assignments. They feel they can keep track of everything in their heads and do not need the extra work of writing things down. However, the use of a daily assignment sheet is often very helpful even for students who are capable of organizing themselves. This lesson consists of a project in which students keep track of their daily assignments.

**Introductory Activities:**

a. Have students describe any methods they use for recording daily assignments – notebooks, assignment sheets, specific pages, etc.

b. Have students discuss which classes tend to give daily assignments, as compared to those that assign long-term projects or include participation as the major activity. How do daily assignments help students learn the material?

**Activity:**

Students are to keep track of their daily assignments for at least one week. You may wish to target only one or two classes at first, depending on the student and the likelihood of good record-keeping. The information on the worksheet "Managing Daily Assignments" includes the date, subject, specific assignment, room for a summary of the class's activity, notation for any homework, and a square to be marked off when the homework (if assigned) is done. You may wish to add other information that is pertinent to your situation.

**Discussion:** After students have participated in this project for at least one week, discuss how helpful the assignment sheet is. Students may have ideas for adding other information or designing their own daily assignment sheet.

1. What classes tended to give daily assignments?

2. Why would briefly recording a summary of the class activity for that day be helpful?

3. What other information would be helpful to monitor on an assignment sheet?

4. Do you have a good idea what your grade or class performance is for each class?

5. How would an assignment sheet be helpful in case you were absent?

6. How would keeping an assignment sheet also help someone else keep up with homework?

**Extension Activities:**

1. Have students design a personal daily/weekly assignment sheet. Tell them to include their own personal touches such as a logo, motto, or any drawing that reflects their personality. Run off copies if possible and encourage students to use them.

2. Include good record-keeping as part of a class grade. Keep students posted often as to their performance in class.

3. At the end of the week, give a quiz on information that should have been kept on the assignment sheet, such as class summary information. Allow students to use their assignment sheets to answer the quiz questions!

**Evaluation:**

    a. List two ways that keeping a daily assignment sheet can help a student get better grades.

    b. List three to five pieces of information that should be included on a daily assignment sheet.

**Teacher Notes:**

_____

_____

_____

_____

_____

_____

Name _____ Date_____

# Managing Daily Assignments

**Directions:** Complete the following assignment sheet. Record all necessary information.


Date _____ Subject _____ Assignment _____

Summary of class: _____

Homework? _____ Done ☐


Date _____ Subject _____ Assignment _____

Summary of class: _____

Homework? _____ Done ☐


Date _____ Subject _____ Assignment _____

Summary of class: _____

Homework? _____ Done ☐


Date _____ Subject _____ Assignment _____

Summary of class: _____

Homework? _____ Done ☐


Date _____ Subject _____ Assignment _____

Summary of class: _____

Homework? _____ Done ☐

# III-27 Managing Long-Term Assignments

**Objective:** The student will plan a long-term (e.g., several weeks' duration) assignment using a calendar and other resources.

**Comments:**

Planning and carrying out a longer assignment requires more effort than maintaining daily work. Especially if the student is given a lot of independence, he or she must organize the project, make deadlines, obtain materials, and keep on track. In this lesson, students are given an assignment to organize.

**Introductory Activities:**

a. Have students give examples of some long-term (at least several weeks, possibly a semester) assignments or projects.

b. Have students give examples of materials or resources that might be involved in a long-term assignment. **(library research, interviewing people, using a computer, etc.)**

**Activity:**

**Discussion:** Assume the project is assigned on October 1 and is due on November 30. Students may want to work in small groups so that they can discuss when they think certain deadlines should be made. Compare deadlines and activities that the students come up with. There is no "right" or "wrong" time schedule, but students should keep certain factors in mind; for example, when the library is open (weekends?), what materials need to be purchased, and how much time might be needed for revisions, etc.

1. After making a careful schedule, what problems could potentially come up that would throw things off? **(getting sick, someone not doing his or her part, etc.)**

2. Where would be a good place to keep the calendar?

3. What shopping or purchasing would you need to do?

4. What plans would you need to make to get access to a computer or typewriter?

5. What materials would you need for a map or other visual aids?

6. What might you put on the cover?

7. Can you think of other items or dates you should include on the calendar?

**Extension Activities:**

Have students organize a similar long-term plan for the following assignments. What tasks are involved? What materials are needed?

a. Prepare a fact sheet on all 50 states. Due in one month.

b. Design and give a "creative" book report. Due in three weeks.

c. Research and prepare a meal from another country. Due in two weeks.

d. Write and perform a play for another class. Due in one month.

e. Make a diorama of a scene from a favorite movie. Due in three weeks.

**Evaluation:**

a. Give examples of two or three long-term assignments or projects.

b. Select one of your examples and list the tasks and materials involved.

c. Using a calendar, make a sample outline of when each task in your example should be completed.

# Managing Long-Term Assignments

**Directions:** Here is Amy's long-term assignment for English and history. Help her plan how she will manage her time so that she will complete the project on time. Use the calendar on the next page to help assign dates for the tasks.

**Project:** Write a research paper on a topic about the Civil War.

**Due:** in two months

**Tasks:**
- pick a topic
- find three sources
- outline is due in one month
- notes should be on 3 x 5 cards, must be turned in after outline
- need to turn in one rough draft
- need at least one map and two pictures or visual aids
- final copy must be typed or on computer
- must have a cover

**Need to:**
- go to the library to do research
- get cards
- read books and other sources
- get lab time on the computer
- buy a cover for the report

## October

| S | M | T | W | TH | F | S |
|---|---|---|---|----|---|---|
|   |   |   |   | 1 | 2 | 3 |
| 4 | 5 | 6 | 7 | 8 | 9 | 10 |
| 11 | 12 | 13 | 14 | 15 | 16 | 17 |
| 18 | 19 | 20 | 21 | 22 | 23 | 24 |
| 25 | 26 | 27 | 28 | 29 | 30 | 31 |

Notes:

## November

| S | M | T | W | TH | F | S |
|---|---|---|---|----|---|---|
| 1 | 2 | 3 | 4 | 5 | 6 | 7 |
| 8 | 9 | 10 | 11 | 12 | 13 | 14 |
| 15 | 16 | 17 | 18 | 19 | 20 | 21 |
| 22 | 23 | 24 | 25 | 26 | 27 | 28 |
| 29 | 30 |   |   |   |   |   |

Notes:

# III-28 Completing Assignments

**Objective:** The student will identify completed assignments and maintain a personal record of completed assignments for a designated period of time.

**Comments:**

Sometimes students may attempt an assignment but not complete it to specification. Turning in a partially completed assignment or doing an inadequate job on a task are problem areas for many students. Students are to identify correctly completed tasks in this activity.

**Introductory Activities:**
   a. Have students give ideas for what a teacher looks for in a completed assignment. **(name on paper, neatness, all parts completed, directions followed, etc.)**
   b. Have students give examples of what types of assignments would need to be completed in their various classes. **(e.g., writing a paper, reading an entire book, painting a picture, etc.)**

**Activity:**

On the worksheet "Completing Assignments," students are to read the assignments given and the description of what the character actually did. Then they are to determine whether or not the assignment was completed and write *yes* or *no* on the line.

**Answers: 1.** no; **2.** no; **3.** yes; **4.** no; **5.** yes

**Discussion:** After completing the worksheet, have students discuss why the characters did or did not complete their assignments.
   1. Why didn't the character complete the science assignment in example 1? **(didn't read the entire assignment)**
   2. What was wrong with the assignment turned in by the character in example 2? **(didn't follow directions)**
   3. What could the girl have done in example 4 to complete the assignment? **(find sandpaper, finish staining)**
   4. How do you know the student in example 5 completed the assignment correctly? **(the word "library" appears on the articles, there are five of them)**
   5. What are some difficulties that you have from time to time with completing assignments in school?
   6. What could you do to improve your completion of assignments?
   7. Are there particular classes for which you have difficulty completing the work?

**Extension Activities:**
   1. Collect various examples of daily, weekly, or monthly assignment sheets. How does each show assignment completion?
   2. Have students keep track of their assignment completion on a regular basis – for at least a month. Teach them to calculate their percentage each week:

$$\frac{\text{number of assignments completed}}{\text{number of assignments given}}$$

**Evaluation:**

    a. Calculate the approximate percentage of assignments you have completed over the past two weeks. (Use your assignment sheets if necessary to calculate this percentage.)

    b. List two specific ways you could improve your percentage of completed assignments.

**Teacher Notes:**

_____

_____

_____

_____

_____

_____

# Completing Assignments

**Directions:** Did the following students complete the assignments they were given? Write *yes* or *no* next to each.

**1.** Class: Science
  Assignment: Read Ch. 14, pp. 81-89

  _____

**2.** Class: Reading
  Assignment: Write a paragraph about a character in the story we read in class.

  _____

**3.** Class: Math
  Assignment: Copy each problem! Solve page 54 (1-10).

  _____

**4.** Class: Woodworking
  Assignment: Finish sanding and staining the wooden box.

  _____

**5.** Class: Social Studies
  Assignment: Collect five news articles about the new library being built downtown.

  _____

## III-29 Good Behavior

**Objective:** The student will recognize and state behaviors that are characteristic of "good" students.

**Comments:**

Most students are probably able to come up with a list of behaviors they think are teacher-pleasing or characteristic of students who never get in trouble. But having "good behavior" is more than just being quiet or not getting caught! In this lesson, several examples are given of what would constitute good student behavior.

**Introductory Activities:**

a. Have students list two examples of good student behavior they have observed recently.

b. Have students list two examples of poor student behavior they have observed recently.

c. Have students speculate on what the consequences were of the examples they listed.

**Activity:**

Students are given a list of student behaviors on the worksheet "Good Behavior." They are to determine which they think are examples of good student behavior and mark them with a check mark.

**Answers: 1.** yes; **2.** yes; **3.** yes; **4.** no; **5.** yes; **6.** yes; **7.** no; **8.** no; **9.** no; **10.** yes; **11.** no; **12.** yes; **13.** yes; **14.** no; **15.** yes

**Discussion:** After students have completed the worksheet, discuss why the behaviors were or were not examples of good student behavior. Discuss why the circumstances give clues as to whether or not the behavior would be appropriate at that time or not.

1. Why would being early to class be an example of good student behavior?

2. What would be the problem with situation 4?

3. Why would situation 9 be a problem in some classes? (**some teachers want extra time spent on their class material**)

4. Why would situation 10 be a good idea – in the right circumstances? (**good use of free time**)

5. How much depends on what each individual teacher will tolerate? (**a lot!**)

6. How can you tell what teachers expect of you and your behavior in their classes? (**usually they will give expectations at the beginning of the year; also observe who gets rewarded and punished in class**)

**Extension Activities:**

1. Have students add more items to the list. What other good student behaviors are important?

2. Have students perform skits demonstrating these behaviors (a) once the "right" way and (b) once the "wrong" way.

3. Select one good student behavior and design a management program for a week or two. For example, make it a point to stand outside your classroom and then award extra points for students who politely greet you each day and/or are in their seat when the bell rings, etc.

**Evaluation:**

a. List five to eight examples of good student behaviors.

b. Select one good student behavior you feel is important and you could improve on. Design a plan you could carry out for at least one week to work on this behavior.

**Teacher Notes:**

_____

_____

_____

_____

_____

_____

# Good Behavior

**Directions:** Which of the following behaviors are examples of good student behaviors? Put a check mark in front of them.

_____ **1.** being on time to class

_____ **2.** being early for class

_____ **3.** saying hello to your teacher before class

_____ **4.** getting up to sharpen your pencil while the teacher is giving directions for the assignment

_____ **5.** asking questions in math if you don't understand what to do

_____ **6.** having extra paper

_____ **7.** coming to class with comic books to read in case you get bored

_____ **8.** getting up to talk to a friend in the hallway during class

_____ **9.** doing your social studies during math class while the teacher is talking

_____ **10.** bringing a reading book in case there is extra time at the end of class

_____ **11.** putting your head down to sleep

_____ **12.** copying notes from the board

_____ **13.** raising your hand to answer questions

_____ **14.** making jokes to get attention

_____ **15.** offering to help another student who is having trouble

# III-30 Getting Along With Authority

**Objective:** Given specific situations, the student will give examples of ways to get along with authority figures.

**Comments:**

Teachers, principals, and even cafeteria workers who give instructions are sometimes seen as threatening authority figures. Some students in particular have difficulty handling being given specific instructions, especially if they have been involved in a problem. Nevertheless, being respectful to authority figures is an essential student skill.

**Introductory Activities:**

a. Have students list at least five adults who are authority figures at home, school, or work.

b. Have students list at least three examples of commands or requests that they have heard given by an authority figure in the past day or two.

**Activity:**

Students are given four examples of students who have been given instructions by an authority figure at school. They are to draw a picture on the worksheet "Getting Along With Authority" to demonstrate how they would handle each situation if they were the student in the example.

**Materials:** pen or pencil, perhaps markers

**Answers:** *(examples)* **1.** "We'll be quiet. Sorry." **2.** "We'll respect your decision." **3.** "We'll try to be patient and just wait." **4.** "We'll have to study tonight."

**Discussion:** Have students share their drawings and responses to the situations on the worksheet. Emphasize that the responses should be respectful, even if they don't agree with what the adult has decided to do.

1. Would you have to say something in every case or would just being quiet be a way of showing respect? **(no verbal response is required in any of them)**

2. If you disagreed with the comments/decision of the authority figure, how could you explain your feelings and remain respectful? **(ask if this is a good time to talk about, offer alternatives, calmly explain yourself, etc.)**

3. Should you always just accept what you are told to avoid a conflict? **(consider each situation – how big of a deal is it really?)**

4. If you think someone is wrong, how could you persuade him or her to listen to you? **(approach him or her at the right time, in the right way; be logical)**

5. Why is it important to get along with your teachers?

6. Why is it important to get along with the principal?

7. Why is it important to get along with your parents, boss, or other adults who have some authority over you?

**Extension Activities:**

1. Have students write a story as if they were principal/teacher for a day. What would they expect of the students? What orders would they expect to be followed? Let students have some fun with this!

2. Play "You Are the Boss." Devise possible problem situations for students to examine and make a decision. For example, how would they handle employees who habitually come in late? What about having to choose between two good candidates who both need a job?

**Evaluation:**

How would you handle the following situations?

a. Your science teacher tells you that you must re-do your entire science project because you didn't follow the guidelines. The project is due in two days.

b. Your principal calls you into the office because some students said you were involved in a fight before school. You were not even there, but the principal is on the phone to your parents and he is angry!

c. Your tennis coach says you are not trying hard enough. He wants you to practice several extra hours including Saturday mornings. You think you are devoting enough time to this and are trying as hard as you can.

**Teacher Notes:**

_____

_____

_____

_____

_____

_____

# Getting Along With Authority

**Directions:** How could the following students get along with the authority figure in each situation below? Draw or explain your ideas on the back of this sheet.

1.

You kids are making too much noise out here in the hall. I'm trying to have class! Please quiet down.

2.

I know you think it is unfair for the entire class to be punished because one person pulled the fire alarm, but that is my decision.

PRINCIPAL'S OFFICE

3.

Everyone at this table is eating last today. It's your turn to be last.

4.

I've changed my mind; the big test will be tomorrow instead of next week.

TEST TOMORROW

# III-31 Asking Good Questions

**Objective:** The student will pose relevant questions given a situation that needs more clarification.

**Comments:**

Asking good questions is an important school skill. Not only must the student take initiative to ask the question, but he or she must also ask the question politely and clearly. For example, how many times have you heard "I don't know what to do," instead of "Could you explain how this fraction is reduced to that fraction?" Helping students narrow their questions to what they really need to know is a specific, important skill.

**Introductory Activities:**

    a. Tell students: "Take out a piece of paper and a pencil." Listen for their comments. What questions did that simple command raise?

    b. Have students list the types of questions they just asked. Were they specific? ("Are we having a test?") General? ("What's going on?")

    c. Have students discuss what class or classes they most often ask questions in or have questions about.

**Activity:**

On the worksheet "Asking Good Questions," students are given examples of characters who need to ask questions to clarify an assignment or get more information. They are to write a good question that asks for appropriate information.

    **Answers:** *(examples)* **1.** "Could you explain how you got a 7 for that answer?" **2.** "When is the book report due?" **3.** "Do we need to bring our gloves?" **4.** "Would it be okay for me to bring in a CD to listen to during class?" **5.** "Would there be a time when I could talk to you about being a lawyer?" **6.** "Do you want us to outline Chapter 3 also?"

    **Discussion:** Have students compare their questions for the situations on the worksheet. Tell them to try to make specific, rather than general, questions.

    1. Why do you think that simply saying "I don't know what to do," or asking "What are we supposed to do?" is not a good way to get information? **(too general, gives the answerer of the question a bigger job)**

    2. Do you think that Frank in situation 3 will get into trouble because he wasn't listening? Is there any way he could ask a question and not get into trouble?

    3. How could Doris in situation 4 ask her question in a way that would get her in trouble? **(be demanding, whiney)**

    4. Why isn't it a good time for Renee, in situation 5, to ask the lawyer a lot of detailed questions? **(the speaker is leaving)**

    5. Do you think most teachers or people in general mind being asked questions?

    6. What are some things you should keep in mind before you ask a question? **(know what you want to find out, make sure the situation is a good time, etc.)**

    7. Is it better to not ask a question at all rather than ask a question you think is dumb or silly? **(hopefully, most teachers would insist that there aren't any "dumb" questions if students truly do not understand)**

**Extension Activities:**

1. When appropriate, have students rephrase questions that are too general while they are in class. Teach them to collect their thoughts and zero in on what information they need to know.

2. Give students the following assignment: Have them raise their hands to ask at least one question in each class for a day or two. The question could be for clarification, asking for more information, or asking for the teacher's opinion on something.

**Evaluation:**

Rewrite the following general questions to make them more specific:

a. **In math:** "What is our assignment?"

b. **In English:** "What is our book report supposed to be about?"

c. **In P.E.:** "What are we doing today?"

d. **In social studies:** "What chapter are we working on?"

**Teacher Notes:**

_____

_____

_____

_____

_____

_____

## Asking Good Questions

**Directions:** Help each student below ask a question about something he or she wants to know. Write your questions next to each student.

1. Sara is working on her math. She doesn't understand how the teacher got the answer that's on the board.

   _____

   _____

   _____

2. Donald doesn't remember when the book report is due.

   _____

   _____

   _____

3. Frank wasn't listening when the P.E teacher told the students everything they need to bring for the softball game after school.

   _____

   _____

   _____

4. Doris wants to know if she could bring in some music for the class to listen to while they are working on an art project.

   _____

   _____

   _____

5. Renee is interested in learning more about being a lawyer. The guest speaker who works for a law firm is just about to leave.

   _____

   _____

   _____

6. Ruth finished her outline, but she isn't sure if she was supposed to do Chapter 3 as well as Chapter 2.

   _____

   _____

   _____

# III-32 Asking for Help

**Objective:** The student will identify appropriate ways and times to ask for extra help.

**Introductory Activities:**

    a. Have students think about a recent time when they needed help on a project or assignment. What type of help did they need? Who helped them? How did they ask for help?

    b. Have students list different ways they can get extra help on their work. **(peer tutors, extra assignments, learning programs, etc.)**

**Activity:**

    **Answers: 1.** no; **2.** no; **3.** yes; **4.** yes; **5.** no; **6.** no

    **Discussion:** Have students discuss why the examples are or are not appropriate times and ways to ask for help. In some cases, it may simply be a matter of good intentions but bad timing!

    1. What is the problem with the example in situation 1? **(bad timing, general question)**

    2. What is the problem with situation 2? **(didn't give the teacher much time to help)**

    3. What could be a potential problem with situation 3? **(the teacher may not have time to help right then)**

    4. If the teacher didn't have time, what else could a student do in situation 3? **(study with a friend, set up an appointment to meet with the teacher later)**

    5. How would going over flash cards in situation 4 be helpful? **(allow the student extra practice)**

    6. Why wouldn't the student admit to having a problem in situation 5? **(embarrassed)**

    7. Would it have been better to admit that you were the one with the problem, rather than saying it is a friend's problem? **(probably; you are the one who wants help)**

    8. What problem could occur in situation 6? **(get in trouble for being disruptive)**

    9. What would be a better way to ask for help in situation 6? **(ask someone next to you, try the program again, wait quietly, raise your hand, etc.)**

**Extension Activity:**

Have students observe quietly how many times other students request help of a teacher in a given classroom. Have them note (if possible) the different approaches taken – raising hand, demanding help, asking for help quietly, etc. After students ask for help, encourage students to thank the teacher or other individual involved for giving help.

**Evaluation:**

Your class has been studying the planets. You will be having a test on material you have learned in class about characteristics of the planets. Unfortunately, you have been sick for a few days with the flu and have missed some notes.

    a. What are some specific ways you could get extra help?

    b. When would be a good time to ask for extra help?

    c. What specific questions would you ask?

Name _____ Date_____

# Asking for Help

**Directions:** Which of the following examples are good ways to ask for help? Put a check mark next to those that are appropriate.

_____ 1. The teacher just walked into the classroom with an armload of books and papers. You run up to him, grab him by the arm, and demand: "I need help! I don't understand what to do!"

_____ 2. Mrs. James told the class that she was available after school on Mondays, Tuesdays, and Wednesdays until 5:00 if anyone needed help on his or her science projects. You go to her office at 4:55 on Wednesday and have a list of 20 questions for her.

_____ 3. You realize you have lost a week's worth of math assignments. You have a test coming up, and want to make sure you are studying correctly. You stay after class for a few minutes to ask the teacher if she has time to help you.

_____ 4. You want more practice on learning about elements in your science class. When the teacher asks if anyone has a question, you raise your hand and say, "I would like more practice on naming the elements. May I borrow the flash cards from the back of the room?"

_____ 5. Your rocket experiment completely flopped. You think you followed the directions, but nothing seemed to go right. You don't really want the teacher to know how bad it was, so you say that a friend of yours has a problem.

_____ 6. The computer program you booted up won't work right. The teacher in the lab seems too busy to help you, so you press a key that makes a beeping sound until she notices you and comes over.

# Section IV

---

# Practical Living Skills

## IV-1 What Do You Need to Know?

**Objective:** Given a situation, the student will identify what information is needed to complete the task.

**Comments:**

No matter how simple a task may appear at first, there is often a need to clarify what needs to be done to complete it. This is a matter of thinking through what is needed to accomplish the task – defining expectations, knowing what to get, doing things in sequence, etc. This activity requires students to decide what information is needed to complete a given task.

**Introductory Activities:**

a. Tell students they are going to prepare a five-course dinner for some people. After they recover from the shock, ask them what information is missing in order to complete this task. List their ideas.

b. Ask students to pretend they are going to take a cruise around the world next summer. What type of information would they need to find out to make plans for this task?

**Activity:**

**Answers:** *(examples)* **1.** shoe size; **2.** how many people will be there; **3.** salary, hours, benefits; **4.** how long it should be, what type of book; **5.** age of boy, interests; **6.** what type of computer; **7.** how many will be there, what you will be serving; **8.** care instructions

**Discussion:** Have students compare their ideas for what information is needed. There should be several different ideas for each one.

1. Why is it important to think about what information is needed before diving into a task? **(would save time, avoid mistakes)**

2. In situation 3, how could you prepare yourself to do well at an interview by finding out appropriate information? **(ask better questions, bring résumé if necessary)**

3. What information is important to know when buying a gift for someone? **(what they are like, their interests, how much money you have to spend)**

4. What might happen if you didn't have enough information to complete a task? **(make mistakes, take time to find the information)**

5. Why do you think people are hesitant sometimes to ask for information, such as stopping to ask for directions? **(feel that it will embarrass them)**

**Expansion Activities:**

1. Have students think of tasks but leave out at least one vital piece of information. Write the tasks on slips of paper, exchange them, and have students identify missing information.

2. Have students identify at least three tasks that are usually done at home or at school. What information is needed to complete these tasks?

**Evaluation:**

What information is needed to complete the following tasks?

a. decorating a room for a birthday party

b. feeding your neighbor's pets while she's away for the weekend

c. buying jeans for a friend

**Teacher Notes:**

_____

_____

_____

_____

_____

_____

Name _____  Date_____

# What Do You Need to Know?

**Directions:** Read the following situations. What information is necessary to carry out the task? Write your ideas on the lines next to each item.

| **Situation** | **What Information Is Needed?** |
|---|---|
| **1.** You are buying new shoes. | _____ <br> _____ |
| **2.** You are planning a birthday party for your mother. | _____ <br> _____ |
| **3.** You are applying for a job as a waiter/waitress at a pizza place. | _____ <br> _____ |
| **4.** You are supposed to write a book report. | _____ <br> _____ |
| **5.** You are buying a gift for your nephew. | _____ <br> _____ |
| **6.** You want to buy a new game for your computer. | _____ <br> _____ |
| **7.** You are cooking dinner for your family tonight. | _____ <br> _____ |
| **8.** You have some seeds to plant outside in your garden. | _____ <br> _____ |

## IV-2 Where to Get Information

**Objective:** Given a situation, the student will identify an appropriate source of obtaining information.

**Comments:**

Once it is established that more information is needed, the problem remains of finding out where to get the answers. In this lesson, students are given situations and must decide where the missing information can be found.

**Introductory Activities:**

a. Ask students where they would go to find out what was being served for lunch that day.

b. Ask students who they would talk to in order to find out what time basketball practice is this weekend.

c. Ask students what source they would use to find out who the 19th president was.

**Activity:**

**Answers:** *(examples)* **1.** television program guide or newspaper; **2.** weather report on TV; **3.** newspaper; **4.** look at wrapper on candy bar; **5.** encyclopedia; **6.** sports magazine; **7.** dictionary; **8.** local bookstore

**Discussion:** Compare responses. Students may have somewhat similar ideas for sources.

1. Did most of your responses involve people, places, or paper?

2. Who is someone whom you consider to be a good source of information about school? sports? life?

3. Why is the public library a good source of information? (**many types of materials are stored there**)

4. Do you think it is just as important to know where to find answers as it is to know the answers?

5. What is a good way to remember what things you need to look up or find out? (**jot down notes, make yourself a list**)

6. Are most of the sources you wrote down easy to obtain or accessible?

**Extension Activities:**

1. Set up a learning center or display table of almanacs or books of lists, etc. Allow students time to browse through them. Make the assignment to write 10 to 15 questions based on interesting facts they have found. Devise a "scavenger hunt" in which students on teams must go through resource books to find specific information.

2. Make a *Jeopardy*-type game with five to eight different categories. Have students write questions ranging from easy to difficult for each of the spaces on the board. (See the example on the next page.) Make sure students have a verified answer for each of their questions! Play the game with two teams.

| Sports | Animals | People | Music | Movies | History |
|--------|---------|--------|-------|--------|---------|
| 10 | 10 | 10 | 10 | 10 | 10 |
| 20 | 20 | 20 | 20 | 20 | 20 |
| 30 | 30 | 30 | 30 | 30 | 30 |
| 40 | 40 | 40 | 40 | 40 | 40 |
| 50 | 50 | 50 | 50 | 50 | 50 |

*Example:* 10-point question for **People** – Name all four science teachers in our school.

### Evaluation:

List an appropriate source for the following situations:

a. You want to know if your painful arm is broken.

b. You are having trouble starting your motorcycle and aren't sure what the problem is.

c. You are interested in tie-dyeing a shirt, but have never done it before.

### Teacher Notes:

_____

_____

_____

_____

_____

_____

# Where to Get Information

**Directions:** Here is a list of information you need to find out about. Write the name of an appropriate source where you could get the answer.

1. What's on TV on Thursday at 9 P.M. on channel 4?

_____

_____

2. What will the high temperature be for tomorrow?

_____

_____

3. What pet dogs are for sale at the pet store?

_____

_____

4. How many calories are in a Butterfinger® candy bar?

_____

_____

5. What is the population of Zaire, West Africa?

_____

_____

6. Who is the first-string quarterback on the Green Bay Packers football team?

_____

_____

7. What are several meanings for the word *row*?

_____

_____

8. What are the current top three fiction bestsellers in the nation?

_____

_____

# IV-3 Information from Newspapers

**Objective:** The student will identify three to five sources of information obtained from newspapers.

**Comments:**

The newspaper is a source of an incredible amount of information – world news, national news, weather, sports, editorials… and so on. In this lesson, students are to use a newspaper to locate information.

**Introductory Activities:**

a. Have students list as many newspapers as they can think of.

b. Have students list different features or sections of the newspaper.

**Activity:**

Using a local newspaper (or whatever newspaper is convenient for class use), have students find the answers to the questions on the worksheet "Information from Newspapers."

**Materials:** pen or pencil, newspaper

**Discussion:** Answers for many of the questions will vary. Have students share their findings.

1. Were you surprised at how many different types of information were contained in the newspaper?

2. How is your newspaper organized? Are there different sections? What parts are always the same?

3. What is an editorial?

4. Who is the advice columnist?

5. How often do you read from the newspaper? What parts do you usually read?

6. Are there any special features in your newspaper?

**Extension Activities:**

1. Have students compare several newspapers, including some that are directed to special interests or organizations. What features are common to all? Which are particularly appealing and why?

2. Have students create their own class newspaper. Have fun designing and planning a unique publication!

**Evaluation:**

a. List five types of information that could be found in a typical newspaper.

b. List the names of three newspapers.

Name _____ Date_____

# Information from Newspapers

**Directions:** Using your local (or other designated) newspaper, find out the following information.

1. What is the name of the newspaper?

   _____

2. What is the date? _____

3. What is the headline? _____

4. What is a sports story about?_____

5. What is the weather forecast for today? _____

6. What are the names of two comics? _____

   _____

7. What is one editorial about? _____

8. What does your horoscope say for today? _____

   _____

9. What is one car that is for sale? Find the price, condition, and other facts.

   _____

10. What is one house that is for sale? Find the price, location, and special features.

    _____

11. What is one sale that is going on this week at a large store?

    _____

12. What is one problem discussed in the advice column?_____

    _____

13. How many sections are in your paper? _____

14. On the back of this sheet, describe one photograph and write the caption under it.

15. How many births/deaths/weddings are reported?_____

# IV-4 Information from Magazines

**Objective:** The student will identify three to five sources of information obtained from magazines.

**Comments:**

Most students are probably familiar with certain teen magazines. Strolling through the supermarket, one can see lots of magazines aimed at different populations. In this lesson, students are to examine different magazines and discover what types of information can be obtained from them.

**Introductory Activities:**

a. Have students list several different magazines with which they are familiar.

b. Have students list their favorite magazine and explain what they particularly like about it.

**Activity:**

On the worksheet "Information from Magazines," students will match the magazine with the type of information typically contained within it. Even if students are unfamiliar with the magazine, they should be able to figure out the contents based on the title.

**Answers: 1.** d; **2.** c; **3.** g; **4.** b; **5.** e; **6.** h; **7.** a; **8.** f

**Discussion:** Go over the answers to the worksheet. Discuss how the clues given indicated which magazine they matched.

1. Which magazines do people in your family read or subscribe to?

2. What is the benefit of reading magazines for information rather than a newspaper? **(more photographs, lengthier articles, different and more in-depth types of stories and features)**

3. What are some of the more unusual magazines you have heard of?

4. How does the cover of a magazine draw your interest? What types of photographs or pictures would be portrayed on a cover?

**Extension Activities:**

1. Have students bring in samples of lots of different types of magazines. Discuss what makes them appealing and to whom they would appeal.

2. Have students design a cover for a magazine they would like to see created. Who would be their target audience? Who (or what) will they feature on the cover?

3. Have students read a magazine they normally would not be interested in. Is the information clearly written and intriguing enough that – even though they may not be interested in the topic – they are still able to understand and appreciate the material?

**Evaluation:**

a. List five to ten different types of magazines (by title).

b. List a topic or type of information that would be obtained from each magazine listed in (a).

# Information from Magazines

**Directions:** Match each magazine listed on the left with an example on the right of information you might find in the magazine.

_____ **1.** *People*

_____ **2.** *Time*

_____ **3.** *Horse Illustrated*

_____ **4.** *TV Guide*

_____ **5.** *New Woman*

_____ **6.** *Sports Illustrated*

_____ **7.** *Bon Appetit*

_____ **8.** *National Geographic*

**a.** recipe for a fancy chocolate dessert

**b.** description of new fall television shows

**c.** what the president is doing

**d.** what Winona Ryder is doing

**e.** how to take care of your kids and keep your job

**f.** how people in New Guinea live and play

**g.** benefits of different types of saddles

**h.** predictions for the Super Bowl

# IV-5 Information from Books

**Objective:** The student will identify three to five types of information that can be obtained from books.

**Comments:**

Books are probably one of the most common sources of information. There are books available on almost any topic you can imagine. In this lesson, students are to go to a library and find examples of books on various topics.

**Introductory Activities:**

    a. Have students list three topics they are interested in learning more about. Then, if they are familiar with some books, have them list a good book that would give information about each topic.

    b. Have students give examples of a book they have read recently that they particularly enjoyed. What was the name of the book, what type (fiction/nonfiction, etc.) of book was it, and what information did they learn from it?

**Activity:**

Students are to consider each subject listed on the worksheet "Information from Books" and browse through the local or school library to find the location of books on these topics. They are to give an example of a book that would provide information on the topic and then give an example of what type of information they could find from the book. You may need to help familiarize students with the layout of the library and where certain nonfiction books are found. Students may also do well on this activity if they work in small groups.

    **Materials:** pen or pencil, access to a library

    **Answers:** *(examples)* **1.** how to care for iguanas; **2.** where to vacation in Florida; **3.** what planes were used in World War II; **4.** how to take better outdoor pictures; **5.** what are some healthy recipes for chicken; **6.** where did President Lincoln grow up; **7.** how did the writer feel about his/her parents; **8.** what are the rules for playing golf

    **Discussion:** Have students go over the books and information they obtained from this activity. Allow students time to check out books they found – perhaps the books will spark some interest in new topics.

1. What did you find interesting or surprising about the books that were available on these topics?

2. How did you choose the book you selected as representative of each topic? What appealed to you about one book rather than another?

3. As you were looking through the shelves of books, what other topics or books distracted you? What else did you find intriguing?

4. When doing a research paper or project, why is it a good idea to use more than one source?

5. What is a problem with using older books as references? (**information can be outdated**)

**Extension Activities:**

1. Have students make a display of books that give information about a topic of their choice. Encourage them to use posters, lists of questions, models, and other aids to make an attractive display about a topic.

2. Have students write and display book reviews or book reports about topics interesting to them or relevant to something they are studying.

**Evaluation:**

What are three pieces of information you could learn from books with the following titles:

*How to Build Your Own Backyard Birdhouse*

*All About Animals of Australia*

*Magic and Card Tricks*

**Teacher Notes:**

_____

_____

_____

_____

_____

_____

# Information from Books

**Directions:** Spend some time in your school or local library. Find an example of each category of book listed below. Then list at least one type of information you could learn from the book.

| Subject | Example (Book Title) | What Information |
|---|---|---|
| **1.** Animals | | |
| **2.** Travel | | |
| **3.** Airplanes | | |
| **4.** Photography | | |
| **5.** Cooking | | |
| **6.** Biography | | |
| **7.** Autobiography | | |
| **8.** Sports | | |

# IV-6 Information from Other People

**Objective:** Given a situation, the student will identify an appropriate person who could provide information to answer the questions.

**Comments:**

People are a wonderful resource for information. People can teach skills, explain how to do things, give opinions about experiences they have had, and make recommendations. Students should not overlook this very important source of information.

**Introductory Activities:**

a. Ask students to give names of people (famous or not, living or deceased) whom they would like to have the opportunity to sit and talk with for an hour. Who would they choose? What would they ask?

b. Ask students to tell about anecdotes in which a person helped them learn to do something or learn about something. How did this person assist them?

**Activity:**

Students are to list a person who would be an appropriate source of information to answer the questions on the worksheet "Information from Other People." In some cases, the name of a specific person (if known) is an acceptable answer. In other cases, a general *type* of person (someone of a certain age, someone who works a certain job, etc.) is sufficient.

**Answers:** *(examples)* **1.** a veteran; **2.** a pilot; **3.** a music teacher; **4.** someone who works at the Department of Motor Vehicles; **5.** someone who has visited France; **6.** a friend who visited the Grand Canyon last summer; **7.** a pitcher for a professional baseball team; **8.** an English teacher; **9.** someone who lived in Spain; **10.** salesperson at a bike shop

**Discussion:** Discuss and compare responses to the questions on the worksheet. Allow students time to share their experiences with types of situations presented.

1. How is talking to a person for information easier or better in some ways than using a book or other written source? **(can get feedback right away, can actually "see" how something is done, etc.)**

2. Just because someone is able to do something well, does that mean he or she is good at teaching or explaining to someone else? **(no)**

3. Do you think you learn or understand better when someone explains something or do you prefer to read instructions, think about them, try them out, and learn by doing?

4. Why is it important to keep in mind that someone's opinion of a task or event may differ from someone else's? **(both express what their perception was, neither may be true or both may be partially true; keep in mind that the person is explaining only what he or she perceived)**

5. What is also important to keep in mind when dealing with a person who has a job to do, for example, a salesperson for example 10? **(that person may not be entirely unbiased!)**

6. Before you consider a person's opinion or judgment on something, what should you know about the person? **(qualifications, reputation, experience, reliability, etc.)**

**Extension Activities:**

1. Invite people to visit your class and talk about what they do or specific skills they have. Prior to the visit, have students list questions they would like to learn about.

2. Have students write letters (fan mail?) to individuals whom they would like to learn more about. Sometimes celebrities will respond by sending at least a photo or form letter.

3. Encourage students to take lessons. School functions sometimes permit lessons in sports, music, and drama for very low cost. Let students know that teachers of many types of subjects are excellent resources for learning new skills.

**Evaluation:**

Who would be an appropriate person to help with the following tasks or questions?

a. What is necessary to adopt a stray kitten from the animal shelter?

b. How old do you have to be to own a BB gun?

c. What customs or celebrations are performed in Germany during December?

**Teacher Notes:**

_____

_____

_____

_____

_____

# Information from Other People

**Directions:** Who (specifically) or what kind of person (job, age, etc.) could give you information about the following topics? Write your answers on the lines.

**1.** What was the Vietnam war like?

_____

**2.** How do you fly an airplane?

_____

**3.** How do you play a guitar?

_____

**4.** What do you need to get or do to obtain a learner's permit for driving?

_____

**5.** What are some sights to see or visit in France?

_____

**6.** What is there to do at the Grand Canyon?

_____

**7.** How do you throw a curve ball?

_____

**8.** Is my story well written and interesting?

_____

**9.** Who would be a good tutor for Spanish class?

_____

**10.** What is the best kind of bike to get for riding cross country?

_____

# IV-7 Information from Television

**Objective:** The student will identify three to five types of information that can be obtained from television.

**Comments:**

Television is probably one of the more common sources of information as it is readily available and appealing to viewers. In this lesson students are to identify types of information that can be obtained from television.

**Introductory Activities:**

   a. Have students list their top three favorite television shows.

   b. Ask students to indicate what type of information can be gotten from the shows they picked.

   c. Ask students to think of two or three shows that are primarily geared towards providing information. What information is given?

**Activity:**

**Answers:** *(examples)* **1.** news bulletin; **2.** sports program; **3.** talk show; **4.** game show; **5.** educational or discovery program; **6.** news/trial

**Discussion:** Students may have some variety in their answers to the worksheet. Have them explain what clues were given in the cartoons to hint at the type of program.

   1. Do you think most people watch television for pleasure or with the intent of learning something?

   2. What programs have you watched that you think give a lot of information?

   3. What type of information are you interested in learning about from television?

   4. Do you have a television in the classroom? If so, how is it used?

   5. How can television be used to provide information in a way that is different from radio, books, or people?

**Extension Activities:**

   1. For a homework assignment, have students watch a specified show on some relevant topic – perhaps a documentary or educational program. In class, have students write a summary of what they remember. Compare students' writings. How accurate and how varied were their summaries?

   2. Tape a provocative talk show episode. Have students watch the show, and periodically stop the program to have students write an opinion, evaluate a comment, or predict what they think will occur next.

   3. If you have the equipment available, have students write, produce, and act in a television production about something of relevance to them, the school, or your community. Don't forget to include commercials!

**Evaluation:**

What type of information would the following television programs provide for the viewer? a. an exercise show; b. a documentary about bullfighting in Spain; c. a debate between political candidates.

# Information from Television

**Directions:** All of these television programs are giving information. What type of program is shown? Write your answer below each picture.

1. _____
   _____

2. _____
   _____

3. _____
   _____

4. _____
   _____

5. _____
   _____

6. _____
   _____

## IV-8 Other Sources of Information

**Objective:** The student will identify five to ten other sources of information.

**Comments:**

There are many other sources of information available to the general public. Students can learn from self-instructional videos, going on a tour, or exploring a learning center. Information is everywhere! In this lesson, students are given numerous other sources of information.

**Introductory Activities:**

a. Have students list five different sources for getting the local weather report.

b. Have students give three to five types of information that can be obtained over the telephone.

c. Have students list other sources of information (other than those already discussed) usually available to them.

**Activity:**

Students are given a word search on the worksheet "Other Sources of Information" that includes various sources of information. They are to find the word and circle it. Words are found in horizontal, vertical, or backwards positions.

**Answers:**

```
l  a  c  f  e  e  d  i  u  g  r  u  o  t  z
a  d  i  c  t  i  o  n  a  r  y  e  l  m  i
n  e  w  t  i  u  y  l  i  h  l  e  i  w  v
g  m  i  l  c  m  i  s  l  t  c  i  c  c  f
u  m  g  l  z  w  i  e  g  m  s  i  g  o  p
a  u  d  i  o  b  o  o  k  s  d  n  k  m  t
g  s  t  b  o  c  m  i  v  h  l  s  i  p  a
e  e  x  r  t  o  l  m  i  c  x  t  i  u  r
t  u  g  a  o  s  s  p  d  h  i  r  t  t  t
a  m  x  r  u  h  i  l  e  c  t  u  r  e  g
p  h  i  y  r  a  d  i  o  g  h  c  l  r  a
e  h  i  m  h  o  m  s  s  e  h  t  o  h  l
s  e  n  c  y  c  l  o  p  e  d  i  a  h  l
r  a  k  t  c  h  o  e  r  i  l  o  h  m  e
m  l  e  a  r  n  i  n  g  c  e  n  t  e  r
h  i  m  w  t  o  m  h  l  c  x  s  h  o  y
```

**Discussion:** After students have completed the word search, discuss how each item provides information.

1. What other sources of information can you think of that are not listed?

2. What are some examples of instructions that provide information? (**assembling a bicycle, playing a game, etc.**)

3. What information could you learn from going through an art gallery or museum? (**something about the exhibits, the artists, the conditions under which the pieces were produced, etc.**)

4. What types of videos are available in your library? What subjects are represented?

**Extension Activities:**

1. Have students select a source and give an oral presentation in class demonstrating how it provides information.

2. Take a tour through a nearby visitors' attraction in your community. Afterwards, summarize what information was presented and evaluate the trip.

3. Make it a class project to listen to some language tapes for a few minutes at the beginning or end of each class. Practice some conversational phrases with each other.

**Evaluation:**

List at least five sources of information (other than those previously considered in lessons).

**Teacher Notes:**

_____

_____

_____

_____

_____

_____

# Other Sources of Information

**Directions:** Below is a list of other sources of information. Find and circle each one in the word search. The words can be found in horizontal, vertical, or backwards positions.

| | | | |
|---|---|---|---|
| radio | library | encyclopedia | dictionary |
| museum | learning center | videos | tour guide |
| art gallery | lecture | zoo tour | instructions |
| audiobooks | language tapes | computer | |

```
l  a  c  f  e  e  d  i  u  g  r  u  o  t  z
a  d  i  c  t  i  o  n  a  r  y  e  l  m  i
n  e  w  t  i  u  y  l  i  h  l  e  i  w  v
g  m  i  l  c  m  i  s  l  t  c  i  c  c  f
u  m  g  l  z  w  i  e  g  m  s  i  g  o  p
a  u  d  i  o  b  o  o  k  s  d  n  k  m  t
g  s  t  b  o  c  m  i  v  h  l  s  i  p  a
e  e  x  r  t  o  l  m  i  c  x  t  i  u  r
t  u  g  a  o  s  s  p  d  h  i  r  t  t  t
a  m  x  r  u  h  i  l  e  c  t  u  r  e  g
p  h  i  y  r  a  d  i  o  g  h  c  l  r  a
e  h  i  m  h  o  m  s  s  e  h  t  o  h  l
s  e  n  c  y  c  l  o  p  e  d  i  a  h  l
r  a  k  t  c  h  o  e  r  i  l  o  h  m  e
m  l  e  a  r  n  i  n  g  c  e  n  t  e  r
h  i  m  w  t  o  m  h  l  c  x  s  h  o  y
```

# IV-9 What Is a Budget?

**Objective:** The student will be able to explain the following terms as they relate to a budget: earned income, deductions, fixed expenses, and flexible expenses.

**Comments:**

Understanding the purpose of a budget and how to devise one that will work for the individual is a harder task than it seems. Many of us have the tendency to spend everything that comes in – and more! In this lesson, students are introduced to some basic terms that relate to devising a budget.

**Introductory Activities:**

a. Ask students how many of them get an allowance or get money from working either at a job or for doing specific chores.

b. Have students volunteer to tell about how they allocate the money they receive.

c. Ask students to help come up with a definition for the term *budget*. **(a plan for what you will do with income and expenses)**

d. Provide definitions for the following terms:

*income* – money that comes in or is earned

*expenses* – money that you must pay out

*fixed expenses* – payments that are always the same amount of money; predictable

*flexible expenses* – payouts of money that can change, they are not always the same amount

*deductions* – money that is taken out of a paycheck to go to other designated sources (such as taxes or insurance)

**Activity:**

With teacher assistance, students are to familiarize themselves with terms on the worksheet "What Is a Budget?" as they relate to money and budgeting. Students are then to categorize the terms into one of four categories – earned income, deductions, fixed expenses, and flexible expenses. The number of answers under each category is shown by the number of lines.

Be sure that students understand the selection of answers (a - p):

a – money that is usually taken out of a check to pay for federal services

b – money that is earned by working more than the usual number of hours

c – expenses that go toward buying and maintaining clothing

d – money that is usually deducted for state services

e – how much money a person earns each hour

f – the amount of money paid each month (usually) for a car

g – taxes that are usually deducted from a paycheck to go towards the person's retirement or other work-related benefits

h – payment for phone calls and services

i – money paid toward a house

j – money that is not from working, but still provides ability to buy things

k – utilities (often a fixed expense)

l – expenses incurred from traveling by car

m – expenses that go toward running a house; for example, getting your carpets cleaned, mowing the grass, home repairs, etc.

n – amount of money spent either eating out or from groceries

o – expenses for leisure activities such as movies, roller skating, etc.

p – money that is taken (usually from a paycheck) to go towards membership in a union, which is an organization that works to improve conditions of the members

**Answers:** *(you may make changes if conditions are different in your area)*
1. Earned Income: b, e, j; **2.** Deductions: a, d, g, p; **3.** Fixed Expenses: f, i, k; **4.** Flexible Expenses: c, h, m, n, l, o

**Discussion:** Discuss why the items under each category would be an example of that category. In some cases, fixed and flexible items might differ.

1. What are other deductions sometimes taken directly from a paycheck? **(insurance, automatic payments, savings, etc.)**

2. If you were trying to tighten your budget, what area(s) would you concentrate on first? Why? **(probably flexible expenses because you would have more control over those items)**

3. Why would the cost of flexible items go up or down? **(seasonal considerations, one-time purchases, etc.)**

4. How would a budget help you in planning for your expenses? **(you would be able to decide ahead of time how much money you wanted to put toward something)**

5. How would a budget help you account for where your money goes? **(you can see exactly how much is spent in each category)**

6. Do you think savings is an important part of a budget? Why? **(yes! prepare for emergencies, plan for something you will need to pay for later)**

7. When would be a good time to make a budget? **(when your income stabilizes or has changed)**

## Extension Activities:

1. Have students find or think of other budgets other than personal and family budgets, such as school corporation, the U.S. government, local parks and recreation department, etc. How is the money allocated?

2. Have students interview their parents about a budget. What guidelines do they use? What does most of the money go for? What percentage goes for housing and food? Do they have a savings plan?

## Evaluation:

a. What is the purpose of a budget?

b. Give an example of *income*.

c. Give an example of a *fixed expense*.

d. Give an example of a *flexible expense*.

e. Give an example of a *deduction*.

# What Is a Budget?

**Directions:** Below is a list of terms that have something to do with earning and spending money. Put each into one of the following categories: (1) earned income, (2) deductions from income, (3) fixed expenses, and (4) flexible expenses.

a. federal taxes

b. overtime pay

c. clothing

d. state taxes

e. hourly wages

f. car payment

g. social security

h. phone bill

i. house payment

j. money from gifts

k. electric and water bill

l. gas for car

m. household expenses

n. food

o. recreation expenses

p. union dues

**1. EARNED INCOME**

_____

_____

_____

**2. DEDUCTIONS**

_____

_____

_____

_____

**3. FIXED EXPENSES**

_____

_____

_____

**4. FLEXIBLE EXPENSES**

_____

_____

_____

_____

_____

# IV-10 Making a Budget

**Objective:** The student will complete a suggested budget by calculating the percentage of money designated for each of several categories.

**Comments:**

Budgets can and should be tailored to fit the needs and goals of the individual. What is important (or necessary) for one person may have little or no value for another. In this lesson, students are given guidelines to complete a budget.

**Introductory Activities:**

a. Have students estimate how much money they have for income each month. (This may be based on allowance, working part-time, savings designated for spending, etc.)

b. Have students prioritize at least three to five items they would include in a personal budget.

**Activity:**

Students are to complete a fictitious budget, based on a monthly income of $2,000. Using the questions and guidelines on the worksheet "Making a Budget," students should be able to calculate the percentage for each category. One point that students need to understand is converting a percentage to a decimal for ease in multiplication. Make sure that students follow the example.

**Materials:** pen or pencil, calculator

**Answers: 1.** $24,000; **2.** $1,320; **3.** $700; **4.** $175; **5.** $70; **6.** $105; **7.** $70; **8.** $70; **9.** $70; **10.** $49; **11.** $35; **12.** $35; **13.** $21

**Discussion:** Have students share other "tricks" or ways to multiply to make finding the percentages easier.

1. Why is it important to work with take-home pay rather than the gross (total) amount when making a budget? **(that is the "disposable" income, the rest is never seen)**

2. Why is it helpful to use percentage when making a budget? **(shows relative amounts of money designated to each account)**

3. What percentage do you think you spend most of your money on?

4. What do you think takes up most of people's money? **(probably housing)**

**Extension Activities:**

1. Invite a banker or obtain personal finance information. What percentages are common or suggested for the main categories?

2. Have students make a personal budget. What categories should they include? How much money can they allocate to each? Then have them try it out for a month and make adjustments as necessary. Evaluate how well they estimated costs!

**Evaluation:**

Fred's paycheck is $3,500 for the month. His deductions total $1,200. His fixed and flexible expenses are equal. How much would he spend on each? **($1,150)**

Name _____ Date_____

# Making a Budget

**Directions:** Use this planning sheet to help Ed make a personal budget. He makes $2,000 a month (before deductions). Write your answers on the lines. Use the back of this sheet for your work.

GAS    HOUSE    FOOD    FUN

**1.** What is Ed's yearly pay?

_____

**2.** If his deductions total $680, how much does Ed bring home each month?

_____

**3.** Ed has several fixed expenses. His apartment costs $550 a month and utilities (water and electricity) are $70 a month. How much is left now?

_____

Ed would like to budget the remaining amount of his money. He wants to designate a certain percentage for each of the following categories. Remember that a percent can be changed to a decimal for ease in figuring out the dollar amount.

**Example:** 25% would be x .25; 15% would be x .15; and so on.

| Category | Percent | Multiply by | Dollar amount |
|---|---|---|---|
| **4.** food | 25% | .25 | _____ |
| **5.** clothing | 10% | _____ | _____ |
| **6.** car/transportation | 15% | _____ | _____ |
| **7.** household expenses | 10% | _____ | _____ |
| **8.** savings | 10% | _____ | _____ |
| **9.** church/charity | 10% | _____ | _____ |
| **10.** phone | 7% | _____ | _____ |
| **11.** medical/dental | 5% | _____ | _____ |
| **12.** charge cards | 5% | _____ | _____ |
| **13.** recreation | 3% | _____ | _____ |

# IV-11 Paying Interest

**Objective:** The student will calculate how much interest is added to a purchase in given situations.

**Comments:**

When people borrow money, especially from a bank or other commercial loan institution, usually a certain amount of interest is added to the transaction. In this lesson, students are introduced to the terms *principal* and *interest* and are given situations in which they must calculate how much money is added to the purchase price when interest is involved.

**Introductory Activities:**

   a. Ask students to lend you $10.00 in cash. Tell them that you'll pay the money back sometime next week. Wait to see how many of them want to add a "service charge" or interest to the loan.

   b. Ask students for their ideas about why people or banks charge interest when money is borrowed. **(the privilege of using someone else's money for awhile)**

   c. Define *principal*. **(the main amount borrowed)**

   d. Define *interest*. **(a charge – usually a percentage – added to the amount borrowed)**

**Activity:**

Be sure students understand how to convert percentage to a decimal for purposes of multiplying (principal times interest) to find the total amount to be repaid. In the examples on the worksheet "Paying Interest," they will need to convert 4%, 7%, 8%, and 10% to .04, .07, .08, and .10 (which will be multiplied by the principal amount).

**Materials:** pen or pencil, calculator

**Answers:**  **1.** p = $6500, i = $260, t = $6760

**2.** p = $35, i = $3.50, t = $38.50

**3.** p = $10,000, i = $800, t = 10,800

**4.** p = $18,500, i = $1295, t = 19,795

**Discussion:** Go over the problems on the worksheet, making sure that students understand how to solve the problems and can make corrections if they got an incorrect answer.

1. Why is it important to find out the interest rate when purchasing something? **(it adds significantly to the price)**

2. Would it ever be cheaper to buy an item with a higher purchase price but with a lower interest rate? **(maybe – you'd have to compare to figure out the bottom line each way)**

3. What are some items you would buy or transactions you would make that will probably have interest added? **(cars, credit cards, loans, mortgage, etc.)**

4. How is interest different from just having a service charge added to the cost of something? **(the more the amount of money involved, the higher the percentage of interest; a service charge might not be so high or so profitable for the bank)**

**Extension Activities:**

1. Have students collect examples of sales ads in which interest is charged on the items; for example, cars, other vehicles, clothing on layaway, etc. Figure out the total cost if the amount is financed for a year.

2. Make a poster comparing the actual cost of one item with different interest rates.

3. Find out the percentage charged on several major credit cards.

**Evaluation:**

Pretend you have borrowed $1,350 for a new snowmobile. You must pay back the loan plus 9% interest.

a. What is the amount of the principal? **($1,350)**

b. What is the amount of interest to pay back? **($121.50)**

c. What is the total amount of money you will have to repay? **($1,471.50)**

**Teacher Notes:**

_____

_____

_____

_____

_____

_____

Name _____ Date_____

# Paying Interest

**Directions:** Read the following situations. Figure out the *principal,* the amount of *interest* paid, and the *total amount* that must be repaid. Use the space below each problem for your work.

1. Tom borrowed $6,500 to buy a used car. He must pay 4% interest.

   Principal_____ Interest_____ Total _____

2. Elana borrowed $35 from her sister to buy some jeans. Her sister wants her to pay back the loan with 10% interest.

   Principal_____ Interest_____ Total _____

3. Mr. and Mrs. Martinez borrowed $10,000 to take a vacation in the Rocky Mountains. The bank charges them 8% interest.

   Principal_____ Interest_____ Total _____

4. Juan borrowed $18,500 to make a down payment on a house. He must pay back 7% interest.

   Principal_____ Interest_____ Total _____

# IV-12 Making Payments

**Objective:** Given the appropriate information, the student will calculate the amount of money due when an item is purchased by a payment plan.

**Comments:**

Many purchases can only be made when the purchaser can make payments, thus spreading out the bills over a predetermined amount of time. What must be considered, however, is how much the purchase actually costs when all of the payments are totaled. Students are given problems to solve in this lesson that involve making payments.

**Introductory Activities:**

a. Tell students you would like to borrow $100 from them and will pay them back with interest, but they'll have to wait five years to get it. Wait for their response. (Some will probably realize that they'll be waiting a long time before getting any money back!)

b. Have students now suggest a reasonable payment schedule for paying back the money. **(possibly a monthly bill)**

**Activity:**

Students are given four situations on the worksheet "Making Payments" that involve a person making payments. They are to figure out how much the total amount paid will add up to.

**Materials:** pen or pencil, calculator

**Answers: 1.** $12,192; **2.** $103; **3.** $344; **4.** $450

**Discussion:** After completing the worksheet, students should discuss how they arrived at their answers. Clear up any confusion about how to solve the problems.

1. Why is a payment plan a good way for some people to make a purchase? **(they may not have enough money all at once to buy something)**

2. What are some items you can buy using payment plans? **(large appliances, cars, televisions, furniture, etc.)**

3. Why do you think making payments sounds like a good idea for many people? **(the monthly payment is small, it doesn't seem like you would be paying very much)**

4. If no interest is charged, how could making payments be better than paying for the entire purchase at one time? **(you can put your money in a savings account and earn interest while you are waiting to make your payments)**

**Extension Activities:**

1. Have students look at or bring in payment books from a loan (be sure parents give permission if they bring in personal loan payment booklets!). Find out the interest rate and total cost of the item financed.

2. Have students figure out the monthly payment on items that are advertised in newspapers. Be sure to calculate the total amount that will have to be repaid.

**Evaluation:**

Victor wants to buy a new bike. He has the following options:

1. He can pay $200 right now and take the bike home.

2. He can put down $50 and make 12 payments of $15 each.

3. He can pay 1/2 now and the balance plus 8% interest in six months.

**Answer the following questions:**

a. Which option should Victor choose to pay the least amount of money? How much would he pay? **(option 1 – $200)**

b. Which option would cost the most? How much would he pay? **(option 2 – $230)**

c. Which option should Victor choose if he only has $70 right now? **(option 2)**

d. Which option should Victor choose if he wants the bike fairly soon but doesn't have all of the cash right now? How much would he pay? **(option 3 – $208)**

# Making Payments

**Directions:** For each situation given below, figure out what information is required and then solve each problem. Use the space for your work.

1. Pete has payments of $254 on a car each month for 4 years. How much does he owe?

   _____

2. Ali owes $1,236 on some furniture. He has to pay every month for one year. How much will he pay each month if all payments are the same amount?

   _____

3. Rosa borrowed $2,064 from her parents to pay off some college expenses. Her parents want her to pay them back, but they will not charge her any interest. She will make 6 equal payments to them. How much will each be?

   _____

4. Carol's payments on a pedigreed dog are $25 a month for 18 months. How much will her puppy cost?

   _____

# IV-13 "On Sale"

**Objective:** The student will calculate the sale price of a given item.

**Comments:**

Buying "on sale" can result in substantial savings. Students can benefit from being able to figure out the sale price of items they are interested in purchasing. In this lesson, students are given the task of calculating the price of an item that has been marked down or is on sale.

**Introductory Activities:**

a. Have students discuss what items they are interested in at the moment that are on sale. What are they and where is the sale?

b. Have students offer what would be considered a good sale price for some common items such as a popular compact disc, personal computer, designer jeans, a perm, and a videogame. What would be the regular full-price cost of these items?

**Activity:**

Students are given four items on the worksheet "On Sale." The original price and the amount of the discount (percentage or fraction) is given. Students are to figure out the sale price. Make sure students remember how to use percentages (multiply by the equivalent decimal) and equivalent fractions (1/2 = 50% = .50 and 1/3 = 33% = .33). Make sure students realize there are TWO STEPS involved in these examples – they must calculate the amount of the discount *and* subtract it from the original price!

**Materials:** pen or pencil, calculator

**Answers:** **1.** $8.00   $72.00;   **2.** $55.50   $27.75;   **3.** $4.50   $13.50;
**4.** $8.91   $18.09;   $5.94   $12.06;   $11.88   $24.12

**Discussion:** Students may have some trouble with the mathematical calculations on these problems. If so, provide them with a helpful chart (perhaps on the board?) that shows the specific steps for solving these problems. (**1.** What is the original price? **2.** What is the amount of the discount – use decimals! **3.** Subtract the discount from the original price.) If necessary, provide a chart of common equivalences between fractions and decimals.

1. In problem 1, why is it relatively easy to figure out a 10% discount?

2. In problem 2, there is a half-price sale. Why do you need to know the price of both sweaters in order to figure out what each sweater would cost? **(you must add them both, then take half to find out what each one would cost)**

3. In problem 4, everything is 1/3 off. What is the decimal you can use to multiply by 1/3? **(.33)**

4. Why do stores have sales? **(to get rid of old merchandise, get people to come to the store, promote other items, etc.)**

5. What are some items that go on sale seasonally? **(snowmobiles, swimsuits, towels, etc.)**

6. What are the pros and cons of waiting to buy something until it is on sale? **(pro – get a good price; con – not so good of a selection, what you want might be gone)**

7. If something is sold "as is," how is that different from "on sale"? **(probably damaged)**

## Extension Activities:

1. Have students walk through a mall and take an informal inventory of what is on sale. How do the stores promote their sale items?

2. Have students become detectives. Search for the same item that is sold in several different stores (e.g., a 2-liter bottle of soda, item of clothing). What is the range of prices for the item? What is the average price? What is the best sale price?

3. Have students visit an outlet mall or store if there is one near you. Compare prices. What is the approximate discount for buying something that is "irregular" or not of the same quality?

## Evaluation:

You are in a shoe store where there is a "buy one, get one at 1/2 price" sale. The shoes you like cost $35.00.

a. How much would the second pair cost? **($17.50)**

b. What would your total cost be? **($52.50)**

## Teacher Notes:

_____

_____

_____

_____

_____

_____

Name _____ Date_____

# "On Sale"

**Directions:** The following items are on sale! The regular prices are shown as well as the amount of the discount. For each problem, figure out the sale price. Use the back of this sheet for your work.

**1.**

Discount: _____

Sale Price: _____

**2.**

Price for two sweaters:_____

Sale Price:_____
(for each sweater)

**3.**

Discount: _____

Sale Price: _____

**4.**

14K GOLD JEWELRY

EVERYTHING 1/3 OFF

$27   $18   $36

Discount:   _____   _____   _____

Sale Price:   _____   _____   _____

# IV-14 Unit Pricing

**Objective:** Given several examples, the student will be able to identify the unit used and the unit price.

**Comments:**

When is a "deal" a real deal? Although some buys may sound good, it is not until you really know what you are getting for your money that you can decide if it is truly a good purchase. In this lesson, students are introduced to the concept of figuring out the cost of an item based on the unit price – how much one ounce, one pound, one gallon, etc., costs.

**Introductory Activities:**

a. Tell students that you have a deal for them – they can either have 5 cans of soda for $3.75 or a 12-pack for $6.00. Which is the better deal? Why? **(the unit price on the first is 75 cents, the second is 50 cents)**

b. Have students explain how they figured out which was the better buy. Hopefully, they will understand that it boils down to how much you would have to pay for a single can.

c. Define *unit pricing*. **(how much the price is for only one of a group of items)**

**Activity:**

On the worksheet "Unit Pricing," students are to figure out what unit is being purchased (one can of soup, one candy bar, etc.) and the price for one item. Students may need a calculator to solve the problems. Be sure students have the unit correctly identified. Also, explain how you want the answer written if it does not come out evenly (for example, three cans for $1.00 would probably be 33 cents; .6666 would be rounded off to .67).

**Materials:** pen or pencil, calculator

**Answers: 1.** one can, 33 cents; **2.** one folder, 25 cents; **3.** one pizza, $4.00 **4.** one CD, $11.67; **5.** one candy bar, 24 cents; **6.** one gallon, $1.15; **7.** one pair of socks, $2.33; **8.** one drink, 25 cents

**Discussion:** Be sure students understand how the correct answers were reached on the worksheet. Discuss any points of confusion.

1. Why is unit pricing helpful when you are comparing different brands of the same product? **(lets you see exactly how much the item costs when compared equally)**

2. What are some common units used when you buy food items? **(ounce, pound, etc.)**

3. What are some items usually packaged in quantities? **(soda, socks, small cereal packages, notebooks, pencils, gum, soap, etc.)**

4. Why isn't bigger always the best buy? **(you might be paying more for each unit)**

5. Should you always get the item with the cheapest unit cost? What other factors should you consider? **(freshness, quality, taste, etc.)**

**Extension Activities:**

1. Have students bring in and set up a display table of grocery items. Figure out the unit cost of each.

2. Find and bring in items that come in different sizes, for example, cereal boxes, soda cans and bottles, etc. Set up an activity for students to figure the unit cost of each and the better buy.

**Evaluation:**

Which is the better buy? Why?

a. three pads of lined paper, each pad containing 50 sheets for $3.00

**or**

b. 1 Super-Duper pad of lined paper with 250 sheets for $4.25

**(b) is the better buy – each sheet is 1.7 cents compared to 2 cents each for (a)**

**Teacher Notes:**

_____

_____

_____

_____

_____

_____

# Unit Pricing

**Directions:** For each example below, write the *unit* that is used and the *unit price* for each.

**1.** Chicken noodle soup: three cans for $1.00

Unit _____ Unit price _____

**2.** Pocket folders: 12 for $3.00

Unit _____ Unit price _____

**3.** Three pizzas for $12.00

Unit _____ Unit price _____

**4.** Buy 2 CD's, get one FREE! Your cost: $35.00

Unit _____ Unit price _____

**5.** Bag of candy: 6 bars for $1.44

Unit _____ Unit price _____

**6.** 20 gallons of gas for $23.00

Unit _____ Unit price _____

**7.** Three pairs of socks for $7.00

Unit _____ Unit price _____

**8.** Boxed drinks: 9 for $2.30

Unit _____ Unit price _____

## IV-15 Sales Tax

**Objective:** The student will be able to calculate sales tax (given) on several examples.

**Comments:**

Most purchases involve another slight expense – sales tax. This amount varies from state to state and students should be aware of the amount for their particular state. Some cities also add other taxes to generate revenue for roads, stadiums, and other specific causes. In this lesson, students are given problems to figure out which involve adding sales tax.

**Introductory Activities:**

a. Tell students that when a customer purchases something at a store, usually the cashier will ring up an additional charge. Ask students if they know what this is. **(sales tax)**

b. Ask students if they know what the amount of sales tax is for their state. Find out!

**Activity:**

Students are given ten items on the worksheet "Sales Tax" and the amount of sales tax that should be added to the item. They are to calculate the total cost of the item. Be sure that students can convert the percentage of sales tax (written as a percent) to a decimal for ease in multiplication. Also be sure that students understand they must add the sales tax to the original cost of the item.

**Materials:** pen or pencil, calculator

**Answers:** *(some numbers are rounded off)*

1. sales tax = $1,077.30; total = $20,109.60
2. sales tax = $1.38; total = $28.88
3. sales tax = $3.96; total = $53.46
4. sales tax = $1.00; total = $26.00
5. sales tax = $4.80; total = $84.75
6. sales tax = $2.80; total = $42.80
7. sales tax = $3.25; total = $68.25
8. sales tax = $1.40; total = $21.35
9. sales tax = $ .07; total = $ 1.23
10. sales tax = $11.92; total = $160.92

**Discussion:** Make sure students understand the concept of "rounding" off the decimals to the hundreds place when working with money. Go over any specific problems students had with the math or with understanding how to figure out the problems.

1. Why isn't sales tax just added to the cost of the item when the price is posted? **(sales tax varies from place to place, this would change the total amount)**

2. Why do some states or cities have higher sales taxes? **(it may be more expensive to live there, they may want to generate revenue for a specific community project)**

3. What are some other added expenses that are tacked on to some purchases besides sales tax? **(for a car – delivery fee, license, options, etc.)**

4. Some places (a professional basketball game, for example) include the sales tax in the posted price of the item. What are some reasons why they would do this? **(they may anticipate having to serve a large crowd, want to expedite the sales, easier to give change, etc.)**

## Extension Activities:

1. Have students find out (and make a map or chart of) the sales tax percentages in the 50 states. How does your state compare to surrounding states?

2. Have students use the range of sales tax percentages and calculate what the same item would cost in various states.

## Evaluation:

a. What is the percentage of sales tax in your state?

b. What would the total cost be for these items including sales tax?

   a bicycle for $235.00

   a watch for $49.00

## Teacher Notes:

_____

_____

_____

_____

_____

_____

# Sales Tax

**Directions:** Figure out the cost of each item with the indicated sales tax. Use the back of this sheet for your work.

| Item | Sales Tax (%) | Total Cost |
|------|---------------|------------|
| **1.** Car: $17,955 | 6% _____ | _____ |
| **2.** Purse: $27.50 | 5% _____ | _____ |
| **3.** Suitcase: $49.50 | 8% _____ | _____ |
| **4.** Football: $25.00 | 4% _____ | _____ |
| **5.** Boots: $79.95 | 6% _____ | _____ |
| **6.** Ticket to a Play: $40.00 | 7% _____ | _____ |
| **7.** Rollerblades: $65.00 | 5% _____ | _____ |
| **8.** Calculator: $19.95 | 7% _____ | _____ |
| **9.** Gallon of Gas: $1.16 | 6% _____ | _____ |
| **10.** Exercise Equipment: $149.00 | 8% _____ | _____ |

## IV-16 Writing a Check

**Objective:** Given the appropriate information, the student will correctly write a sample check.

**Comments:**

Some students may already have an active checking account; others may want to open one when they have incoming money or need to write checks for purchases. In this lesson, students are introduced to the information required on a check and are given practice in writing sample checks.

**Introductory Activities:**

    a. Have students describe checks they have seen in use. **(personalized checks, humorous checks, checks with cartoons on them, etc.)**

    b. Have students list occasions on which they or their parents have written checks. Why was a check used rather than cash or a charge?

    c. Draw or make a large blank check for purposes of demonstration. Include blanks for: (1) the date, (2) the party to whom the check is written, (3) the dollar amount in numbers, (4) the amount in words, (5) signature, and (6) memo or purpose. Explain the purpose of each and demonstrate how each is used.

**Activity:**

    **Discussion:** Check over students' checks to make sure all information is filled out properly. Answer any questions about the checks.

    1. How is using a check convenient for many people? **(don't have to carry cash, can keep track of spending, etc.)**

    2. What types of places will usually take a check? **(grocery stores, department stores, gas stations, etc.)**

    3. What identification is sometimes required to write or cash a check? **(driver's license, credit card)**

    4. What happens if you write a check and don't have enough money in your account to cover it? **(it will "bounce" or be returned with a substantial service charge added)**

    5. What is a "blank check"? **(a check that is signed, but the amount is not filled in)**

**Extension Activities:**

    1. Invite a banker to speak to the class or obtain literature from a local bank about opening a checking account. Find out what options are available for the customer. Is a minimum balance required? How much does it cost to maintain the account? List other questions.

    2. Almost every interest group has a series of checks that appeal to them. Collect cancelled checks and display them.

**Evaluation:**

    a. What are two benefits of using a checking account?

    b. Write a check to your teacher for $100.

# Writing a Check

**Directions:** Use the blank checks on the next sheet to write checks for the following amounts and purposes. Look at the example for help. Use today's date.

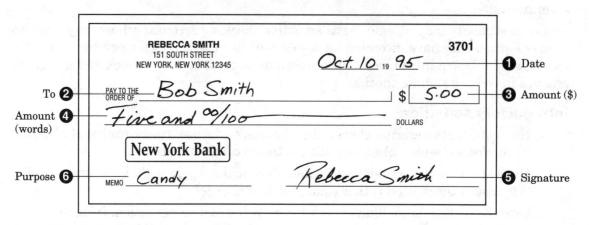

**REBECCA SMITH**
151 SOUTH STREET
NEW YORK, NEW YORK 12345

**3701**

**❶ Date** — *Oct. 10* 19 *95*

**To ❷** PAY TO THE ORDER OF *Bob Smith* $ *5.00* — **❸ Amount ($)**

**Amount ❹** (words) *Five and °°/100* DOLLARS

New York Bank

**Purpose ❻** MEMO *Candy* *Rebecca Smith* — **❺ Signature**

**1.** Write a check to the Hobby Castle for $9.93 for a model airplane.

**2.** Write a check to Ms. Beamon for $17.54 for the class cookie sale.

**3.** Write a check to Friendly Fones for $39.00 for a new bedroom phone.

**4.** Write a check to Towne Outlet Store for $52.30 for school supplies.

---

**3702**

_____ 19 _____

PAY TO THE
ORDER OF _____ $ [        ]

_____ DOLLARS

[Bank]

MEMO _____ _____

---

**3703**

_____ 19 _____

PAY TO THE
ORDER OF _____ $ [        ]

_____ DOLLARS

[Bank]

MEMO _____ _____

---

**3704**

_____ 19 _____

PAY TO THE
ORDER OF _____ $ [        ]

_____ DOLLARS

[Bank]

MEMO _____ _____

---

**3705**

_____ 19 _____

PAY TO THE
ORDER OF _____ $ [        ]

_____ DOLLARS

[Bank]

MEMO _____ _____

# IV-17 Maintaining a Checking Account

**Objective:** The student will be able to correctly enter sample checks into a checking account ledger.

**Comments:**

Not only must students know how to fill out a check, they must also learn to keep careful accounting records of how much money they have in the checking account. In this lesson, students are given a fabricated checking record to enter into a ledger.

**Introductory Activities:**

a. Have students raise their hands if they have a checking account.

b. Have students raise their hands if they would like to have a checking account.

c. Ask students to list some responsibilities they would have to live up to if they had a checking account. (**maintaining accuracy, making sure they have the money in the account**)

**Activity:**

Using the worksheet "Maintaining a Checking Account," students are to complete a checking ledger based on having an opening balance of $150.00 and subsequently subtracting checks and a service charge and adding a deposit. You may wish to go through the first check notation in the register together as an example.

**Materials:** pen or pencil, calculator

**Answers:** The ledger should resemble the following:

| | | | |
|---|---|---|---|
| 101 | 10/1/95 | Fred's Discount Shop | 8.89 |
| | | (balance) | 141.11 |
| 102 | 10/1/95 | Polly's Pizza | 15.42 |
| | | (balance) | 125.69 |
| 103 | 10/2/95 | Northfield High School | 17.00 |
| | | (balance) | 108.69 |
| 104 | void | | |
| 105 | 10/3/95 | Harvell Oil Company | 40.30 |
| | | (balance) | 68.39 |
| Dep. | 10/3/95 | +150.00 | 218.39 |
| 106 | 10/4/95 | Mrs. Violet Chandler | 10.50 |
| | | (balance) | 207.89 |
| Serv. Ch. | 10/5/95 | | 8.00 |
| | | (balance) | 199.89 |

**Discussion:** Make sure students understand how to maintain the ledger and answer any questions they have about doing the math. Students may ask about the column with the check mark. Many people use this to reconcile their checks by placing a check mark in the column after the bank has cashed and returned the check.

1. How often do you think you should make sure your math is accurate? (**after every few checks at least**)

2. How could you check your math? (**use a calculator**)

3. How could you use monthly bank statements to make sure your records are accurate? (**check your balance with the balance that the statement shows – after subtracting the checks that have not been cashed already**)

4. What do you think are some common sources of error? (**not lining up the decimal point, forgetting to subtract an amount, just making mathematical mistakes**)

5. What should you do if you make a mistake on a check? (**write "void" across it, or if it is minor you can change it and put your initial next to the mistake**)

6. Sometimes there is a service charge as a penalty added if you do not have enough money in your account and the check "bounces." How could you avoid this? (**some banks have overdraft protection, also check your balance periodically to make sure you are still okay**)

### Extension Activities:

1. Obtain examples of typical monthly bank statements. Have students figure out what information is contained on it and how this could help make sure their personal banking records are accurate.

2. Compare the features of checking accounts at two or three local banks. Find out which would be the best for students to start out with. Find out the policy for being overdrawn, overdraft protection, and any other relevant features.

### Evaluation:

You open a checking account with a deposit of $100.00. Your first check is written for $37.92. What is your balance? (**$62.08**)

Name _____ Date_____

# Maintaining a Checking Account

**Directions:** Complete the following ledger from your checking account. Give yourself a starting balance of $150.00 in the first deposit column.

Write check #101 on 10/1/95 to Fred's Discount Shop for $8.89

Write check #102 on 10/1/95 to Polly's Pizza for $15.42

Write check #103 on 10/2/95 to Northfield High School for $17.00

Void check #104 – you made a mistake in the amount

Write check #105 on 10/3/95 to Harvell Oil Company for $40.30

Deposit $150.00 on 10/3/95

Write check #106 on 10/4/95 to Mrs. Violet Chandler for $10.50

Subtract a service charge of $8.00 on 10/5/95

| NUMBER | DATE | DESCRIPTION OF TRANSACTION | PAYMENT/DEBIT (−) | ✔ | FEE (IF ANY) (−) | DEPOSIT/CREDIT (+) | BALANCE $ |
|---|---|---|---|---|---|---|---|
| | | | | | | | |
| | | | | | | | |
| | | | | | | | |
| | | | | | | | |
| | | | | | | | |
| | | | | | | | |
| | | | | | | | |
| | | | | | | | |
| | | | | | | | |
| | | | | | | | |
| | | | | | | | |
| | | | | | | | |
| | | | | | | | |

# IV-18 Credit Cards

**Objective:** The student will use a sample credit card to answer information about its use.

**Comments:**

It is getting easier and easier for students to obtain credit cards. Unfortunately, the benefits seem to overshadow the risks that can be involved with easy credit. In this lesson, students are given a sample credit card and are asked to answer questions about its use.

**Introductory Activities:**

a. Have students list the names of familiar major credit cards.

b. Have students tell the percentage of interest charged on credit cards that they or their parents have or cards that have been advertised.

c. Have students figure out how much interest would be paid on a balance of $4,890 if the interest rate was 22%. **($1,075.80)** Does this seem like a lot?

**Activity:**

Have students examine the information about the sample credit card on the worksheet "Credit Cards." Explain what the numbers refer to.

> *credit limit* – how much you can charge on the account; *annual percentage rate* – the amount of interest charged annually on the balance of a credit card account; *annual fee* – how much you pay each year for the privilege of having the card; *valid dates* – when you first got the card and when it will expire; *account number* – the 16-digit number that is the number of your account on this card

**Answers: 1.** 5231 0004 3214 3268; **2.** $10,000; **3.** $17.90; **4.** once a year; **5.** February, 1998; **6.** General Card; **7.** $209; **8.** $375 + 67.13 = $442.13 (rounded off)

**Discussion:** Make sure students can calculate the interest rate (some numbers are rounded up). Answer any questions they have about the worksheet.

1. How is the use of a credit card helpful? **(convenient, gives you extra time for payment)**

2. How is use of a credit card more flexible than using a check? **(you can spend money that you don't actually have yet; some places will take credit cards but not checks)**

3. What should you be aware of before running up a huge credit card bill? **(how much the percentage rate will add to your bill)**

**Extension Activities:**

1. Have students collect and compare features of having a major credit card. Compare items such as the annual fee, percentage rate of interest, other benefits, etc. You may want to have students draw enlargements of the cards and list the features on posters.

2. Have students make a list of 50 local stores or nearby places that will accept a credit card.

**Evaluation:**

Write a paragraph listing several pros and cons of using a credit card for purchases.

# Credit Cards

**Directions:** Look at the sample credit card below. Then answer the questions.

Credit Limit: $10,000

Annual Percentage Rate: 17.9%

Annual Fee: $50.00

1. What is the account number on this credit card?

    _____

2. How much can you charge on this card?

    _____

3. If you charged $100, how much interest would you have to pay in a year?

    _____

4. How often do you have to pay the $50 fee?

    _____

5. When does this card expire?

    _____

6. What type of credit card (name) is this?

    _____

7. If your balance is $219 and you have to make a minimum payment of $10, what would your new balance be (before interest is added)?

    _____

8. If your balance is $375, what would you owe after you figure out the interest you are being charged?

    _____

## IV-19 What Is a Savings Account?

**Objective:** The student will be able to explain basic similarities and differences between a checking account and a savings account.

**Comments:**

Students may have had a savings account established for them when they were young. A savings account has the added benefit over a checking account of paying interest on money that is in the account. However, usually there is a minimum amount that must be kept in the account to get the interest rate. In this lesson, some features of a savings account are discussed and a savings account is compared to a checking account.

**Introductory Activities:**

a. Have students raise their hands if they have a savings account. Ask when the account was first established.

b. Have students explain what they know about how a savings account is different from a checking account. You may want to divide the chalkboard into two parts, titling one "Checking" and the other "Savings."

**Activity:**

Go over some features of a savings account, including:

– Most savings accounts are established for the purpose of leaving the money in the account, not taking it out.

– Most savings accounts pay a higher rate of interest than a checking account.

– Most savings accounts will have a service charge if the balance is below a predetermined amount.

– Money can be withdrawn from a savings account at any time.

– Banks will send a monthly statement recording all activity from a savings account (similar to a checking account).

Then distribute the worksheet "What Is a Savings Account?"

**Answers:** *(there may be some difference in answers, depending on the bank accounts your students use or are familiar with)* **1.** C, S; **2.** C, S; **3.** S; **4.** C; **5.** C; **6.** S; **7.** C, S; **8.** C, S; **9.** C, S; **10.** C

**Discussion:** Make sure students have an understanding of the basic differences and commonalities between typical checking and savings accounts. Again, specifics may differ.

1. Why do you think many people have both types of accounts? **(may have different needs; enough money to keep in a savings account but need to write bills often)**

2. How would monthly statements on both types of accounts be helpful to make sure your accounting is accurate? **(the statements keep track of all transactions, gives you something to go on to check your own records)**

3. How do bank cards or bank machine cards make getting to your money even easier? **(most operate 24 hours, don't have to wait for a teller, etc.)**

**Extension Activities:**

1. Have students find out and compare interest rates at banks for checking and savings accounts. What are the specific terms involved for each account?

2. If you had a lot of money to invest, what might be a better alternative than a savings account to make more money? Find out about certificates of deposit, money market accounts, life insurance, etc.

**Evaluation:**

a. What are two ways a savings account is different from a checking account?

b. What are two ways a savings account is similar to a checking account?

**Teacher Notes:**

_____

_____

_____

_____

_____

Name _____ Date_____

# What Is a Savings Account?

**Directions:** Read the following descriptions of the bank account. Write "C" if it could refer to a checking account. Write "S" if it could refer to a savings account. Some of the items will have both.

**C = checking**       **S = savings**

_____ **1.** You can deposit money into this account.

_____ **2.** You can take money out of this account.

_____ **3.** You usually get a better interest rate.

_____ **4.** You can write checks from this account.

_____ **5.** You probably would use this account very often.

_____ **6.** If you had a large amount of money and weren't planning to spend it soon, you'd use this account.

_____ **7.** You have to have a minimum balance.

_____ **8.** You get a statement each month that tells how much money you have in the account.

_____ **9.** You may have to pay a service charge if you don't have a large enough balance.

_____ **10.** You would use this account if you have a lot of bills to pay.

## IV-20 Applying for a Loan

**Objective:** The student will list at least five pieces of information a bank would evaluate before approving a personal loan for an individual.

**Comments:**

Having a good credit history is important. Banks have access to information about how well a person pays back previous loans, amounts borrowed, and other bank information. It is also important for a person to have a reliable source of income to show that he or she can repay the loan. In this lesson, students are to consider the process of getting a loan – from the bank's point of view.

**Introductory Activities:**

a. Have students list situations in which someone might need to get a loan. **(making a large purchase such as a house, going to college, financing a vacation, etc.)**

b. Ask students to list types of information they think a bank or loan officer might want to know about a person before deciding whether or not to loan him or her the money.

**Activity:**

On the worksheet "Applying for a Loan," students are given a list of questions to consider about financial situations and ability to repay a loan. They are to speculate about why each particular question would be important from the bank's point of view.

**Answers:** *(examples)* **1.** establishes previous credit history with the bank; **2.** credit history; **3.** they want to know how much you were able to pay back previously; **4.** credit record; **5.** source of paying back the money; **6.** if you are financially able to pay back the money; **7.** same as 6; **8.** they want to know if you are going to be around for awhile or if you have a history of taking off often; **9.** hopefully you have some responsibility to care for them; **10.** they want to know of someone to contact, perhaps to ask about you; **11.** they would not approve a loan that might not hold its value – e.g., to go gambling; **12.** want to know your plan for repayment; **13.** they want to make sure you have something of value they can take if you don't have the money; **14.** they want the name of a responsible party who could cover your debt; **15.** they want to know how much money other people or agencies will want; **16.** this shows what you own that could be converted to cash if necessary

**Discussion:** Go over the questions as a class. Talk about why these questions are important to getting a loan and repaying the loan.

1. How does the bank benefit from loaning you money? **(they charge interest)**

2. How can a bank decide if you are a good risk or not? **(check your credit history)**

3. Why is having a steady job and the same address for several years an important consideration? **(it shows you have some stability in your life)**

4. What might happen if you were not able to make your loan payments? **(a few notices at first, eventually you could be taken to court, your car may be taken by the bank, etc.)**

5. If a friend asked you to co-sign a loan for him or her, what would you want to know about your friend? **(probably some of these same questions)**

## Extension Activities:

1. Have students complete a loan application from a local bank or car dealership. (See the example here.) What information is requested?

| FIRST NAME | MIDDLE | LAST | SOC.SEC.# | BIRTH DATE Mo. Day Yr. | PHONE # |
| --- | --- | --- | --- | --- | --- |

| ADDRESS | CITY | COUNTY | STATE | ZIP | LIVED THERE Yrs. Mos. |
| --- | --- | --- | --- | --- | --- |

| PREVIOUS ADDRESS | CITY | COUNTY | STATE | ZIP | LIVED THERE Yrs. Mos. |
| --- | --- | --- | --- | --- | --- |

EMPLOYED ☐ NAME OF BUSINESS   ADDRESS   CITY   STATE   ZIP   HOW LONG?
SELF-EMPL. ☐
OTHER ☐

| TRADE OR OCCUPATION | BADGE OR DEPT. # | SALARY WAGES BEFORE TAXES | PREVIOUS EMPLOYER & ADDRESS | HOW LONG? |
| --- | --- | --- | --- | --- |

| SPOUSE'S NAME | MIDDLE | LAST | SOC.SEC.# | BIRTH DATE Mo. Day Yr. | PHONE |
| --- | --- | --- | --- | --- | --- |

EMPLOYED ☐ NAME OF BUSINESS   ADDRESS   CITY   STATE   ZIP   HOW LONG? Yrs. Mos.
SELF-EMPL. ☐
OTHER ☐

| TRADE OR OCCUPATION | BADGE OR DEPT. # | SALARY WAGES BEFORE TAXES | PREVIOUS EMPLOYER & ADDRESS | HOW LONG? Yrs. Mos. |
| --- | --- | --- | --- | --- |

RENT BY MONTH ☐   LANDLORD OR MORTGAGE HOLDER (Name, Address, & Phone)   MONTHLY PAYMENT OR RENT $
LEASE ☐
OWN ☐   MORTGAGE AMOUNT $

SIGNATURE

INDIVIDUAL ☐   PARTNERSHIP ☐   CORPORATION ☐   PAYMENT DATE DESIRED

2. Have students contact a bank to find out what information is revealed on a personal credit history. It is interesting to find out exactly what information a bank has access to! If possible, you may want to have one printed out (anonymously) to examine it.

## Evaluation:

List three factors that would be important in getting a bank loan.

# Applying for a Loan

**Directions:** Before a bank will give you a loan, you may have to answer some questions or provide information about your money management. Read the following questions that you may be asked. Why would each question be important?

1. Have you taken out other loans with this bank?

   _____

2. Have you paid them back? _____

3. How much was the loan for? _____

4. Do you pay your bills on time?_____

5. Do you have a steady job?_____

6. How much do you make a month/year?_____

7. Do you have any other source of income? _____

8. Have you lived at the same address for three years or more?

   _____

9. Do you have a family? _____

10. What is the name of a relative?

    _____

11. What is the purpose of this loan? _____

12. How will you pay it back?_____

13. What collateral do you have in case you can't pay it back?

    _____

14. Is there someone who will co-sign your loan to take responsibility for it if you don't pay?

    _____

15. How much money do you owe to other banks or other people?

    _____

16. What property do you own – cars, houses, land, etc.?

    _____

# IV-21 Local Transportation

**Objective:** The student will describe forms of transportation available in the community.

**Comments:**

Getting around independently is a worthy goal of any member of a community. While some students may have bicycles or ride a school bus to get where they want to go, there are usually other modes of transportation that are available and should be investigated. These may include public buses, a subway system, taxis, and so on. In this lesson, students are to target places they frequently go to and note what form of transportation they use.

**Introductory Activities:**

   a. Have students list ways people can get around in their community.

   b. Have students put a check mark next to the ways they have used.

   c. Have students put a dollar sign ($) next to the ways that cost money.

   d. Have students put the letter "A" next to the ways that require an adult's help.

**Activity:**

Encourage students not to put down the same answer for all items. If necessary, have students put an alternative mode of travel for the items if their first choice tends to be the same.

   **Discussion:** If your community is small, many students probably get around by foot, bike, or with the help of an adult driver. Encourage students to think about alternative modes of transportation. Is there a public bus system that could get them around? Do they ever carpool with a friend's parents? Look for alternatives!

   1. Do you feel your town/community has adequate public transportation?

   2. Are there any places you would like to be able to get to but can't? Is it because you need an adult, need money, or haven't learned to use that particular transportation system?

   3. Do you feel you are able to use public transportation without major problems?

   4. How much do you rely on adults or older siblings who drive to get you around?

   5. Do you plan to have a car or access to a car when you are old enough? How?

   6. Other than going to a friend's house or to school, where do you normally go on a regular basis that requires transportation?

**Extension Activities:**

   1. Have students conduct a survey of their classmates regarding how they travel (a) to school, and (b) for fun.

   2. Have students compile a list of facts about public transportation in their community. Find out about rates, availability, schedules, etc.

**Evaluation:**

   a. List three forms of transportation available to you in your community.

   b. Describe how each form listed in (a) is used by you and/or by others.

# Local Transportation

**Directions:** List ten places you go to periodically in your community or have recently visited. How do you get there? Write your answers on the lines below.

**Place**                                                    **Mode of Travel**

1. _____        _____

   _____

2. _____        _____

   _____

3. _____        _____

   _____

4. _____        _____

   _____

5. _____        _____

   _____

6. _____        _____

   _____

7. _____        _____

   _____

8. _____        _____

   _____

9. _____        _____

   _____

10. _____        _____

    _____

# IV-22 Forms of Transportation

**Objective:** The student will list at least ten different forms of common transportation.

**Comments:**

There are many methods of getting around. While some of the more common methods may be car, bus, or bicycle, there are a lot of other organized transportation systems such as public buses, subways, or taxis – depending on where you live. In this lesson, students are asked to think about different forms of transportation.

**Introductory Activities:**

a. Have students list different forms of transportation.

b. Have students put a check mark by those they have ever used or been on.

**Activity:**

**Answers:** *(Across)* **1.** ambulance; **3.** horse; **5.** skis; **6.** bicycle; **7.** boat; **9.** snowmobile; **11.** taxi; **12.** subway; **15.** golf cart; **16.** van *(Down)* **2.** car; **3.** helicopter; **4.** bus; **8.** train; **9.** skates; **10.** moped; **13.** wagon; **14.** motorcycle

**Discussion:** Go over the answers to the crossword puzzle. Students will probably not have any trouble with this one!

1. What factors determine what type of transportation is used in an area? (**weather, seasons, cost, population, etc.**)

2. What are the benefits of using public transportation rather than a personal vehicle? (**cost, reliability, don't have to worry about maintenance or parking, etc.**)

3. What are some benefits of using a personal vehicle rather than public transportation? (**freedom to go where you want, travel with friends, etc.**)

4. Why is it good to have or know about alternative forms of transportation? (**in case of emergency, checking out cost**)

5. How much do these factors enter into your decision about what method of transportation to use: cost, safety, convenience, availability?

**Extension Activities:**

1. Have students make a poster depicting various forms of transportation. Research the history of the vehicle or system.

2. Have students find out the cost of owning/operating a personal car for one year. Compare this to the amount of money needed to operate a school bus/commercial airplane/train.

3. Choose a city for a theoretical destination. Compare the costs of traveling to that city by car, bus, train, and airplane.

4. Other countries might have unusual forms of transportation (e.g., gondolas in Venice, camels in Egypt). Pick a country to investigate and find out how its citizens get around.

**Evaluation:**

Choose one form of transportation and write a paragraph giving the pros and cons of using this form of travel.

# Forms of Transportation

**Directions:** Complete the following crossword puzzle with the terms in the box below. Use the clues to help you.

| | | | |
|---|---|---|---|
| subway | ambulance | skates | horse |
| helicopter | bicycle | snowmobile | bus |
| car | moped | motorcycle | van |
| golf cart | train | skis | taxi |
| | wagon | boat | |

**Across**
1. emergency vehicle
3. animal that can be ridden
5. boards strapped to your feet
6. two-wheeled vehicle
7. vehicle that goes on water
9. vehicle used on snow
11. cab
12. train that goes underground
15. vehicle used on golf course
16. roomy vehicle, larger than a car

**Down**
2. automobile
3. air vehicle that can fly up and down
4. vehicle that can carry many people at one time
8. vehicle that goes on a track
9. shoes with wheels
10. bicycle with a motor
13. small vehicle pulled by a handle
14. motorized two-wheeled vehicle

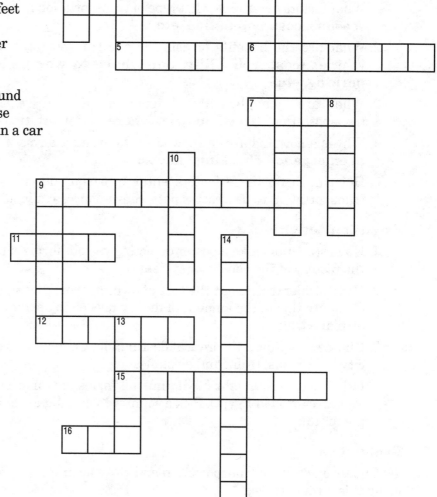

# IV-23 Planning a Trip

**Objective:** The student will list at least five considerations necessary for planning a trip.

**Comments:**

Whether planning to travel across the city, across the state, or across the country, one must consider the expense of travel. There are costs involved, not only in the actual travel, but in meals, motels, and expenses for sight-seeing when the destination is reached. This lesson lists factors that must be considered when traveling.

**Introductory Activities:**

  a. Ask students to list a place they would like to travel to someday. Allow time for them to share their ideas.

  b. Have students list some ideas of what they would have to plan for before actually taking the trip. (Assume that money is not a problem.)

**Activity:**

You may wish to narrow the scope of this assignment by having students select a site within your state or possibly within another designated area. You may wish to have students work in small groups on this project.

  **Materials:** pen or pencil, various guide books to cities or places

  **Discussion:** Students may come up with other items or considerations that are involved in taking a trip **(tipping a taxi driver, car repairs, etc.).**

  1. Why did you select the particular destination for this project? Was this a pleasure trip? sightseeing? to visit someone?

  2. How could you figure out the number of miles involved in the trip? **(atlas, map)**

  3. If you drove and used 29 cents/mile as your estimated cost, how much would the trip cost to drive there and back?

  4. Why is it usually cheaper to visit some places in the off season? **(not so busy)**

  5. What are some other ways you can reduce the cost of a trip? **(stay with friends, take a bus, pack your own food, etc.)**

**Extension Activities:**

  1. Have students contact a travel agency to collect brochures of interesting places to visit. Find out about ups and downs of costs and how you can save money by taking advantage of "package deals."

  2. Find out about trips that are offered to school groups at a discount rate. How much money is saved by traveling this way rather than as an individual?

  3. Have students collect photos and postcards of their designated trip. Make a display of the sights and adventures.

  4. Research motel chains. Find out the relative costs of staying in several different motels in a given city.

**Evaluation:**

  a. List five factors to consider in planning a trip.

  b. List three cost considerations (involving money) you would have to keep in mind when taking a trip. **(meals, gas, tickets, tipping, shopping, etc.)**

# Planning a Trip

**Directions:** Select a destination for your trip. Then do some research to find the answers to the following questions.

Destination (local/state/national/international):

_____

Specific destination: _____

Length of time spent traveling: _____

Mode(s) of travel:_____

Number of miles traveled:_____  Cost of travel: _____

Number of meals involved: _____  Cost of meals: _____

Clothing required (list): _____

_____

_____

Travel items (list):_____

_____

Number of suitcases needed: _____

Activities at destination: _____

_____

People to visit: _____

_____

Things to see: _____

_____

Tourist attractions:_____

Who will accompany you on the trip: _____

Spending money:_____

Hotel/motel accommodations:_____

Cost per night: _____

Other considerations (parking at airport, tips, etc.):_____

_____

Timetable (leaving, arriving, returning):_____

_____

# IV-24 Estimating Costs

**Objective:** The student will estimate costs associated with travel (e.g., meals, motel, attractions) given a designated destination.

**Comments:**

There are a lot of "hidden" costs involved in traveling, but adjustments can be made by staying in a less costly motel, eating at economical restaurants, traveling with others, etc. In this lesson, students are to compare travel expenses to a specified destination by manipulating several variables.

**Introductory Activities:**

a. Have the class select four major cities that would be interesting to visit (e.g., New York, Los Angeles, Denver, Chicago).

b. Have the class select a specified time for which they would like to pretend (or actually would like to visit someday) to visit that city.

**Activity:**

Students should be divided into groups and assigned a major city to visit for a week (or whatever length of time you decide). Their object is to plan a visit to that city and estimate the costs involved on the worksheet "Estimating Costs." You may wish to have each group take a different city to compare how much it would cost a typical tourist to visit different places, or you may wish to have each group use the same city as the destination and plan the excursion differently. Students will probably need to get guide books for the city selected. It would also be helpful to have brochures on motel chains or other travel information.

**Materials:** pen or pencil, guide books for cities, maps, brochures on major motel chains, other travel information

**Discussion:** Students will probably have a lot of information to share on their "discoveries" about their cities. Hopefully, they will also be somewhat enlightened as to how expensive meals and lodging can be.

1. Why are some cities more expensive to visit than others?

2. Did you find any good airfare rates?

3. What was the cheapest available way to get to your city?

4. What sights would you want to see in your selected city?

5. Who or what agencies can help you in planning a trip? **(travel agent, AAA)**

6. What was the range of prices for hotels or motels in the area?

7. What were some rates for rental cars? What determines the prices? **(kind of car, length of rental, adding insurance, etc.)**

**Extension Activities:**

1. Have students obtain and collect guide books for other interesting places. How much more would it cost to visit some places in Europe or other continents?

2. Have students find listings or books containing Bed and Breakfast establishments. Many of them are quite interesting, historic, and unique! Compare rates and places.

3. Some motel or hotel chains put out brochures advertising their amenities – a pool, spa/exercise room, elaborate room service, free breakfast, free newspaper, etc. Have students investigate what special attractions some places of lodging offer.

**Evaluation:**

Pretend you are a travel agent working with a customer who would like to visit the city you have just studied. What advice would you offer him or her in planning a trip? What should he or she see there? What questions would you ask the customer to find out what the specific needs are?

**Teacher Notes:**

_____

_____

_____

_____

_____

_____

Names _____

# Estimating Costs

**Directions:** Divide into groups. Each group will select a destination or target city (e.g., Chicago, New York, Denver, Los Angeles). Pretend you will spend one week at the selected city. Answer the following questions based on your city.

1. How much will it cost to get to your city?

_____

_____

2. How will you travel to get there?

_____

3. How much would a hotel cost for your stay?

_____

4. How much would meals cost?

_____

5. What will you want to do or see in the city? What do you estimate these attractions will cost?

_____

_____

_____

_____

6. What will a rental car cost (per day/per week)?

_____

7. What other expenses might you have to consider? Estimate them.

_____

_____

_____

_____

# IV-25 Using a Timetable

**Objective:** The student will be able to read a given timetable of a public transportation system and solve situational problems.

**Comments:**

Reading a timetable is a useful skill for anyone who uses public transportation to get around. Decisions about arrival times, how long a layover may be, making transfers, and planning one's schedule around possible departures and arrivals are all considerations the user must be able to understand. This lesson provides a sample timetable and problems for the student to solve.

**Introductory Activities:**

a. Have students list vehicles or transportation systems that use a timetable. **(public buses, trains, UPS, subways, etc.)**

b. Have students list information that would probably be contained on a typical timetable. **(vehicle number, arrival time, departure time, names of the stops, etc.)**

**Activity:**

**Materials:** pen or pencil, perhaps a clock or clock manipulative

**Answers: 1.** 12:15 P.M.; **2.** A, B; **3.** C, D; **4.** 40 minutes; **5.** A–12 minutes, B–8 minutes, C–15 minutes, D–10 minutes; **6.** 38 minutes **7.** A,B (C might be cutting it close!); **8.** 1 hour, 33 minutes

**Discussion:** Go over all of the problems with students, making sure they understand how to find the answers if they had any difficulty.

1. Why is it important to know how long of a layover there will be at a stop? **(in case you need to change trains, get off, etc.)**

2. How would knowing the schedule ahead of time help you plan your trip? **(you'd know when to be there, what time you'll arrive, plan alternatives if necessary)**

3. Do trains (or buses or airplanes or anything else with a timetable) always adhere to the schedule? **(sometimes they may run late or early)**

4. Why should you allow extra time to make connections? **(because sometimes they are not on schedule)**

**Extension Activities:**

1. Have students bring in sample timetables from public transportation systems. Have them write and exchange problems and situations with each other.

2. Using a timetable, give students a destination and time limit. Have them plan an efficient route.

**Evaluation:**

a. What are some systems of transportation that use a timetable?

b. What are three to five pieces of information contained on a typical timetable?

Name _____  Date_____

# Using a Timetable

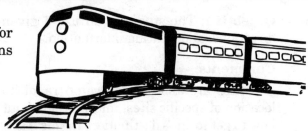

**Directions:** Below is a sample timetable for trains in City X. Answer the following questions based on the timetable.

| Train | Leaves Fortville | Arrives Downtown | Leaves Downtown | Arrives River Ridge |
|-------|------------------|------------------|-----------------|---------------------|
| A | 8:02 A.M. | 8:53 A.M. | 9:05 A.M. | 9:40 A.M. |
| B | 11:30 A.M. | 12:15 P.M. | 12:23 P.M. | 1:03 P.M. |
| C | 1:29 P.M. | 2:09 P.M. | 2:24 P.M. | 2:56 P.M. |
| D | 6:15 P.M. | 6:57 P.M. | 7:07 P.M. | 7:45 P.M. |

**1.** What time does Train B arrive downtown?

_____

**2.** Which trains arrive at River Ridge before 2:00?

_____

**3.** Which trains could you take leaving from Fortville after noon?

_____

**4.** How long is the ride from Fortville to downtown on Train C?

_____

**5.** How many minutes does each train stay at the downtown station?

_____

**6.** How long does it take for Train D to get from downtown to River Ridge?

_____

**7.** If you needed to be at River Ridge before 3:00 P.M., which trains would you take?

_____

**8.** How long is your ride from Fortville to River Ridge on Train B?

_____

# IV-26 Reading a Map

**Objective:** The student will use a given map to answer questions about distance, directions, and locating information.

**Comments:**

Maps are another source of travel information. They can provide the user with location of specific sites, information about distance between points, and a good idea of how to get to one's destination. In this lesson, students are given a small map of a portion of Washington, D.C. to answer questions.

**Introductory Activities:**

a. Have students list various types of maps and their uses. (**weather map, road map, population map, etc.**)

b. Have students tell about maps they have used recently or are familiar with. (**map of the school, city map, etc.**)

**Activity:**

Students should examine the partial map of Washington, D.C. on the worksheet "Reading a Map." Make sure students can read the information on the map and are familiar with the scale of miles and compass.

**Materials:** pen or pencil, ruler

**Answers: 1.** Lincoln Memorial; **2.** Supreme Court, Library of Congress; **3.** southeast; **4.** one inch = 1/2 mile; **5.** *(example)* go east on Constitution Avenue to 7th Street, turn south/right until you get to Independence Avenue, turn east/left; **6.** Constitution Avenue, Independence Avenue; **7.** National Museum of American History; **8.** northeast

**Discussion:** Answer any questions students may have about the activity.

1. How could a map help someone get around in an unfamiliar place?

2. What information does a compass give? (**directions – north, south, east, west**)

3. Why is knowing the scale of miles important? (**gives distance**)

4. What other transportation information might be given on a city map? (**bus lines, subway stops, etc.**)

5. What other information might be contained on a map key? (**parks, roads, restrooms, phones**)

6. Where are some places that would distribute maps? (**zoo, museum, etc.**)

**Extension Activities:**

1. Have students collect various maps and make a display.

2. WHERE AM I? Give a map to students with a starting point and a set of directions. See if they end up at the intended destination.

3. Have students make a map of their neighborhood, community, state, or other relevant place.

**Evaluation:**

Have students refer to the Washington, D.C. map on the worksheet to answer the following questions:

   a. About how far is it from 7th Street to 17th Street? **(one mile)**

   b. What direction is the Vietnam Veterans Memorial from the National Museum of American History? **(west)**

   c. What is the highway number of Constitution Avenue? **(50)**

   d. What direction do the numbered streets run? **(north – south)**

**Teacher Notes:**

_____

_____

_____

_____

_____

_____

Name _____ Date _____

# Reading a Map

**Directions:** Below is a map of highlights of Washington, D.C. Use the map to answer the questions below.

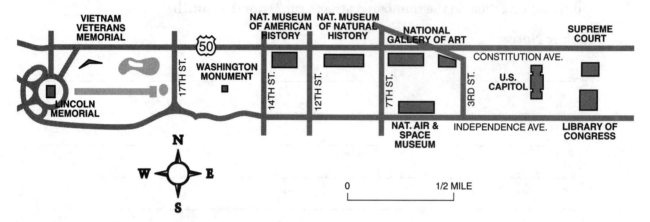

**1.** What national monument is on the west side of this map?

_____

**2.** What two buildings are on the east side of this map?

_____

**3.** What direction is the U.S. Capitol building in relation to the Supreme Court building?

_____

**4.** What is the scale of miles?

_____

**5.** Give directions from the National Museum of Natural History to the National Air and Space Museum.

_____

_____

**6.** What two major avenues run east and west?

_____

**7.** What building is between 14th street and 12th street?

_____

**8.** Where is the Vietnam Veterans Memorial in relation to the Lincoln Memorial?

_____

# IV-27 Right vs. Privilege

**Objective:** The student will list at least three reasons why driving is an activity that is to be taken seriously.

**Comments:**

Driving is an activity that most teenagers look forward to – and maybe come to expect. Depending on the individual circumstances, some young drivers have access to their parents' cars or even manage to get one of their own. In the wrong hands, however, driving can be dangerous. Students should be cautioned to revere driving with respect: it is a privilege, *not* a right.

**Introductory Activities:**

a. Have students define the word *right* (in the context of driving). (**something that you are entitled to – you can expect it!**)

b. Have students define the word *privilege.* (**having or enjoying something special**)

**Activity:**

**Discussion:** Have students discuss their thoughts about the cartoon and possible consequences of the girl's actions.

1. If you were Samantha's mother, would you ask any further questions about where the gas went from the night before?

2. If you were Samantha's mother, would you be so quick to hand over the keys and credit card? Why or why not?

3. How do you know that Samantha is not a careful driver? (**broken turn signal**)

4. How do you know that Samantha has been stopped by the police before? (**she said "oh no, not again"**)

5. What "rights" does Samantha think she is entitled to related to driving a car? (**apparently the right to have it maintained by her mother, the right to speed, annoy other drivers, etc.**)

6. What consequences do you think Samantha will face from the state trooper? (**at least a warning, probably a ticket**)

7. What consequences do you think Samantha will/should face from her mother? (**suspended driving privileges would be fair, but it seems as though her mother is pretty lenient**)

**Extension Activities:**

1. Have students obtain a copy of the rules of the road for driving for your state from your local license branch. Have them find out what the requirements are for obtaining a driver's license in your state.

2. Have students interview their parents or close adult friend. At what age did the person learn to drive/get a license/get a car?

**Evaluation:**

a. In the context of driving a car, explain the difference between the right to drive and having the privilege of driving.

b. Write a paragraph giving at least three reasons why driving is a serious activity.

# Right vs. Privilege

**Directions:** Read the following cartoon story. Pretend you are Samantha's parent. What would you do?

## IV-28 Choosing Your Driver

**Objective:** The student will list at least three characteristics of a responsible driver.

**Comments:**

Students may not have the privilege to be a driver, but they will often find themselves a passenger. Trusting the driver of the car to be alert, careful, law abiding, and sober is the responsibility of the passenger. In this lesson, students are to examine characteristics of potential drivers and decide whether or not they think they would be safe.

**Introductory Activities:**

a. Have students think of someone who they would consider to be a good driver.

b. Have students list characteristics of the person they had in mind that would demonstrate why or how that person is a good driver.

**Activity:**

**Answers:** *(suggested)* **1.** yes – concerned about safety; **2.** no – unafraid of speed; **3.** no – inattentive; **4.** yes – appears to be safe; **5.** no – never ride with someone who has been drinking; **6.** no – Amy is not in good shape to drive; **7.** yes – concerned about taking care of his car; **8.** no – his reactions will be impaired

**Discussion:** Have students talk about their answers and why they would or would not feel safe riding in a car with the driver described.

1. Do you feel it is important to wear a seatbelt? Do you know of anyone who was injured or killed in a car accident because of not wearing a seatbelt?

2. How can excessive speed be dangerous? **(might lose control, have to react more quickly)**

3. What are other distractions besides a loud radio that can affect paying attention to your driving? **(drinking or eating, petting a dog, trying to put on makeup in the mirror, etc.)**

4. Do you know of anyone who was involved in a drinking and driving accident?

5. What are some weather conditions that can affect driving? **(fog, rain, glare from the sun, etc.)**

6. What are some characteristics of a good driver? **(reacts quickly, thinks, is a skillful driver, etc.)**

**Extension Activities:**

1. Have students survey five drivers. Include the length of time the person has been driving on your survey. What are three pieces of advice about driving that each would give to a new driver?

2. The National Safety Council publishes defensive driving course materials. Have students browse through this or similar publications and list at least ten helpful tips for driving under atypical situations (or driving "defensively").

**Evaluation:**

a. List three characteristics or behaviors of a good driver.

b. List three characteristics or behaviors of a poor driver.

# Choosing Your Driver

**Directions:** Would you ride in a car with this person as your driver? Write YES or NO next to each description. Then explain why or why not.

1. Jaime makes all of the passengers in his car wear their seatbelts and lock their door.

    _____

2. Wanda just borrowed her sister's sports car. She wants you to see how fast it can go.

    _____

3. Julie drives with one hand on the steering wheel and one adjusting the radio station – which is LOUD. She thinks she will get attention from the boys who drive close by.

    _____

4. Yolanda always stays within the speed limit and concentrates on her driving.

    _____

5. Ray has had three beers at a party. He says he feels fine and will be happy to give you a ride home.

    _____

6. A big snowstorm is due. The roads are already icy and there is low visibility. Amy is a new driver and nervous.

    _____

7. Alfred has had his license for over a year. He just finished paying for his car and is very proud of it. He always tries to park where it won't get hit.

    _____

8. Kevin says he can drive better after he has smoked a joint. He'll be glad to prove it to you!

    _____

# IV-29 Drinking and Driving

**Objective:** The student will be able to state his or her opinion regarding drinking and driving.

**Comments:**

Drinking and driving is a very dangerous, deadly combination. In fact, drinking and driving is the leading cause of death for teens. In this lesson, students are to react to statements about drinking and driving.

**Introductory Activities:**

a. Ask students to show (by raising hands) if they think drinking and driving is one of the top ten leading causes of death among teens.

b. Ask students to raise their hands if they think drinking and driving is one of the top three leading causes of death among teens.

c. Ask students to raise their hands if they think drinking and driving is the leading cause of death among teens.

**Activity:**

Students are given ten opinion statements on the worksheet "Drinking and Driving" to express their agreement/disagreement. Comments will be discussed after students have completed the survey.

**Discussion:** Have students volunteer to express their opinions about the statements. Be aware that students may have alcohol-related problems in their families and probably a few have had experience with alcohol-related tragedies. You may want to make adjustments for sensitive students.

1. Do you know of someone who was involved as a driver in an alcohol-related accident?

2. Do you know of someone who was involved as a passenger in an alcohol-related accident?

3. What is meant by a "designated driver"? **(someone who will not drink in order to drive the passengers home safely)**

4. What are some alternatives to getting around if you or your driver have been drinking at a party or somewhere away from home? **(calling someone else, calling a taxi, spending the night, etc.)**

5. How do students feel about assemblies or presentations that are geared to preventing students from drinking and driving? Are they taken seriously?

6. How much of a factor (deterrent or advocate) are parents in drinking and driving? Would you be afraid to tell your parents that you had been drinking? How would your parents react?

**Extension Activities:**

1. Find out if there is a S.A.D.D. (Students Against Drunk Driving) group at your school. How many students are involved? How could you start one? (Contact SADD, P.O. Box 800, Marlborough, MA 01752; phone: 508-481-3568.)

2. Invite a medical person (doctor, EMT, etc.) to visit school to talk about alcohol-related car accidents they have dealt with.

3. Have students write and conduct a student survey about student drinking and driving in your school.

4. Have students find out what *blood-alcohol level* (BAC) means and what the illegal BAC in your state is. **(This is the percentage of alcohol in the blood and is measured in blood, breath, or urine.)**

5. Many communities will print results of court cases in the newspaper as part of the public record. Have students look through the list and calculate how many are related to drunk driving. What penalties were determined for each case?

## Evaluation:

a. What is the leading cause of death among teens?

b. Write a paragraph expressing your opinion about drinking and driving.

## Teacher Notes:

_____

_____

_____

_____

_____

_____

# Drinking and Driving

**Directions:** Read the following statements. Circle AGREE or DISAGREE to show how you feel or react to the statement.

**1.** You should never drink alcohol and then drive.                                    **Agree   Disagree**

**2.** You should never ride in a car with someone who drinks and drives.                **Agree   Disagree**

**3.** Drinking and driving is the leading cause of death for teens.                     **Agree   Disagree**

**4.** If most of my close friends were drinking at a party and then one                 **Agree   Disagree**
offered to drive home, I would drink too, even if I knew I would
ride home with one of them.

**5.** It is embarrassing to call your parents to come pick you up at a party.           **Agree   Disagree**

**6.** I know of someone who was killed or injured in a                                  **Agree   Disagree**
drunk-driving accident.

**7.** My parents don't care if I drink as long as I don't drive.                        **Agree   Disagree**

**8.** I would stop drinking if I had a close call with a drunk driver.                  **Agree   Disagree**

**9.** I am familiar with the alcohol education taught in health                         **Agree   Disagree**
class or other program as it relates to drinking.

**10.** If adults brought in wrecked cars from drunk-driving accidents,                  **Agree   Disagree**
students would laugh.

# IV-30 Cost of Maintaining a Car

**Objective:** The student will be able to obtain estimates of typical car maintenance and repairs.

**Comments:**

It would be great if there were no costs involved after the purchase of the car; however, the bills are just beginning. Students should become familiar with routine maintenance involved in having a car (oil change, windshield wiper fluid, coolant level, air pressure in tires, etc.) as well as how much some major work might cost (brake or muffler replacement, dents, air conditioning, etc.). In this lesson, students are to select a car to "own" and research how much maintenance would cost.

**Introductory Activities:**

    a. Have students list types of maintenance that is done on a car.

    b. Have students list major repairs they are familiar with that have been done on their own or a family car.

**Activity:**

Students are to select a type of car they would like to use as the basis of researching maintenance cost on the worksheet "Cost of Maintaining a Car." You may wish to limit them to something realistic (within a modest budget) or you may allow them to select a luxury car. To complete this activity, students will need access to information about their selected car and will need to visit or make phone calls to insurance companies, garages, car maintenance shops, gas stations, and/or auto parts stores. Some students may already be familiar with how to work on their own cars or have friends or family members who are good at this.

    **Materials:** brochures on cars (available from car dealers), advertisements from auto parts stores, other newspaper ads for oil change specials, etc.

    **Discussion:** Students will need to do some individual calling and research to complete this activity. It will be interesting to compare the prices on different makes and models of cars.

    1. Why is it important to know what grade or type of gas your car should run on?

    2. Compare the range of cost for auto parts on common replacement parts such as belts, spark plugs, headlights, etc. Does it cost more to have a luxury car?

    3. How much can you save by doing a routine maintenance job yourself? Is it worth the time?

    4. How could you learn how to do some routine maintenance?

    5. Why is it important to get more than one estimate on a major repair job?

**Extension Activities:**

    1. Have students obtain an owner's manual for a car. What routine maintenance is recommended? How often should maintenance jobs be performed?

    2. Give students a list of auto parts. Send them out to compare prices in different auto supply stores. Where are the best buys?

3. Have students figure out what it costs to keep gas in an economy car, mid-sized car, and luxury car for one year. (Make assumptions such as the size of the tank, how many miles would be put on in one year, and what grade of gas is recommended.)

4. Have students figure out what it would cost to keep a car for one year, given limits such as mileage, etc. Include insurance, maintenance, gas, wear-and-tear, etc.

**Evaluation:**

a. List three maintenance jobs that should be done routinely to keep a car running well.

b. List three major repairs that could be necessary on a car.

**Teacher Notes:**

_____

_____

_____

_____

_____

_____

# Cost of Maintaining a Car

**Directions:** Congratulations! You've got your own car! Now let's see if you can afford to keep it. Find out what each of the following situations would cost you. First, some specific information about your car:

Purchase price:_____

New or used? _____

Describe the car (make, model, year): _____

Cost of license plates:_____

Insurance company: _____     Cost for 6 months: _____

1. You notice your gas gauge is on empty. You pull into the gas station and put 20 gallons into the tank, which fills it up.

    **a.** What grade of gas will you use? _____

    **b.** How much is one gallon of gas? _____

    **c.** How much will it cost to fill the tank?_____

2. You are driving along when you hear a funny squeaking noise in the engine. You find out it is the fan belt. You and a friend decide to fix it yourself. How much will the fan belt cost?

    _____

3. At night you are pulled over by a police officer because your car has a headlight out. What will this part cost if you decide to fix it yourself?

    _____

4. It's time for an oil change. You decide to go to a quick oil-change station. What will it cost for this service?

    _____

5. It has been rainy for a week. You take your car through a car wash. How much does this cost?

    _____

6. After you coasted through three stop signs, you decide to have your brakes looked at. Bad news – you need a complete brake replacement. What's the price on this?

    _____

## IV-31 Car Insurance

**Objective:** The student will be able to identify common information from a sample insurance policy.

**Comments:**

Having insurance on one's car is not only a good idea, it is a requirement in some states. Students may or may not realize that because they are young, they will have to pay a higher premium. Other factors, such as what the vehicle is used for, how many miles are put on the vehicle each year, the year and type of car, and the number and severity of accidents and claims, all contribute to the price one must pay for insurance. In this lesson, students are introduced to some common terms used when talking about car insurance and are given a sample insurance policy to examine.

**Introductory Activities:**

a. Ask students to predict the reaction that their parents would have if they found out their vehicle was stolen. (Some may have stories to tell about incidents in which this has happened!)

b. Have students name insurance companies they have heard of or are used by their families.

c. Explain the following terms by definition and example:

   *bodily injury liability* – when you are responsible for injuring another person with your vehicle

   *property damage liability* – when you are responsible for damaging another person's property

   *uninsured motorists protection* – when your vehicle is damaged by another driver who does not have insurance

   *automobile collision insurance* – protection from damage to your car

   *automobile comprehensive insurance* – protection for anything else that can happen to your car such as damage from fire, theft, weather, etc.

   *deductible* – a certain amount of money you have to pay towards damages; the insurance company will pay the rest

**Activity:**

**Answers: 1.** State Insurance Company; **2.** Pete Smith; **3.** November 9, 1995; **4.** May 9, 1996; **5.** 3; **6.** New Yorker; **7.** all 3; **8.** all 3; **9.** 2 and 3; **10.** it says that the policy premium does not indicate any driver under age 25; **11.** pleasure; **12.** work; **13.** good driver, multiple cars; **14.** have a good driving record (no tickets)

**Discussion:** Answer any questions the students may have about the worksheet.

1. Why wouldn't you have comprehensive insurance on an older car? (**it might not be worth it if the car itself wasn't worth very much**)

2. Why is it a good idea to shop around for an insurance company? (**some offer better rates than others, special discounts, etc.**)

3. If you were to have a minor accident, why is it important to get an estimate on the damage? (**so the insurance company will know how much to pay**)

4. Why do you think there is a deductible on the collision insurance? **(might make you more careful if you knew you have to pay for some of it!)**

5. Why would insurance rates be lower for people who drive less than 7,500 miles a year? **(the less they drive, the less chance they would have of being involved in an accident)**

6. Why would insurance rates be lower for a driver over the age of 25? **(they would probably be more experienced drivers, may have families they are responsible for, drive primarily to work, etc.)**

### Extension Activities:

1. Invite an insurance company representative to talk to the class. Topics might include the importance of being a careful driver, how to protect your car from theft, and different insurance options.

2. Compare the insurance rates for several different types of cars. Include a "hot" sports car, expensive luxury car, four-door sedan, and economy vehicle.

### Evaluation:

a. Explain what is meant by "collision" insurance.

b. Explain what is meant by "comprehensive" insurance.

c. List at least three factors that would affect the insurance rate you have to pay.

### Teacher Notes:

_____

_____

_____

_____

_____

_____

# Car Insurance

**Directions:** Below is a sample car insurance policy. Look it over and then answer the questions on the next sheet.

| **STATE INSURANCE COMPANY** | ISSUED OCT 9, 1995 |
|---|---|

Policy # 0 12 782837 05/09          FROM NOV 9, 1995

Name of insured     Pete Smith         TO MAY 9, 1996

| Vehicle | Year | Make and Serial No. | Lienholder |
|---|---|---|---|
| 1 | 87 | Bronco IFMDU2744 | |
| 2 | 89 | Firebird IG2FS2157 | |
| 3 | 91 | New Yorker IC3XC66 | First National Bank |

### Your Coverages and Limits of Liability

| | Coverage |
|---|---|
| 1 2 3 | Bodily Injury Liability<br>$50,000 each person – $100,000 each occurrence |
| 1 2 3 | Property Damage Liability<br>– $25,000 each occurrence |
| 1 2 3 | Uninsured Motorists/Bodily Injury<br>$50,000 each person – $100,000 each accident |
| 1 2 3 | Automobile Collision<br>Less deductible of $100.00 each occurrence |
|    2 3 | Automobile Comprehensive |

Your policy premium does not indicate any driver under age 25

| | |
|---|---|
| 1 2 3 | No unmarried driver under 25 |
| 1 | Over 7500 miles a year, for pleasure |
|    2 3 | Over 7500 miles a year, work |

Good driver rate applied       Yes

Multiple Car Discount       Yes

## Car Insurance, continued

**Questions:**

1. What is the name of the insurance company?

   _____

2. What is the name of the insured person?

   _____

3. When does the insurance policy go into effect? _____

4. When does the insurance policy end? _____

5. How many vehicles does the insured person own?

   _____

6. Which car is not completely paid for yet?

   _____

7. Which vehicles are covered for damaging other people's property? Which vehicles are covered for damage to the car?

   _____

8. Which vehicles are covered for fire, theft, and anything else that would affect the car?

   _____

9. How do you know the insured person is over age 25?

   _____

10. What is the Bronco used primarily for?

    _____

11. What are the other two vehicles used for?

    _____

12. What are the two discounts given?

    _____

13. How would you get a good driver discount?

    _____

# IV-32 A Place to Live

**Objective:** The student will identify possible appropriate housing arrangements for given characters.

**Comments:**

Housing does not necessarily mean living in a house – there are all sorts of living arrangements that can suit people in various situations. In this lesson, students must match the character with an appropriate accommodation.

**Introductory Activities:**

    a. Ask students to share their ideas about where they expect to live after they have completed their schooling or are working somewhere.

    b. Have students list different types of housing or living arrangements for adults or people who are "on their own."

**Activity:**

On the worksheet "A Place to Live," students are to match the characters (who are given specific needs or situations as clues) with a housing possibility. Explain that not everyone can afford (or wants) to live in a house. Some people need to live close to their place of employment, or on a bus line, or want to live with friends, or need to save money by staying with relatives.

    **Answers: 1.** c; **2.** e; **3.** a; **4.** d; **5.** f; **6.** b

    **Discussion:** Go over the answers on the worksheet. Some answers may fit more than one character, but in order to make the answers come out even, the clues need to fit one particular response.

    1. Why do many people start out by renting an apartment rather than buying a house? **(easier to get out of, cheaper payments, etc.)**

    2. What are some disadvantages to living in an apartment? **(neighbors, parking, restrictions on pets, etc.)**

    3. What are some advantages/disadvantages to living with relatives? **(save money, but may not have privacy)**

    4. Why do you think some housing places have restrictions on kids or pets? **(tend to cause more damage, may annoy neighbors)**

    5. How would you handle problem neighbors if you lived in an apartment? **(talk to manager, talk to the other tenants, talk to the problem people, etc.)**

    6. How could you be a good neighbor to your neighbors? **(be considerate)**

    7. How would you go about finding a place to live? **(check classifieds, friends' recommendations, etc.)**

**Extension Activities:**

    1. Have students collect information on local apartment complexes. Compile and compare prices and amenities offered – how much is a one-bedroom apartment? two-bedroom? a pool? game room? allow pets?

    2. Have students prepare and carry out an interview of someone who has recently taken a job, moved out of his or her parents' home, and/or is living independently. Find out if there were any surprises about finding a place to live or what is involved in living independently.

**Evaluation:**

Consider your needs and probable income. Make a list of what considerations will influence your choice of living arrangements when you are on your own.

**Teacher Notes:**

_____

_____

_____

_____

_____

_____

Name _____ Date_____

# A Place to Live

**Directions:** Match the person on the left with a good place for him or her to live on the right. Write the letter of your answer on the line.

_____ 1. Sally is going to college part-time at night. She works during the day. She shares a car with her sisters at home. She gets along pretty well with her parents.

**a.** Westwood Apartments – close to town and right on a public bus line.

**b.** Deluxe Mobile Homes – have your own small yard and share a community playground.

_____ 2. David has a full-time job with good hours. He doesn't want to live alone, but he wants his own room. He has several good friends who are in the same situation.

**c.** Live at home with parents and siblings.

**d.** Stay with Aunt Mary who lives in a big city, has lots of room, and won't charge any rent.

_____ 3. Pete doesn't have a car, so he needs to live close to his job. He works during the day.

**e.** Share an apartment with one or two friends.

**f.** Rent a room in a large house with several smaller apartments. You can stay only one month or as long as you like.

_____ 4. Alison wants to go to school in another city where she can get the classes she wants. She hopes she can save some money by staying with someone she knows.

_____ 5. Monroe moved to a new town. He would like to stay there for awhile, but he doesn't know the area well and doesn't really know where he would like to settle permanently.

_____ 6. Shanelle wants her own place, and she really would like a yard, even if it is small. She has a small child and would like privacy.

# IV-33 Home Upkeep

**Objective:** The student will list 10 to 15 routine jobs that are necessary for properly upkeeping a house or residence.

**Comments:**

It takes work to keep a place looking nice! Students may not realize how much work is involved in general cleaning, routine maintenance, and making improvements. In this lesson, students must make a list of inside and outside jobs that are necessary to keep a residence looking acceptable.

**Introductory Activities:**

    a. Give students a blank sheet of paper and have them draw an abandoned house. Discuss what clues they gave that the house was abandoned.

    b. Make a class list of maintenance work that would need to be done to improve their abandoned houses. Students may also have drawn a neglected yard to go with the house. Include yardwork!

**Activity:**

Students are given a list of items or rooms on the worksheet "Home Upkeep" that routinely need attention, such as the yard, carpet, plumbing, etc. They are to list at least one specific routine job that needs to be done to keep the area functional, clean, and neat.

    **Answers:** *(examples)* **OUTSIDE:** mow the lawn, replace shingles, clean windows, paint fence, clean up after pets, weed, keep debris out of driveway; **INSIDE:** wash walls, clean carpet, clean appliances, flush pipes, dust and vacuum, clean windows, clean out refrigerator, wash sheets, wax the kitchen floor, clean toilets

    **Discussion:** Students may vary somewhat on the jobs they listed for the specific areas. Have students share their ideas.

    1. Why is it important to keep your home looking nice? **(looks as though you are responsible, keeps property values up, safer environment)**

    2. How could letting your home deteriorate affect safety? **(things may fall apart, someone could get injured, a child may get into a place where he or she could get hurt, etc.)**

    3. What goes through your mind when you see a house or apartment that used to be quite nice but is now run-down? **(the owners didn't care, perhaps couldn't afford to keep it up)**

    4. Why do you think some people would rather live in an apartment or condominium than keep up with a house? **(may be older, unable to physically do the work, don't want to spend the time)**

    5. Some people enjoy doing yardwork. Why? **(like to be outside, enjoy watching things that they have planted grow, etc.)**

    6. What extra responsibility do pet owners have? **(keep their yards clean, exercise their pets, make sure the houses are clean if the pets are kept indoors, etc.)**

**Extension Activities:**

1. Have students make an extensive shopping list of items needed for a thorough cleaning (top to bottom!) of a house or apartment. Then do some research at a local store and figure out what it would cost.

2. From the list of jobs in (1), have students find out how long it actually takes to do the job (specify the particulars – clean the carpets in 4 rooms, wax one 9 x 12 kitchen tile floor, etc.). You may want to take a class average. It would also be interesting to have students take before and after pictures of their projects!

**Evaluation:**

a. List five to ten general routine jobs for keeping a residence livable and comfortable.

b. List two to three reasons why it is important to keep your living quarters looking nice.

**Teacher Notes:**

_____

_____

_____

_____

_____

_____

# Home Upkeep

**Directions:** There is a lot to do to keep your place looking nice. List at least one job that needs to be done occasionally next to each clue word below.

**OUTSIDE**

yard_____

roof _____

windows_____

fence _____

pets _____

garden _____

driveway _____

**INSIDE**

walls _____

carpet _____

appliances _____

pipes, plumbing _____

dusting, vacuuming _____

windows_____

refrigerator _____

bedroom _____

kitchen _____

bathroom _____

# IV-34 Home Repairs

**Objective:** The student will make a list of home repairs that are routinely necessary and available resources for making the repairs.

**Comments:**

Unfortunately, things break, burn out, get lost, or fall apart with old age. Part of independent living is recognizing when there is a maintenance problem and taking steps to repair the damage. It isn't necessary to call in a professional in every case, but on the other hand, it is important to know when something is beyond your skills! In this lesson, students are to identify home repair problems and offer solutions.

**Introductory Activities:**

    a. Have students make a class list of everything they can think of that can go wrong in a house or apartment.

    b. Have students identify the last two or three things that needed to be repaired around their house.

**Activity:**

Students are to read the short story on the worksheet "Home Repairs" about a man who is faced with numerous housing repairs and to list them. Then they are to make a tentative list of a professional who may need to be called or jot down what supplies they may need to get to do the job themselves.

> **Answers:** *(examples)* broken coffee maker/take to appliance repair; burned out light/replace with new bulb; spill on carpet/clean with towel; broken garbage disposal/call appliance repair; no hot water/call plumber; dirty windows/clean them; gutters filled with leaves/clean them out; loose hand rail/tighten loose parts; broken cord/replace cord

> **Discussion:** Hopefully, no one really has this bad of a day! Students may differ on what jobs they think should be done by a hired professional. It is expensive to call a service person for every little job. Students hopefully will realize the importance of learning to do a few home repairs on their own.

1. Why is it a good idea to be able to do some home repairs by yourself? (**save money, save time waiting for repair person to show up**)

2. Why is it a good idea to call a professional service person to do some home repairs? (**get a guarantee, may do a better job, have the right tools and supplies, do the job faster, etc.**)

3. Why is it important to keep warranties on major appliances such as a refrigerator or oven? (**it shows when and where you purchased the appliance, tells what is covered, may entitle you to free service within the warranty period, etc.**)

4. When shopping around for service, what qualifications do you think are important to find out about before having someone do the work? (**if they are recommended to do a good job, provide a guarantee of their work, reasonable price, efficient workers, etc.**)

**Extension Activities:**

1. Have students watch a movie or television show parodying the hassles of being homeowners, such as *The Money Pit* or "Home Improvement."

2. Have students find out how much an electrician, plumber, carpenter, and/or appliance repair person charge for their services.

3. Have students obtain some books on do-it-yourself home maintenance and evaluate the books. Are they easy to understand? Are the directions accurate? Would they be helpful in making repairs?

4. Have students opt to learn one maintenance task from a friend, parents, older sibling, or other volunteer teacher. Expect a demonstration or report on this new learning!

**Evaluation:**

a. List five typical home repairs that will probably be necessary at some point.

b. List three to five professional service people whom you could call for repairs. Describe the type of maintenance or repair that the person would do.

**Teacher Notes:**

_____

_____

_____

_____

_____

# Home Repairs

**Directions:** Below is a story about Pete, who is having a very bad day. Make a list of all the repairs he needs to do something about and then make a list of who he should call or what he should do. You can use the back of this page to write your lists.

Pete's alarm went off, early in the morning. He rubbed his eyes and went into the kitchen to make coffee, but for some reason the coffee maker wasn't working. He decided to drink some orange juice. He opened the refrigerator, but found that the light had burned out and he couldn't see what was inside. He grabbed some juice, but as he turned around his dog knocked into him and he spilled the juice all over the kitchen carpet. He had some cereal for breakfast, and was going to dump the remains down his garbage disposal, but when he turned on the switch, nothing happened. He also realized that he was missing a spoon. He decided to wash his dishes, but when he turned on the faucet, only cold water came out – no hot water! There went his long morning shower! His dog was barking at something outside and Pete went to look, but he couldn't see through the dirty windows. Leaves were falling all over the yard. He managed to wipe a little spot in the window on the second floor, where he could see that the gutters were completely filled with leaves. He turned to go back down the steps but his hand slipped on the stair rail, which was loose. He tried to turn on the light at the bottom of the stairs, but his dog had chewed up the cord to the lamp. No light! He decided he would head on to work – where hopefully everything was in working order!

## IV-35 Care of Clothing

**Objective:** The student will demonstrate knowledge of how to care for or repair various clothing items.

**Comments:**

We all probably wish that our clothes would be self-cleaning (and put themselves on hangers and go into the closet on their own); however, in order to look presentable we must periodically clean and repair whatever is necessary. In this lesson, students must think about how to take care of various items of clothing.

**Introductory Activities:**

    a. Have students tell what they do with their clothes when they are done wearing them for the day. (Try not to be shocked!)

    b. Have students tell who is primarily responsible for taking care of their clothes right now.

**Activity:**

Students are given a list of typical clothing maintenance or repairs on the worksheet "Care of Clothing." They are to suggest a way to take care of the problem.

**Answers:** *(examples)* **1.** take jacket to dry cleaner; **2.** replace the zipper; **3.** sew on the button; **4.** hand wash the shirt; **5.** hook them together before throwing them into the wash; **6.** sew the rip; **7.** wash it off; **8.** spray pre-wash cleaner on the spot; **9.** replace the shoelaces; **10.** sew the hem; **11.** iron the shirt; **12.** sew the hole shut

**Discussion:** Some students may have more practical knowledge about doing minor repairs and cleaning than others do. Have students share their knowledge with the class.

1. Why aren't you wearing the same clothes now that you had five years ago? **(outgrow them, styles change, clothes wear out, etc.)**

2. Why is it a good idea to take good care of your clothes? **(they will last longer, look better)**

3. Do you have a system now for taking care of your clothes? How does it work? How could it be improved?

4. When you shop for clothes, what things do you consider – cost, style, care, etc.?

5. What sources could you check if you weren't sure how to clean a specific stain? **(clothing care books, call a cleaner)**

**Extension Activities:**

1. Have students write the specific steps for operating a washing machine and dryer.

2. Have students check advertisements or make phone calls to find out the cost of having clothing items dry cleaned.

3. Have students run a load of clothing through a local coin-operated laundry machine.

4. Supply students with a needle, thread, a button, and swatch of fabric and have them practice sewing it on!

5. Have students write a short story entitled something like: "I Am Joe's Shirt" – describing a day in the life of a shirt from the shirt's point of view.

6. Have students compile a booklet of helpful cleaning hints. Copy and distribute the tips to students.

## Evaluation:

a. List five typical clothing repairs that need to be done periodically .

b. List three typical clothing cleaning tasks that need to be done periodically .

## Teacher Notes:

_____

_____

_____

_____

_____

_____

# Care of Clothing

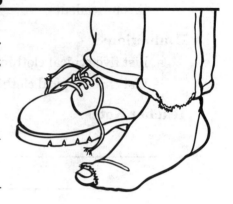

**Directions:** Below is a list of clothing maintenance or repairs that need to be done. Write your suggestion for what needs to be done.

1. Your suit jacket needs to be cleaned, but it says "Dry Clean Only" on the label.

   _____

2. Your skirt has a broken zipper on the side.

   _____

3. There is a button missing from your favorite shirt.

   _____

4. Your new red and white T-shirt is dirty but you are afraid if you wash it, it will come out pink.

   _____

5. Whenever you wash a pair of socks, you seem to lose one of them.

   _____

6. There is a little rip in one of your shirts.

   _____

7. You spilled some ketchup on a tie.

   _____

8. You were playing a little too roughly, and got some blood on your jeans.

   _____

9. The end of your shoelace has completely unraveled and you can't get it through the hole anymore.

   _____

10. The hem of your slacks is coming out.

    _____

11. Your dress shirt is wrinkled.

    _____

12. There is a hole in the toe of your sock.

    _____

# IV-36 Nutrition

**Objective:** Given guidelines, the student will plan a nutritious meal.

**Comments:**

In our hurried pace of life, planning and eating nutritious meals sometimes goes by the wayside. It may be easier to grab a little bag of potato chips and a candy bar than to take the time to eat something more healthy and full of vitamins. In this lesson, students are introduced to the food guide pyramid and will use that as a guideline to plan nutritious meals.

**Introductory Activities:**

a. Ask students to list the last ten things they can think of that they have eaten.

b. Have students put a check mark next to the items they think are considered nutritious.

c. Define *nutritious*. **(describing foods that contain nutrients – substances in food that provide material for maintaining the body and keeping it healthy; specific nutrients include fats, proteins, minerals, vitamins, and carbohydrates)**

d. Have students reconsider the items they checked in ("b") to see if they want to change their answers.

**Activity:**

**Materials:** pen or pencil, books on nutrition, calorie-counter booklets, etc.

**Discussion:** Have students share their ideas on nutritious meals. They could exchange papers or evaluate volunteers' ideas as a class. Make sure students included items from the food pyramid guide.

1. Why is it important especially for children to eat nutritious meals? **(their bodies are still growing)**

2. What are some benefits to eating well? **(you'll feel better, maintain your weight, have a stronger body, fewer cavities, etc.)**

3. Not all foods that are good for you taste bad. What are some foods you like that you know are good for you?

4. Some menus in restaurants are marked "heart smart." What does that mean? **(low in fat, won't clog your arteries)**

5. What are some physical or health conditions that some people have that require special diets? **(heart diseases, obesity, diabetes, hyperactivity, etc.)**

**Extension Activities:**

1. Have students find out the number of calories contained in 20 food items (e.g., candy bar, apple, serving of lettuce, etc.).

2. Have students find out the number of grams of fat in the same items.

3. Have students find out the recommended caloric intake for their age, weight, sex, and activity level.

4. Assign students the task of keeping track of everything that is eaten for one week. Look for trends. Are the foods nutritious?

5. Challenge students to take one week to give up fatty foods and eat only healthful foods. How do they feel at the end of the week?

6. Talk to school cafeteria personnel to find out what the school's specific nutritious guidelines are.

7. Have students research a topic involving nutrition. What foods are high in specific nutrients?

8. Prepare a book of nutritious meals using healthful guidelines.

9. Have students write to child-care organizations that promote nutrition in third world countries. How do they help feed underprivileged children?

10. Have students make a chart showing the nutritional value (including calories, vitamins, serving size, etc.) of several common foods.

### Evaluation:

a. What are some guidelines to include when planning a nutritious meal?

b. Give an example of at least one item in each group of the food group pyramid.

### Teacher Notes:

_____

_____

_____

_____

_____

_____

Name _____ Date_____

# Nutrition

**Directions:** Using the food guide pyramid, plan one day of nutritious meals – breakfast, lunch, dinner, and snacks.

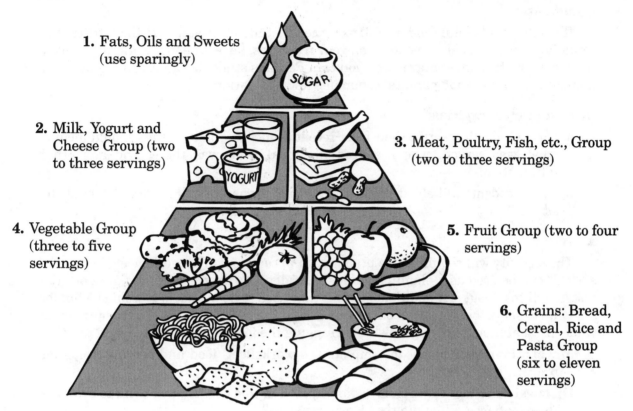

**1.** Fats, Oils and Sweets (use sparingly)

**2.** Milk, Yogurt and Cheese Group (two to three servings)

**3.** Meat, Poultry, Fish, etc., Group (two to three servings)

**4.** Vegetable Group (three to five servings)

**5.** Fruit Group (two to four servings)

**6.** Grains: Bread, Cereal, Rice and Pasta Group (six to eleven servings)

| **Breakfast** | **Lunch** | **Dinner** | **Snacks** |
|---|---|---|---|
| _____ | _____ | _____ | _____ |
| _____ | _____ | _____ | _____ |
| _____ | _____ | _____ | _____ |
| _____ | _____ | _____ | _____ |
| _____ | _____ | _____ | _____ |
| _____ | _____ | _____ | _____ |
| _____ | _____ | _____ | _____ |
| _____ | _____ | _____ | _____ |

# IV-37 Preparing a Meal

**Objective:** The student will participate in a group project by preparing a nutritious meal.

**Comments:**

It would be a helpful (and useful) exercise for students to step into the kitchen and actually prepare a meal. Depending on your resources, have students work in groups to carry out this task in whatever way you can. Perhaps students can prepare a meal for "homework" and include parental comments and evaluation!

**Introductory Activities:**

    a. Have students describe their most recent dinner at home. Details should include what was served, who prepared the meal, who was there, and any other information.

    b. Have students tell about the last meal they prepared. Ask for details about the situation.

**Activity:**

This activity will require some preparation to carry out. The worksheet "Preparing a Meal" can be used as a planning guide for students to devise a menu, figure out the cost, and think about any additional details that need to be included. It would be fun for students to serve their meals to others, who could then "rate" the meal as to nutritional value, presentation (adding garnishes, arranging the food on a plate, etc.), and taste!

    **Materials:** pen or pencil to complete the worksheet, food and serving items for preparing the food

    **Discussion:** After students have participated in this activity, ask them to evaluate the experience. What did they learn from this?

    1. On what special occasions has your family prepared a particularly fancy meal? **(Thanksgiving dinner, special guest, etc.)**

    2. What are the usual procedures for preparing a meal at your house?

    3. How many times a week do you or your family eat meals out?

    4. Who is primarily responsible for preparing meals at your house?

    5. Do you enjoy preparing meals? Why or why not?

**Extension Activities:**

    1. Have students compile a cookbook of favorite easy-to-prepare recipes.

    2. Have students occasionally make and bring in nutritious snacks for the class.

    3. Encourage students to take a community class in cooking – perhaps Japanese cooking or using a crock pot, etc.

    4. Have students plan and prepare a meal for their family. Note what comments are made!

**Evaluation:**

List two to three benefits of preparing a meal rather than eating out. **(may be less expensive, suited to tastes, nutritious foods, home atmosphere, etc.)**

# Preparing a Meal

**Directions:** Have students work in groups to prepare a nutritious meal to share with others. They can use this worksheet to plan and evaluate this activity.

Group Members: _____

_____

Cost/Total or Per Person

Main Course: _____    _____

# of servings:_____    _____

Vegetables/Fruit: _____    _____

Bread/Cereals: _____    _____

Milk Group: _____    _____

Dessert: _____    _____

Beverage:_____    _____

Other necessary items (napkins, silverware, etc.):

_____    _____

TOTAL:  $ _____

Rate:   Nutritional Value _____     Presentation _____     Taste _____

from 0 = poor to 5 = excellent

# IV-38 Shopping

**Objective:** The student will identify items commonly found at various retail stores.

**Comments:**

Maintaining a home also involves shopping for items to keep things going. In this lesson, students are asked to think about what items would be found in given stores.

**Introductory Activities:**

    a. Ask students to list at least five items they recently have shopped for and/or purchased.

    b. Ask students to list the stores they visited to make their purchases.

**Activity:**

    **Answers: 1.** f; **2.** h; **3.** c; **4.** j; **5.** g; **6.** b; **7.** d; **8.** i; **9.** a; **10.** e

    **Discussion:** Be sure to have students share their ideas on the additional items that could be bought at the stores.

    1. Besides actually going to a store, what are some other ways to shop or make purchases? **(catalog shopping, orders by mail, television, etc.)**

    2. Do you enjoy shopping? Why do you think some people love to shop so much?

    3. How do you choose what stores you are going to shop at? What considerations go through your mind? **(what is on sale, quality of merchandise, etc.)**

    4. When you have lots of items to buy, what kind of planning do you need to make? **(where the stores are located, what else you can get at one store, etc.)**

    5. What are some ways to save money when shopping? **(look for sales, buy in quantity, use coupons, etc.)**

**Extension Activities:**

    1. Have students write a holiday or birthday gift list. Then indicate what stores Santa or your friends would have to visit!

    2. Compare prices at stores that carry the same product, such as generic aspirin, candy bars, shoelaces, etc., at a grocery store, pharmacy, and convenience store.

    3. Write a paragraph about being turned loose in a store for three hours with unlimited money. What would you go for?

**Evaluation:**

Here is Danny's shopping list: 12 pens, a 2-liter bottle of soda, and a candy bar. Below are the prices at three different stores. If Danny only wants to make one stop, where would he get the best overall deal? **(grocery store)**

| **Drug Store** | **Grocery Store** | **Convenience Store** |
|---|---|---|
| 12 pens/$1.00 | pens 10 cents each | pens 3 for $1.00 |
| soda for 1.19 | soda for 79 cents | soda for 99 cents |
| candy bars 4/$1.00 | candy 3/$1.00 | candy 35¢/each |

**total cost =**    **$2.44**         **$2.32**         **$5.34**

# Shopping

**Directions:** On the left side is a list of ten common stores for shopping. On the right side, match an item you would be able to purchase at that store. Be careful – some may match with more than one, so think carefully and use the clues. Then, add at least two additional items you could purchase at each store.

_____ **1.** Pharmacy

  _____

  _____

_____ **2.** Clothing Store

  _____

  _____

_____ **3.** Grocery Store

  _____

  _____

_____ **4.** Shoe Store

  _____

  _____

_____ **5.** Auto Parts Store

  _____

  _____

_____ **6.** Gift Shop

  _____

  _____

_____ **7.** Pet Store

  _____

  _____

_____ **8.** Sporting Goods Store

  _____

  _____

_____ **9.** Toy Store

  _____

  _____

_____ **10.** Jewelry Store

  _____

  _____

**a.** teddy bear

**b.** greeting card

**c.** apples

**d.** leash

**e.** diamond ring

**f.** prescription pills

**g.** spark plugs

**h.** sweater

**i.** tennis racquet

**j.** tennis shoes

## IV-39 Using Classified Ads

**Objective:** The student will use classified ads to answer questions about housing.

**Comments:**

Many times housing can be located through classified ads. Some information that is given may include the monthly rent, special features such as a pool or tennis courts, the location, and whether or not utilities are included. Students are given sample classified ads for housing and are asked to answer questions about the ad.

**Introductory Activities:**

a. Have students list apartment complexes that are located in or near their community.

b. Have students list places that a potential renter would look to find available housing. **(notices on a community bulletin board, newspapers, etc.)**

**Activity:**

Make sure students are familiar with the terms *security deposit, utilities, appliances, deposit,* and *references.* They are to answer questions about the classified ads on the worksheet "Using Classified Ads."

**Answers: 1.** someone who likes to play golf or needs to live close to the city; **2.** cost; **3.** $348; **4.** the tenant doesn't have to pay a separate bill for heat, water, electricity; **5.** no – it's upstairs; **6.** heat, water, appliances; **7.** newly remodeled; **8.** someone who wanted a yard; **9.** to make sure the person is reliable; **10.** the tenant's car could be parked close to the house, not on the street

**Discussion:** Some students may live in apartments or rooms in a house and can relate their experiences. Emphasize that classified ads only give partial information and that people who are looking for a place to live would probably want to check out the neighborhood and see what the apartment is like.

1. Why do some apartment complexes have a model apartment for people to see? **(they can show you exactly what the apartment is like without bothering tenants)**

2. What information is important to check out when using a classified ad to find a place to live? **(the cost, what's available, location of the apartment)**

3. What information would you have to find out by actually going to the apartment, rather than asking over the phone? **(the view, the neighbors, the actual condition of the apartment, etc.)**

4. What special incentives do some apartments give to encourage people to move in? **(offer one month free rent, no damage deposit, etc.)**

5. What changes can you make to an apartment? **(curtains, perhaps paint the walls a different color)**

6. Why do some rental housing places have restrictions on children and pets? **(damage, noise)**

7. Why would some people want to live in a furnished apartment? **(they may move often, not have furniture, just need a short-term place to stay for awhile)**

**Extension Activities:**

1. Have students make a list of questions that someone should ask before renting an apartment. What information should he or she make sure to find out about?

2. Interview an apartment manager. What are his or her most common complaints about renters?

3. Interview a tenant of an apartment. (Perhaps you could have a parent or friend volunteer to do this.) Find out what he or she likes about living in an apartment. What are his or her most common complaints of living in an apartment? What are the best things?

**Evaluation:**

Write a classified ad that contains the following information: There is a 2-bedroom apartment for rent for $400 a month. Small pets are allowed, but no children. The apartment is part of a complex that offers a pool, tennis courts, and game room to its tenants. Heat is included in the rent. It is close to schools and a shopping mall. There is a bus line within walking distance.

**Teacher Notes:**

_____

_____

_____

_____

_____

_____

Name _____ Date _____

# Using Classified Ads

**Directions:** Read the following sample classified ads. Then answer the questions.

## Apts., Unfurnished

NORTHWIND COMPLEX On golf course, 1 or 2 bedrooms, 10 minutes to city. Phone 1-219-555-8296.

_____

ONE bedroom, stove, refrigerator and utilities furnished. Rent weekly. $87. Phone 123-2959.

_____

TWO bedroom upper, small but nice. Heat, water and appliances. $350 a month. Security deposit. Phone 333-3333 from 9 A.M. to 5 P.M.

_____

DOWNTOWN, upstairs, newly remodeled, $325, tenant pays utilities. Phone 888-2932.

## Houses, Duplexes

Small 2-bedroom cottage, yard, off-street parking. NO PETS. Deposit, references. $350 a month. Phone 999-8291.

1. Who might be interested in this type of apartment?

_____

2. What information is missing from this ad that might be helpful?

_____

3. How much would it cost per month to rent this apartment?

_____

4. What does "utilities furnished" mean?

_____

5. If you had trouble with steps, would this be a good apartment?

_____

6. What comes furnished with this apartment?

_____

7. What is special about this apartment?

_____

8. Who might be interested in this type of housing?

_____

9. Why would references be required?

_____

10. Why is "off street parking" important?

_____

# Section V

**Vocational Skills**

# V-1 What Are You Good At?

**Objective:** The student will identify at least 20 things that he or she feels he or she can do well. This may include accomplishments, personality attributes, talents, etc.

**Comments:**

In beginning the search for a job and hopefully a career, the student may begin by looking at his or her own skills and interests. While not everyone is lucky enough to find his or her job fascinating, it is a worthwhile endeavor to take inventory of what one is able to do well and is interested in doing. Perhaps later there will be some overlap between the job and the interest. In this lesson, students are to make a list of what they feel are their skills, talents, and/or things that they are knowledgeable about.

**Introductory Activities:**

  a. Define *skill*. (**something someone is able to do well; this can be an acquired thing with learning**)

  b. Define *talent*. (**a natural ability to do something well; this is something that you have or you don't – it can be developed and enhanced, but it is more of something that is within the person**)

  c. Define *job*. (**a task that is performed usually for money; can be short-lived and may not involve a lot of training or skill**)

  d. Define *career*. (**a profession, usually involving training, which may last throughout a person's life**)

**Activity:**

  **Discussion:** Provide time for students to share their ideas about their skills and interests. If some students say they cannot think of any, encourage classmates who know them to help them out.

  1. Do you have skills or talents that seem to run in your family? If so, what?

  2. Why do you think people in the same family might have similar interests? (**availability of resources**)

  3. How did you become good at the things you are proficient in now? (**practice, good teaching, asking questions, etc.**)

  4. Do you need other people to tell you that you are good at something or is it enough for you to recognize your skills yourself?

  5. What are some skills that can be learned if you are willing to become a student or apprentice?

  6. What are some examples of talents that some people just naturally possess? (**musical ability, athletic ability, etc.**)

  7. What are some skills you have developed within the last year?

  8. How did you learn a new skill?

**Extension Activities:**

1. Encourage students to take part in a workshop, mini-course, correspondence class, YMCA/YWCA evening class, cooking class at the community center, etc. Many classes are free or are available for a small charge. Learn a new skill!

2. Help students offer their services for free to become an apprentice to someone who does something they are interested in or would like to learn more about. Try to help students hook up with an auto repair shop, riding stable, artist, etc.

**Evaluation:**

a. List two skills in which you are competent that you have learned or developed in the past year.

b. List two talents you possess.

**Teacher Notes:**

_____

_____

_____

_____

_____

_____

Name _____ Date_____

# What Are You Good At?

**Directions:** Make a list for yourself of 20 to 25 (or more) things you are able to do well. Don't limit yourself to only things you can make or compete at; include things you know a lot about and your personality strengths.

**Examples:**

I am good with children.

I can fix things – a bike, VCR, etc.

I know a lot about astronauts and the space program.

1. _____
2. _____
3. _____
4. _____
5. _____
6. _____
7. _____
8. _____
9. _____
10. _____
11. _____
12. _____
13. _____
14. _____
15. _____

16. _____
17. _____
18. _____
19. _____
20. _____
21. _____
22. _____
23. _____
24. _____
25. _____
_____
_____
_____
_____

## V-2 My Interests

**Objective:** The students will identify at least five to ten different interests that he or she currently has.

**Comments:**

Some jobs come with a rather predictable work environment; a pilot, for example, may have a regular route, is responsible for the welfare of others, must be cool in a crisis, and should be familiar with the technology of the plane. A person who enjoys none of those qualifications would probably not seek a job in which he or she would be piloting an airplane. In this lesson, students are to identify some characteristics of a job that appeal to them.

**Introductory Activities:**

    a. Have students write one career that is of interest to them.

    b. Have students list at least three to five interests or skills that a person who performs that job would probably have.

**Activity:**

    **Discussion:** Clarify any items the students are unsure about. Remind them that this is just a preference list; there is no wrong or right.

    1. What do you think are some major considerations for someone looking for a job? **(depends on the individual and his or her needs at the time – money, security, outlet for creativity, etc.)**

    2. Why are school years a good time to develop and pursue interests? **(find out what you like and dislike; what you're good at)**

    3. What new interests have you discovered about yourself recently? How did you come to make these discoveries?

    4. What are some ways you could take advantage of opportunities to try new things? **(read, volunteer, take a summer job, etc.)**

**Extension Activities:**

    1. Have students look over the preferences they select. Have them identify at least one career that seems to fit their interests.

    2. Assign a class project to select 50 careers. Provide a 10-sentence summary for each career that describes the probable characteristics of someone in that career.

    3. Have students begin a personal career file: collect news articles, school information, brochures, etc., on interesting careers. Find out the salary, available training, and working conditions associated with that career.

**Evaluation:**

    a. List three of your main career interests at this time.

    b. Write a paragraph describing a time when you explored or tried something new and found out something about yourself.

Name _____ Date_____

# My Interests

**Directions:** Read the following list of interests you may have. Circle those that appeal to you.

1. working with pets

2. working with children

3. being inside

4. being outside

5. being around people

6. moving around

7. sitting at a desk to work

8. teaching someone how to do something

9. traveling

10. driving

11. taking care of things

12. working under high pressure, excitement

13. having a calm, predictable environment

14. being creative

15. following a set schedule each day

16. doing lots of different tasks

17. doing the same task over and over

18. being responsible for the welfare/safety of others

19. making lots of money

20. using a computer

21. having a chance to learn new skills

22. helping other people

23. supervising other people

24. working whatever hours I want

25. getting raises and promotions

## V-3 Hobbies

**Objective:** The student will describe how a specific hobby can be related or turned into a career.

**Comments:**

Sometimes things we do for fun and pure enjoyment can pay off in terms of being a vocational choice. Some hobbies are engaged in because they are a pleasant "break" from a demanding career (doctors playing golf?), and sometimes turning a hobby into a business can take away the enjoyment of the hobby. In some circumstances, however, it is nice to think of your work as something you truly enjoy doing. In this lesson, students are to specify how certain hobbies may be turned into careers.

**Introductory Activities:**

a. Define *hobby*. **(an activity that is engaged in primarily for entertainment)**

b. Have students list five to ten hobbies with which they are familiar.

**Activity:**

Students are to match the hobby on the left side of the worksheet "Hobbies" with a possible career listed on the right side that could grow from that hobby. Make sure students understand what is usually involved in the hobbies listed.

**Answers: 1.** f; **2.** h; **3.** c; **4.** d; **5.** i; **6.** e; **7.** g; **8.** k; **9.** a; **10.** l; **11.** j; **12.** b

**Discussion:** Make sure students did not have any trouble completing the worksheet.

1. What are some other examples of hobbies that can turn into careers?

2. Do you personally know of any people who have turned a hobby into a business or career?

3. Some people choose hobbies that are very different from their jobs. For example, a woman who works at a desk all day might go jogging for fun. What are some other examples of hobbies that would complement certain types of jobs?

4. What are some collections you can think of? **(stamps, dolls, antique cars)**

5. What would be the value of becoming an "expert" in a certain field of study if it was not part of your job?

6. What are some sports hobbies you can think of?

7. How could the sports as a hobby be turned into a career other than by actually participating in the sport as a professional? **(advertising, sales of related merchandise, etc.)**

8. Why do people invest time and money in hobbies? **(serious fun!)**

9. Think of some very exciting careers – race car driving, modeling, working on television, etc. Do you think the people who are involved in these careers may have begun by dabbling in the career as a hobby? How?

10. Do you think people who are involved in exciting careers would have very different activities for their hobbies?

**Extension Activities:**

    1. Organize a "Hobby Fair" for your class. Have students (or parents or adult friends or other interested community people) bring in collections, pictures, posters, brochures, etc., about their hobby.

    2. Assign students the task of researching a new hobby. Let them find out about it and report back to the class.

    3. Invite speakers to class to talk about their hobbies. How does the hobby fit into their life as a balance or supplement for their career? Does the speaker wish that the hobby could be his or her career?

**Evaluation:**

    a. List three personal hobbies.

    b. Describe how each of your hobbies could turn into a career for you.

**Teacher Notes:**

_____

_____

_____

_____

_____

_____

# Hobbies

**Directions:** Below is a list of some hobbies that people have turned into careers. Match the hobby with the career that it could turn into.

_____ **1.** refinishing furniture

_____ **2.** collecting antiques

_____ **3.** training dogs

_____ **4.** painting with watercolors

_____ **5.** writing poetry

_____ **6.** cooking fancy meals

_____ **7.** playing football

_____ **8.** planting and growing flowers

_____ **9.** sewing

_____ **10.** doing aerobic dancing

_____ **11.** repairing cars

_____ **12.** horseback riding

**a.** selling patterns at a fabric shop; helping customers with their sewing needs

**b.** working at a store that sells saddles and bridles

**c.** working for the police department K-9 (canine) unit

**d.** selling paintings at an art gallery

**e.** running a catering business

**f.** selling furniture made of wood; doing repairs involving woodworking

**g.** coaching a high school sports team

**h.** working in a museum as a guide

**i.** being a freelance writer selling work to magazines

**j.** working in an auto body shop

**k.** managing a florist shop

**l.** teaching exercise classes at a health spa

# V-4 Realistic Vocational Goals

**Objective:** The student will identify problems with characters who have unrealistic career goals.

**Comments:**

Many children want to grow up to be actresses, sports heroes, rock stars, and millionaires! It seems glamorous and attainable to a child who doesn't realize that the odds are against him or her. In this lesson, examples are given of characters who have somewhat unrealistic aspirations.

**Introductory Activities:**

    a. Have students volunteer to tell when they were 5 or 6 years old, what they wanted to be when they were grown up.

    b. Have students raise their hands if they have changed their minds about a career since they were little. If so, why?

**Activity:**

    **Answers:** *(examples)* **1.** a small town may not support a huge factory/he doesn't mention having any resources to open a factory; **2.** it appears as though the girl doesn't have much musical ability; **3.** the product is not good; **4.** he doesn't know much about his product; **5.** he did not research the business – it may be a total scam; **6.** he doesn't seem bright enough to be a scientist

    **Discussion:** Have students explain how they selected the problems in each example. Some assumptions have to be made about the characters since not a lot of facts are given.

    1. Is it wrong to have high aspirations? Why not plan to become a sports hero or rock star since some people obviously make it? **(try to be realistic – some make it, but many more do not)**

    2. What types of skills or talents do you think are important when choosing a career? **(things that will fit into the career)**

    3. Why is it important to know a lot about your product if you are selling it? **(so you can be convincing to your customers)**

    4. What lack of skills seems apparent in examples 2 and 6? **(musical/ability, general intelligence)**

    5. Do you think having someone tell you "You'll never make it" can work in a positive sense? How? **(might give the person incentive to try to beat the odds)**

    6. What advice do you think someone who "beat the odds" would give to others who want to be where they are? **(keep trying, don't give up, etc.)**

    7. What are some things you could be doing right now to help yourself towards whatever career or goal you are interested in?

**Extension Activities:**

    1. Have students find and read interviews given by people who are successful in their fields. What advice do they offer to people who want to be successful?

    2. Have students make a bulletin board emphasizing the importance of hard work toward achieving a goal. Use a "ladder" with words, such as *education, taking a risk, talking to people, learning, listening,* etc., written on the rungs.

**Evaluation:**

What is at least one realistic career goal for the following characters:

a. Joel loves music. He knows all of the artists and bands that are currently on the Top 40 list. He can't play an instrument, but he has a great memory for songs. *(examples:* **disc jockey, record store owner or manager)**

b. Rachel is good with numbers. She always has her checkbook balanced and handles investments for her family. She enjoys learning about how to make money by investing in the stock market. *(examples:* **stock market investor, accountant, financial advisor)**

c. Marta was abused as a child. She spent a lot of time in courts and eventually grew up in a foster home. Now she wants to help protect children from the type of abuse that she lived through. *(examples:* **lawyer, social worker)**

d. Tomas enjoys taking pictures. He has several cameras and has taken classes in photography. He would rather be behind a camera than anywhere else. *(examples:* **studio photographer, freelance photographer for books/ calendars/magazines)**

# Realistic Vocational Goals

**Directions:** The characters below are going to run into difficulty as they prepare for a career. What problem(s) do you see in each case? Write your ideas on the lines.

1. It doesn't matter that I live in a town of 2,500 people – I'm going to become a business whiz and open a huge factory and make millions.

2. I know Madonna won't be around forever. The world will be ready for the next great rock star! ME!

3. How hard can it be to sell jewelry? I'll get this special "starter kit" and I'm on my way!

4. Howdy. I'm selling...uhhhhh...well, let's see. Oh, heating products. Would you like to buy some?

5. You tell me it costs only $10,000 to buy into this fast-growing business? What's the name of it again? Sure, I'll throw in my life savings to buy in.

6. Yeah, I can be a rocket scientist. How do you spell "moon"?

# V-5 Academic Strengths

**Objective:** The student will review past and present report cards and state at least two academic strengths.

**Comments:**

School records are important, especially since most high school transcripts will play a part in the student's further education. If students are in high school, you may be able to track their past records through your central office. Some students may have past report cards at home and you may need to get parent permission to view them. Many schools send home standardized test information at the end of the school year as well. In this lesson, students are to look at their grades and determine which subject or subjects are a "strength." They may wish to view future career possibilities in light of what they are interested in and excel at in school.

**Introductory Activities:**

    a. Have students tell about their best year in school. When was it? Why was it good?

    b. Have students write what they think is their best subject in school.

**Activity:**

Using past report cards and any other objective information about students' performance, students should summarize the information on the worksheet "Academic Strengths." Many report cards contain places to record attendance, which can affect school performance. Have students list semester or yearly grades for the main academic subjects and include other appropriate subjects in the last column. Make sure you do not embarrass students who may not have good grades.

    **Materials:** reports cards, standardized test results (if available), attendance reports, pen or pencil

    **Discussion:** Since grades may be a rather personal issue with some students, have students volunteer to reveal their thoughts and answer questions. Have students go over the discussion questions at the bottom of the worksheet.

**Extension Activities:**

    1. Have students find out if there is a connection between attendance and grades. If possible, provide students with information about attendance and grades from anonymous students in their class. Do good students have good attendance? Do poor students have poor attendance? Have them define their terms and decide what limits support their conclusions.

    2. Have students interview teachers in the school or collect examples of grading procedures for their classes. How much control does a student have over the grade he or she gets in a class? (Some teachers may grade on a contract basis; others use percentage of points, etc.)

**Evaluation:**

    a. List two of your academic strengths as indicated by report card grades.

    b. Select one of your memorable classes and grades. Explain in a paragraph what you remember about that class. Why was it memorable? Was the grade you received a fair one? Why?

# Academic Strengths

**Directions:** Using old report cards and standardized testing if available, complete the following academic profile of your grades over the past few years. Be objective!

| School Year | Attendance (exc./good/poor) | Grades | | | | |
|---|---|---|---|---|---|---|
| | | **Math** | **Rdg./Eng.** | **Science** | **Soc. St.** | **Other** |
| | | | | | | |
| | | | | | | |
| | | | | | | |
| | | | | | | |
| | | | | | | |
| | | | | | | |
| | | | | | | |

1. How was my attendance overall?

2. In what areas do I have the best grades?

3. Is this an area that I am interested in learning more about?

4. In what areas do I have the worst grades?

5. What is my explanation for those grades?

6. Do I feel these grades are a fair representation of my abilities and knowledge in these areas?

7. At this point, am I interested in further education, such as college?

8. Am I interested in further education, such as technical or vocational training?

9. Are there ways to improve my grades? How?

10. Am I interested in putting more effort into academic classes if it would improve my chances for further education?

# V-6 Teacher Recommendations

**Objective:** The student will accurately report and summarize teacher comments on past report cards.

**Comments:**

Teacher recommendations and comments on report cards can be very enlightening. Although they are subjective, the comments still reflect how a professional in a position of authority and evaluation viewed the student's performance. Having students read the comments, especially if they are available over the course of several years, can be quite enlightening. Again, having the student look for trends and strengths – not finding excuses or blaming others – is the purpose of this lesson.

**Introductory Activities:**

a. Have students think of or write the names of two teachers with whom he or she got along particularly well.

b. Have students write or indicate what comments these teachers had about the academic and behavioral performances of the student while he or she was in the class.

**Activity:**

**Materials:** report cards, informal notes or reports, pen or pencil

**Discussion:** Some students may have a particularly vivid memory of a good or bad encounter with a teacher and with the comments made from this encounter. While we wish that every teacher was positive, optimistic, and objective, we must admit that there are times (and students) that are negative and seem hopeless. As students discuss their thoughts, allow them to express their opinions. Go over the discussion questions on the worksheet.

**Extension Activities:**

1. If this activity is workable, have students return to interview a particularly favorite teacher – perhaps from several years in the past. Now that several years have passed, what did the teacher think would happen to the student? Was he or she correct in the predictions? Did the student live up to the expectations?

2. Have students tell about particularly good moments in which a teacher encouraged or gave an important comment to a student.

3. Have students write a thank-you note to a teacher who in some way encouraged or gave a kind comment to them.

**Evaluation:**

a. What are at least two strengths that are evident based on teacher comments or recommendations about your performance in school?

b. What are at least two cautions or weak areas that your teachers have reported about your performance in school?

c. Write a paragraph about a teacher comment or recommendation that in some way affected you in a positive way.

# Teacher Recommendations

**Directions:** Again, you will need to refer to report cards or teacher reports to objectively complete this activity. Answer the following questions to the best of your ability.

| School Year | Teacher | Comments (Academic/Behavioral) |
|---|---|---|
| | | |
| | | |
| | | |
| | | |
| | | |
| | | |

1. Were there any particular years you remember as being very good for you as far as getting along with teachers? Was there anything special about that year/those years?

2. What comments do your teachers have about your academic strengths?

3. What comments do your teachers have about your effort?

4. What comments do your teachers have about your behavior in class?

5. Do you see any patterns or trends to the comments made?

6. Do you agree with the comments made by your teachers? Why or why not?

7. What specific recommendations have your teachers made about your ability to succeed in college, technical school, or whatever further education you are interested in?

8. Have teachers made informal comments to you about what they think your likelihood of success will be? What other comments have they made about your abilities/attitude/effort?

## V-7 Choosing Classes

**Objective:** The student will indicate at least five choices of future classes that interest him or her and are appropriate selections.

**Comments:**

Remember when students' favorite classes were always lunch and gym? As students get older and approach the time at which they must make some necessary pre-vocational decisions, suddenly it really is important to think about what classes will help them towards their goals. In this lesson, students are to think about possible classes and activities that fictional characters should take in order to pursue their goals.

**Introductory Activities:**

a. Have students list at least one class they are thinking about enrolling in during the next year or two.

b. Have students tell or write why they are looking forward to this class.

c. After completing (b), have students raise their hands if they selected the class because it sounded like "fun." Then have them raise their hands if they selected the class because it was part of a "career plan."

**Activity:**

**Answers:** *(examples)* **1. a.** yes; **b.** yes – work at a kennel or veterinarian's office to see if he likes the work; **c.** drawing (some careers involve medical drawings for textbooks); **2. a.** home economics, food preparation and nutrition; **b.** yes – she shouldn't limit herself – she may become interested in another career or interested in working with caring for children rather than adults; **c.** don't do it – she probably won't be successful; **3. a.** if he is keeping them up; **b.** what kind of a worker Antonio is – does he show up on time?; **c.** any classes that will help Antonio with independence after school – business classes, auto mechanics classes, food preparation, etc.

**Discussion:** Go through each of the three examples on the worksheet. Not all details were provided, so students must make some assumptions about the students. Allow students time to express their opinions about what these students should do.

1. Why would it be helpful for Ralph to take science classes in high school? **(he will need to take science in college!)**

2. Does every elective that Ralph take need to be relevant to his future career plans? **(no – in fact it's a good idea to use the time to keep exploring different options and try out different activities)**

3. What might happen if Maria decides she is tired of working at a nursing home but hasn't had any other sort of training? **(she'll probably quit and start from ground-zero)**

4. Why is it important for Maria to take other classes such as business or child care? **(she may want to have other options if she decides she doesn't want to work in the nursing home forever)**

5. Why shouldn't anyone take classes based on who is in the class? **(except for the obvious social reasons, it may not have any relevance to what the student wants to accomplish)**

6. Why is Antonio's situation a pretty good one? **(he's still in school, but he also gets some work experience)**

## Extension Activities:

1. Invite a school counselor to visit your class to talk about special types of programs (such as work-study, job shadowing, volunteering in classrooms for credit, etc.) available to students. Sometimes just knowing about inventive, exciting programs that are in the not-too-distant future is a good incentive for students who are thinking about quitting to stay in school.

2. Invite an upperclass student (senior, junior) from the high school to visit your class to talk about what classes are particularly interesting or useful for him or her. A peer may have a lot more influence over the expectations of a student than a teacher. Students may not be aware of some classes that are particularly new and very exciting.

## Evaluation:

a. List at least three possible classes you are interested in taking in the future.

b. For each class listed in (a), write one reason why you are interested in that class.

Name _____ Date_____

# Choosing Classes

**Directions:** The following characters are planning classes for the rest of their high school education. Pretend you are their counselor and help them make appropriate selections.

1. Ralph wants to finish high school and then go on to college to study veterinary medicine. His grades are pretty good and he is willing to put time in to study.

**a.** Should Ralph take a lot of science classes?_____

**b.** Would you suggest that Ralph do some volunteer work? What?

_____

**c.** Ralph is also interested in art. What electives might Ralph want to take?

_____

2. Maria doesn't know if she wants to go to any type of school after high school. She already has a part-time job in a nursing home and would like to work there full-time. Her grades are C's, but she doesn't enjoy school or put much effort into her classes.

**a.** What type of classes might Maria do well with?

_____

**b.** Would you suggest that Maria take some business classes or child care classes? Why?

_____

**c.** If Maria wanted to take Advanced Physics because her boyfriend is enrolling in the class, what would you tell Maria?

_____

3. Antonio is involved in a special work/study program that allows him to take classes in the morning and then work at a vocational training school program in the afternoon. As long as he keeps his grades up, he can continue in this program until he graduates.

**a.** What would you want to know about Antonio's grades?

_____

**b.** What information might you want to know from the vocational school instructors?

_____

**c.** What classes might you suggest Antonio take at the high school?

_____

# V-8 Having a Disability

**Objective:** The student will explain how a person with a disability could make adaptations to do well in school or on the job.

**Comments:**

Just because a person has a disability (physical, emotional, learning, etc.) does not mean he or she can not still achieve success at school or on the job. There are many adaptations that can and must be made for people who are differently-abled. In this lesson, students are given examples of characters who have a disability. They are to explain how the character is coping with school and work in spite of the disability.

**Introductory Activities:**

    a. Have students make a list of disabilities with which they are familiar.

    b. Have students look over their list and note how many were physical disabilities.

    c. Have students give examples of any individuals they know who have a disability and how that person functions with adaptations, if necessary.

**Activity:**

Students are to read five examples on the worksheet "Having a Disability" about people with disabilities in a school or work situation. They are to identify the disability and explain how the character is coping with it in each setting.

    **Answers:** *(examples)* **1.** physically disabled/uses elevator; **2.** learning disability/taped material; **3.** epilepsy/medication; **4.** emotional disability/small class; **5.** deaf/ hearing aid, translator

    **Discussion:** Go through each example and clarify each disability if students are unfamiliar with the basic handicapping condition.

    1. Do you know of anyone with a disabling condition? What?

    2. Does this person's disability stop this person from doing what he or she wants or needs to do in any way?

    3. What special adaptations (if any) are made for this person?

    4. Do you think having a disability should stop someone from succeeding in school?

    5. What are some ways schools can help a person with a disability?

    6. What types of jobs might be out of the realm of possibility for the characters on this page? Why?

**Extension Activities:**

    1. Have students work in groups and research a handicapping condition. Have them find the definition of the handicap, ways that people with this disability can overcome or work around it, famous people who have had this condition, and other topics. Ideas may include: deaf, blind, cerebral palsy, epilepsy, mental retardation, emotional disturbance, physically challenged, etc.

    2. Have students volunteer to spend time working in a classroom with handicapped children. The experience may be quite enlightening!

    3. Have students read selected books written by or about people with handicaps. What limits (if any) did the people put on themselves?

4. Find out what community resources are available to help people with disabilities. Is there a group home? Sheltered workshop? Vocational training?

5. If you know of someone who would be willing to come in to talk to the class about his or her disability and how it affects everyday life, invite this person to school. Prepare your class for appropriate questions. Perhaps someone in your class has a disability – be sensitive to his or her feelings.

**Evaluation:**

a. List examples of at least three common disabilities.

b. For each, give an example of how a person with that disability might still perform school and work tasks.

**Teacher Notes:**

_____

_____

_____

_____

_____

_____

Name _____  Date_____

# Having a Disability

**Directions:** Read the accounts of the following students. Identify each disability. Then explain how each is coping with his or her situation at school and on the job.

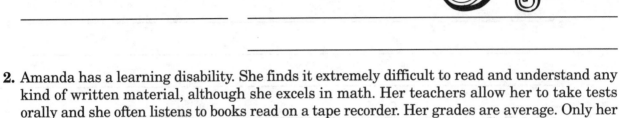

1. Mark is in a wheelchair. He was injured in an accident many years ago, but has complete use of his upper body. At school he has classes on the first floor and uses the school elevator to get where he needs to go. He attends regular classes at school.

   _____          _____

   _____

2. Amanda has a learning disability. She finds it extremely difficult to read and understand any kind of written material, although she excels in math. Her teachers allow her to take tests orally and she often listens to books read on a tape recorder. Her grades are average. Only her closest friends even realize that she has a disability.

   _____          _____

   _____

3. Charlie has epilepsy. He cannot get a driver's license, but he has no other restrictions. His seizures are completely controlled with medication. He does average or above-average work at school and has two part-time jobs: delivering the local newspaper and helping his uncle at a gas station.

   _____          _____

   _____

4. Kanisha is in a class with other students who have not done well in a traditional class setting. She has an emotional handicap that prevents her from learning as easily as some other students. The class is small and she takes most of her academics from one teacher. They also do some "job shadowing" several times a week in which Kanisha can assist people at the local hospital.

   _____          _____

   _____

5. Eric is partially deaf. He has a small hearing aid in both ears and communicates primarily through signing. He attends several regular classes with the help of a translator. After school Eric helps out at the YMCA with teaching swimming to young children with and without handicaps.

   _____          _____

   _____

# V-9 Finishing High School

**Objective:** The student will give at least two reasons why it is important or beneficial to complete high school.

**Comments:**

There are a lot of reasons why teenagers drop out of high school. Among these are the facts of pregnancy, poor grades, truancy, getting into trouble at school, boredom, seeing no relevance, and a simple lack of motivation. In this lesson, students are asked to respond to comments about completing high school.

**Introductory Activities:**

a. Have students raise their hands if they intend to graduate from high school.

b. Have students raise their hands if they have a close friend who has dropped out of high school.

c. Have students raise their hands if they have a brother or sister who has already dropped out of high school.

**Activity:**

Students are to read the twelve statements on the worksheet "Finishing High School." They are to circle AGREE or DISAGREE to show how they feel about the statement. They are all opinion statements, so inform students that they will not be scored "right" or "wrong."

> **Discussion:** It may be quite surprising to hear your students' views on completing high school. While some may be overly optimistic that they of course will complete high school (even with poor attendance, poor grades, low motivation), others – particularly those without support from home – may already be planning to quit. Without being judgmental or "preachy," listen to the students' comments and opinions. Extension activities may prove to be quite enlightening to some of these students!

1. What do you think is the main purpose of high school?

2. If someone close to you has dropped out of school, why would that make it more likely that an individual would also drop out of school? **(that's their model, may think of this as "freedom," the individual may already have a job)**

3. Do you think there is a connection between the amount of education a person has and his or her earning potential?

4. What other kinds of training are available after high school besides a regular four-year college program? **(two-year degrees, vocational schools, apprentice programs, etc.)**

5. Do you feel your parents value a high school education?

6. Why is a high school degree sometimes important to a parent or grandparent who never got one? **(they might feel as though they have missed an opportunity)**

7. What are some ways that classes and schools try to make learning more relevant? **(offer on-the-job programs, work/study, etc.)**

8. Do you know of anyone who has completed the GED program? What comments did this person have about the program?

9. If someone has quit high school, how easy do you think it would be to return – especially after having a baby or working for awhile? **(probably difficult – new responsibilities, less time, more stresses)**

10. What advice would you give to someone who was struggling in high school, but still wanted to stay in and try to finish? **(get help – talk to a counselor, teachers, get tutoring, etc.)**

## Extension Activities:

1. If possible, have a counselor come in to explain the GED (equivalency) program. Some students may think this is an easy way to get through high school. Find out about the history of the program (military program during World War II), the restrictions, time involved, level of material, and commitment of time that is necessary to complete the program.

2. Have students research the earning potential of students with and without high school degrees.

3. Have students find out reasons why teenagers drop out of high school. How many plan to return? How many actually return?

4. Invite speakers to your class who have made the decision (or felt it was necessary) to drop out of high school. Do they regret the decision? What factors were involved in their life at the time? What are they doing today?

## Evaluation:

a. List at least two reasons why it is beneficial to complete high school.

b. List at least two reasons why teenagers may choose to drop out of high school.

c. Write a paragraph explaining your intentions about finishing high school.

Name _____  Date_____

# Finishing High School

**Directions:** Complete the following survey by expressing your opinions and reactions to the following statements about high school. Circle *agree* or *disagree* after each statement.

1. It is important to have a high school diploma.  **Agree**   **Disagree**

2. You can still get a good job without a high school degree.  **Agree**   **Disagree**

3. High school is a waste of time if you don't plan to go to college.  **Agree**   **Disagree**

4. Most high school classes don't have any practical value.  **Agree**   **Disagree**

5. It is easy to get a GED (equivalency degree) if you drop out of school and then want to get a degree.  **Agree**   **Disagree**

6. There are ways to get help if you want to finish high school.  **Agree**   **Disagree**

7. A lot of my friends either have quit school or intend to quit high school.  **Agree**   **Disagree**

8. One or both of my parents did not finish high school.  **Agree**   **Disagree**

9. I have a brother or sister who quit school.  **Agree**   **Disagree**

10. I would consider leaving high school, but only if I had a job already lined up.  **Agree**   **Disagree**

11. The only reason I am in high school is because of the activities and my friends.  **Agree**   **Disagree**

12. If you really want to get a high school diploma, you will find a way.  **Agree**   **Disagree**

# V-10 Extracurricular Activities

**Objective:** The student will list at least five to ten extracurricular activities available at his or her school and how involvement in those activities is beneficial to vocational planning.

**Comments:**

Schools, no matter how small, generally offer a range of extracurricular activities for students to participate in. Many colleges look for evidence of participation as part of the application process. It is important for students to be well-rounded, to try different things, and to be part of groups. Getting involved and being part of a team are important qualities to future employers. Plus, it can be fun! In this lesson, students are to complete a word search that includes many examples of extracurricular activities.

**Introductory Activities:**

Have students guess which activity you are referring to by giving the following clues:

a. "Go! Team! Go!" (**cheerleading**)

b. "Would you please grant an interview, Ms. Principal?" (**school paper**)

c. "There are other ways to have fun without drinking!" (**Students Against Drunk Driving – S.A.D.D.**)

**Activity:**

Students are to try to find the words in the word search puzzle "Extracurricular Activities." They are all examples of typical extracurricular activities at schools. Inform students that not all of the activities may be available at your school. Clarify any terms with which students are unfamiliar.

**Answers:**

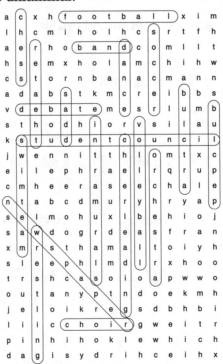

**Discussion:** After completing the activity, have students talk about which activities they are interested in or involved in. Perhaps some students are unaware of the activities available at your school.

1. What are some of the benefits of being involved in an extracurricular activity? **(fun, be on a team, learn a new skill, etc.)**

2. What might it cost you in terms of time and money to become involved in an extracurricular activity? **(time for practices, travel time, money for uniforms, etc.)**

3. What is fun about being part of a team? **(other people accept you, support you, might enjoy being on a winning team, etc.)**

4. What skills might you learn from being a part of a group that an employer would be interested in? **(how well you get along with others, are you a leader, can you learn new things)**

5. Why do you think potential employers want to know which activities you were involved in when you were in high school? **(want to know your interests, what type of skills you have, etc.)**

6. Are there certain groups at your school that are considered to be "desirable"? What?

7. Are there certain groups at your school that are laughed at or not respected?

8. If you were going to start a new extracurricular organization at your school, what would it be?

## Extension Activities:

1. Have students research and then prepare a display showing the different activities available at your school. They may want to interview people who are involved in the club or group (or they may be a member themselves), find out the restrictions, membership responsibilities, services provided, skills taught, etc.

2. Encourage students to join an activity – perhaps something they never really gave any serious thought to before. Give it a try!

## Evaluation:

a. List five to ten extracurricular activities available at your school.

b. For each, specify at least one skill that would be used when performing that activity.

c. Select one of your activities and explain how (or why) an employer might be interested to know you were involved in that activity at school.

# Extracurricular Activities

**Directions:** There are a lot of extracurricular activities in the word search below. Can you find them all? Look for the words horizontally, vertically, diagonally – and backwards!!

```
a  c  x  h  f  o  o  t  b  a  l  l  x  i  m
l  h  c  m  i  h  o  l  h  c  s  r  t  f  h
a  e  r  h  o  b  a  n  d  c  o  m  l  l  t
h  s  e  m  x  h  o  l  a  m  c  h  i  h  w
c  s  t  o  r  n  b  a  n  a  c  m  a  n  n
a  d  a  b  s  t  k  m  c  r  e  i  b  b  s
v  d  e  b  a  t  e  m  e  s  r  l  u  m  b
s  t  h  o  d  h  i  o  r  v  s  i  l  a  u
k  s  t  u  d  e  n  t  c  o  u  n  c  i  l
j  w  e  n  n  i  t  t  h  l  o  m  t  x  c
e  i  l  e  p  h  r  a  e  l  r  q  r  u  p
c  m  h  e  e  r  a  s  e  e  c  h  a  l  e
n  t  a  b  c  d  m  u  r  y  h  r  y  a  p
s  e  l  m  o  h  u  x  l  b  e  h  i  o  j
s  a  w  d  o  g  r  d  e  a  s  f  r  a  n
x  m  r  s  t  h  a  m  a  l  t  o  i  y  h
s  l  e  e  p  h  l  m  d  l  r  x  h  o  o
t  r  s  h  c  a  s  o  i  o  a  p  w  w  o
o  u  t  a  n  y  p  t  n  d  o  e  k  m  h
j  e  l  o  i  k  r  e  g  s  d  b  h  b  i
l  i  i  c  c  h  o  i  r  g  w  e  i  t  r
p  i  n  h  i  h  o  k  l  e  w  h  i  c  h
d  a  g  i  s  y  d  r  i  h  c  e  i  h  x
```

band
orchestra
football
volleyball
theater
dance
wrestling
SADD
intramurals
choir
debate
chess
pep club
student council
swim team
cheerleading
newspaper
art club
soccer

# V-11 Post-School Planning

**Objective:** Given a post-school goal, the student will identify at least two steps that should be taken to prepare for that goal.

**Comments:**

Whether a student chooses to attend college, find a job, seek vocational training, or get married and keep a house, it is important to begin making plans to achieve those goals – especially if they are related to high school performance. In this lesson, students are to complete paragraphs indicating plans for reaching a post-high school goal.

**Introductory Activities:**

 a. Ask students to write a possible/probable post-school goal for themselves.

 b. Have students indicate if their high school performance and records have any direct affect on attaining that goal.

**Activity:**

**Answers:** *(examples)* **1.** information; **2.** interested; **3.** letter; **4.** scholarship; **5.** office; **6.** appointment; **7.** decision; **8.** college; **9.** information; **10.** when/where; **11.** well; **12.** accepted

**Discussion:** Go over the answers on the worksheet and clarify any questions.

1. When is a good time for students to start thinking and making plans for what they will do after high school? **(during high school or even earlier)**

2. What are some other options for life after high school besides college or working? **(getting married, raising a family, taking an extended vacation if you have the money!)**

3. Why do you think the prospect of leaving high school and entering the world of work is exciting for some people? **(represents freedom, adulthood, a paycheck, application of learned skills, etc.)**

4. Why do you think some people are excited about going to college and facing more learning? **(it will provide them with a more specific work goal, more directed studies, etc.)**

5. If someone is planning to go to college, why is it necessary to start planning early? **(need time to take tests, must adhere to deadlines, complete applications, etc.)**

6. Why is it a good idea to visit colleges? **(you can see what the campus is like, find out about programs offered, etc.)**

**Extension Activities:**

1. Have students select a college and write a letter requesting information about programs and an application. These can be used later to form a class file if the student is not really interested in the college. Find out what information is needed to attend the college, the cost per year, housing costs, and academic/ entrance requirements.

2. Arrange for the counselor to give a "tour" of school resources for students. Show students where to find material about schools and training, scholarship information, vertical files containing pertinent information, etc.

3. Send away (or ask the counselor) for college entrance test information (SAT, ACT). Explain why this is required for certain colleges, how often it is given, and what the scores mean.

## Evaluation:

List at least two steps that should be taken in preparation for the following post-school goals:

a. attending Harvard University

b. working at a local factory

c. taking classes through correspondence school

## Teacher Notes:

_____

_____

_____

_____

_____

_____

Name _____ Date_____

# Post-School Planning

**Directions:** The following students are making plans for what they want to do after they complete high school. Fill in the blanks to complete the paragraphs. (More than one answer may be appropriate.)

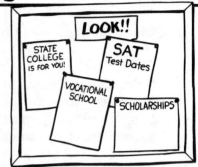

Shawnell is definitely interested in attending college. She wants to get more

**(1)** _____ about the college to know whether or not it will

have the program she is **(2)** _____ in. She has decided to

write a **(3)** _____ to get more information about the

college.

\*\*\*

Frank's family does not have a lot of money. Frank gets good grades, however, and

he hopes he might get a **(4)** _____ to help pay for his way.

There is a bulletin board near the **(5)** _____

at his school. There are often lists of scholarships available.

\*\*\*

Dianne isn't sure what to do after high school. She made an

**(6)** _____ to talk to her counselor. She thinks this person

can help her make some **(7)** _____ about

what to do.

\*\*\*

Antonio doesn't want to go to a four-year college, but there is a vocational

**(8)** _____ near him that will give him the training he

wants. He called the school to ask for **(9)** _____ about

what programs are available there.

\*\*\*

Kevin wants to go to a university in another state. The university requires him to

take a test called the SAT. Kevin must find out **(10)** _____

the test is given. He knows that he needs to do **(11)** _____

on the test to help him get **(12)** _____ to the school.

## V-12 Searching for a Job

**Objective:** The student will identify at least five ways to begin searching for a job.

**Comments:**

For many students, it may seem overwhelming at first to enter the world of work after the structure and safety of high school life. Some may already have jobs lined up, but many probably must go in "cold" – beginning that search for the first real job. Students are given examples of ways to begin looking for a job in this lesson.

**Introductory Activities:**

a. Have students raise their hands if they are planning to inherit the family fortune after they finish high school and never work another day in their life again.

b. Have students raise their hands if they are already working somewhere and plan to continue to work there after high school.

c. Have students raise their hands if they have a good idea of what they will be doing right after high school.

d. Have students raise their hands if they think they could benefit from some help getting a job after high school.

**Activity:**

**Answers:** *(examples)* **1.** find out if there is an opening at a business in your area for which you are qualified; **2.** list your skills and have employers contact you; **3.** your friend/relative may know the person who does the hiring and put in a good word for you; **4.** this lets the employers know you are available; **5.** a counselor can help match you with a job; **6.** there may be a job placement service after training is completed; **7.** a social worker may be able to find you a position; **8.** this can help someone get a foot in the door, sometimes businesses will hire temporary helpers

**Discussion:** Have students share their ideas and/or experiences with getting a job. They may have additional suggestions as well.

1. How much time do you think is involved in job-hunting? **(could be a lot!)**

2. What are some ways you can be systematic about looking for a job? **(keep a list of places you have tried or want to try)**

3. Who are you probably competing with to find a job? **(other recent graduates, unemployed adults in the community, other skilled workers, people who have been laid-off in your area, etc.)**

4. Do you think the job will come to you or will you have to do some work to find a job? **(unless they are in a family business, they will probably have to do some work)**

5. How could job-hunting be a discouraging experience? **(getting turned down, being told you don't have enough experience)**

6. If the place you are interested in working at requires experience, how could you go about getting experience if they won't hire you? **(find something somewhat related)**

**Extension Activities:**

1. Have students interview five adults to find out how they got their first job.

2. Go through your local paper's classified ads for employment. Have students systematically go through them to find what types of jobs are available, the range of salaries, which are entry-level positions, how many require specific experience, and if some will provide training. For how many of the jobs are students qualified right now?

3. Contact an employment agency to find out the terms for finding a job through this means. Is a fee involved? How much? What types of jobs are listed?

**Evaluation:**

a. List two possible jobs in which you are interested.

b. List three ways you could begin a search for finding one of those jobs listed in (a).

**Teacher Notes:**

_____

_____

_____

_____

_____

_____

# Searching for a Job

**Directions:** Below is a list of ways to find a job. Write an example of how the method could help you (or someone you know) find a job.

1. reading the classifieds in the newspaper

   _____

   _____

2. putting your own ad in the paper

   _____

   _____

3. asking friends and relatives if they know of any openings where they work

   _____

   _____

4. going to businesses, factories, and other places of work and asking for applications

   _____

   _____

5. talking to a counselor at an employment agency

   _____

   _____

6. signing up for job training in your community

   _____

   _____

7. finding out if you are eligible for any government-sponsored work programs

   _____

   _____

8. working for a temporary-help agency

   _____

   _____

# V-13 A Résumé

**Objective:** The student will construct a brief résumé including education, work experience, interests, and other relevant information.

**Comments:**

A résumé is a simple one-page document that introduces the hopeful employee to the prospective employer. Although the format may vary, information that is usually included might be: personal information, work experience, education, and references. In this lesson, students examine a sample résumé.

**Introductory Activities:**

a. Define *résumé*. **(a brief account of one's work experience and qualifications)**

b. Ask students to give their ideas of what an employer would want to know about them before hiring them for a job.

**Activity:**

**Answers: 1.** high school graduate; **2.** he has a wide variety of interests and abilities – is athletic, musical, probably smart!; **3.** probably a favorite teacher, owner of the construction company he worked for; **4.** he was given some responsibility, is able to make repairs; **5.** 18 (in 1994)

**Discussion:** Answer any questions about the information Michael included on his résumé. Then go over the following questions.

1. Why is it usually important to keep the information on a résumé to only one page? **(gives a lot of information in a little space, employers don't have to spend a lot of time reading it)**

2. Why should a résumé be neat and easy to read? **(it's the first impression you give of yourself)**

3. Why it is helpful to list the duties you performed on your jobs? **(so the employer will know exactly what you were responsible for)**

4. Why is it good to include some personal interests and achievements? **(this may set you apart from other applicants, shows your strengths)**

5. What personal information might you include on a résumé? **(birthday, family information, phone, address, etc.)**

**Extension Activities:**

1. Collect and display different examples of résumés. Discuss with students what is distinctive about each. What information is common to them all?

2. Have students compose a personal résumé. Have them experiment with different styles. Display them to the class, with permission.

**Evaluation:**

a. What are you most proud of that you would include on your résumé?

b. What references would be most helpful on your résumé?

c. What are some unique things about you that would set you apart from others on your résumé?

# A Résumé

**Directions:** Below is a sample résumé for a character. Look it over carefully and then answer the questions below.

---

**Michael A. Kenner**
1124 North Orchard Street
Milwaukee, WI 53213
(414) 476-9988

Education
Graduate of Milwaukee North High School, 1994

Extracurricular Activities
Football team, 1992-1994
Swing Choir, 1991-1994
Debate Team, 1993-1994
Chess Club, 1992-1993

References
Camille T. Sabato, teacher (414) 883-2959
Alexander Smith, Smith Construction owner (414) 783-2990

Work Experience
Smith Construction Company, summer 1993, Carpenter's assistant
Dairy Barn, after school 1992-1994, Assistant manager
Pete's Bike Repairs, summers 1991-1992, Helped take orders,
   minor repairs

Interests
bike riding, sports, hunting

Personal Information
Born May 20, 1976
Oldest of three children

---

1. What do you know about Michael's education? _____

_____

2. What can you tell about Michael from his interests and extracurricular activities?

_____

3. Why do you think he selected the references he did?_____

_____

4. What do you know about him from his work experiences?_____

_____

5. How old is Michael? _____

## V-14 Interviewing

**Objective:** The student will give at least five important considerations to keep in mind during the interviewing process.

**Comments:**

The interview is the first step in the door towards getting a job. It is at this point that the prospective employee has a chance to make a face-to-face impression with someone who may have the authority to hire him or her for the job. In this lesson, the student is to evaluate ten different steps in the interviewing process and state appropriate ways to handle each step.

**Introductory Activities:**

    a. Ask students to give their opinions as to what a job interview is .

    b. Ask students to give reasons why making a good impression at an interview is important.

**Activity:**

Students are to complete the worksheet "Interviewing" by providing the character with appropriate comments (or actions) related to performing well at an interview. Students can add to the drawings, put in conversation, or simply write out their advice.

**Materials:** pen or pencil, markers (for drawing)

**Answers:** *(examples)* **1.** be polite, be specific; **2.** be on time or early; **3.** dress for the type of job – don't overdo it, don't look too casual; **4.** "Good morning" not "Yo"; **5.** express interest, don't ask about salary right away; **6.** tell why you came for the job; **7.** tell what you have done that might be relevant; **8.** express some personality; **9.** "Thank you for your time"; **10.** thank them for the interview, reaffirm your interest in the position

**Discussion:** Go through each of the steps and talk about what would be considered appropriate or inappropriate at each point.

1. Why is it important to be on time or early for an interview? (**their time is valuable, you want to appear conscientious!**)

2. What would be appropriate dress if you were applying for a job at an office? (**dress or skirt; shirt and tie**)

3. What would be appropriate dress if you were applying for a counselor's position at a sports camp for kids? (**something more casual**)

4. Why would it be important to ask questions about the position? (**shows that you are interested, have given it some thought**)

5. Why shouldn't you ask about the salary right away? (**it would appear as though that was your only reason for wanting the job**)

6. If the interviewer tells you right away that you won't get the job, why should you still be polite when you leave? (**there might be another job opening later**)

7. Why is it a good idea to send a follow-up letter or make a phone call? (**to find out what they have decided, make another good impression**)

**Extension Activities:**

1. Practice mock interviews with students taking turns interviewing each other. Have them fabricate the type of job they are offering and make a list of questions. Have students participate by interviewing and evaluating the interviews of others.

2. Have students work in groups to illustrate various positive and negative points about being a good interviewee. Videotape the skits and have students evaluate them. This can be a fun activity!

3. Invite a business friend to talk to the class about what he or she looks for in a person who is interviewing for a job. What specific things turn them off? What is impressive?

**Evaluation:**

a. What are some important things to prepare for before the interview?

b. What are some ways to make a good impression during the interview?

c. Why is an appropriate appearance very important during an interview?

**Teacher Notes:**

_____

_____

_____

_____

_____

_____

# Interviewing

**Directions:** Alison is interviewing for a job as a typist in a business office. What advice would you give her at each step of her interviewing process?

**1.** Calling to set up a time: _____

_____

**2.** Being on time:

_____

_____

_____

**3.** Appropriate appearance:

_____

_____

_____

**4.** Polite greeting:

_____

_____

_____

**5.** Asking good questions about the position:

_____

_____

_____

**6.** Explaining her interest in the job: _____

_____

**7.** Stating her qualifications:

_____

_____

_____

**8.** Telling personal things about herself that are interesting and unique:

_____

_____

**9.** Politely leaving:

_____

_____

**10.** Sending a follow-up letter:

_____

_____

# V-15 Having a Good Attitude

**Objective:** The student will rewrite comments reflecting a bad attitude toward work to make them positive or acceptable.

**Comments:**

Not every job is a worker's dream. Some jobs, especially entry-level positions, might involve doing tasks that are less than glamorous, low in pay, and may be tedious. Employees who have the attitude that they are "too good" for the job (and express this feeling) are probably not going to last long. Students need to realize that having a good attitude is important on any job. In this lesson, students are to rewrite negative comments to make them reflect a better attitude.

**Introductory Activities:**

    a. Present students with the following scenario: "You just started a new job. Your boss comes to you and says that she noticed you were late. She warns you not to let it happen again. What will you do?" Write students' responses on the board.

    b. Next to each response, decide if it reflects a "positive attitude" (taking the criticism politely, without defiance, etc.) or a "negative attitude" (responding in a sullen or defiant manner).

    c. Have students speculate what might happen to the employee if each of the possible responses listed was followed.

**Activity:**

The characters on the worksheet "Having a Good Attitude" reflect a "negative" attitude in terms of being defiant, lazy, self-seeking, or appearing "too good" for the position. Students are to decide what is wrong with the attitude expressed and then rewrite the characters' comments to reflect a better attitude. Students may argue that the employee is in the right and should not have to put up with unfair treatment, etc. For the sake of completing the worksheet, inform students that there will be a lesson later on handling problems with the boss.

    **Answers:** *(examples)* **1.** At least this job is a start and I'm getting a paycheck. **2.** I can learn to go to bed earlier at night. **3.** I'll try to keep my mouth shut when I'm upset around that man. **4.** I'll do the best I can, even though the work is dull. **5.** If I do good work on this job, I'll probably get to do something better later. **6.** Fred will understand that I need this job. **7.** If I'm caught not doing my share, my coworkers won't help me out when I need it. **8.** I'll put the earring back in at 5:01.

    **Discussion:** Students may feel the employee has a right to pick and choose whatever job he or she wants. Indeed, if someone is in a position to have a lot of choice, there is no reason to stay at a job that makes life miserable. On the other hand, if one is beginning the world of work, it is crucial to make a good impression, practice good work skills, and learn the social skills needed to be a good employee – if only to work one's way out of that job into a better one.

    1. If someone feels he or she is "too good" to do a certain job, what other options does he or she have? **(look for something else, put up with it for the time being, etc.)**

    2. If you have no other work options at the moment and are stuck in a low-paying, boring job, what could you do? **(learn to adapt, try to make it as interesting for yourself as you can)**

3. Why do some people feel work rules have to bend to fit their personal rules – such as what time they will start, what they will wear, etc.? **(they probably have been used to "calling the shots" and haven't been used to following school rules either)**

4. Is getting a paycheck the only reason to stick out a job you don't like? **(it might be enough in some cases, but it's also a good idea to stay around long enough to get a good recommendation and experience)**

5. How can you reflect a good attitude towards your coworkers? **(be friendly, do your share, be positive about the work)**

6. If you bring a bad attitude to work with you, how does that affect the people you work with? **(might rub off)**

7. How does the bad attitude affect your job performance? **(probably makes you not want to care or do a good job)**

8. Can you think of any ways to change a bad attitude? **(realize that you need the job more than it needs you, calm yourself down and rethink your goals, etc.)**

**Extension Activities:**

1. Have students talk to their parents about their work. If their parent is an employer, have them give examples of employees who have good attitudes on the job. If their parent is primarily an employee, look for examples of how they reflect a good attitude. Share these ideas with the class.

2. Collect, write, and display positive attitude comments around the room. These can be useful for school situations as well as work. Colorful signs that display sayings such as "I can do that!" or "Here's my best work!" can reflect a positive attitude about your classroom.

**Evaluation:**

Rewrite the following comments to reflect a more positive attitude:

a. This work is stupid. Whoever thought of doing this was really an idiot.

b. No one will notice if I leave ten minutes early again. I work hard enough that I am owed that time anyway.

c. I don't care that the boss said to do it his way – I think my own way is better.

# Having a Good Attitude

**Directions:** What is wrong with the attitude expressed by the employees below? Rewrite their comments to reflect a better attitude!

1. There's no way I would work at that place – they hardly pay anything and the work is too hard. I'm better than that!

_____
_____
_____
_____

2. I'm not taking any job where I have to get up before noon.

_____
_____
_____
_____

3. I don't like that boss. He reminds me of a teacher I used to hate.

_____
_____
_____

4. This work is boring. Forget it!

_____
_____
_____

5. I like animals, but cleaning out all these cages is not what I had in mind. I wanted to play with them and pet them.

_____
_____
_____

6. I can't work overtime! I have a date with Fred!

_____
_____
_____

7. If I work slowly enough, the others will get my work done.

_____
_____
_____

8. I'm not taking out the earring. I don't agree with the dress code, so I won't follow it!

_____
_____
_____

# V-16 Being a Good Employee

**Objective:** The student will select the better of two employees given example workers and state why.

**Comments:**

Having a good attitude is only one factor in being a good employee. There are a lot of other factors such as being punctual, performing well, getting along with the boss, getting along with coworkers, and so on. In this lesson, students are given pairs of employees to compare and must select the better one.

**Introductory Activities:**

a. Have students list characteristics of a good employee (you may start the list with "good attitude"). Students can give examples.

b. Have students list characteristics of a poor employee. They can add specific examples if they choose.

**Activity:**

**Answers: 1.** second/comes to work ready to work; **2.** first/is recognized for performance; **3.** first/team player; **4.** second/polite and respectful to boss; **5.** first/gets along with coworkers; **6.** second/comes to work on time

**Discussion:** Go over the examples on the worksheet and have students explain what characteristic the "good employee" is demonstrating.

1. How would you feel if the first worker in example 1 was a brain surgeon who was going to operate on you today? **(frightened!)**

2. Why is it important to be mentally and physically ready to work? **(you owe that to your employer, it's important in order to do a good job)**

3. In example 2, why do you think the second employee never gets noticed? **(maybe she never does anything well)**

4. In example 3, the second worker says the company does not care. Who else does not care? **(the worker)**

5. Both employees greeted the boss in example 4, but what is the difference? **(one was sarcastic, the other was sincere)**

6. Do you think the second employee is being phoney or just trying to get in good with the boss? **(could be, it all depends on the attitude of the employee)**

7. What characteristic is demonstrated in example 6? **(being on time)**

**Extension Activities:**

1. Have students write and present (or videotape) a humorous skit in which two employees are vying for the same position. Both could go overboard trying to impress the boss.

2. Have students come up with a checklist for at least ten skills they think are indicative of a good employee. Which of these skills also apply to being a good student?

**Evaluation:**

a. List at least five characteristics of a good employee.

b. Choose one characteristic and explain how this contributes to being an effective employee and producing a better product or service.

# Being a Good Employee

**Directions:** Read the comments of each pair of employees below. Circle the one who is the better employee of the two. Explain why with your classmates.

1. - yawn - I was out til 3 A.M. last night. I hope I don't have to do anything hard today!

I'm ready to work! I'm saving my fun for this weekend!

2. Wow! I got another award for doing excellent work!

The boss never notices how hard I work!

3. I know not getting that contract is bad, but let's work together and try to get the next one.

This company isn't going anywhere. Nobody cares.

4. Good morning, Mr. Sledge. (What a jerk!)

Good morning! What would you like me to do first today?

5. Hi, Mabel. Hi, Pete. How are you doing today? Frank, do you need a hand with that?

If you don't do your share, I won't either.

6. Hey. I'm only ten minutes late today!

I like to get myself organized before everybody else gets here.

# V-17 Getting Along with the Boss

**Objective:** Given a hypothetical problem situation involving an employer, the student will suggest an appropriate response to handle the situation.

**Comments:**

It is not always easy to get along with others, but when that person happens to be your boss, it is an especially delicate situation. It is not always right to back down, especially when you feel you are in the right. But these situations must be handled with respect and with a clear mind. In this lesson, students are given situations to consider and come up with a solution for handling a difficult boss.

**Introductory Activities:**

a. Have students raise their hands if they have ever been given instructions to follow that seemed to make no sense whatsoever.

b. Have students raise their hands if they had to work with someone who had authority over them, but for whom they had no respect. Allow time to elaborate.

c. Have students raise their hands if they had to work with someone who had a bad temper or was overly sensitive about things. How did they handle this situation?

**Activity:**

**Answers:** *(examples)* **1.** I will if I can, but could I have some extra time to get my previous assignments done first? **2.** If you give me a minute to explain, I think I can make it more clear. **3.** I would be happy to stay another time, but I have plans I need to take care of tonight. **4.** ignore – wait for calmness; **5.** I would appreciate it if you would ask me about that first, and please don't refer to me as "honey"; **6.** Apparently we are having some office personality problems – how would you like us to handle this?

**Discussion:** Allow students the opportunity to share their responses and raise questions about how best to handle each situation.

1. In the first example, the boss complimented the worker and seemed to be rewarding her efficiency by giving her more work. Should the worker protest?

2. Is it ever right to argue with the boss? What if you strongly feel you are right and he or she is wrong?

3. If you couldn't go to your boss with a problem, who else might be available to consult with? **(a mediator, another worker in the same position, another employer who might have the same status in the office, etc.)**

4. How could you make your position known (as in example 3), and not be taken advantage of, but still be cooperative? **(explain that you have obligations also, the request is unreasonable especially since the boss is leaving to play golf)**

5. Is a boss allowed to have a temper tantrum, as in example 4? **(sometimes – they are human)**

6. Why might it be a good idea to check with a coworker about what to do before you do something you are not sure about? **(the other employees might clue you in as to how best to handle the situation)**

7. What is the real problem with example 6? **(the boss doesn't want to become involved in the office problems)**

8. If you truly could not get along with your immediate supervisor or boss, what alternatives might there be? **(ask for a transfer within the company, look for another job with the same qualifications, etc.)**

## Extension Activities:

1. Have students look through business publications for articles about how to manage others. From a boss's perspective, what are some qualities that inspire respect? What makes a good manager of people?

2. Have students role-play ways to handle a difficult work situation. Show one with disastrous results, and then rework the skit to handle the same situation more appropriately.

3. Devise some "sticky" situations. Send three or four students out of the room while they are set up. Have each of the students return individually, and see how they choose to respond to each situation. Are the reactions quite different?

## Evaluation:

What is an appropriate way to handle the following situation?

Your boss sends you out to pick up some coffee and donuts for a business meeting with five other people. He forgets to give you any money and never mentions paying you back for the breakfast. He now is preoccupied with some other tasks, but you want to be repaid for the $20 you spent for him.

# Getting Along with the Boss

**Directions:** Here are examples of some bosses who are not the easiest to get along with. Write an example of something you as the employee could do to handle the situation or draw a picture on another sheet of paper.

1. Here – I know you can handle these ten extra cases. You're so efficient.

2. I don't understand your position on this. It's not clearly written. Would you please re-do it?

3. I know it's 5:30, but would you please stay an extra three hours to finish this project? I need to golf with my buddies.

4. WHY ISN'T ANYONE AROUND HERE WORKING AS HARD AS I AM? THERE'S A LOT TO BE DONE! WE NEED TO TIGHTEN UP! NAG, NAG, NAG, NAG!

5. This is my secretary. She won't mind doing your work for you, will you, honey?

6. I don't know why you all can't get along and work out your own problems. All you do is complain about each other. I've had enough of it.

# V-18 You Are the Boss

**Objective:** The student will supply appropriate responses for hypothetical work situations as if he or she were the boss.

**Comments:**

It can be fun to be on the "other side" of a decision-making situation. Instead of making complaints about the boss, students are going to "be" the boss. In this lesson, they are to handle typical situations and try to arrive at a resolution.

**Introductory Activities:**

a. Have students think about past "bosses" they have had. In some cases, this may be a part-time job supervisor, a coach or teacher, or perhaps an adult relative who supervised their work. Have them write the name of someone whom they thought was a particularly good "boss."

b. Have students list several reasons why they considered this person to be a good boss.

c. Have students think about any situations in which they have supervised someone else. Give time for them to tell about these situations.

**Activity:**

Students are to assume the role of the boss in the situations on the worksheet "You Are the Boss." They are to write/state how they would handle the problem presented. Some of the situations may be vague or nonspecific; in those cases, let students make assumptions as long as they can justify their answers.

**Answers:** *(examples)* **1.** answers will vary; you might want to wait to fill the position for some better applicants; **2.** report the problem to your supervisor; **3.** inform Mary that her skills are in need of immediate help, refer her to a night course in English, get her a spell-checker, etc.; **4.** continue to do your job, ignore the tantrums, put your findings in writing and let him deal with it, etc.;. **5.** if there are customer complaints, inform him that there is a dress code and he must tune it down during working hours (but perhaps tell him you admire his taste for parties!); **6.** talk to her in private, tell her that you have had complaints from other employees; **7.** calmly explain that you need to have easy access to the files in order to efficiently do your job, give her one more chance

**Discussion:** Students may have some varied answers to the situations on the worksheet. Discuss the pros and cons of what the students have come up with.

1. Would you enjoy being a boss or do you prefer to take instructions from others?

2. What do you think would be the best thing(s) about being the one in charge?

3. What do you think would be the hardest thing(s) about being in charge of others? **(the responsibility)**

4. If someone wanted to be popular and have everyone like him or her, what would be a drawback to being a boss? **(making unpopular decisions)**

5. What do you think is the single most important quality about being a good boss? Efficiency? Having respect of employees? Being fair?

**Extension Activities:**

1. Have students role-play being the boss. Come up with some unusual situations and allow students time to think about what they would do, then demonstrate in front of the class.

2. Give students opportunities to take leadership positions in class occasionally — perhaps let them take turns being teacher for a day (with limits!). They may think being in charge is "fun and games," but hard work and conscientious planning are necessary to seriously teach or put out a product!

**Evaluation:**

a. List three to five qualities of a good boss.

b. How would you handle the following situation: You have been asked to fire your best friend from the job because he or she has been caught stealing money from the cash fund. Your friend denies it and is extremely upset, but you have seen the evidence and you, too, believe that stealing has been going on.

**Teacher Notes:**

_____

_____

_____

_____

_____

_____

# You Are the Boss

**Directions:** Now you are in charge! How would you handle the following situations?

1. You have two applicants for the same position. One is very creative, but he has a poor attitude. You think it might be difficult for the other employees to get along with him. The other applicant is very reliable and has good references, but seems boring and not very energetic. What will you do?

   _____

   _____

2. You really liked the work that Tom had been doing – until he got heavily involved in alcohol. Now his attendance is poor and he is often late to work. Everyone is aware of the problem, but Tom continues to deny that there is anything wrong.

   _____

   _____

3. Mary is a good worker, but she can't spell. What's worse, she doesn't ask questions about assignments when she doesn't understand what to do – she just goes ahead and does what she thinks is right. Almost everything she does has to be re-done, either by Mary or someone else.

   _____

   _____

4. George cannot take criticism. Whenever you have to tell him to make a correction, he flies off the handle and becomes irate and defensive. It's getting so you hate to find any mistakes because you dislike confronting him so much.

   _____

   _____

5. Ricardo is bright and intelligent – but he's been coming to work with green and pink striped hair and outfits that look like something out of the circus. He is friendly and outgoing, but his appearance is just too much!

   _____

   _____

6. Andrea comes to work but mostly just to talk about her problems. She will corner another employee and go on and on about every little thing that is happening at home. People can't get their own work done because of her constant talking!

   _____

   _____

7. You have asked Mrs. Riley to change the way she files your work, but she won't do it. She insists that her way is better. But you can't find anything. The more you insist, the less she listens to you.

   _____

   _____

# V-19 Getting Work Experience

**Objective:** The student will list several ways to get work experience.

**Comments:**

There are opportunities available all around for young people to get work experience – which is sometimes a prerequisite for someone to hire them for another job! Some of the jobs may not pay much (and some may involve volunteering just for the experience), but the experience gained can be beneficial and look great on a résumé. In this lesson, students are to think of lots of ways they can gain work or leadership experience.

**Introductory Activities:**

a. Have students think of ways or times when they have been in a leadership position. List them.

b. Have students raise their hands if they have ever baby-sat, cleaned out a garage, walked a dog, or washed a car. Inform them that they have work experience!

**Activity:**

**Discussion:** Ask students to share their ideas. See if students can come up with at least 20 different ways they can gain work experience.

1. How many of the ways you thought of involved earning money for your services?

2. How important is it for you to have money for what you do? Would you consider working for free if you got good experience?

3. What are some unusual experiences you have had that would apply to a job you might eventually do?

4. What are some organized volunteer programs in your community? (**Meals-on-Wheels, hospital gift shop, etc.**)

5. What does the fact that you have done part-time work and volunteer work say about you to a potential employer? (**you are creative, resourceful, and are interested in others, etc.**)

**Extension Activities:**

1. Have students find out about volunteer programs in the community. Encourage them to sign up to give it a try for the experience.

2. Set up peer tutoring or cross-age tutoring within your school. Provide training for helping the students learn to be tutors and start them off with a volunteer experience.

3. Have students contact some local businesses to find out if there are part-time work/study positions available. Some businesses will work with a school as "partners in education."

**Evaluation:**

a. List at least five possible work/leadership experiences you have already participated in or would consider doing.

b. What are at least two reasons why volunteering is a helpful experience both for you and the agency for which you are working?

# Getting Work Experience

**Directions:** Below is a partial list of ways you can get some work experience that might help you with future jobs. Add to the list with your own ideas.

1. work for your parents' office or business

2. ask your relatives for part-time work

3. be a camp counselor in the summer for children

4. volunteer to work with handicapped children after school

5. teach a Sunday School class for children

6. help out on a farm

7. tutor children at your school

8. offer to care for neighbors' pets/houses while they are on vacation

9. be a library assistant at your local library

10. become involved in summer sports programs as a manager, batboy, etc.

11. _____

12. _____

13. _____

14. _____

15. _____

16. _____

17. _____

18. _____

19. _____

20. _____

# V-20 Changing Jobs: Why?

**Objective:** The student will identify several reasons why people change jobs.

**Comments:**

There are lots of reasons why people change jobs – it may be due to work environment, boredom with the job, additional training that qualifies one for a new job, or change in location. Most people do not keep the same job (or even career) for their entire working life. It is important to keep options open and if the opportunity to move to another job that is in some respects better presents itself, it is perfectly acceptable to do so. In this lesson, students are given examples of people who are ready or desiring to change jobs.

**Introductory Activities:**

a. Ask students to give examples from personal experience of their parents or relatives of times when they changed jobs.

b. Ask students to give reasons why people might change jobs.

c. After listing reasons, have students try to categorize them; e.g., personal reasons, professional concerns, etc.

**Activity:**

**Answers: 1.** c; **2.** b; **3.** d; **4.** a; **5.** f; **6.** e

**Discussion:** After students have completed the worksheet, see how the reasons compare with the reasons students listed in the introductory activities. What other reasons did they give that were not on the worksheet?

1. Some people keep the same job for their whole lives. Why? **(no other options, enjoy the work, work for family, etc.)**

2. What are some good or positive reasons for job changes?

3. What are some negative reasons for changing a job?

4. What else might change with a new job that demands more responsibility? **(more money, power, respect, time demands, etc.)**

5. What stresses might be involved in a job change? **(moving, getting to know different people, learning a new job, etc.)**

**Extension Activities:**

1. Have students interview at least five adults who have had job changes. Find out the sequence of jobs – have most been improvements? Were they the same types of jobs? What contributed to making a job change?

2. Have students prepare a bulletin board entitled "Climbing the Ladder of Success" (or similar theme) showing how an entry-level position can lead (with additional training, skills, and some luck) to different positions. For example, a principal may have started out by being an assistant to a teacher, then became a student teacher, teacher/coach for a high school, and eventually a principal. Have students find out other "paths" that careers can follow.

**Evaluation:**

a. List three to five reasons why a person may want to change jobs.

b. Write a paragraph explaining at least one negative aspect and one positive aspect of changing jobs.

# Changing Jobs: Why?

**Directions:** Match the person who is changing jobs with the reason why he or she wants a job change.

_____ 1. I'm bored with my present position of planting seedlings. I would like to do something different, like plan how a garden will look when it is finished.

**a.** higher pay

_____ 2. I just can't work with that woman anymore. She criticizes everything I do. I go home feeling like I'm worthless.

**b.** get away from an unpleasant situation

**c.** more interesting job

_____ 3. It's too far to work at that supermarket. Now that one is open one block from my home, I'm going to apply for a job there.

**d.** better location

**e.** benefits

**f.** more responsibility

_____ 4. Hey! I can make $2 more an hour for the same job at that factory. It's time for a change!

_____ 5. Now that I've completed this training, I should be eligible for a supervisor's position.

_____ 6. If I guarantee that I will stay on the new job for a year, they will pay for my training and get me started in this new office. Sounds good to me!

# V-21 Changing Jobs: How?

**Objective:** The student will list at least three ways or steps that a person can take to make a job change.

**Comments:**

Once the decision to change jobs has been reached, it is then time to begin the job search all over again; however, there is one difference – now the person has had at least one job and has experience! Even if the experience was negative and the person realizes that this is not the job for him or her, at least that is a starting point. In this lesson, students will complete paragraphs to indicate how to go about changing jobs by improving skills, getting additional training, or using other available resources to make that change.

**Introductory Activities:**

    a. Have students write a probable job they are capable of holding right now or perhaps work at part-time.

    b. Have students indicate by raising hands if they would like to keep that same job for the rest of their lives. Why or why not?

**Activity:**

Students are to complete the worksheet "Changing Jobs: How?" by filling in the blanks in paragraphs with words from the selection at the bottom of the page. When completed, the paragraphs will give ideas for ways to make a job change.

**Answers: 1.** experience; **2.** training; **3.** help; **4.** recommendation; **5.** job; **6.** classifieds; **7.** move; **8.** consider; **9.** night; **10.** quit

**Discussion:** Changing jobs does not indicate that you are disloyal or hard to get along with – it may only indicate that you are willing to move up or move on to something else that comes along that is better for you. Have students discuss the following questions.

1. If you are happy with your present job, why even bother looking for something else? **(it may not meet your needs for the future, you may want to earn more money, have more prestige, etc.)**

2. What are some jobs that have built-in advancement? **(some entry-level jobs provide training, management positions, etc.)**

3. Do you think some companies would like to keep their good employees so they make arrangements for them to stay to have a better job? Why? **(yes – good employees are hard to find!)**

4. If you knew that your boss could recommend you for a better position within the same company, how could you go about using this resource? **(ask for an evaluation, talk to boss about your desire to change jobs, etc.)**

5. What are some ways to get additional skills that would qualify you for a better job within a company? **(ask around, check with the personnel office, look for in-service opportunities, etc.)**

6. Sometimes factories or businesses close and the job goes with it. If your position is terminated because of those factors, how would this affect your looking for another job? **(still use the references, explain that it was not your fault that you're out of a job, etc.)**

**Extension Activities:**

1. Have students check with their parents or other adults who work and bring in examples of on-the-job or in-service training that is available to employees. How does this help both the employee and the company?

2. Find out what evening school courses are available at local community colleges. How could a person maintain a day job and still get training to help him or her advance to another position?

**Evaluation:**

a. List two or three ways a person could change jobs once already employed.

b. Write a paragraph explaining how satisfactory (or superior) job performance on a present job can benefit someone when they are changing jobs.

**Teacher Notes:**

_____

_____

_____

_____

_____

_____

Name _____    Date_____

# Changing Jobs: How?

**Directions:** Fill in the blanks in the following paragraphs
to find some ways to change jobs. Use the words in the word box
at the bottom of the page.

You are bored with your present job. If you could get some

more **(1)** _____ , you would be

qualified to do something else. You might want to find out about

some **(2)** _____ that is offered on your

present job that would help you move on to something new.

***

You like your boss and do very well at what you do. Perhaps your boss can

**(3)** _____ you find another job at the same place. You can

always ask for a good **(4)** _____ from him or her. This will

help you find another **(5)** _____ .

***

There is nothing in your town besides the same old jobs. You look through the

**(6)** _____ and find out that you can do a similar, but more

interesting job if you are willing to **(7)** _____

to another city. You are alone and don't have a family, so you might

**(8)**_____ it!

***

If you are willing to go to school at **(9)** _____ ,

you can take some evening classes in a new area that interests you. This way you

won't have to **(10)** _____ your present job, but you

can try out something new.

***

| | | | |
|---|---|---|---|
| recommendation | training | experience | classifieds |
| quit | night | help | move |
| job | consider | | |

# V-22 A Job Application

**Objective:** The student will complete a sample job application accurately and neatly.

**Comments:**

Most job searches begin with an application. This requests information regarding the applicant's education, work experience, and personal information. A student should be prepared when entering the world of work to have the necessary information. Also, an application should be filled out completely, honestly, and neatly. All of these are factors in making a good first impression – which is often what the application serves as. In this lesson, students are to work on completing a job application.

**Introductory Activities:**

a. Ask students how many of them have ever walked into a place of business, threw out their arms and yelled, "I'm ready to work! When do I start?" and have gotten a job?

b. Ask students to explain why filling out a job application is usually the way many companies begin their search for employees.

c. Ask students to list what information they think is generally included on a job application.

**Activity:**

Students are to complete the sample application for employment on the worksheet "A Job Application." They will need to know or obtain their social security number, names and phone numbers of references, and dates of previous employment.

**Discussion:** Have students ask for clarification about any parts of which they are unsure. They may need a day to get missing information such as their social security number. Encourage students to write as legibly as possible. Also inform them to be honest and accurate on the application.

1. Why is it very important to write legibly on the application? **(the reader needs to know how to contact you or the references, has to be able to read the information)**

2. What else can help make a good first impression on the application? **(using one color of ink or even typing it, staying within the lines, overall neat appearance)**

3. Why would an employer want to know of any physical defects? **(they need to know if you can perform the job you are applying for)**

4. What are some jobs that require someone to be over 18? **(serving alcohol)**

5. Why would they want to know your hobbies or interests? **(to see what kinds of activities you are involved in)**

6. Why would they want to know if you have a criminal record? **(the job may involve handling money or checks, involve some sort of security, etc.)**

7. Why are you not to include activities that indicate your race or religion? **(should not be a factor in getting the job)**

8. Why is it important to have good references from your previous employers? **(they probably will be contacted)**

9. Why would they want to know how many days were lost from work? **(they want to know if attendance will be a problem)**

10. What factors are prohibited from being discriminated against as written on the top of the application? **(race, creed, color, national origin, ancestry, age, sex, physical or mental handicaps, etc.)**

**Extension Activities:**

1. Collect and bring in examples of applications for employment from several businesses or organizations. Have students check them out and figure out what things are similar about each.

2. Have students prepare a personal information sheet they can use to complete applications. Have them record references, names and addresses of previous employers, etc.

**Evaluation:**

How would you revise the following responses to an application for employment:

1. What interests you in working for our company?

   I am hoping to get free food and be able to talk to my friends while I am working.

2. What are your hobbies or special interests?

   I have no hobbies. I am interested in boys.

3. What is your reason for leaving your last job?

   My boss was a jerk.

# A Job Application

**Directions:** Here is a sample job application for an entry-level position at a fast-food restaurant. Complete the application to the best of your ability.

## BURGER HAVEN

AN EQUAL OPPORTUNITY EMPLOYER - M/F/H

RESTAURANT OPERATIONS
HOURLY EMPLOYEE

# APPLICATION FOR EMPLOYMENT

Discrimination in employment because of race, creed, color, national origin, ancestry, age, sex, physical or mental handicaps, or liability for service in the armed forces of the U.S. is prohibited by federal legislation and/or by laws against discrimination in some states.

### PERSONAL

| LAST NAME | FIRST | MIDDLE INITIAL | PHONE |

STREET ADDRESS | CITY | STATE | ZIP CODE

SOCIAL SECURITY NUMBER

NAME AND PHONE OF PERSON TO BE NOTIFIED FOR EMERGENCY

KNOWN PHYSICAL DEFECTS WHICH COULD AFFECT YOUR ABILITY TO PERFORM POSITION BEING APPLIED FOR

IS YOUR CITIZENSHIP OR IMMIGRATION STATUS SUCH THAT YOU CAN LAWFULLY WORK IN THE U.S.? ☐ YES ☐ NO
IF HIRED CONTINUED EMPLOYMENT MAY BE DEPENDENT UPON PROOF OF CITIZENSHIP OR PRESENTATION OF AN ALIEN REGISTRATION NUMBER.

ARE YOU ☐ 14 - 15 ☐ 16 - 17 ☐ 18 OR OLDER     IF UNDER 18, PROOF OF AGE MUST BE PROVIDED PRIOR TO HIRING

### EDUCATION

| NAME OF SCHOOL AND ADDRESS | # OF YEARS COMPLETED | GRADUATED YES | GRADUATED NO | NUMBER OF COLLEGE CREDIT HOURS | MAJOR | AVERAGE |
|---|---|---|---|---|---|---|
| JUNIOR HIGH | | | | | | |
| HIGH SCHOOL | | | | | | |
| COLLEGE | | | | | | |
| OTHER | | | | | | |

EXTRACURRICULAR ACTIVITIES

CURRENTLY ENROLLED IN HIGH SCHOOL/WORK/STUDY PROGRAM     ☐ YES     ☐ NO

### GENERAL/ACTIVITIES

DATE AVAILABLE TO START

| DAYS AND HOURS AVAILABLE TO WORK | DAY | SUNDAY | MONDAY | TUESDAY | WEDNESDAY | THURSDAY | FRIDAY | SATURDAY |
|---|---|---|---|---|---|---|---|---|
| | FROM | | | | | | | |
| | TO | | | | | | | |

WHAT INTERESTED YOU IN BURGER HAVEN?

WHAT ARE YOUR HOBBIES, SPECIAL INTERESTS, AND ACTIVITIES?
(Do not include those indicating race, creed, nationality or religion)

HAVE YOU EVER BEEN CONVICTED OF A FELONY OR MISDEMEANOR OTHER THAN A TRAFFIC VIOLATION? ☐ NO ☐ YES
IF YES STATE CHARGE, COURT, DATE AND DISPOSITION OF CASE

| COMPANY NO. 1 (Present or most recent employer) | | | ADDRESS/PHONE NUMBER | |
|---|---|---|---|---|
| EMPLOYED (Month & Year) | | RATE OF PAY | | AVERAGE NUMBER OF HOURS WORKED PER WEEK |
| FROM          TO | | START          ENDING | | |
| POSITIONS HELD | | | SUPERVISOR'S NAME/POSITION | |
| DESCRIBE YOUR DUTIES | | | | |
| MAY WE CONTACT THIS EMPLOYER? ☐ YES   ☐ NO | DAYS LOST FROM WORK | | | |
| REASON FOR LEAVING | | | | |

| COMPANY NO. 2 (Present or most recent employer) | | | ADDRESS/PHONE NUMBER | |
|---|---|---|---|---|
| EMPLOYED (Month & Year) | | RATE OF PAY | | AVERAGE NUMBER OF HOURS WORKED PER WEEK |
| FROM          TO | | START          ENDING | | |
| POSITIONS HELD | | | SUPERVISOR'S NAME/POSITION | |
| DESCRIBE YOUR DUTIES | | | | |
| MAY WE CONTACT THIS EMPLOYER? ☐ YES   ☐ NO | DAYS LOST FROM WORK | | | |
| REASON FOR LEAVING | | | | |

THE INFORMATION I AM PRESENTING IN THIS APPLICATION IS TRUE AND CORRECT TO THE BEST OF MY KNOWLEDGE, AND I UNDERSTAND THAT ANY FALSIFICATION OR MISREPRESENTATION HEREIN COULD RESULT IN MY DISCHARGE IN THE EVENT I AM EMPLOYED BY BURGER HAVEN. I AUTHORIZE BURGER HAVEN OR ITS REPRESENTATIVES TO CONTACT ALL FORMER EMPLOYERS AND TO FURTHER INQUIRE AS TO ANY INFORMATION GIVEN BY ME ON THIS APPLICATION.

APPLICANT'S SIGNATURE _____   DATE: _____

## DO NOT WRITE BELOW THIS LINE - FOR BURGER HAVEN USE ONLY

| COMPANY NO. 1 REFERENCE CHECK | | | | GOOD | AVERAGE | POOR |
|---|---|---|---|---|---|---|
| APPLICANT ELIGIBLE FOR REHIRE: ☐ YES ☐ NO | | | ATTENDANCE: | ☐ | ☐ | ☐ |
| DATES OF EMPLOYMENT VERIFIED ☐ YES ☐ NO | | | PERFORMANCE: | ☐ | ☐ | ☐ |
| CHECKED BY | | CONTACTED | DATE: | | | |

| COMPANY NO. 2 REFERENCE CHECK | | | | GOOD | AVERAGE | POOR |
|---|---|---|---|---|---|---|
| APPLICANT ELIGIBLE FOR REHIRE: ☐ YES ☐ NO | | | ATTENDANCE: | ☐ | ☐ | ☐ |
| DATES OF EMPLOYMENT VERIFIED ☐ YES ☐ NO | | | PERFORMANCE: | ☐ | ☐ | ☐ |
| CHECKED BY | | CONTACTED | DATE: | | | |

MANAGER 'S/INTERVIEWER'S NOTES:

# Section VI

## Lifestyle Choices

# VI-1 What Are Values?

**Objective:** The student will list at least five common values and give an example of each.

**Comments:**

Each of us has a value system. There are certain things we place great importance upon and we act accordingly. Our values may be gained from our parents, our experiences, our education, and other sources, but it is important to know what we value. In this lesson, students are introduced to the concept of values and are given examples.

**Introductory Activities:**

a. Tell students you are going to say some words. Have them write one word that comes to mind that seems to include your examples.

| | |
|---|---|
| $1,000,000...gold coins...winning the lottery | MONEY, WEALTH |
| mom...dad...uncle...brother...Aunt Ginny | FAMILY |
| blue ribbon...trophy...diploma | ACHIEVEMENT |

b. Define *value.* (**something of great importance to someone**)

**Activity:**

On the worksheet "What Are Values?" students are to match examples of values in action with the value listed.

**Answers: 1.** e; **2.** h; **3.** c; **4.** i; **5.** b; **6.** g; **7.** j; **8.** a; **9.** k; **10.** d; **11.** l; **12.** f

**Discussion:** Have students discuss any of the items that are unclear to them. Explain that these are just examples – there are lots of other ways to demonstrate the value.

1. Which of the values on the worksheet are important to you?

2. What are some other examples of demonstrating the values on the worksheet?

3. Which values do you think would be important to these people: teacher? lawyer? model? elderly person? mother? athlete?

**Extension Activities:**

1. Have students collect or record bumper stickers they have seen or heard of. What values are indicated by the stickers? What clues were given?

2. Listen to speeches by politicians or school board members (elections times are good times to work on this activity). What values are brought up?

**Evaluation:**

a. List five to seven common values.

b. For each value listed in (a), give an example of how someone could demonstrate that value.

# What Are Values?

**Directions:** Match the value on the left with an example on the right of someone demonstrating that value.

_____ **1.** HEALTH

_____ **2.** WEALTH

_____ **3.** FAMILY

_____ **4.** FRIENDSHIP

_____ **5.** HUMOR

_____ **6.** EDUCATION

_____ **7.** BEAUTY

_____ **8.** SPACE

_____ **9.** FOOD

_____ **10.** EXERCISE

_____ **11.** MUSIC

_____ **12.** HAPPINESS

**a.** wanting to have your own bedroom

**b.** watching a comedy show on television

**c.** spending time at the movies with your brothers and sisters

**d.** working out at a health spa three times a week

**e.** making sure you have had your flu shot

**f.** doing things you enjoy, allowing yourself to have fun

**g.** going to graduate school

**h.** opening a savings account

**i.** sticking up for your friend, even when nobody else will

**j.** planting flowers in front of your house

**k.** preparing a gourmet meal

**l.** learning to play the piano

# VI-2 Values Important to Me

**Objective:** The student will state or list at least five values that are personally important to him or her.

**Comments:**

Everyone has values, whether they are specifically stated or not. Just by observing a person and listening to what he or she says, you can determine some things that are of great importance to that person. In this lesson, students are to think about specific values that are meaningful to them.

**Introductory Activities:**

a. Have students write the name of a person who is important to them.

b. Have students write an important possession.

c. Have students write what they think is the most important characteristic a person can have.

**Activity:**

**Discussion:** Since this is an individual activity, responses will be quite different. It might be interesting to find out (with a show of hands) which items were most often selected as being important to students within the class.

1. Why are the things that people value different for everyone? **(people have had different upbringings, different experiences, etc.)**

2. What values do you think are probably the same for most people? **(health, happiness, etc.)**

3. What people or kinds of people would not value wealth? **(clergy, homeless?)**

4. What problems could arise between people who have very different value systems? **(depends on the value, but there could be a lot of conflicts)**

5. Do you think a person's values change as the person gets older? Why? **(probably – needs change as they get older, need to have a job, money)**

6. How could a traumatic experience such as being saved from a life-threatening situation affect a person's values? **(they might tend to value life/health more)**

**Extension Activities:**

1. Have students consider the items on the worksheet and try to reduce them to a single word, e.g., doing well in school, being well-educated could both be covered by EDUCATION.

2. Have students add items to the list. Which are the result of specific experiences they have had?

3. Have students conduct a survey of a cross-section of the population: adults, students, elementary children. Make a list of ten items to give as the survey. Which values are more predominant in certain age groups? (e.g., do children value health and wealth? Do adults value being good at sports?)

**Evaluation:**

a. List five personal values.

b. Give an example for each value in (a) of how you demonstrate that value in your life.

# Values Important to Me

**Directions:** Put a check mark next to the items on the list that are somewhat important to you. Put two marks next to those that are extremely important to you. Leave items blank if you are not particularly interested in that value.

_____ 1. having a lot of money

_____ 2. doing well in school

_____ 3. having a lot of friends

_____ 4. having one close friend

_____ 5. getting along with my parents

_____ 6. getting along with my family

_____ 7. having time to myself

_____ 8. not worrying about having enough to eat

_____ 9. getting/having a good job

_____ 10. liking my job

_____ 11. respecting myself

_____ 12. being respected by others

_____ 13. having my own space/room

_____ 14. being good at something

_____ 15. having a clean room

_____ 16. breathing clean air

_____ 17. recycling

_____ 18. being well-educated

_____ 19. being in good health

_____ 20. being handsome/pretty

_____ 21. knowing that someone loves me

_____ 22. being in love

_____ 23. having nice clothes

_____ 24. having a lot of possessions

_____ 25. being in good physical shape

_____ 26. having a boyfriend/girlfriend

_____ 27. being good at sports

_____ 28. helping others

_____ 29. being recognized for helping others

_____ 30. believing in God

_____ 31. being happy

_____ 32. being right about something

_____ 33. being able to handle responsibility

_____ 34. setting goals for myself

_____ 35. having control of what happens to me

# VI-3 Forming Values

**Objective:** The student will state reasons why an individual might hold on to a certain value.

**Comments:**

Sometimes an experience or goal can help determine what value is important to an individual. An impoverished third-world child might value food and clothing because these items are not readily available. Someone who set a goal of college or a particular job might value these aspirations. In this lesson, students are given examples of individuals who have specific values.

**Introductory Activities:**

   a. Have students think of one thing their parents or important adults taught them that they still value highly today.

   b. Have students think of a specific event (good or bad) that has influenced their having a value today.

**Activity:**

On the worksheet "Forming Values," students are to read the examples and decide why the person in the example holds a particular value and why.

**Answers:** *(examples)* **1.** children/death of one; **2.** track achievement/he's good at it!; **3.** friendship/examples of kindness have affected her; **4.** safety/lack of safety at previous school; **5.** physical health/restrained for 6 weeks; **6.** education/worked hard to get it

**Discussion:** Students' responses may differ slightly on the worksheet, but should reflect basically the same values. Allow students time to elaborate if they know of a similar example of someone forming a value from a particular experience.

1. What are some other values that might be traced to a specific incident? **(hunger, poverty, etc.)**

2. What are some values that might be formed by a good experience? **(friendship from having some good friends, wealth from good business investments, etc.)**

3. Some values may be acquired from the teaching or experience of older people, such as parents or teachers. What are some examples of these experiences? **(going through a war or depression)**

4. What are some values that may be formed from specific teachings? **(religious beliefs, ways to organize and run a house, prejudices towards specific groups of people, etc.)**

5. What are other sources of information that might help someone form values? **(movies, books, newspaper accounts of events, etc.)**

## Extension Activities:

1. Have students look for examples of tragedies (floods, fires) and victories (sports events, Olympics, human interest stories) in the newspaper or magazines. What values are displayed in these? Look/listen for quotes from people in these situations.

2. Show a movie or video to students in which a specific value is promoted. (For example, *Brian's Song* shows great friendship, *Lean on Me* promotes educational excellence.) Discuss how the characters came to cherish the values promoted.

## Evaluation:

Write a paragraph telling about an event in your life that helped shape a value for you.

## Teacher Notes:

_____

_____

_____

_____

_____

_____

# Forming Values

**Directions:** Read each example below. Why do you think the person in each example holds that particular value?

1. Mrs. Kinsey had three children. After her youngest child was killed in a car accident, she became very protective of the remaining two. Not a day goes by that she doesn't involve herself with the children.

   Value: _____ Why: _____

2. Mark began running track when he was in elementary school. It was not long before he began winning events and competing in state meets. Now Mark runs every single day – either jogging outside in good weather or inside on the indoor track at the high school. He is determined to break the record that he set last year.

   Value: _____ Why: _____

3. Carol moved to a new city with her parents. She didn't know anyone and felt quite lost. She was befriended by an outgoing, popular girl – Jayne. Jayne began saving a place for Carol at the lunch table, riding to school with her, and finding activities that Carol could join to get to know people. Carol is thrilled that Jayne has been so kind to her.

   Value: _____ Why: _____

4. Yosely was a student at an inner city school. Guns and violence were a way of life for him. When his mother moved the family to another city to live with relatives, Yosely attended a school that was small, quiet, and safe. Yosely is happy to go to school now.

   Value: _____ Why: _____

5. Tomas had surgery on his leg to remove a bone growth. For six weeks he had to live with a scratchy, cumbersome cast on his leg. He couldn't move around easily and was tired of feeling so helpless and restrained. When the cast was finally taken off, Tomas wanted to walk everywhere.

   Value: _____ Why: _____

6. Sandy wanted to go to college to become a nurse. She didn't have a lot of money, but she worked two part-time jobs at night after high school. She was awarded a scholarship from her high school to attend the nursing program. She was ecstatic!

   Value: _____ Why: _____

# VI-4 Values in Action

**Objective:** The student will identify what value(s) is/are demonstrated by deciding on a course of action in a given situation.

**Comments:**

It's hard to know exactly what you would do in a hypothetical situation. However, thinking ahead of time of what you wish you would do is often quite revealing in itself. In this lesson, students are to decide what they think they would do in hypothetical situations and tell what value they are demonstrating.

**Introductory Activities:**

a. What person do you think of when you hear the word "honesty"? Why?

b. What person do you think of when you hear the word "intelligent"? Why?

c. What person do you think of when you hear the word "fairness"? Why?

**Activity:**

Have students read the situations on the worksheet "Values in Action" and come up with a response as to what they think they would do. They should also try to decide what value they would be demonstrating by their actions.

> **Discussion:** Have students share their ideas about the situations on the worksheet. Have other students in the class try to decide what values are demonstrated. Do they agree with what the student selected as the value?
>
> 1. Are you the kind of person who can decide quickly what you will do in a situation or do you need time to think?
>
> 2. Do you think if you are sure of your values, it would make decisions very clear-cut for you? Are most situations black and white? **(probably not – you must always consider the details involved)**
>
> 3. Who is a person whom you greatly admire because of his or her values? What are those values?
>
> 4. Even if you don't particularly care for a person because of his or her personality or other characteristics, do you find that you can admire the values he or she has? Give examples.

**Extension Activities:**

1. Have students watch the nightly news on television (or tape it and play it for the class as a group project). What values in action are evident in the broadcast?

2. Have students make a conscious effort to observe themselves displaying their values in day-to-day life. Have them record instances in which they reflect their values at home, school, work, and with friends.

**Evaluation:**

Choose one of the following values:

> friendship          achievement          justice          peace

Write a paragraph describing how you have incorporated that value into a recent situation in which you were involved. Provide the details and outcome of the situation.

# Values in Action

**Directions:** What would you do in these situations? What value(s) would you be demonstrating by what you do?

1. You are walking downtown when a man who appears to be homeless comes up to you and asks for a dollar. Before you can even answer, another man interrupts and says, "Don't give him any money; tell him to get a job." What will you do?

   Value:_____

   _____

2. Your house is on fire and you have time to run in for only one trip. If you turn right, you can get to your bedroom where your special possessions are. If you turn left, you can get to your workroom where all of your school projects are. What are you going to get?

   Value:_____

   _____

3. You notice a neighborhood bully picking on a smaller boy from your class. You don't really know or like the small boy, but it annoys you that the larger boy thinks he can act like that. Are you going to do anything? What?

   Value:_____

   _____

4. Your friends want you to join them in breaking into a house and looking for money and valuables. You are running short on cash and would like to have some to buy your mother a nice gift for her birthday. Still, you aren't sure you want to be involved in a robbery, even if it seems safe. What will you do?

   Value:_____

   _____

5. Your father wants you to work around the house this weekend. You would rather go out on a date with a new person you are interested in. Your father is counting on you. Your new friend is waiting for your answer. What will you do?

   Value:_____

   _____

# VI-5 Smoking – Is It for Me?

**Objective:** The student will identify several reasons why people choose to smoke or not smoke.

**Comments:**

By this age, many students are probably already smoking and are tired of listening to adults lecture them about the dangers of this habit. There are lots of reasons why smoking is unhealthy. On the other hand, the decision to smoke or refrain from smoking is tied into factors such as peer pressure, parents' attitudes about smoking, desire to appear "cool" or mature, etc. At this point, students have probably already made up their minds. If we can educate them as to the facts about smoking, perhaps some of them will make informed decisions about smoking.

**Introductory Activities:**

Have students complete a secret survey by indicating: 1. if they consider themselves to be smokers; 2. if one or both of their parents smoke; and 3. if they know of someone who wishes he or she could quit smoking but is having difficulty.

**Activity:**

On the worksheet "Smoking – Is It for Me?," students are to read the situations that involve smokers/non-smokers and indicate the essence of the situation.

**Answers:** *(examples)* **1.** enjoys smoking; **2.** had experience with father's death from cancer; **3.** smell is offensive; **4.** wants to appear "cool"; **5.** image - wants to appear older; **6.** probably addicted; **7.** has health problems; **8.** smokes from nervous tension

**Discussion:** Students probably have some personal anecdotes either pro or con regarding smoking. Allow them equal time to express their opinions, but feel free to question the basis of their decisions.

1. If you smoke now, do you think you will still be smoking in ten years? Why or why not?

2. Do you believe there are serious dangers associated with smoking?

3. Does knowing the facts about the dangers of smoking affect your decision to smoke or not to smoke?

4. If parents smoke, do you think that would increase the chances of the children in the family smoking? Why?

5. What experiences do you know of people who have tried to quit smoking? What success stories are you aware of?

6. About what percentage of the people you hang around with would you classify as smokers?

7. About what percentage of people who are smokers do you think would like to quit?

**Extension Activities:**

1. Assign students the task of finding out recent facts and statistics about smoking. What diseases are associated with smoking? How is nicotine addictive?

2. Have students take a pro/con stance as to whether the government should regulate smoking and the rights of smokers.

3. Have students calculate how much money would be spent on cigarettes if a person smoked two packs a day for one year.

4. Cigarette smoking is associated with at least 85 percent of all cases of lung cancer. It is also a leading cause of heart disease. Obtain information from your local heart association or cancer centers about smoking. Get the facts.

5. Have students research the different ways and effects of quitting smoking (hypnosis, behavior modification, etc.). What results and conclusions can they reach?

6. Collect different forms of advertising for cigarette ads. What is the point of each? To whom does each appeal? How effective is it?

7. What brand(s) of cigarettes are popular among students? Research the amount of tar and nicotine in some popular brands. What exactly is being taken into the body?

**Evaluation:**

a. List at least three reasons why people choose to smoke.

b. List at least three reasons why people choose not to smoke.

**Teacher Notes:**

_____

_____

_____

_____

_____

_____

Name _____     Date _____

# Smoking – Is It for Me?

**Directions:** What reasons do these people give for smoking or not smoking? Write your answer on the lines.

1. I've been smoking for over 30 years and I feel fine. I have no reason to give up smoking. I enjoy it.

_____

2. I've just spent five years watching my father die from lung cancer. There's no way I will ever smoke. He smoked, but I won't.

_____

3.  Pewwww! Open the window!

_____

4. Hey, I'm cool. See those guys looking at me?

_____

5.  You're kidding – you're not 18? Smoking makes you look so much older!

_____

6. I must have another cigarette. I'll quit tomorrow. Where are my cigarettes?

_____

7. (Cough! Cough! Cough!!)

_____

8.  I'm so nervous! What if I don't get the job?

_____

# VI-6 Marijuana and Other Drugs

**Objective:** The student will be able to give factual information about specific drugs.

**Comments:**

As with smoking, the choice to smoke marijuana and do other drugs is one that may already be made on the part of the student. Peer pressure, availability, lack of thought, and other facts play a part in this decision. There are many programs available to fight drug abuse. Hopefully, your school and community are aware of the problem and are taking steps to combat this widespread problem. In this lesson, students are given factual information about some commonly abused drugs.

**Introductory Activities:**

a. On a scale of 1 to 10 (with 10 the most severe), have students rate the drug problem as they see it in their school.

b. On a scale of 1 to 10, have students rate the drug problem as they think the adults (parents, teachers, school administrators, police) in the community would perceive it.

c. Have students volunteer to explain any discrepancy between (a) and (b).

**Activity:**

Students are given on the worksheet "Marijuana and Other Drugs" a short paragraph to read about several commonly abused drugs. Questions about them are contained in the discussion below.

**Discussion:** Some students may not want to reveal their thoughts about drug usage, particularly if they are known to be users in their crowd. Encourage them to at least answer the factual questions.

1. How would you answer people who say that smoking marijuana is no more harmful than smoking cigarettes? **(it contains more cancer-causing agents than cigarettes)**

2. The marijuana produced today is from 5 to 20 times stronger than that from a decade ago. How would you answer people who argue that they used marijuana and it never hurt them any? **(they probably had a less-potent product)**

3. Cocaine is sometimes promoted as a recreational drug, often used by yuppies for fun. What are some of the dangers of using cocaine? **(damage to the membrane of the nose, disruption of the heart and respiratory functions)**

4. What is the problem with unsterile equipment associated with drug use? **(it can be a way to get AIDS or other diseases)**

5. How can unborn children be victims of drug abuse? **(pregnant women can have premature or addicted children)**

6. What is an example of an inhalant? **(aerosol spray cans, paint cans, containers of cleaning fluid, etc.)**

7. What are some immediate effects of inhaling vapors? **(nausea, sneezing, nosebleeds, etc.)**

8. What are hallucinations? **(perceptions of an object or event that does not really exist, usually due to drugs)**

9. Have you heard of anyone having "flashbacks" due to previous drug use?

10. Many of these drugs have legitimate medical uses. Can you think of any? **(pain control, antidepressant uses, diet control, etc.)**

11. How can being involved with drugs negatively affect your performance in school or at work? **(memory loss, attitude, depression, etc.)**

**Extension Activities:**

1. Interview a social worker in a drug treatment center. Listen to anecdotes of people whose lives have been affected by being controlled by drug abuse.

2. Research the drug problem in your community. What steps are being taken to recognize and prevent this situation?

3. What educational programs are in the schools at the elementary, middle school, and high school level? How effective are they?

4. Have students research specific drugs. Find out the causes, effects, and problems associated with each.

5. Have students design a puppet show to present to younger children about alternatives to drug use.

6. Have students research the price of drug abuse in personal pain, business loss, affects on the family, courts, hospitals, and social agencies.

7. Find out the community penalties for possession of controlled substances. If possible, talk to a police officer involved with this aspect of drugs in your community. Do you think the penalties are severe enough?

8. What drug rehabilitation programs are available in your community? Contact your local mental health agency or hospital to get more information.

**Evaluation:**

a. List at least three drugs that are commonly abused.

b. For each drug in (a), describe the possible effects.

# Marijuana and Other Drugs

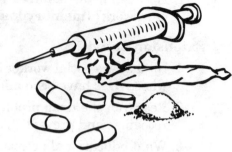

**Directions:** Below is information about some specific drugs and the effects they have. Read each paragraph carefully and be prepared to answer questions about them.

## 1. Cannabis (*generic name*: marijuana)

The use of cannabis may affect your short-term memory and ability to understand things. It can reduce your ability to perform tasks requiring concentration, such as driving a car. It is damaging to the lungs and contains more cancer-causing agents than cigarettes.

## 2. Cocaine

Cocaine is usually sold as a white powder that is inhaled through the nasal passages, although it can be injected or smoked. It stimulates the central nervous system which is evidenced by dilated pupils; and raised blood pressure, heart rate, respiratory rate, and body temperature. Chronic use can cause damage to the mucous membrane of the nose. If injected with unsterile equipment, the user can get AIDS and other diseases. The use of cocaine can cause death by disrupting the brain's control of the heart and respiration.

## 3. Narcotics (heroin, codeine, morphine, opium, etc.)

These drugs produce a feeling of euphoria followed by drowsiness, nausea, and vomiting. An overdose can affect breathing and lead to convulsions, coma, and possibly death. Tolerance develops rapidly. Addiction in pregnant women can lead to premature, stillborn, or addicted children.

## 4. Inhalants (nitrous oxide, hydrocarbons, etc.)

When vapors are inhaled, the immediate effects can include nausea, sneezing, nosebleeds, and lack of coordination. They can also decrease heart and respiratory rates. Long-term use may result in disorientation, violent behavior, brain hemorrhage, or death. Repeated sniffing can permanently damage the nervous system.

## 5. Hallucinogens (LSD, PCP, etc.)

LSD can produce illusions and hallucinations. These sensations and feelings can change rapidly and the user may experience panic, confusion, and loss of control. Chronic users of PCP report memory problems, speech difficulties, and mood disorders including depression, anxiety, and violent behavior.

# VI-7 Teens and Drinking

**Objective:** The student will be familiar with recent statistics involving attitudes of teens toward drinking.

**Comments:**

This lesson is adapted from a survey published in *USA Weekend* from August 1994. Teenagers wrote in to reveal their thoughts and experiences with alcohol. While it is unscientific, the opinions are probably in line with many communities around the country. Use this information to find out about your students' perceptions and experiences with alcohol.

**Introductory Activities:**

   a. Ask students to indicate how many of them feel there is a problem with drinking or alcohol among teens in the community.

   b. Ask students to indicate whether they think *drugs* or *alcohol* is a larger problem.

**Activity:**

Students are to fill in missing information about teens and alcohol. Again, this is adapted from an unscientific survey about the opinions and experiences of teenagers with drinking. Without giving students any additional information, have them complete the worksheet "Teens and Drinking." Then compare the answers with the ones from the teens on the survey.

   **Materials:** pen or pencil, copy of the survey (see extension activities)

   **Answers: 1.** private homes; **2.** 21; **3.** 60%; **4.** it doesn't interest them; **5.** recreational (includes to get drunk, celebrate, enjoy the taste, relax, etc.); **6.** they are smaller, takes less alcohol to become drunk, takes longer for alcohol to leave their system because of lower amount of the enzyme that breaks down alcohol; **7.** eaten, food; **8.** 1.5, 5, 12; **9.** beer; **10.** .06; .04; **11.** drinking and driving; **12.** parents

   **Discussion:** Go over the students' ideas on the worksheet and then compare them to the results on the survey. Are they close?

1. What is good about students drinking in private homes? **(might be supervised, might not drive)**

2. What are ways that teenagers can get alcohol? **(parents, friends, etc.)**

3. How is peer pressure a factor in drinking?

4. How is boredom a factor in drinking?

5. How is rebellion a factor in drinking?

6. If parents drink, do you think their children are more likely to drink? Are they likely to have easier access to alcohol?

7. Children of alcoholic parents have a greater likelihood of becoming alcoholics themselves. How might this affect a teenager? **(be conscious of it, don't use your parents as role models)**

8. Have you or someone you know had a bad experience involving alcohol? How did it turn out?

9. Do you think most parents know that their children drink? Do they care?

10. What stand does your school take on teenage drinking? Is there a chapter of Students Against Drunk Driving (SADD) in your school?

11. Should athletes be required to sign a pledge against drinking? Why or why not?

## Extension Activities:

1. Reprints of the survey and the results can be obtained from Avery Business Services, 39 Fort Point Street, East Norwalk, CT 06855. One copy is $1.60. Find out more about what the teens reported.

2. Have students make a list (or poster) of alternatives to drinking. Where are places they can go to, activities they can participate in? How can they better spend their time?

3. Have a representative from AA (Alcoholics Anonymous) or Alateen talk to your class. What are some of the devastating effects of being an alcoholic or having alcoholics in the family?

## Evaluation:

Write a paragraph explaining your opinion on the use of alcohol among teenagers. Does your opinion reflect the majority of the students at your school?

## Teacher Notes:

_____

_____

_____

_____

_____

_____

# Teens and Drinking

**Directions:** See how much you know about teens and alcohol. Fill in each blank with what you think is the correct answer. This activity is taken from a survey from *USA Weekend*, August 1994.

**1.** The most common place for teenagers to drink is

_____.

**2.** The legal age to buy or possess alcohol is _____ across the nation.

**3.** Students in high school estimate that _____ percent of their classmates drink.

**4.** The reasons that 65% of the non-drinkers give for not drinking is

_____.

**5.** Teens who drink (94% of those on the survey) gave this as a reason:

_____.

**6.** Females get drunk faster than males because _____

_____.

**7.** How fast alcohol is absorbed into the blood depends on what you've _____lately.

The less _____, the faster you get drunk.

**8.** A "drink" consists of: _____ oz. of liquor, _____ oz. of wine, or _____ oz. of beer.

**9.** The alcoholic beverage that teenagers drink most often is _____ .

**10.** In most states, a blood-alcohol level of .10 is considered legally drunk. If you have had two

drinks in two hours, you're at _____ if you weigh 120 pounds, or _____ if you weigh 180 pounds.

**11.** The leading cause of death for teens is _____ .

**12.** The single most important factor in reducing alcohol abuse is _____ .

# VI-8 Changing Your Appearance

**Objective:** The students will state at least three to five ways that a person could make changes in his or her appearance.

**Comments:**

Perhaps we all dream of waking up one morning and being that beautiful or handsome creature to whom everyone is attracted. We are often our own worst critics when it comes to judging our appearance. We might feel we are too tall, too fat, not pretty enough, etc. While physical appearance is only one dimension (and perhaps not even that important!), there are some things that can be changed to improve one's physical appearance. In this lesson, some of those changes are investigated.

**Introductory Activities:**

   a. Have students raise their hands if they have ever used a tanning booth.

   b. Have students raise their hands if they have ever experimented with hair color.

   c. Have students raise their hands if they are wearing contact lenses.

   d. Have students raise their hands if they are wearing braces.

**Activity:**

Several ways to change one's physical appearance are listed on the worksheet "Changing Your Appearance." Students are to match the change desired with a way that could promote or make that change. Be sure students understand that these are not desirable changes for everyone; they are merely suggestions that one might investigate if they wanted to make physical changes.

**Answers: 1.** c; **2.** h; **3.** g; **4.** l; **5.** e; **6.** a; **7.** k; **8.** d; **9.** i; **10.** b; **11.** j; **12.** f

**Discussion:** Avoid focusing on students who may have particular problems with their physical appearance, e.g., excessive acne, obesity, etc. Try to keep things on general terms.

1. Do you think men or women are more conscious of how they look and how to improve their looks?

2. What are some ways that are different for men vs. women?

3. If someone really wanted to change his or her appearance, what might stop him or her? **(money to visit a doctor or get a fashionable hair style, not knowing how to go about starting an exercise program, etc.)**

4. What are some physical problems that are common to most students? **(probably pimples, improper eating habits, need for straightening teeth, etc.)**

5. If someone didn't have a lot of money, how could he or she still be fashionable? **(do some of the hair styling at home or with friends, buy fewer but better clothes, etc.)**

6. Is it important for girls to wear a lot of makeup? **(depends on the individual case – some look better without a lot on)**

**Extension Activities:**

1. Invite a beauty specialist to come to the school to do a face/hair makeover on some volunteers. Have him or her point out techniques for enhancing one's best features to look good.

2. Have students find out the cost (and duration) of basic orthodontic work.

3. Contact lenses are now quite affordable. Have students contact a local eye care specialist to find out the cost of getting contacts.

4. Have students take a pro/con view of plastic surgery procedures. What are the costs, benefits, risks, results?

5. Have students research the effects of visiting a tanning booth.

6. Have some ambitious students put together a fashion show for both boys and girls. What "look" is popular right now? Recruit a few "models" to demonstrate good fashion looks. Have fun!

**Evaluation:**

a. List three to five physical changes that a person could make in his or her appearance.

b. Write a paragraph explaining what you like best about your appearance and what you would change if you could (or what you are working on changing).

**Teacher Notes:**

_____

_____

_____

_____

_____

_____

Name _____ Date _____

# Changing Your Appearance

**Directions:** Match the item on the left that is a condition you would like to change with the idea on the right that shows a way to make that change.

BEFORE    AFTER

_____ 1. You want your hair to be shorter.

_____ 2. You want your hair to look blonder and curlier.

_____ 3. You hate wearing glasses.

_____ 4. Your striped shirts make you look heavy.

_____ 5. You are heavy!

_____ 6. Your teeth are crooked.

_____ 7. Your skin is very pale.

_____ 8. You have pimples all over your face.

_____ 9. Your eyebrows are very bushy.

_____ 10. Your skin is blotchy.

_____ 11. You are very thin and have no muscle tone.

_____ 12. People tell you that you dress very sloppily.

**a.** braces or other orthodontic appliance

**b.** use facial makeup to even out the color of your face

**c.** get a haircut

**d.** use acne medication and/or visit a dermatologist

**e.** watch what you eat, try to lose weight carefully

**f.** update your wardrobe by buying some new clothes; get advice from salesperson

**g.** try some contact lenses

**h.** try some hair coloring, get a perm

**i.** thin your eyebrows with a tweezer

**j.** start an exercise program to build up some muscle

**k.** get outside in the sun a little more

**l.** wear clothes that are more flattering to your body type

# VI-9 Exercise

**Objective:** The student will list at least three forms of exercise that are interesting to him or her.

**Comments:**

It's all too easy to adapt to a sedentary lifestyle – watching TV, movies, playing videogames, etc. Physical fitness is a way for anyone to release tension, get into shape, feel better, and find ways to have a good time with others. In this lesson, students are to think of and participate in some form of exercise.

**Introductory Activities:**

a. Have students raise their hands if they have participated in an organized sport within the last six months.

b. Have students volunteer to tell about their favorite form of exercise.

**Activity:**

Students are to choose one form of exercise (suggestions are on the worksheet "Exercise"; others can be added) and keep track of their participation for at least two weeks. You can make modifications as necessary. Some students may choose to begin walking; others may already be involved in organized team sports; still others may resist any form of exercise and need to be "pushed" a little. Encourage students to choose something they really are interested in doing.

**Materials:** pen or pencil, stopwatch or watch with second hand (to keep track of heart rate)

**Discussion:** After students have completed the activity, discuss their results.

1. Why did you choose the form of exercise that you did?

2. Do you enjoy exercising with someone else or do you prefer working on your own?

3. Was it difficult to find goals to set for yourself?

4. What did you find that you enjoyed about participating in your form of exercise?

5. Was it hard to keep up with the pace you set for yourself (e.g., daily workouts, running a mile, etc.)?

6. What type of exercise programs are provided at school?

7. What are some community fitness programs that are available to most people?

**Extension Activities:**

1. Send away for guidelines from the President's Council on Physical Fitness. What should each age group be able to accomplish?

2. Inspire students by watching videotapes of some recent Olympic events.

3. Find and study some interviews with athletes. To what do they attribute their success? How much time is spent in physical conditioning and training?

**Evaluation:**

a. List three forms of exercise in which you have been involved or are interested.

b. For each form of exercise listed in (a), write a short paragraph describing the exercise, mentioning the benefits, equipment (if any) needed, and why it interests you.

Name _____ Date_____

# Exercise

**Directions:** Below is a list of some forms of exercise in which you might be interested. Select at least one that you can work on and keep track of your involvement and progress for at least two weeks.

jogging                walking                bicycling
hiking                 body building          gymnastics
aerobics               health-spa equipment   weight-lifting
swimming

| Date/Date | Exercise | Number of Minutes | Measure of Progress (weight, heart rate, respiration, etc.) |
|-----------|----------|-------------------|-------------------------------------------------------------|
|           |          |                   |                                                             |
|           |          |                   |                                                             |
|           |          |                   |                                                             |
|           |          |                   |                                                             |
|           |          |                   |                                                             |
|           |          |                   |                                                             |
|           |          |                   |                                                             |
|           |          |                   |                                                             |

# VI-10 Hygiene

**Objective:** The student will define hygiene and list at least three ways good hygiene can be obtained.

**Comments:**

Hygiene is more than simply being clean; it also involves general maintenance of good health. This includes nutrition, exercise, and taking care of oneself. Maintaining good hygiene is important not only to look good and feel good for yourself, but to make a good impression on others. In this lesson, students are to state reasons why good hygiene is important in given examples.

**Introductory Activities:**

a. Define *hygiene.* **(the state of maintaining good personal health, including nutrition, exercise, and regular physical and dental check-ups)**

b. Ask students to list ways that people can achieve good hygiene.

**Activity:**

Students are to read the examples on the worksheet "Hygiene" and then decide why good hygiene is important in each case. They are to identify the problem and offer a solution.

**Answers:** *(examples)* **1.** he probably smells bad and is dirty/plan to apply for the job at a time when he appears better; **2.** her hands may be dirty/wash hands before preparing food; **3.** doesn't take care of his teeth/make a dentist appointment; **4.** smoking may offend others/be aware of when other people will be around, wash clothes and hair often; **5.** does not eat balanced meals/be more conscious of eating habits

**Discussion:** Listen to students' ideas for various solutions to the problems.

1. Why do you think having good hygiene makes a better impression upon potential employers? **(you are more attractive, it's important especially if you deal directly with customers)**

2. Why is it important to have clean hands when you're working around food? **(don't want to transfer germs to others)**

3. What are some consequences of never going to the dentist? **(problems with teeth and gums, may lose your teeth to decay, bad breath, etc.)**

4. How do you feel about people who smell bad because of smoke? Is it anyone's business besides their own? **(this should open up a lively discussion of personal rights! Let students express their opinions)**

5. If someone works around other people and there are restrictions against smoking, what could that person do as an alternative? **(chew gum, limit smoking to before and after work or in designated places, etc.)**

6. What is wrong with Ben's meals? **(only consists of chocolate)**

7. How do you know that Ben's diet is not good for him? **(he is gaining weight, lacks energy)**

8. How does having good hygiene affect the individual person? **(lots of positive benefits – feel better, look better)**

9. How does having good hygiene affect people around you? **(makes you more desirable to be around)**

**Extension Activities:**

1. Have students review their day. What specific instances of practicing good hygiene come to mind?

2. Look for signs and other examples of good hygiene practices being promoted in work or school places. For example, "NO SMOKING" signs, signs that employees must wash their hands, etc.

**Evaluation:**

a. Define *hygiene*.

b. List three examples of practicing good hygiene.

**Teacher Notes:**

_____

_____

_____

_____

_____

_____

# Hygiene

**Directions:** Read each short story below in which each person has a problem with some aspect of hygiene. Then write why good hygiene is important in each case and what each person should do.

1. Robbie is applying for a job at a store where he will check out customers and help bag their purchases. Before applying for the job, Robbie played basketball with some friends for an hour, helped a friend change the oil on his car, and then realized he didn't have time to take a shower.

   **Problem (Why?):** _____

   **Solution:** _____

2. Angela loves to cook and often has friends come over to eat with her. Sometimes, though, she doesn't bother to wash her hands before preparing the food.

   **Problem (Why?):** _____

   **Solution:** _____

3. Ray always leaves the house in a rush to get to school each day. He has time to grab a bowl of cereal or some toast, but he doesn't seem to have time to brush his teeth or floss. The right side of his jaw hurts and he is afraid to go to the dentist – he might have to have some painful dental work done!

   **Problem (Why?):** _____

   **Solution:** _____

4. JoAnn smokes as often as she can. People at work are starting to complain about the smell of smoke on her hair, clothes, and breath. Whenever she walks into a room, people know that JoAnn is there.

   **Problem (Why?):** _____

   **Solution:** _____

5. Ben eats chocolate for breakfast, chocolate for lunch, and chocolate for dinner. Sometimes he complains of not having a lot of energy and of not being hungry for more nutritious foods. He is starting to gain weight as well.

   **Problem (Why?):** _____

   **Solution:** _____

# VI-11 Personal Check-Up

**Objective:** The student will complete a personal survey that inventories his or her personal hygiene practices.

## Comments:

It is important for students to realize they must take some action themselves to maintain good health. This involves going to the doctor (when necessary), visiting the dentist, getting sufficient exercise and sleep, and any other practices that help keep them healthy. In this lesson, students will complete a personal survey.

## Introductory Activities:

a. Have students raise their hands if they have been to the dentist in the last year.

b. Have students raise their hands if they have had their vision checked in the last year.

c. Have students raise their hands if they know their height and weight.

d. Have students raise their hands if they have been to the doctor for a routine check-up in the past year.

## Activity:

Students are to complete a survey on the worksheet "Personal Check-Up" requesting personal information about their hygiene practices. Since this is of a personal nature, inform students that it is for their own benefit but you expect them to complete it honestly.

**Discussion:** Inform students that they don't need to put down exact dates of their last appointments, but that the survey is simply to have them think about some good health practices and the last time they paid attention to them.

1. If someone is healthy and strong, is it still necessary to eat right, get sleep, and visit the dentist? (**yes – age will catch up with them, prevention is important**)

2. Why is it important to go to the dentist regularly? (**this can prevent tooth decay**)

3. Why is it important to have your vision checked periodically, especially while you are still in school? (**your vision can still change, if you need glasses or other corrections this can help you while in school and need to see to read**)

4. What forms of exercise are promoted in school? (**physical education, intramural activities, sports**)

5. How much responsibility do you take for what you eat? Is most of what you eat determined by your parents or the school?

6. Why is a regular amount of sleep important? (**helps you study better, stay alert**)

7. What are some other items you would add to your own checklist for maintaining good hygiene?

**Extension Activities:**

1. Have students set personal hygienic goals for themselves – for example, make that needed dental appointment, get a change in hair style, begin exercising, etc.

2. Have students record their sleeping habits (hours, length, quality of sleep) for a week or two. When sleeping is regular, do they feel more refreshed? What prevents them from getting to sleep at regular times?

**Evaluation:**

a. List at least three items you think are important for good personal hygiene.

b. List at least one thing you could do to improve your personal hygiene in the next month.

**Teacher Notes:**

_____

_____

_____

_____

_____

# Personal Check-Up

**Directions:** How often do you get a personal check-up? Answer the following questions as honestly as you can.

## Cleanliness

1. How often do you take a bath or shower?

   _____

2. How often do you wash your hair? _____

3. How often do you cut your fingernails and toenails? _____

## Dental Care

4. How often do you brush your teeth?_____

5. How often do you floss? _____

6. How often do you visit your dentist for cleaning or other dental work? _____

## Medical Care

7. When was the last time you had your vision checked? _____

8. When was your last physical check-up? _____

9. Do you have any physical condition that should be followed by a medical doctor?_____

10. Do you take all required medicines correctly? _____

## Exercise

11. Do you exercise regularly? _____

    What activities do you participate in? _____

12. Are you overweight or underweight? _____

## Nutrition

13. How many of your meals are probably balanced or nutritious? _____

14. Do you eat a lot of snacks, chocolates, or food that have little nutritional value?_____

15. Do you eat good, nutritious meals regularly? _____

## Rest

16. How many hours of sleep do you normally get each night? _____

17. Do you sleep well or do you have trouble getting to sleep, waking up, etc.?

    _____

18. Do you take any medication to help you get to sleep? _____

19. Is your sleeping schedule fairly regular? _____

## Other

20. How often do you get your hair cut (or styled)?_____

21. How often do you buy new clothes? _____

22. Do you feel you don't have enough time to fit everything into your schedule?

    _____

# VI-12 Being Sexually Active

**Objective:** The student will identify several common arguments for and against being sexually active as teens.

**Comments:**

Many teens see nothing wrong with being sexually active. However, with the onset of sexually-transmitted diseases, including AIDS, teens are more cautious and hopefully more informed than those from even a decade ago. Teens who are proud of their virginity and stand against the pressure of having sex when they don't really want to are making the news. Still, there are teens who will make the choice to become sexually active, even if it is not in their best interests. In this lesson, reasons that people give for and against being sexually active as teens are examined.

**Introductory Activities:**

Have students make some guesses as to the following information. (This information is taken from the article, "Virgin Cool," *Newsweek,* October 17, 1994.)

a. At what age do you think most boys have their first sexual intercourse? **(16.6)**

b. At what age do you think most girls have their first sexual intercourse? **(17.4)**

c. How many (what percentage) do you think remain virgins throughout their teenage years? **(20%)**

**Activity:**

Students are given a list of comments on the worksheet "Being Sexually Active." They are to circle whether or not they agree with the statement and then add their own comments. Again, due to the private nature of the questions, some students may not wish to volunteer their thoughts.

> **Discussion:** Students may want to talk about their own personal experiences with sex. Depending on your class, either encourage them to speak out or ask them to speak in general terms to avoid embarrassing anyone. Their thoughts are important.

1. How much of a factor is peer pressure in deciding to be sexually active as a teen?

2. Do you think there are either positive or negative feelings among your peers about deciding to be sexually active?

3. What do you think are teens' biggest fears about being sexually active? **(diseases, pregnancy, AIDS, emotional distress, being caught, etc.)**

4. Do you think it would be difficult to say no to a sexual involvement if you really didn't want to become involved?

5. How has the increased incidence of sexually-transmitted diseases and AIDS affected teens' decision to wait to have sex?

**Extension Activities:**

1. Find out what sex education classes are offered in your high school. What information is given about being sexually active? What reasons are given to wait?

2. Have students use teen magazines as resources to compile some information about sexual activity in teens. List some questions to research, such as: what reasons do teens give to wait, how many choose to wait until marriage to have sex, what are some ways to handle problem situations and still remain "cool."

3. Students may be embarrassed or shy about asking questions of a sexual nature. Give students the opportunity to privately write any questions they are concerned about. Try to provide an appropriate time to discuss their concerns.

## Evaluation:

a. List at least two reasons why some teens believe that being sexually active is okay.

b. List at least two reasons why some teens believe it is not in their best interests to be sexually active now.

c. Write a paragraph explaining your position on teens and sexual activity. (*Note:* You may wish to make this a non-graded assignment or a private journal entry.)

## Teacher Notes:

_____

_____

_____

_____

_____

_____

# Being Sexually Active

**Directions:** Here are comments that reflect some attitudes of teens about being sexually active. Do you agree or disagree with them? Circle your choice and then add your comments on the back of this sheet.

1. "If our relationship is based totally on sex, there *is* no relationship."  **Agree    Disagree**

2. "If a boy tells me that I have to have sex with him to show him that I love him, it's a signal right there! I will not have anyone put that kind of rule on me!"  **Agree    Disagree**

3. "If you really love someone, like enough to think about marrying him or her someday, sex is okay."  **Agree    Disagree**

4. "Sex is okay as long as you practice 'safe sex.' As long as you use a condom, you'll be okay."  **Agree    Disagree**

5. "There's nothing wrong with virginity."  **Agree    Disagree**

6. "Teenagers today have to think about getting AIDS and HIV. We have to be more responsible than our parents were at our age."  **Agree    Disagree**

7. "Most kids don't have sex until they are about 17. That's old enough to make responsible decisions."  **Agree    Disagree**

8. "After my boyfriend and I had sex, he seemed to lose interest in me. I felt like I had been used. That hurt more than anything else."  **Agree    Disagree**

9. "I know of several kids my age who have already had babies. I don't want to have to deal with that. I want to stay young, stay a kid, and have fun for as long as I can."  **Agree    Disagree**

10. "It's not a big deal to say you chose to abstain from sex. It's becoming more and more accepted. It's a good thing."  **Agree    Disagree**

11. "Having premarital sex is totally against my religion. I just don't believe it is morally right."  **Agree    Disagree**

12. "If it feels good, do it."  **Agree    Disagree**

# VI-13 Healthy Dating

**Objective:** The student will give at least five examples of ways teens can have fun together, primarily in a non-sexual manner.

**Comments:**

Dating is a time for teens to get to know members of the opposite sex. There are many things available for creative teens to do for the purpose of just having fun, being relaxed together without the pressure of long-term commitment, and testing out one's values. In this lesson, students are given suggestions for dates and can come up with their own ideas.

**Introductory Activities:**

    a. Have students indicate by raising hands how many of them have friends who date regularly.

    b. Have students raise their hands to indicate they date regularly.

    c. Have students list several activities that teens in their school or community like to do on dates.

**Activity:**

Students are to read a list of possible activities for dating on the worksheet "Healthy Dating" and to put an X next to those that sound appealing. They can also add their own ideas.

    **Discussion:** Students may insist that some of the ideas are not fun at all. If they think about it, however, there are lots of activities that may not seem fun in themselves, but because of with whom you are doing them. Ask students to include their own ideas.

    1. What, in your opinion, is a good definition of a "date"?

    2. What kinds of activities are provided for dating at your school? church? community center?

    3. Would you ever go out on a date with someone you didn't like because you'd get to go somewhere you wanted to go?

    4. Would you go out on a date with someone whom your friends really didn't like, but who you were interested in getting to know?

    5. What would you do if you were asked out by someone your parents didn't approve of?

    6. Would you go out with someone who was five years older than you? How about five years younger?

    7. Would you go out on a date with someone whom you knew would only be just a friend?

    8. Why is it important to get to know all aspects of a person, especially when you are starting to become seriously interested in that person?

    9. What does it tell you about a person if he or she wants to include family members in your activities?

    10. What does it tell you about a person if he or she likes to try new things?

    11. What does it tell you about a person if he or she is kind to animals?

12. What does it tell you about a person if he or she doesn't like to listen to your side of the story?

13. What does it tell you about a person if he or she thinks everyone else is a bad driver, is stupid, doesn't know what's going on, etc.?

14. Do you think it's okay to date more than one person at a time?

**Extension Activities:**

1. Have students figure out the average cost of a date, including factors such as: meals, activity, night of the week, transportation, etc.

2. Have students write a paragraph describing a "dream date." Have them stop to consider what they really think is important. Is it where they go? How much money is spent? Who they are with?

**Evaluation:**

a. List at least five activities that would be appealing to you on a date.

b. List at least five qualities that you would look for in someone you were interested in dating.

**Teacher Notes:**

_____

_____

_____

_____

_____

_____

# Healthy Dating

**Directions:** There are a lot of things to do with someone whose company you enjoy. Put an X next to the ideas on the list below that sound appealing to you.

_____ 1. join a bowling league

_____ 2. learn to line dance

_____ 3. learn to play poker

_____ 4. ride every roller coaster in an amusement park

_____ 5. go horseback riding

_____ 6. ride bikes through the parks

_____ 7. volunteer to work at a nursing home together

_____ 8. go to your favorite ice cream store and resolve to try every single flavor (a different one with each visit)

_____ 9. see a movie with subtitles

_____ 10. include his or her little sister while you go out

_____ 11. help set up a lemonade stand to raise money for charity

_____ 12. walk through the cow barn at the 4-H fair

_____ 13. wash his or her father's car

_____ 14. build a birdhouse together

_____ 15. join a summer theater group

_____ 16. play board games

_____ 17. take a craft class

_____ 18. learn to cook a gourmet meal and share cleanup chores

_____ 19. give each other lots of "what would you do if…" situations

_____ 20. brush each other's hair with a soft brush

# VI-14 Rate the Date

**Objective:** Given various dating examples, the student will rate each on a scale of 1 to 10 and give reasons for his or her rating.

## Comments:

We have probably all had dating disasters that now appear humorous (when you can look back on it). On the other hand, don't you remember a few times when you remember a moment you wish you could relive again and again? Some students may not actually be dating, but they can still identify good and bad aspects of going on a date. In this lesson, they are to read some episodes of students on dates and then rate them according to a scale.

## Introductory Activities:

    a. Ask students to volunteer to describe the most awful dating experience they had. (Encourage humor!)

    b. Ask students to tell about a particularly fun or interesting date they had.

## Activity:

Students are to read the anecdotes of seven different dates and then score them (1 to 10, 1 = disaster, 10 = wonderful) on the worksheet "Rate the Date." They will discuss their rating scales.

    1. In example 1, what factors were not important to the girl on this date? **(rain, cold)**

    2. What factors were important to her? **(considerate date)**

    3. In example 2, what did Jennifer do that the boy found annoying? **(ignored him)**

    4. In example 3, what was important to the girl? **(seeing the movie)** What did she find irritating? **(the boy's behavior)**

    5. In example 4, why did Amy surprise the boy? **(she turned out to be a lot of fun)**

    6. Did you rate the date pretty high in example 5? Why? **(probably – both people had a good time)**

    7. Do you think Janine was inconsiderate in example 6? Do you think the boy will ever ask her out again? **(ordered expensive items, didn't thank him/probably not)**

    8. In example 7, what could have prevented that date from going so bad? **(Jeff could have tried to avoid the fight)**

    9. What factors did you include in your ratings? What did you consider to be important about a good date?

    10. Do you need to spend a lot of money to have a good date?

    11. What do you appreciate from the other person when you go on a date? **(courtesy)**

    12. Would you go out on a "blind date"? What information would you want to know ahead of time?

    13. Do you think girls and boys should split the cost of dating?

**Extension Activities:**

1. Set up a "Dating Game" in which students ask questions of each other, but do not know to whom they are talking. (You could use a room divider, having students answer in writing, etc.) Students might find it interesting to determine what girls/boys find appealing about them.

2. Have students conduct an informal survey or poll asking ten friends or classmates to tell the best thing/worst thing they had happen to them while on a date. Information should remain confidential, of course, and be used simply for fun.

**Evaluation:**

Rate the following date. Include what factors you used to determine your rating.

"I was really excited about going on my first date with Bill – on a ride in his brother's four-seater airplane. I had never been in an airplane, so I was really excited. What I didn't know was that I would get so airsick I spent the whole time vomiting into a little bag. I was so embarrassed, but I remembered to thank Bill and his brother and told them that I would always remember this very memorable experience. Bill couldn't stop laughing. He said I was a great sport and that our next date would be on the ground."

# Rate the Date

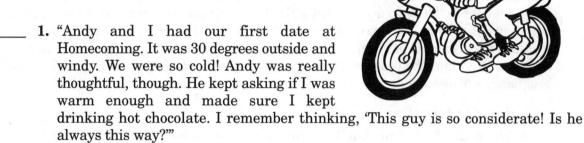

**Directions:** Rate each date described below on a scale of 1 to 10, with 1 being a disaster and 10 being wonderful. Think about what you are considering to be important!

_____ **1.** "Andy and I had our first date at Homecoming. It was 30 degrees outside and windy. We were so cold! Andy was really thoughtful, though. He kept asking if I was warm enough and made sure I kept drinking hot chocolate. I remember thinking, 'This guy is so considerate! Is he always this way?'"

_____ **2.** "Jennifer and I had been going out casually for awhile, so I felt like I knew her pretty well. But one night we double-dated with her best friend and her boyfriend. Jennifer and the girlfriend talked and laughed with each other the whole night. The other guy and I felt like we weren't even there! They kept talking about people and things we didn't know anything about."

_____ **3.** "I had been looking forward to going to the movies with Ricardo. I really wanted to see the movie! But all he wanted to do was hang all over me and make out. I couldn't wait until it was over. I went back the next day to see the movie I had missed while I was being pawed."

_____ **4.** "People told me Amy would really be a dud because she's so quiet. I just found myself talking and telling her things about myself that I had never told anyone else. She's such a good listener – I was fascinated just sitting around in the library, talking for hours."

_____ **5.** "Pete and I took off on his motorcycle and went all around the county. It was a blast. We both love to be outdoors and feeling free! We made plans to work on fixing up his car next weekend."

_____ **6.** "I don't think Janine dates very much. When we went out to dinner, she ordered the most expensive items on the menu. I hardly had enough cash to pay for it. Then when it was over, she didn't even thank me."

_____ **7.** "Jeff and I went roller skating at the community rink. Another guy he knew from high school knocked into him, so Jeff shoved him back. One thing led to another until there was a full-fledged fight and the cops came. That date really made an impression on me!"

# VI-15 Teenage Pregnancy

**Objective:** The student will demonstrate knowledge of facts about teenage pregnancy.

**Comments:**

Teenage pregnancy is a by-product of unprotected sexual activity. Sometimes it is seen as a means to an end ("He'll marry me if I'm carrying his child."), fulfillment of an emotional need ("I'll have my own little child to love and need me."), or sometimes as a tragic mistake ("How can I go to college now?"). One must realize that teenage pregnancy includes the father of the child, two sets of parents, many decisions that must be made, and goals that must be readjusted. In this lesson, some aspects of dealing with teenage pregnancy are discussed.

**Introductory Activities:**

    a. Write the first comment that comes to your mind when you hear: teenage pregnancy.

    b. Were your comments positive or negative?

**Activity:**

Students are to read the short story on the worksheet "Teenage Pregnancy" about Paula, a girl who became pregnant in eighth grade. The story is true. In the story, Paula had a miscarriage, which came as a welcome relief to all involved. Discuss aspects of the story and the questions below.

    **Answers:** *(examples)* **1.** not using birth control or perhaps choosing to have sex; **2.** she was very scared; **3.** comforting, sympathetic; **4.** brought them closer; **5.** frightened, relieved; **6.** concerned about her reputation; **7.** no – both too immature

    **Discussion:** You may have students in your class who are pregnant, have been pregnant, or have someone in their family who has been in this situation. Be sensitive to their situations.

1. How does pregnancy put teenage girls at a disadvantage? (**must consider dropping out of school, cost of a baby**)

2. What are some reasons why teenagers might try to get pregnant? (**think it will give them self-esteem, attention from the father, attention from friends, someone to love them, etc.**)

3. How do you think a girl would feel who did not want to become pregnant but does become pregnant? (**discouraged, embarrassed, frightened, panicky, etc.**)

4. How is teenage pregnancy perceived at your school or in your community?

5. What restrictions would being pregnant place on a girl who wanted to stay in school? (**child care, being tired**)

6. If someone did not have a supportive family who would help with the baby, what additional problems would a teenage mother face? (**housing, child care, having to work, dropping out of school, etc.**)

7. What responsibility do you think the father should accept?

8. Birth defects are more likely to occur in very young teenage mothers. How would this make motherhood even more complicated?

9. Teenage marriages have a very high divorce rate. With this in mind, would you suggest the boy and girl get married just because she is pregnant?

10. Two out of three pregnant teenagers drop out of school. How would this complicate a girl's future? (**hard to find a job**)

11. In many states a boy who is 16 can be charged with statutory rape or child molesting if he has intercourse with a girl under 16. This can involve court sentencing and child support, not to mention ill-will between the parties involved. How can this complicate a pregnancy?

## Extension Activities:

1. Have students estimate the cost of having and maintaining a child for one year. (Include cost of food, clothes, medical attention, and child care.)

2. Have students find out about the abortion laws in your state. What is an abortion? How is it performed? How much does it cost?

3. Have students find out about abortion alternatives in your state or community. What resources are available to help with pregnant teenagers who want to give up their babies for adoption?

4. Check with your administrator for permission, and then invite a local medical doctor to talk to your class about the risks of teenage pregnancy, labor and delivery concerns, and responsible sexual behavior. Students may "turn off" lectures from their teachers, but hearing the same information from a medical professional who "has been there" may wake up a few students.

## Evaluation:

How could teen pregnancy affect the following factors:

staying in high school

getting a job

relationship between the father and mother

financial matters

free time

# Teenage Pregnancy

**Directions:** Read the story about Paula. Then answer the questions on the next page.

     Paula was a pretty, lively 15-year-old girl. She and her boyfriend, Todd, had been dating since the beginning of summer. They had been sexually active most of the summer. Neither one used any kind of birth control. Paula had been in a lot of trouble in school, and was in a special class for at-risk kids. She had gotten to be pretty close to her teacher, Mrs. Armstrong. One day Paula came to school acting wild and silly. She made jokes and laughed at everything. Paula and her girlfriend, Alyssa, began writing notes back and forth and laughing hysterically. Finally Mrs. Armstrong called Paula out into the hall to ask her what was wrong. It only took about ten seconds for Paula to burst into tears and sob uncontrollably. She had just done a home pregnancy test that morning which confirmed her fears: she was pregnant. Mrs. Armstrong held Paula in her arms while Paula wailed with grief. Her parents, she feared, would *never* understand. Her dad would kill her and Todd. She'd be kicked out of the house, she'd be out on the streets, she'd have a baby . . . a baby! Mrs. Armstrong drove Paula to her mother's house. It turned out that Paula's mother was quite a bit more understanding than Paula had given her credit for. Soon all three of them were crying, and deciding how to deal with this situation.

     Over the next few days, Paula's mother took a positive stance. She took her daughter to a doctor, who confirmed the pregnancy. They started Paula on prenatal vitamins, talked to Todd and his parents about the situation, and made a major decision: Paula would have the baby and it would stay in the family. Somehow they would work it out. Paula and her mother even went out shopping to buy some baby clothes and a crib. They felt they could handle this situation. Paula even began looking forward to having a baby.

     A few days later, Paula began bleeding. She felt her body cramping and could hardly breathe with the pain. Her mother took her to the hospital. The bleeding continued, as did the pain. She was having a miscarriage. The doctor explained that many times teenagers do miscarry with their first pregnancy. This was the case. The pregnancy was over.

     Paula spent a few days in the hospital and then two weeks at home recovering. She felt awkward at first returning to school. She knew that a lot of people were talking about her. She had her girlfriend lined up to fight anybody who wanted to say something to her face. (She was unable to fight until she was completely healed.) No one did. A few months later, Paula and Todd broke up. They both decided that they wanted to date other people. The pregnancy just seemed like a bad dream.

## Teenage Pregnancy, continued

**Directions:** Answer these questions about Paula and Todd.

**1.** What was the first mistake Paula made?

_____

_____

**2.** Why do you think Paula was laughing and acting so silly when something very serious was happening?

_____

_____

**3.** What do you think about the way Mrs. Armstrong handled the situation?

_____

_____

**4.** How did this experience affect Paula and her mother?

_____

_____

**5.** How do you think Paula felt about having a miscarriage?

_____

_____

**6.** Why do you think Paula wanted to fight anyone who had comments about her?

_____

_____

**7.** Do you think Paula and Todd should have talked about marriage?

_____

_____

# VI-16 HIV and AIDS

**Objective:** The student will identify facts about HIV and AIDS.

**Comments:**

Teens are now at-risk for the HIV infection and AIDS. Many people who are now in their 20s and 30s were infected when they were in their teens – it just took ten years or longer for it to show up. In this lesson, some facts about HIV and AIDS are presented.

**Introductory Activities:**

a. Ask students to write what HIV stands for.

b. Ask students to write what AIDS stands for.

If students are not sure, go over the following introductory information:

HIV stands for *human immunodeficiency virus*. This is the virus that causes AIDS – *acquired immunodeficiency syndrome*. Primarily AIDS affects a person by making your body unable to fight diseases and infections, which then kills you.

**Activity:**

Several paragraphs of information about HIV and AIDS are presented on the worksheet "HIV and AIDS." After reading the paragraphs, students are to match the question at the bottom of the page with the paragraph that answers the question.

**Answers: 1.** d; **2.** f; **3.** a; **4.** h; **5.** c; **6.** e; **7.** g; **8.** b

**Discussion:** Students may already have some experience with people they know who have the disease or have formed some opinions about people with AIDS.

1. When do you think students should be taught about AIDS? Is elementary school too young?

2. Why don't many high school students know the facts about AIDS? **(don't listen, don't think it will affect them)**

3. Do you think most students are more concerned about drunk driving than about AIDS? **(it might seem more realistic)**

4. Do you think students are better informed about AIDS than their parents? **(probably)**

5. Do you know of anyone with AIDS?

6. Why do you think so many people still don't know the facts about how to avoid getting AIDS or how it is passed from one person to another? **(think it won't happen to them)**

7. Is the fear of AIDS a real fear for you, or do you think it is something that will never touch your life?

8. How would you feel if a new student came to your school and you found out he or she had AIDS?

9. How would you feel if you found out your little brother had AIDS?

10. Do you think more money should be given from the government for finding a cure for AIDS? What about money for cancer or heart disease?

**Extension Activities:**

1. Have students read the story of Ryan White, a hemophiliac 16-year-old boy who died from AIDS (*People* Magazine, May 30, 1988). They will read what it was like for a teenager who experienced the pain, emotional suffering, and challenges from this disease.

2. Have students contact the local Red Cross for information about HIV and AIDS. Do a presentation for the class.

3. Have students research articles about people's personal encounters with people with AIDS. Try to "humanize" the disease.

**Evaluation:**

a. What is AIDS?

b. What are some symptoms of AIDS?

c. How can you protect yourself from getting AIDS?

d. Is there a cure for AIDS?

**Teacher Notes:**

_____

_____

_____

_____

_____

_____

# HIV and AIDS

**Directions:** Here are some facts and figures about HIV and AIDS. After reading each paragraph, match it with the question below that it answers. Write the number of the question on the line next to the paragraph.

_____ **1.** AIDS stands for acquired immunodeficiency syndrome, which is a disease caused by a virus (HIV). A blood test can tell whether or not you have been infected with HIV. You may not show any symptoms for many years.

_____ **2.** There are several ways the AIDS virus can be spread. They include: unprotected sex (without a condom) with someone who is infected with the AIDS virus; sharing drug needles or syringes with someone who is infected; and passing the infection from mother to baby during pregnancy, childbirth, or possibly breast feeding. At one time people were getting the AIDS virus through blood transfusions, but now blood is tested carefully before it is used.

_____ **3.** There is no cure for AIDS. Eventually, it will kill you.

_____ **4.** You are not safe from AIDS even if you are not gay. Anytime you have sex with someone you are at risk if the other person is infected. The more sexual partners involved, the greater your chance of becoming infected.

_____ **5.** There are some symptoms of AIDS, such as swollen glands, coughing, fever, or diarrhea. But these are symptoms of other common illnesses, too. The only way to know for sure is through a blood test.

_____ **6.** Here are some ways to protect yourself from getting AIDS: don't do drugs, don't have sex, don't be afraid to say NO. Wait for the right time, the right place, and the right person.

_____ **7.** You will not get AIDS from drinking fountains, a hug, coughing, sneezing, spitting, mosquitoes, or from sharing utensils (forks, cups, etc.). It is not spread through swimming pools, phones, toilets, or shower facilities. You can safely eat food that has been prepared or served by someone who is infected.

_____ **8.** There are a lot of rumors and misinformation about HIV and AIDS. Get the facts. You can get information from your county health department, the American Red Cross, health hotlines, and your doctor.

---

**a.** Is there a cure for AIDS?

**b.** How can I find out the facts about HIV and AIDS?

**c.** What are some symptoms of AIDS?

**d.** What does AIDS stand for?

**e.** How can I protect myself from getting AIDS?

**f.** How is the AIDS virus spread?

**g.** What are some common activities that will not spread the AIDS virus?

**h.** Can you get AIDS if you are not gay?

## VI-17 What's a Reputation?

**Objective:** The student will make assumptions about a character's reputation based on given clues.

**Comments:**

A reputation is a judgment placed upon a person by others. Whether deserved or not, people make decisions about a person's character. In this lesson, students are given comments about others to consider. They are to decide what it tells about the person's reputation.

**Introductory Activities:**

a. Define *reputation*. **(a person's character as judged by other people)**

b. Write one comment you think people say about you to others.

**Activity:**

Students are to read the comments on the worksheet "What's a Reputation?" and make a judgment as to some aspect of the person's reputation.

**Answers:** *(examples)* **1.** she's a good cook; **2.** he is a poor driver; **3.** he knows about cars; **4.** he cheats; **5.** she's a bad player; **6.** he's a good salesman; **7.** she is honest; **8.** he lies; **9.** he's a poor carpenter; **10.** she's fun; **11.** Mrs. Gabler has a bad temper; **12.** he eats a lot

**Discussion:** After students have completed the worksheet, compare their responses. Did they come up with the same conclusions?

1. How do other people come up with ideas about a person's reputation? **(things they observe, things they hear from others)**

2. What is an example of a good reputation?

3. What is an example of a bad reputation?

4. How do other people determine someone's reputation?

5. How does what you say or do reflect your attitudes and ideas? How, in turn, does that affect your reputation? **(that's what gives people something to work with, to decide what they think of you)**

6. How long do you think it takes a stranger to size up a person?

7. How long does it take to gain a reputation? **(in some cases, not very long)**

8. Just because you (or someone else) has a reputation for being or doing something, does that mean it is deserved? How can people be mistaken?

**Extension Activities:**

1. Have students consider some political figures or celebrities. What reputations are they known for? How did they get these reputations?

2. Have students think of famous people (or, if appropriate, students within the school body). Who has a reputation for: being a good sport? being friendly? being rich? being athletic? Have students think of other categories. Try to emphasize the positive.

**Evaluation:**

    a. Define *reputation*.

    b. What clues might help you determine the following characteristics about another person:

       Marguerite is very concerned about her appearance.

       Akim loves to play basketball.

       Jonathan drives too fast.

**Teacher Notes:**

_____

_____

_____

_____

_____

_____

# What's a Reputation?

**Directions:** Read the following comments. What does each tell you about the person's reputation?

1. "She's such a brain!"

_____

2. "Don't ever get in the car with Tom if you value your life."

_____

3. "Fred is the one to ask if you have a question about cars."

_____

4. "Oh, no – do I have to sit next to him in this class? I'll have to hide my paper so he doesn't copy everything."

_____

5. "I hope we don't have to have Sheila on our team. She's awful."

_____

6. "If you want a good deal, buy your cars from Mr. Alvarez."

_____

7. "If Angie says it's true, it's true."

_____

8. "Don't believe anything Mark says."

_____

9. "John built your back porch? I hope it doesn't fall down."

_____

10. "Be sure to invite Kim to the party. She's a lot of fun."

_____

11. "I'm afraid to admit that I messed up on this paper. Mrs. Gabler will have a fit."

_____

12. "Let's make sure we eat dessert before Randy gets here. There won't be any left."

_____

# VI-18 Losing a Good Reputation

**Objective:** The student will identify consequences of losing a good reputation.

**Comments:**

Unfortunately, one mistake or episode can turn a good reputation into a bad one. It seems that people like to look for mistakes and dwell on the episodes we may regret. In this lesson, students are given an example of a nice girl who makes an error in judgment. Students are to think through possible consequences of losing a good reputation.

**Introductory Activities:**

a. Ask students to think of examples of how someone could lose a good reputation.

b. Ask students to think of ways that someone could gain a good reputation.

**Activity:**

Students are to read the short story on the worksheet "Losing a Good Reputation" and then answer questions about the characters' reputations. Additional discussion questions are included.

> **Answers:** *(examples)* **1.** quiet, shy; **2.** someone who gets drunk at parties; **3.** sneaky, parties a lot; **4.** not sure about her friendship with Bridget, not sure about being at the party – then included in the group, sick; **5.** probably - it's quite a change in reputation; **6.** a few months or until she does something to change the reputation/probably

> **Discussion:** The following questions deal more generally with the idea of changing one's reputation.

1. Once a person has lost a good reputation, what could that person do to regain it? **(keep engaging in good behaviors)**

2. Do you think other people enjoying finding mistakes in others? Why?

3. Does it seem unfair that just one mistake or error in judgment can ruin someone's reputation?

4. Is it harder to lose a bad reputation than to lose a good one?

**Extension Activities:**

1. Have students look for articles in newspapers and magazines that describe changes in reputation for famous people. What events or episodes have contributed to a change in reputation? What are the consequences for each person?

2. Select and tape some television shows that depict a character undergoing a reputation change. Discuss with students the reasons why it happened. Was the change for the better or worse?

**Evaluation:**

Have students write a paragraph depicting how someone could lose a good reputation and what the consequences might be.

# Losing A Good Reputation

**Directions:** Read the following story. Then answer the questions.

Jennifer was always quiet and shy until she met Bridget. Bridget was outgoing and had a lot of friends. She was fun and friendly, but didn't get along with her parents. When her parents would leave for an evening, Bridget would break into the bar in the basement and call a few friends to come over. Sometimes Jennifer felt out of place and awkward around Bridget, but she never thought they would get into trouble. One night Bridget invited Jennifer to spend the night. Bridget's parents left and before long, there was a party going on. Jennifer didn't want to seem out of it, so she took a drink. Other kids at the party were all drinking, and it didn't seem bad. Soon she was surrounded by a lot of kids, all of whom seemed to be friendly. Jennifer felt included and happy. Everyone cleared out before the parents returned, but Jennifer still was feeling the effects of the wine she had been drinking. The next morning she woke up nauseous and vomiting. At school on Monday, she found out that a lot of kids had been talking about the party. Jennifer realized she was the topic of conversation. The quiet little girl now was known as someone who was quick to take a drink. The next party had Jennifer at the top of the list. But the word going around was not that she was a lot of fun to talk to; she was fun to talk about.

**1.** What kind of reputation did Jennifer have at the beginning of the story?

_____

**2.** What kind of reputation did she end up with?

_____

**3.** What kind of reputation did Bridget have?

_____

**4.** What kinds of ups and downs did Jennifer go through?

_____

**5.** Do you think she has any regrets about her behavior at the party?

_____

**6.** How long will Jennifer have this reputation? Is it deserved?

_____

## VI-19 Changing Your Reputation

**Objective:** The student will identify reasons or ways for individuals to change a reputation in specific examples.

**Comments:**

Reputations are gained and lost all the time. If someone makes a concerted effort to change a reputation, that can happen. There are also other ways to make changes. Sometimes other people make that determination for us by providing training, guidance, or a model. In this lesson, students are given examples of reputations that have changed and are to determine what factors were involved.

**Introductory Activities:**

   a. Have students give an example of something that could change a good reputation to a bad one.

   b. Have students give an example of something that could change a bad reputation to a good one.

**Activity:**

Students are to read the four examples of reputation-changes on the worksheet "Changing Your Reputation" and decide what was the "old" reputation and now is the "new" reputation.

   **Answers: 1.** good student/apathetic student; **2.** unathletic/good athlete; **3.** school-skipper/regular attender; **4.** unskilled/good worker

   **Discussion:** Have students give their ideas about what caused the changes in the characters' reputations.

   1. In example 1, do you think Cindy cares about the reputation she has amongst her teachers? **(probably not)**

   2. Which reputation is most important to her? **(the one she gets from her friends)**

   3. In example 2, Alfredo went from a negative reputation to a positive one. What qualities – besides athletic ability – do you see in Alfredo? **(dedicated, goal-oriented, etc.)**

   4. Geno, in example 3, had a change in reputation that he had little to do with. Would this still give him a deserved reputation?

   5. What kind of attitude did Maria show on her job? **(willing to learn, willing to go through training)**

   6. Why would it be important for Maria to have a good reputation on the job even though her job is probably an entry-level job? **(she may want to advance later, a good reputation would help her gain a better job later)**

**Extension Activities:**

   1. Have students examine the changes in reputation in several celebrities such as O.J. Simpson, Michael Jackson, Princess Diana, etc. Also look for testimonials of prisoners who have gone straight, people who have undergone moral changes, and other dramatic events. What events caused the changes in reputation? Are the changes for the better? Are they unfair?

   2. Show students the classic movie *My Fair Lady* in which a dramatic transformation is achieved in an uncultured girl. Discuss how her reputation was changed.

**Evaluation:**

    a. List at least three ways a person can change his or her reputation.

    b. List a famous person who has had a change in his or her reputation. What factor(s) were involved in making this change?

**Teacher Notes:**

_____

_____

_____

_____

_____

_____

# Changing Your Reputation

**Directions:** Read the following examples of people who have had a change in reputation. How would these events change what someone thinks of a person?

1. Cindy always had good grades and was a pretty good student. Her teachers liked her because she was bright and polite. As she got older, she started to hang around with a group of girls who liked to party more than they liked to study. When teachers tried to talk with her about what was happening, she ignored them.

**BEFORE    AFTER**

**Old reputation:** _____

**New reputation:**_____

2. Alfredo was picked last on any athletic team. He hated going to gym class because it always made him feel like a loser. Then he joined a karate class after school and began working out. He developed muscles, energy, and a spirit to compete. After a few months, he began trying out for some after-school teams. He found that he enjoyed them and was getting pretty good at them. Other kids began asking him to join them when they played.

**Old reputation:** _____

**New reputation:**_____

3. Geno had a terrible attendance record at school. He just didn't care about attending. Then he found out that the courts decided he had to see a probation officer once a week to discuss some of his other problems. Now that he didn't have a choice, he began attending every day. Now everyone expects him to show up – which he does.

**Old reputation:** _____

**New reputation:**_____

4. Maria was "all thumbs" when it came to typing. She worked at a job in which she had to do some work on a word processor. Her bosses were frustrated, too, at all of her mistakes, although they really liked Maria and wanted to see her succeed. They decided to pay for her to attend night-school classes to learn how to operate a computer. Once she received the training, she understood how to do her job better. Now she looks forward to doing the paperwork!

**Old reputation:** _____

**New reputation:**_____

## VI-20 How You Appear to Others

**Objective:** The student will describe how he or she appears to several other specified individuals.

**Comments:**

We have many sides, many faces. While we may seem sweet and kind to our best friend's mother, we may be nasty and mean to that little brother whom we see every day. We give different people a different view of how we behave and what we think. Sometimes when two people are discussing the same person, the views are entirely different and you wonder if they are talking about the same individual! Part of what makes us complex, interesting individuals is the different attributes we expose to others. In this lesson, students examine the different reputations other people might have of the same person.

**Introductory Activities:**

a. Ask students how they feel about _____ (select a winning football or basketball team). Many students will probably indicate it is their favorite team. Ask why? **(we like to be associated with winners)**

b. Ask students how they feel about _____ (select a team with a somewhat bad reputation). Comments will probably be negative!

**Activity:**

Using the worksheet "How You Appear to Others," students are to examine their reputations in light of how they appear to several different individuals. The individuals chosen are random, and you may wish to add or change the people. Encourage students to be objective!

**Discussion:** Students may consider this a rather personal activity, so ask for volunteers to divulge information if they wish.

1. How much control do you have over your reputation among other people?

2. Do you think your reputation is more accurate when given by people who are close to you, such as a family member or your best friend?

3. Do you think people who know you only through school or work would have valid observations about you? Why? **(they may be more objective, different circumstances)**

4. Do others see you as they want to see you? Are they accurate?

5. Do you think others see you as you would like them to see you? Are you effectively giving them the right information to have whatever reputation you want?

6. Have you ever tried to make a good impression in front of someone and ended feeling like you were being a phoney?

7. When you described your reputation as if you were another person, did you tend to list your accomplishments? your personality? your physical appearance?

8. Are you happy with the reputation you feel most people have given you?

**Extension Activities:**

1. Have students spend some time talking to a close friend about how they appear to others. Find out what their reputation is. Are they surprised?

2. Collect and read some yearbooks (with permission). A lot of the comments may reveal some insights into the people's reputations. It would be interesting to look through those of parents! Again, get permission!

**Evaluation:**

a. In general, what kind of reputation do you think you have among your closest friends?

b. What kind of reputation do you have within your family?

c. What kind of reputation do you have at school or work?

d. Which reputation most reflects you? Why?

**Teacher Notes:**

_____

_____

_____

_____

_____

_____

# How You Appear to Others

**Directions:** Different people have different perceptions of what you are like. Fill in the following information on the picture below. How would you be described, or what would your reputation be described as, by the following individuals?

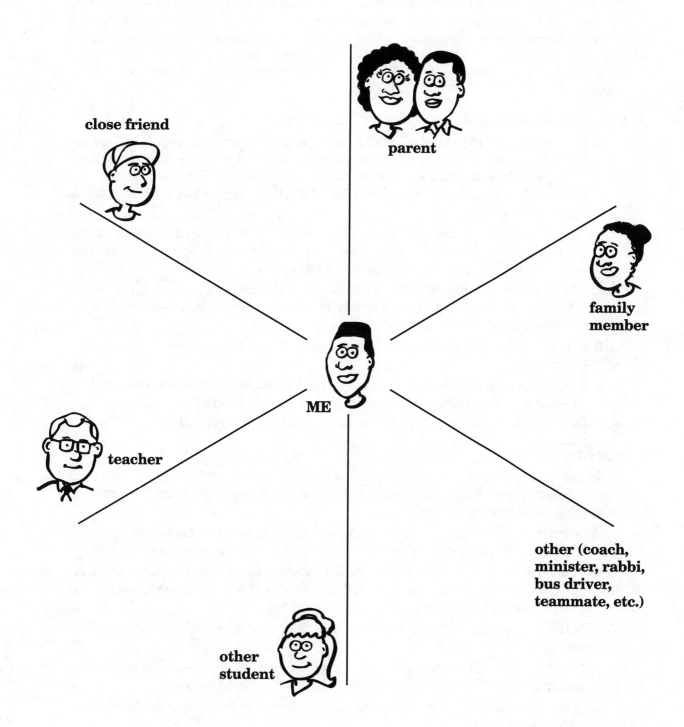

## VI-21 Stress and Stressors

**Objective:** The student will identify the stressor (something that causes us to feel stressed) in given situations.

**Comments:**

Stress is a part of life. Things that make us feel stressed are called stressors. This is not necessarily a negative thing; some people draw more energy, strength, and resourcefulness from being in what others might term a "stressful" situation. What is important is that each student can identify what is stressful and is able to cope with the situation. In this lesson, students are given stressful situations and are to select the stressor.

**Introductory Activities:**

a. Pretend you are in the following situation: Someone is chasing you. He is getting closer and closer. You are running as fast as you can, but your legs are getting tired and you can't go any faster. He is gaining on you! Now he is right behind you! You can hear him breathing! How do you feel? (**students may suggest fear, panic, excitement**)

b. Now let's continue the situation. The person grabs you and you fall down. Suddenly you hear cheering and thousands of people are yelling, "TOUCHDOWN!" Now how do you feel? (**happy**)

c. Did your perception of the situation change after you were given more information? Why? (**in the context, it was not truly a life-threatening situation**)

d. Would you as the runner feel stress, even if you knew it was all a game? (**probably**)

e. Define *stress*. (**a feeling or response that results from some demand or pressure placed upon you; could be pleasant or fearful**)

f. Define *stressor*. (**something that causes you to feel stressed**)

**Activity:**

In this lesson, students are to read on the worksheet "Stress and Stressors" examples of stressful situations. For each, they are to pick out the stressor and identify whether it is "good" or "bad" (pleasant/unpleasant).

**Answers: 1.** test/negative; **2.** accident/negative; **3.** late bus/negative; **4.** school record/positive; **5.** discipline by principal/negative; **6.** too many tasks/negative

**Discussion:** Have students reveal their thoughts about the stressors and their perceptions of each situation. Expand by having them tell about similar situations they have been in. Did they feel similarly stressed?

1. Is there a chance the stress that Otis feels in example 1 would help him perform better? (**yes**)

2. If you knew that Terri took her father's car without permission and then got into an accident, would that increase her level of stress? (**probably**)

3. What if Terri had caused an accident by running into someone else? (**yes, increased stress**)

4. Why would Rolando in example 3 feel anxiety? (**there is nothing he can do about making that bus come faster**)

5. Do you think most athletes feel stress at times? **(probably)**

6. What are some causes of their stress? **(training rigors, desire to achieve, competing against others)**

7. What are some ways your body might show signs of stress, particularly in example 5? **(red face, tightly clenched fists, increased heart rate, etc.)**

8. What could Wendy do in example 6 to relieve her stress? **(take a deep breath, make a plan for getting the work done, cancel the babysitting, etc.)**

## Extension Activities:

1. Have students compile a list of 10 to 15 activities that can be the cause of positive stress.

2. Have students compile a list of 10 to 15 activities that are usually the cause of negative stress. These activities could be at home, school, work, or leisure time.

## Evaluation:

a. Define *stress*.

b. Define *stressor*.

c. Give an example of a situation in which the stressor is positive.

d. Give an example of a situation in which the stressor is negative.

## Teacher Notes:

_____

_____

_____

_____

_____

_____

# Stress and Stressors

**Directions:** Read each situation below. Identify what is stressful (the stressor) about each situation and circle whether or not it is positive or negative.

1. Otis flunked his science test. He has a chance to retake it after school. If he does not get at least a "C" on the test, he will flunk the entire course and end up in summer school.

**Stressor:** _____

**Positive**      **Negative**

2. Terri borrowed her father's car to drive to the library. An elderly driver came out of nowhere and broad-sided the car, leaving a smashed window and bent door. The other driver was hysterical, screaming and crying. Terri stepped out of the car, shaken but not hurt.

**Stressor:** _____

**Positive**      **Negative**

3. Rolando looked at his watch for the third time. If the bus didn't get to the stop in the next minute, he would be late for his first day on the job. Where was that bus?

**Stressor:** _____

**Positive**      **Negative**

4. Christine took a deep breath. If she could do one more push-up, she would set a new school record. Her mouth was dry, her arms ached, but she was determined!

**Stressor:** _____

**Positive**      **Negative**

5. Dale and Karl sat side by side in the principal's office, giving each other occasional glares. "It was your fault," Dale hissed to the other boy. He received only silence. The shadow of the principal loomed over them. "You can come into my office now," boomed the angry voice.

**Stressor:** _____

**Positive**      **Negative**

6. Wendy looked at her assignment sheet. There was homework – lots of it! – assigned in every subject. She had to babysit for the McDermott triplets all evening. And she had promised her mother she could clean the entire house since she had had her friends over the night before. She felt overwhelmed!

**Stressor:** _____

**Positive**      **Negative**

# VI-22 Stressful Events and Situations

**Objective:** The student will identify common life events that are associated with stress.

**Comments:**

Children, as well as adults, feel stress. For them, the stressor may be something as seemingly simple as moving to a new neighborhood or as devastating as experiencing the death of a parent. In this lesson, students are given a list of common stressors among children and are to take note of those that personally affect them.

**Introductory Activities:**

   a. Have students list what they consider to be one of the most stressful situations at home.

   b. Have students list what they consider to be one of the most stressful situations at school.

   c. Have students list what they consider to be one of the most stressful situations among their friends.

**Activity:**

Students are to read a list of stressful situations on the worksheet "Stressful Events and Situations" and indicate those that might be affecting them. Inform them that this is a personal inventory and will not be collected, but that they should be aware of the stresses they are under. Later lessons will discuss combating stress.

   **Discussion:** Since the information is personal, students will not need to share their answers unless they want to discuss them in general terms. Be sensitive to their needs at this time.

   1. Do you feel school puts a lot of stress on its students? How?

   2. Would you rather have parents who put pressure on you to succeed, or parents who were more laid-back and let you work at your own pace?

   3. Do you feel you work or perform well or even better under pressure?

   4. Why would personal health problems affect all other areas of your life?

   5. Why is change – even if it is good or neutral – considered to be stressful? **(have to adapt to new things)**

   6. Do you think winning the lottery would be a stressful event? How? **(very much so! it affects many areas of change in life)**

   7. How could success and achievement cause stress? **(you might feel you have to live up to new expectations)**

**Extension Activities:**

   1. Have students find a more complete list of adult life stressors. Some lists even provide a type of rating that indicates how intense that life event might be. (For example, the death of a spouse is usually at the top of the list with a rating of 100. Divorce, marital separation, being in jail, being fired, retirement, and taking on a mortgage are also important stressors.) Although your students may view adulthood as far off, they or their parents will face these events before they know it.

   2. Have students do a book report on the story of an individual who dealt with (and overcame) a stressful event.

## Evaluation:

    a. List at least ten important stressors that most people encounter in life.

    b. Select a stressor that you can relate to personally and explain how it adds stress to your life. Is that stress positive in any way? How?

## Teacher Notes:

_____

_____

_____

_____

_____

_____

# Stressful Events and Situations

**Directions:** Below is a list of stressful events and situations that occur throughout life. Put a check mark next to those that affect you.

_____ **1.** moving or changing schools

_____ **2.** having difficulty in school with academics

_____ **3.** death of a close friend

_____ **4.** death of a family member

_____ **5.** change in the family (new baby, new siblings)

_____ **6.** family crisis

_____ **7.** family financial problems

_____ **8.** alcohol abuse by family members

_____ **9.** physical and emotional changes of puberty

_____ **10.** domestic violence

_____ **11.** living in a dangerous neighborhood

_____ **12.** living in a single-parent household

_____ **13.** parental separation or divorce

_____ **14.** peer pressure

_____ **15.** personal health problems

_____ **16.** rejection by family members, friends, peers

_____ **17.** ridicule by family members, friends, peers

_____ **18.** change in sleeping habits (more, less, time of day)

_____ **19.** change in eating habits

_____ **20.** unrealistic expectations by parent or teacher

_____ **21.** excessive discipline by parents

_____ **22.** in trouble with the law

_____ **23.** dealing with pregnancy

_____ **24.** finding a job

_____ **25.** getting married

# VI-23 Coping with Stress

**Objective:** The student will be able to list and briefly explain at least three techniques for reducing stress.

**Comments:**

There are many techniques and programs available for stress reduction. These may include everything from talking to yourself to hypnosis. Since our concern is students, the techniques presented in this lesson are fairly simple and straight-forward. They can be learned and practiced within a school setting, with friends, or by individual study.

**Introductory Activities:**
a. Have students list what they consider to be extremely stressful occupations. **(surgeon, airline pilot, spy, etc.)**
b. Have students suggest ways that people engaged in those occupations could handle their stress.

**Activity:**

Students are to read on the worksheet "Coping with Stress" a list of eight ways or techniques that may be helpful in dealing with stress. They are to answer the questions about each technique.

**Answers: a.** he could imagine himself winning; **b.** he could clear his mind of other thoughts; **c.** she could rehearse all aspects of the speech; **d.** he or she could go through the arguments, anticipate all responses of the boss; **e.** encourage yourself not to get down about it; we all make mistakes; **f.** dwell on the times you succeeded, you will succeed again; **g.** you wouldn't be confident enough to take a strong stand; **h.** gain respect for yourself; **i.** train self to stop that line of thought; **j.** an explosive, laser beam; **k.** avoid whenever possible, continue to do your best, it will be over someday; **l.** find someone you can talk to, join Alateen; **m.** practice time management to get everything in; **n.** take a course, ask someone to teach you; **o.** vocabulary, other self-help books; **p.** he or she could think through the problems of the day while moving around; **q.** do something that involves the hands so he won't be tempted to eat

**Discussion:** Be sure to go over all the techniques and explain how each can work. Students may choose to target one to try. Some may already be employing some of the techniques in their experiences with stress.

1. Which of the techniques seem most appealing to you?
2. Which techniques have you already tried or currently use to reduce stress?
3. Can you think of other techniques that are helpful?

**Extension Activities:**

1. Steer students towards biographies of people who have gone through extremely stressful periods of their lives. How did these people cope? People like Anne Frank, Wilma Rudolph, Terry Fox, and survivors of the holocaust have experiences that are incredible.

2. Encourage students to try the techniques when they are in stressful situations. Have them report back to you (or the class) as to the success each has had. Practice them as a class if possible!

**Evaluation:**

    a. List at least three techniques that can be used to reduce stress.

    b. Describe how the techniques in (a) are helpful.

    c. Write a paragraph detailing which technique you find helpful and in what situations you have used it.

**Teacher Notes:**

_____

_____

_____

_____

_____

_____

# Coping with Stress

**Directions:** Here is a list of some ways that can be helpful in managing stressful situations and/or the stressor itself. Read each carefully and then answer the questions.

1. **RELAXATION** – Teach yourself to relax when you are in the stressful situation. Take a few deep breaths, close your eyes, imagine yourself floating.

   **a.** How could this be useful to a person who is about to run a race?

   _____

   **b.** How could this be useful to a person about to take a very important test?

   _____

2. **POSITIVE PRACTICE** – Before engaging in a stressful activity, go over it in your mind. Envision yourself performing each and every step, and always end with success! Do it so many times that it seems natural.

   **c.** How could this technique be used with someone who has to give a speech?

   _____

   **d.** How could this be used with someone who has to present his or her side of a conflict to the boss or administrator?

   _____

3. **TALKING TO YOURSELF** – Get comfortable with the idea of giving yourself "pep talks" when you feel stressed. Keep repeating phrases such as, "You are doing fine! This is something you can handle. You don't even need to worry about this." Say the things you wish someone else would say to you.

   **e.** How could this work in a situation where you made a mistake and are afraid to face your peers?

   _____

   **f.** How could this technique help someone who sometimes succeeds but sometimes doesn't?

   _____

4. **ASSERTIVENESS** – Reduce your stress by standing up for what you believe is right. Handle the level of conflict by practicing saying what you believe and not backing down.

   **g.** Why wouldn't this be a good technique if you weren't really sure how you felt or didn't know enough about the situation?

   _____

   **h.** How would it make you feel to know that others respected what you had to say?

   _____

## Coping with Stress, continued

**5. THOUGHT STOPPING** – When you feel the symptoms of stress creeping in, imagine a lightning bolt flashing through the sky and bombarding that stressor to pieces. Imagine yourself screaming, "STOP! THAT'S ENOUGH!" Forbid yourself to dwell on it anymore. "STOP! STOP! STOP!"

**i.** How could this technique be used for someone who daydreams a lot and ends up thinking about ways he or she is going to mess up or fail?

_____

**j.** What other mental images could be used to block or destroy a thought?

_____

**6. COPING SKILLS** – Pinpoint the stressor and logically decide how you can cope with it. If you have to sit next to that bully every day for the rest of the semester, make your plan as to how you can survive. Will you ignore him? Will you bring up a new, friendly topic of conversation? Will you combine other techniques, such as positive practice, to learn to handle this person in a way of your choosing? If you know there is going to be a problem, plan ahead of time how you will handle it. Then stick to your plan.

**k.** How could you cope with a teacher who is out to get you?

_____

**l.** How could you cope with a stepfather who is an alcoholic?

_____

**m.** How could you cope with a grueling work schedule for the next four weekends?

_____

**7. LEARN NEW SKILLS** – Perhaps the stress comes from inability to perform. If a secretary is worried about making mistakes on the typewriter, taking a course in typing would give her new skills and take care of the problem. People are capable of learning many new things!

**n.** What skills could someone learn who is afraid of working with mechanical things?

_____

**o.** If someone is embarrassed about appearing dumb, what skills could he or she learn to improve this image?

_____

**8. EXERCISE** – Sometimes stress can be greatly alleviated by taking it out physically! Run! Play handball! Work out! Do something to get your body on your side. Take out that energy in a positive, healthy way.

**p.** How could exercise help someone out who worked at a desk all day?

_____

**q.** What exercise would you recommend for someone who likes to eat when they are stressed?

_____

# VI-24 Depression

**Objective:** The student will define depression and identify several symptoms of depression.

**Comments:**

Everyone experiences moods of depression, particularly associated with sadness, grief, loneliness, or other traumatic events. But when the feeling of depression lasts for an extended period of time, it can cause other problems and may require treatment from a specialist. In this lesson, students are given a list of symptoms of depression.

**Introductory Activities:**

a. How would you feel if you came home from school and found out that a fish in your aquarium had died? **(probably sad for a little while)**

b. How would you feel if you came home and your favorite dog had died? **(a little sadder than the fish?)**

c. How would you feel if you found out your favorite uncle had died? **(very sad)**

d. How long do you think you would feel bad about the death of the fish? the dog? the person?

e. What would you think of a person who was still grieving over a dead fish three years later, grieving to the point that he or she couldn't eat, couldn't sleep, and didn't seem to care about anything? **(you'd wonder what the significance was of the fish and also seek professional help)**

f. Define *depression.* **(an emotional state in which the person feels sad, lonely, grieving, or just "down." This is normal for short periods of time. When the symptoms persist, there is concern for a more serious problem.)**

**Activity:**

The term "depression" can refer to a mood that describes the behavior of anyone who is in a state of sadness, grief, or general gloominess. When used to refer to clinical depression, this is a much more serious type of depression that can be associated with other types of disorders and even suicide. In this lesson, students are to examine symptoms or signs of depression by matching them with a comment on the worksheet "Depression." Hopefully this will create an awareness of the problem. Be sure to explain any terms with which students are unfamiliar.

**Answers: 1.** e; **2.** c; **3.** k; **4.** j; **5.** b; **6.** i; **7.** d; **8.** g; **9.** h; **10.** f; **11.** a; **12.** l

**Discussion:** Everyone feels some of the symptoms of depression from time to time. Be sure students understand that this is normal.

1. Can you relate to most of the comments on the worksheet, at least at some time or another in your life?

2. When do you remember being the most depressed?

3. Do you know of anyone who was so depressed that he or she needed professional help?

4. What kinds of treatments are you aware of for depression? **(counseling, medication, perhaps shock therapy)**

5. Why wouldn't it work to just tell someone to "snap out of it!"? **(it may be a chemical problem requiring medical treatment)**

6. Do children experience depression? **(yes)**

7. What are some causes of depression in children? **(children who suffer a significant loss, have low self-esteem, have family problems, or have inherited tendency for depression)**

8. What would you think of someone who was on medication for depression?

9. Are people who are treated for depression "crazy"? **(no, but they may need help)**

10. During the times when you were depressed, what got you out of it or helped a lot?

## Extension Activities:

1. Have students research the treatments for depression. Have them find out in what ways other people (especially families) can help with a depressed individual.

2. Have students make a list of what they think are the most important factors of their lives that are associated with depression. Would a bad haircut make you feel depressed? Would losing a parent to cancer? Have them give this some thought. Answers will differ greatly among students.

## Evaluation:

a. Define and explain *depression*.

b. List at least five symptoms or signs of depression.

# Depression

**Directions:** Below is a list of comments that might indicate a depressed feeling and a list of symptoms of depression. Match the comment on the left with the symptom on the right.

_____ 1. "I don't care how I do on the test. It doesn't matter to me."

_____ 2. "I'm not hungry – I just don't feel like eating anything."

_____ 3. "I used to enjoy playing football, but I don't anymore. I don't enjoy basketball either anymore."

_____ 4. -yawn- "I'm soooooo sleepy."

_____ 5. "I don't feel like going out with my friends. I don't want to be around people."

_____ 6. "I'm trying to think of the right answer, but I just can't seem to stay on one thought for a long time."

_____ 7. "My head hurts. My stomach hurts."

_____ 8. "Nobody likes me – I don't blame them. What's there to like?

_____ 9. "I've been crying for the past three days. I just feel like crying all the time."

_____ 10. "Nothing is going right. Even if I won the contest, I'd probably have to give the prize back."

_____ 11. "Why do you say I'm always in a bad mood? I'm *not* in a bad mood. Now get out of here and leave me alone!

_____ 12. "I can't sleep at night. I just lie there and toss and turn. All night long."

**a.** irritable, crabby

**b.** socially withdrawn

**c.** decreased appetite

**d.** aches and pains

**e.** apathetic, indifferent

**f.** pessimistic, looks at the bad side of things

**g.** low self-esteem

**h.** long, severe crying spells

**i.** inability to concentrate

**j.** mentally and physically tired

**k.** unable to enjoy activities once enjoyed

**l.** insomnia, can't sleep

# VI-25 Suicide

**Objective:** The student will be familiar with facts about suicide.

**Comments:**

Suicide has been termed as the ultimate depression, anger turned inward, or the answer to a seemingly hopeless situation. Researchers believe that children who think about, talk about, and attempt suicide also suffer from depression; but that not all depressed children are suicidal. In this lesson, some facts about suicide (the incidence, methods, and likelihood of occurrence) are presented.

**Introductory Activities:**

a. Ask students if they know of anyone who has tried to commit suicide. Do not ask for personal details, just if they know of a case.

b. Ask students to think of reasons that would explain why someone would try to or want to commit suicide; in other words, what is there about life that would be so awful that death is a better alternative?

**Activity:**

This is a sad lesson. At some time or another, most adolescents have probably imagined their own death, dreaming of how they will be missed after they're gone. The worksheet "Suicide" gives them some things to think about in relation to suicide. You may have students in your class who have attempted suicide, so treat them with care.

**Answers: 1. a.** they won't need them anymore; **b.** preparing a method of death; **c.** this shows what they are thinking about, preoccupied with; **2.** to give a warning, threat, cry for attention; **3.** between 3 P.M. and 6 P.M.; **4.** shooting, hanging, drug overdoses, breathing gas; **5.** guns; **6.** drugs; **7.** three months following a suicide attempt; **8.** 8; **9.** girls, boys; **10.** positive communication, healthy family relationship

**Discussion:** Students may be surprised at some of the answers. Have them speculate as to why these answers make sense.

1. How can friends help someone avoid suicide, even if he or she is very depressed?

2. Are there situations in life that truly are "hopeless" and "unchangeable"?

3. Why do parents make a big deal about keeping alcohol and guns out of reach of children?

4. What reasons do you think someone would give for making a suicide attempt?

5. What are some other examples of suicidal gestures, rather than a real suicide attempt?

6. What celebrities have you heard of who have committed suicide?

7. Suicide and death are permanent. Do you think young children do not fear death because they do not realize that?

8. Can you think of anything in your life that would make you consider suicide?

**Extension Activities:**

1. Have students research the incidence, methods, and reasons for suicide in your community or state.
2. Have students find interviews or testimonials from teenagers who have been on the brink of suicide but were unsuccessful. What thoughts about life and death do they feel now?
3. Find out what agencies and professionals are available for students to contact regarding depression and suicide.

**Evaluation:**

1. Write a paragraph describing what you know about teenage suicide.
2. Your best friend shoves his or her most prized possessions into your hands and says he or she doesn't feel well. You fear the worst. What will you say? What will you do?

**Teacher Notes:**

_____

_____

_____

_____

_____

_____

# Suicide

**Directions:** Following is a questionnaire about suicide. Write your thoughts.

1. How would these symptoms be clues that someone was thinking about suicide?

   **a.** giving away valued possessions

   _____

   **b.** getting a weapon

   _____

   **c.** talking about death, drawing pictures about death, listening to music about death

   _____

2. A *suicidal gesture* is making a statement about a person's emotional state, such as swallowing a bottle of sleeping pills in front of a parent. Why would someone do this?

   _____

3. At what time of day do you think most suicides occur?

   _____

4. What do you think are the most common methods of committing suicide for children and adolescents?

   _____

5. What is the choice of suicide for boys?

   _____

6. What is the choice of suicide for girls?

   _____

7. What is the most crucial time period after a suicide attempt has been made?

   _____

8. Out of every ten children who die from suicide, how many do you think have made previous attempts?

   _____

9. Which group do you think attempts more suicides, girls or boys? Which group has more deaths from suicide, girls or boys?

   _____

10. How can a family reduce the risk of suicide in a son or daughter?

    _____

# VI-26 Getting Help

**Objective:** The student will identify ways that an individual could get help from given sources of assistance.

**Comments:**

Life is not so dismal that there is not someone or something that can help a person out of a stressful or depressing situation. Rather than cave in to stressors that seem unbearable, students should learn ways to draw strength from available resources. In this lesson, students are given a list of resources that could be of use in some stressful situations and are to apply them to given situations.

**Introductory Activities:**

    a. Have students think of a stressful moment or situation with which they are familiar or have recently experienced. Then have them write one possible way they could alleviate that stress.

    b. Have students consider their response to (a). Did they write a person? a place? an agency? a behavior? Try to categorize the responses.

**Activity:**

On the worksheet "Getting Help," students are given individuals who are in stressful situations. They are also given a clue as to a way to help relieve that stressful situation. They are to write a way that the clue could help the individual deal with the stress.

    **Answers:** *(examples)* **1.** talk to a counselor, report the problem; **2.** talk to someone who knows what it is like, ask questions; **3.** get advice and help with setting up a program from the drug counselor; **4.** talk to a doctor, get medication; **5.** read about ways to safely diet; **6.** spend time in prayer and meditation; **7.** talk to friends who may know the boy; **8.** watch the documentary for information; **9.** get ideas from the book about how to change her looks/behavior; **10.** get support (monetary and emotional) from parents

    **Discussion:** Students may have various answers to the situations on the worksheet. Have them share their ideas.

    1. Everyone feels unhealthy stress from time to time. What are some methods to lessen the stress that cost very little in terms of money? (**talking to friends or family, reading, watching TV**)

    2. What are some methods that require a commitment or extensive investment of time or money? (**therapy, programs involving dietary foods, etc.**)

    3. Do you think most people don't want to ask for help when they are in stressful situations? Why? (**pride, embarrassment, etc.**)

    4. Do you think it indicates that someone is weak or not resourceful if they ask for help?

    5. Some people resent it when others tell them they have a problem. Why would they have this sort of reaction? (**don't want to be bothered, don't feel adequate to help, etc.**)

    6. How would you react if someone came to you with a serious problem?

7. If you were the one involved in a serious situation, would you feel free to go to parents, friends, a doctor, or other source? Why or why not?

8. In what situations does doing absolutely nothing take care of some problems? **(health - body may heal, friends - their attitudes may change over time, etc.)**

## Extension Activities:

1. Have students keep a "Mood Journal" for several days or weeks. At certain times during the day, have them record their feelings, thoughts, and general mood. See if they can find any pattern or draw any unscientific conclusions. Does life seem better in the morning? Are problems harder to deal with at the end of the day?

2. Someone once noted that you can detect a person who is depressed because he or she makes you feel depressed by just being around them. Have students be aware of how other people make them feel. Do certain friends make you feel better just by being around them?

## Evaluation:

a. List at least five sources of assistance for stressful situations.

b. Choose two sources from (a) and explain how each source could be helpful in a stressful situation.

# Getting Help

**Directions:** How could each person in the stressful situation described below get help from the source indicated?

1. Francesca is being threatened with abuse by her step-father. *(social service agency)*

   _____

2. Chuck has diabetes. *(person who has been through the disease and treatment)*

   _____

3. Rick has been taking drugs and alcohol for quite awhile. He would like to change these habits. *(drug counselor)*

   _____

4. Jennie is depressed about her acne. *(medical person)*

   _____

5. Alison is worried about putting on too much weight. *(magazine article)*

   _____

6. Kevin is in the hospital where he will soon undergo major surgery. *(prayer, inspirational thoughts)*

   _____

7. Debi needs a date for the dance this weekend and is interested in a new boy who seems shy. *(advice from friends)*

   _____

8. Juan is interested in learning about how a community is dealing with problems of violence in the school. *(TV documentary)*

   _____

9. Karla thinks she is unattractive. She would like to appear more outgoing and noticeable. *(self-help book)*

   _____

10. Gerald is desperate for money. He owes money to some people who are not very understanding. *(parents)*

    _____

## VI-27 You Have Choices!

**Objective:** The student will identify at least three possible choices of action given a stressful situation.

**Comments:**

The sources of stress that students will face will differ among students. Family circumstances, the community in which they live, and their values will all affect the types of choices available to a student. In this lesson, they are given situations to consider and must come up with several possible choices that are available to them.

**Introductory Activities:**

a. Have students write a stressor in their lives that they would consider to be fairly "mild."

b. Have students write a stressor in their lives that they would consider to be "moderate" in intensity.

c. Have students write a stressor that they are most concerned about, or would consider "serious."

**Activity:**

Students are to consider the stressful situations on the worksheet "You Have Choices!" and come up with at least three possible choices to deal with it. Then they are to indicate which would be the best for them to carry out.

> **Discussion:** Have students share their responses if they choose to. Reaffirm that we are all individuals and may not have the same resources available. But in each case, there will hopefully be at least one good choice that will assist the student in dealing with the situation.

1. Do you feel your life is now fairly stress-free compared to when you were younger?

2. Do you think as you get older there will be more serious stressors in your life?

3. How much time have you spent in learning how to deal with stress and pressure in life? Did you have any specific training or lesson in how to deal with it?

4. How does your personal value system or spiritual belief system affect your ability to deal with stress?

5. Do you think going through stressful periods helps you learn to adjust to stress and how to cope with it?

6. Would other people see you as someone who is really able to cope with pressure or not?

7. Do you feel you have adequate resources for help in stressful situations? What are those resources?

**Extension Activities:**

1. Have students construct a "Stress Scale" of their concerns and pressures in their life right now. Emphasize that this is a personal activity and they will not have to share it if they choose not to. Help them construct a hierarchy of their stressors with "mild" or "minor" at the bottom, continuing up through more serious or severe stressors.

2. Have students compile a personal list of resources to combat pressure or stressors in their lives. This could be done in conjunction with extension activity 1. Make sure students realize that there are personal resources available to help them make choices.

3. Have students work in groups to make positive posters with themes of making choices to strengthen oneself rather than giving in to pressure.

## Evaluation:

a. List at least three stressors in your life.

b. Rate the stressors according to the intensity you experience with each.

c. Choose one stressor and list at least three choices you have to deal with that stressor.

# You Have Choices!

**Directions:** Pretend you are in each of the following stressful situations. What are at least three possible choices you have for each? Put a check mark next to the one you think is the best for you.

1. Your parents are furious at your best friend because the two of you got into some trouble. They have forbidden you to get together until further notice. That might be forever!

   _____

   _____

2. Your boyfriend/girlfriend, whom you thought was wonderful, is seeing someone else behind your back. Evidently you are the only one who didn't know.

   _____

   _____

3. You've been working after school at a grocery store for a few weeks now. Suddenly your boss decides that you aren't working hard enough and fires you.

   _____

   _____

4. You just found out you are flunking U.S. History and will be facing summer school.

   _____

   _____

5. Your goal in life is to play on the varsity tennis team. Your best friend made the team, but you didn't.

   _____

   _____

6. Your parents just informed you that your dad is being transferred to the other side of the United States. This means you are giving up your rather nice life here.

   _____

   _____

7. The group you hang around with has gotten involved in using cocaine. It's right there, available to you. Your friends tell you that it's fun, safe, and won't even cost you any money.

   _____

   _____

8. The phone call you just made confirmed your suspicions —the pregnancy test was positive.

   _____

   _____

# Section VII

---

# Problem-Solving Skills

# VII-1 Understanding the Problem Situation

**Objective:** The student will demonstrate understanding of a given problem situation by identifying the problem(s) involved.

## Comments:

Everyone find themselves in problem situations at one time or another. A first step towards resolving the problem is identifying what the problem consists of. Few problems are simple enough to reduce to one little event; most involve larger situations in which several factors interplay to create problems. In this lesson, students are given problem situations to consider and must pick up the specific factors involved in contributing to that problem situation.

## Introductory Activities:

    a. Have students think of one problem situation that is important as it relates to their school.

    b. Have students write the names or positions of the main people involved in the problem situation.

    c. Have students share their ideas and opinions as to what problems face the school at this time.

## Activity:

Students are given four problem situations to read on the worksheet "Understanding the Problem Situation." They then are to list the specific factors contributing to the problem situation. In each case there is no simple single factor that is the problem; there are many contributing forces that affect the situation.

    **Answers:** *(examples)* **1.** some employees don't like the new boss, some do (personality conflicts), there is resentment between employees, the boss seems to have favorites, the atmosphere is tense in the office, there is a loss of personal privileges; **2.** Terry spent a lot of money on Angela which she accepted, they apparently were not communicating about their expectations of the relationship; **3.** the first teacher is a friend of the family, Phyllis's skills have improved to the point that the first teacher is not adequate, the first teacher thinks everything is fine, Phyllis has a chance to take lessons with a better instructor, Phyllis is fearful about talking to the first teacher; **4.** everyone has been cheating without penalty, the person reporting was not involved in this incident (but has cheated before), parents are involved in being upset about the discipline policy, a big deal is being made about something that you think is not even a problem, people have different opinions on what cheating is

    **Discussion:** Have students share their thoughts about the problems involved in each situation. Point out to students that there are several factors contributing to each problem situation.

    1. How could you simplify each of the four problems into simple statements? (**e.g., a new boss contributed to work problems, Angela didn't want to have sex with Terry, Phyllis wanted to dump her tennis coach, the teacher was upset with a class for cheating**)

    2. How does oversimplifying the situations change the whole way you look at the problem? (**it makes you miss a lot of the subtleties that still contribute to the problem**)

3. Do you think most problems involve lots of little factors, rather than one main problem? **(probably – life is complex!)**

4. Is there a simple solution to the problem situation in example 1? Why/why not? **(many people are involved)**

5. Does every person involved in that work situation have some choices? What? **(choice to comply, complain, talk to the boss, etc.)**

6. Does only Angela have the problem in example 2? **(both are involved)**

7. Did Angela owe Terry an explanation of her feelings early on in the relationship?

8. Does Angela owe Terry sex for the expensive dinners and presents?

9. Does Phyllis owe loyalty to the first instructor in example 3?

10. How could Phyllis make the problem worse? **(keep going behind the instructor's back)**

11. In example 4, is the problem with cheating or being caught cheating?

12. What values are esteemed by the students and the teacher?

13. Is there a way to handle this situation so that each and every student is treated fairly? **(not unless everyone confesses)**

14. Should Richard be punished even though he didn't copy from anyone?

15. Should the narrator be punished even though he or she didn't cheat on this assignment? Is the punishment directed toward cheating in general or cheating on this specific activity?

## Extension Activities:

1. Have students role play the situations on the worksheet, taking care to explain how each of the participants might feel under the circumstances. You may want to have several groups of students redo the role plays, showing different endings.

2. Look through headlines of articles in the newspaper. Have students demonstrate how problems are brought to attention through a simple statement, and then elaborated upon in the article to reveal more complex factors going on.

## Evaluation:

Demonstrate how each of these "simple" problems could be expanded to reveal complex factors affecting the situation.

a. You've been cut from the varsity football team.

b. You didn't get a scholarship you were counting on.

c. The rent in your apartment just went up $50 a month.

Name _____ Date _____

# Understanding the Problem Situation

**Directions:** Read the following situations. List several specific factors or problems that contribute to making the entire situation a problem.

1. Everything seemed to be going along fine at Office X until a new supervisor was hired. He wanted the employees to work faster, take no personal phone calls while on the job, and not  talk about things that were not work-related. The entire atmosphere at the office changed. While some workers felt they were pressured unfairly to work harder, others felt rewarded and noticed for their dedication to the company and their performance. Those who liked the new boss were unfriendly to those who did not like the new boss. Every day there were people who talked of quitting, not talking to other employees, and competing to get attention from the boss.

**What problems do you see in this situation?** _____

_____

2. Angela was dating Terry for a few weeks while everything was fun. He spent a lot of money on her every weekend, taking her out to expensive restaurants and buying her gifts. Angela liked Terry a lot as a friend, but wasn't sure she wanted to get more involved. Terry began pressuring her to have sex, and when she resisted, he became angry and hurt. Angela felt confused and hurt, also. Now they are not even talking at all to each other.

**What problems do you see in this situation?** _____

_____

3. Phyllis was taking tennis lessons from a friend of the family who used to play a lot when she was in high school. Phyllis was getting to be quite good – in fact, she was at the point that she was probably better than her instructor. She wanted to move up to a new level of training, but she didn't want to hurt her current instructor (who was planning to set her up in a city tournament). Phyllis found out about an instructor in town who was a professional player for awhile and is excited about taking Phyllis on as a new customer. Phyllis is afraid to talk to the friend of the family about this.

**What problems do you see in this situation?** _____

_____

4. Almost everyone in your English class has been cheating on the last research assignment. They copied from Richard, who was making some money by selling copies to people in the class. You,  however, did not copy from this person this time, although you have in the past. The teacher found out what was going on, and is furious. The school board is threatening to start expulsion procedures and parents are in an uproar about that too. You think it is unfair for everyone to be punished, especially because YOU did not cheat on this assignment. Everyone does it – why should the teacher be upset about this one?

**What problems do you see in this situation?** _____

_____

## VII-2 Coping with Surprises

**Objective:** The student will identify an appropriate coping strategy given problem situations.

**Comments:**

Even though we may make elaborate plans, there are always things that can and do go wrong. Part of being a good problem solver is the ability to cope with mistakes or surprises that happen. This is a time to think, regroup, assess the situation, and attempt to get back on track. In this lesson, students are given problem situations and are asked to identify a coping strategy.

**Introductory Activities:**

Have students consider the following situations. What possible things could go wrong?

a. planning an outdoor wedding

b. inviting your friends out to dinner without checking the prices on the menu

c. having two dates on the same night

**Activity:**

Students are to read on the worksheet "Coping with Surprises" the examples of unpleasant surprises that can happen and to write a way to cope with the situation. Ideally, the students should try to focus on getting "back on track" towards the original plan.

**Answers:** *(examples)* **1.** continue to entertain your friends by watching a movie on TV; **2.** ask the coach for more time if possible; **3.** use humor to announce that you are going to speak from the heart!; **4.** get to a telephone or wait for someone to come to the parking lot and get a ride to a safe place; **5.** make the best of it, have a good time with the ones who are there; **6.** try to find another truck (and another friend!); **7.** explain your situation to the supervisor, get a doctor's excuse; **8.** get up early and get to the school copier or another copier; **9.** get off at the first stop and get going in the right direction, make phone calls if necessary to let people know where you are; **10.** call a friend who is in your class and borrow a book

**Discussion:** Things often go wrong. In each case, have students share their ideas for ways to cope with the problems and get back on track. In some cases, they may just have to accept the situation and make the best of things. In others, they can actually try to do something to find another way to achieve the goal.

1. Why does it seem as though things go wrong at the worst possible time? Is this really true, or does it just seem that way? **(things may be more crucial at an important time)**

2. How can you prepare for mistakes to happen? **(think ahead, go through all of the things that might go wrong)**

3. When things are beyond your control, how can you use your personality to cope? **(show a sense of humor, ask for help, show strength and determination, etc.)**

4. Do you think people are sympathetic to your situation when you are in an embarrassing position? **(probably)**

5. In situations where you learn to cope with the unexpected, how do you think this could turn into a positive experience? **(prepare you for the same type of situation happening again, cause you to be more resourceful, etc.)**

### Extension Activities:

1. Have students locate copies of "Murphy's Law" which is a humorous interpretation of how things go wrong. Have students write a few of their own as they apply to their situations.

2. Have students locate cartoons, such as "The Far Side," which also depict situations in which things go horribly awry. Perhaps you have some artistic students who can draw their own renditions of humorous situations.

### Evaluation:

How could you cope with the following situations:

a. You are in the middle of a math test. Suddenly the batteries in your calculator are dead.

b. You are watching volleyball intramurals after school. A friend comes up to you and says, "Aren't you supposed to be babysitting for Mrs. Peters?" You realize you are an hour late and you totally forgot.

c. You are out on a date at an amusement park with someone you think is really special. He or she sees an old friend and disappears for a very long time. You are not sure if he or she is coming back.

Name _____ Date_____

# Coping with Surprises

**Directions:** Here are some situations in which some unplanned surprises come up. What could you do in each situation to cope with the problem and get yourself back on track?

1. You are showing a video at a party to your friends when suddenly the VCR shuts off and the tape is jammed inside.

   _____

2. You're on the track team, ready to run the biggest race of your season when you notice your shoe lace is about to break and one of the cleats is broken off.

   _____

3. You are giving a speech to ask students to elect you for Student Council president when you realize you have forgotten your notes and don't even know what your next sentence will be.

   _____

4. Your car won't start after play practice in the evening. It's dark, late, and you're alone. The parking lot is nearly empty.

   _____

5. You planned a huge surprise party for your best friend. Everyone said they would come, but only three people show up.

   _____

6. Fred promised you could use his pickup truck for your club's float for the parade. At the last minute, he informs you that he lent it to somebody else.

   _____

7. Your throat hurts a lot. You want to call in sick to work, but you've missed a lot of work lately and you're afraid you'll lose your job.

   _____

8. You're supposed to make copies of your report for the class, but the library copier is broken. It's 8 o'clock at night and nothing is open.

   _____

9. You're running late to get downtown. Accidentally, you find that you are on the wrong bus. You're headed uptown!

   _____

10. You have a huge algebra test tomorrow. You brought every book home from your locker . . . except the algebra book!

   _____

# VII-3 Adjusting to Change

**Objective:** The student will identify positive coping strategies that are necessary to handle changes in situations.

**Comments:**

Life is not predictable. There are often changes in schedules, personnel, resources, timing, and numerous other changes, many of which are unpredictable. Before allowing these unforeseen changes to throw us into a wild frenzy, it is helpful to stop, think, and decide how these changes will affect us. Some things will need to be done immediately; others may take longer. Coping with changes is a sign of maturation as well as a necessary life skill.

**Introductory Activities:**

How difficult would these changes be to adjust to:

a. changing a dentist appointment from 4:00 to 5:00

b. going from blonde hair to black hair

c. transferring to a high school in another state

d. finding out your single parent is getting married again

e. finding out that you have juvenile diabetes

**Activity:**

The worksheet "Adjusting to Change" gives situations that involve changes. Students are to read the two possible responses for each situation and circle the one that better depicts the person coping well with the change.

**Answers: 1.** first; **2.** second; **3.** first; **4.** second; **5.** first; **6.** first

**Discussion:** Students should discuss why the chosen response reflects the better choice of behavior or attitude in the matter and why the other response is not appropriate.

1. How many of the examples involve a change in attitude on the part of the main person? **(really, all of them involve having an attitude of wanting to work out the problem)**

2. Some of the changes were a result of someone else's mistake. Which ones? **(#3, #4)**

3. Even if something is not your responsibility, do you still have a responsibility to deal with the change? **(yes, if you're involved at all)**

4. How could a display of temper cause even bigger problems? **(might anger other employees, make a small problem seem larger, does nothing to solve the problem)**

5. Why do you think many people dislike change? **(they get used to doing something one way, get good at it and don't like to have things done differently)**

6. If you knew that change in the way you did something would be hard at first, but would eventually make your life easier, would you do it? **(hopefully)**

7. What are some technological changes that older people today are resisting or having difficulty with? **(VCRs, computers, bank machines, etc.)**

**Extension Activities:**

1. Have students look at a set of blueprints from the design of a house or other building project. Have them figure out why this is a good time to make changes, if changes are going to be made. What parallels can they determine between blueprints for a building project and planning other types of projects?

2. Have students think of examples of other changes that occur all the time. For example, substitutions of players in a basketball game, food substitutions at lunch, substitute teachers, etc. How do these changes affect others involved?

**Evaluation:**

Write a paragraph describing a change in your life that affected you deeply in some way. Did this change affect others also? Would you view this as a positive change now?

**Teacher Notes:**

_____

_____

_____

_____

_____

_____

Name _____  Date_____

# Adjusting to Change

**Directions:** Below are situations that are causing problems because there has been a change. Read the two possible responses for each and circle the one that shows the better coping response to the change.

---

1. Guess what? Mike, your best employee, just quit. It's too bad there's a big order that's due tomorrow.

   Let's get some ads out to try to hire someone new. Meanwhile, let's get some temporary help.

   What's his problem? How could he do this?

---

2. Your budget is just cut in half.

   I wonder if we can beg for more money from another department?

   I'll go over our expenses and see what we can cut.

---

3. That project is due tomorrow, not next week. I read this wrong!

   I guess I'll be working late tonight.

   It's just impossible. I can't do it.

---

4. Sorry I forgot to tell you, class, but the reports have to be typed.

   TYPED! Mine's already done by hand!

   I'll talk to him after class to see if he can make an exception.

---

5. That machine is broken, you'll have to use the other one.

   Could you go over the directions with me?

   Stupid machine!

---

6. You're now on the night shift.

   I'll need to make plans for sharing the car and getting a babysitter.

   I can't work nights. I'll never stay awake!

---

Name _____

# VII-4 Taking Responsibility for Mistakes

**Objective:** The student will identify mistakes that were made by lack of taking responsibility.

**Comments:**

When someone is given responsibility, it is his or her duty to fulfill that task. When mistakes arise because that responsibility was not taken seriously or was misunderstood, other problems can arise. Mistakes that are the result of foolishness or carelessness can truly be tragedies. In this lesson, students are to match causes and effects of making mistakes due to lack of taking responsibility for a situation.

**Introductory Activities:**

   a. Have students tell about the last task or responsibility that was assigned to them by their parents or other adult (not school-related).

   b. Have students rate how well they carried out that responsibility.

   c. Have students speculate as to what might have happened if they had neglected their responsibility.

**Activity:**

Students are to match on the worksheet "Taking Responsibility for Mistakes" causes of mistakes with the effect that would probably occur from that mistake.

**Answers: 1.** d; **2.** a; **3.** e; **4.** b; **5.** f; **6.** c

**Discussion:** Have students go over their answers on the worksheet and discuss how the problem in each could have been prevented.

   1. If you are given responsibility for a task and then a problem comes up, what new responsibility do you now have? **(responsibility for taking care of that problem)**

   2. On the worksheet, could all of those problems have been prevented if the person had taken more responsibility for doing the job right? **(yes)**

   3. In each case, who would the person report to? **(parent or adult, family, family members, teacher, owner of car, employer)**

   4. How could each individual take responsibility for the action that resulted? **(admit the problem, take steps to make things right)**

   5. In each case, how could the person make things right?

   6. Why might it be embarrassing to let someone know about your mistakes?

   7. What excuses could each person on the worksheet give?

   8. Do you think an employer or family member would rather hear excuses or apologies? Would they rather hear a plan to make things right?

   9. How could each person on the worksheet have done an excellent job at his or her task? **(spent time teaching the child something, walking the dog through the park, cleaning up the kitchen, doing a neat job on the report, driving carefully, delivering pizzas on time and courteously)**

   10. If the individuals had striven to do an excellent job, rather than finding themselves making mistakes, they would be getting credit instead of blame. Do you think that's important in these cases?

**Extension Activities:**

1. Have students find out what awards and incentives are given through businesses to their employees. They can check with their parents or look through the business pages in the paper. Sometimes the paper will print pictures of prominent employees who have taken a special course, done an exemplary job, participated in a special project, etc. Find out what types of recognition are printed.

2. Have students make a list of school awards and incentives given for exemplary work.

3. Sometimes prominent people will give the credit for their success to others, such as a parent, family member, teacher, or coach. Look for examples of stories in which a successful person has credited his or her success to someone else.

**Evaluation:**

a. List at least five responsibilities you have been given, either by a parent, teacher, coach, or other source.

b. State possible mistakes that could occur if you did not take that responsibility seriously and accurately.

**Teacher Notes:**

_____

_____

_____

_____

_____

# Taking Responsibility for Mistakes

**Directions:** Match the cause on the left with the effect on the right. Write the letter on the line next to each cause.

## VII-5 Considering Important Factors

**Objective:** The student will identify examples in which individuals have considered several factors that would affect the outcome of the situation.

**Comments:**

For many decisions, especially minor ones, there is probably little thought or planning that goes into the process of making that decision. But for more important decisions, one must consider a lot of factors. Sometimes how you "feel" at the time is not the way to make a productive decision. One should consider whatever factors are involved in that situation (price, efficiency, other people, deadlines, etc.). In this lesson, students are to identify individuals who have used a systematic plan to make a decision.

**Introductory Activities:**

a. Present students with the following situation: If you had the choice between taking $500 cash or a one-hour shopping spree in your favorite store, which would you choose?

b. Have students list what factors were involved in making their decision.

c. Present students with this situation: There is a $100 bill hidden in the room. How would they go about trying to find it? List some of their "plans."

**Activity:**

Students are to read the situations on the worksheet "Considering Important Factors" that involve an individual making a decision. The students are to decide which examples show the person considering the factors involved in the decision as opposed to those who are haphazard, or without a plan.

**Answers: 1.** no; **2.** yes; **3.** yes; **4.** no; **5.** yes; **6.** no

**Discussion:** Have students give and explain their responses to the worksheet.

1. Did all of the examples show a plan, even if the plan was haphazard or unworkable? **(yes, you could argue that even a bad plan is still a plan)**

2. In situation 1, if the word *some* was changed to *all*, would that be a more systematic plan? **(yes)**

3. What are the important factors to consider in situation 1? **(academic goals, how much money you have to spend, geographic location, etc.)**

4. Do you think this individual will make a good decision or will the decision be made for him? **(sounds like this is a passive person who probably won't get accepted to anything!)**

5. In situation 2, did you think this was a systematic plan? **(yes)**

6. What factors did the person consider to be important? **(work qualifications)**

7. In situation 3, what important factors were considered? **(flight times, rates)**

8. Did the person in situation 4 have a plan? **(sort of – just working on what he felt like)**

9. What could go wrong with that system? **(if you felt like quitting, your work would not get done)**

10. Is situation 5 an important decision? How much time should that decision take? **(it depends on whether it is a dinner for the president or dinner for the family, the person making the decision has eliminated the two main choices already and come up with an alternative)**

11. What factors were important to the person in situation 5? **(quality of meat, what was eaten recently, ease of preparation)**

12. In situation 6, does the individual have a good plan? **(no)**

13. Is a bad plan better than no plan at all, in that case? **(no – by sorting the checks in that manner it will really mess them up; it'll be worse than not doing anything because it might be mistaken for having been done correctly)**

14. Do you think most people put a lot of thought into daily decisions? **(probably not – choose by habit)**

15. Does any decision have important factors that go with it? **(yes)**

16. Does the process of identifying the important factors that go with a decision help make the best decision more clear? **(hopefully)**

## Extension Activities:

1. Have students look through the national news section of the newspaper. What important decisions do government officials have to make? What are some of the important factors that must be considered before making a decision?

2. Have students watch some of the congressional debates on television. What is involved in the decision-making process as far as considering important factors?

3. Have students list five to ten decisions they have directly or indirectly been involved in during the past week. Have them rate the importance of the decision (e.g., setting up the time of a dental appointment vs. selecting a new car) and list the factors involved in making that decision.

## Evaluation:

What factors are involved in making the following decisions:

a. whether to buy a St. Bernard puppy from a pet store or adopt a homeless adult small dog

b. going to a movie you don't really want to see with a person you are interested in or going out to an expensive dinner and special event with someone you really don't like

# Considering Important Factors

**Directions:** Each of these individuals is trying to make a decision. Decide which ones are considering the factors involved and which ones are not. Write YES or NO next to each example.

1. I'm not sure which college to go to. I guess I'll just apply to some of them and see where I get accepted.

_____

2. I can only hire one assistant. I'll go through their résumés, set up interviews with the ones who sound good, and then I'll pick one.

_____

3. There are four flights to New York. I'm going to check the times of arrival and departure to see which fit my schedule. Then I'll check rates for the flights and try to find a good deal.

_____

4. All this homework! I'll work on whatever I feel like for awhile. It will all get done.

_____

5. Should I buy ham or roast beef? Well, let's see...the ham is on sale, but it looks fatty. We had roast beef last night... I think I'll buy hamburger instead. That will be quick to fix for dinner.

_____

6. It's going to take forever to put all these checks in numerical order! I'll throw the ones with even numbers in one pile and odd numbers in the other.

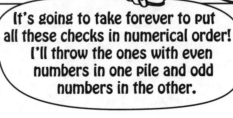

_____

# VII-6 Needs vs. Wants

**Objective:** Given examples, the student will identify a need vs. a want.

**Comments:**

Sometimes it is hard to distinguish between a need and a want. Do we need those new jeans or can we live without them? Is it necessary for survival to have expensive shoes or is it important because everyone else has them? Again, making a good decision must involve considering the factors. You have to have clothes, but you must consider the appropriateness of the occasion, cost, quality, etc. In this lesson, students are given situations that can roughly be divided into wants and needs, and must categorize them.

**Introductory Activities:**

    a. Inform students that Christmas (or Hanukkah) is coming early and they can have five things they want. Have them make their lists.

    b. Inform students they are being sent to the moon for a week. Have them make a list of five items they would take with them.

    c. Have students compare the items on the lists. What would qualify an item as a "want" or a "need"?

    d. Have students come up with working definitions for the terms *want* and *need*. A want could be considered something that would be helpful to have, but not necessary to accomplish a certain goal. A need could be something that is crucial to completion of a goal. In that respect, new shoes may be a want if a person already has shoes for walking around, but specific shoes may be a need if the person must have a certain type of footwear to play a sport.

**Activity:**

Students are to read the statements on the worksheet "Needs vs. Wants" in which a desire for something is expressed. From the context, they are to determine whether the item involved is a "want" or a "need." The purpose of the lesson is not so much to sort through the responses, but to look for additional factors that would indicate what the goal is in each situation.

    **Answers:** *(suggestions – allow for discussion to clarify the student's responses and thinking)* **1.** need (socially expected); **2.** want; **3.** want; **4.** need (proper clothing); **5.** need (medicine); **6.** want; **7.** need (tools for completing assignments); **8.** depends on the situation – since it is the "ultimate" we can assume that the buyer has some choices and "wants" this specific item; **9.** need (hygiene); **10.** want (but depends on the situation – if a car is the only way that the individual can get to school, it would be a "need"); **11.** could be either – does the coursework depend a lot on using a personal computer for assignments?; **12.** need

    **Discussion:** In each of the examples on the worksheet, there are other questions that can and should be asked to clarify the situation. Depending on that situation, either answer could be justified! Encourage students to think!

1. What are some examples of items that would be considered "needs" in terms of social behavior? **(gifts, cards, bridesmaid dresses, taking someone out to dinner, etc.)**

2. Besides oxygen, food, clothing, and shelter, what are some other "needs" that humans have? **(need to be loved, need for friendship, need to play, etc.)**

3. Is it wrong to want something expensive if it is available in a cheaper model? **(not necessarily – if you have the money to buy something nice, it's not a problem)**

4. If your goal was to be the best football player in your school, what might be some of your equipment needs? **(padding, shoes, helmet, etc.)**

5. What would be some of your other needs? **(time for training, good coaching, adequate sleep, proper nutrition, etc.)**

6. Is it wrong to want things? **(not necessarily)**

7. When you make decisions, should you consider "wants" as well as "needs"? **(absolutely! Focus on your goals!)**

## Extension Activities:

1. For each of the examples on the worksheet, have students construct a situation in which the item is a "want" and then a "need." By manipulating the situations, each item could conceivably fit into either category.

2. Have students investigate Abraham Maslow's hierarchy of human needs. Make a chart indicating this theory of what humans need and what is included at each level.

## Evaluation:

a. Give an example of something that is a "need" for you. Explain your example.

b. Give an example of something that is a "want" for you. Explain your example.

Name _____ Date_____

# Needs vs. Wants

**Directions:** Read the following statements. Does each indicate something that the person *needs* or something that the person *wants*? Write the answer on the line.

_____ **1.** I got invited to Sarah's birthday party. I must decide what to get her for a gift.

_____ **2.** That was a great dinner. What shall I order for dessert?

_____ **3.** Oh, that little kitten is so cute. I'll take her home with me.

_____ **4.** This sock has a huge hole in it. I'll get new ones.

_____ **5.** Where is my cough medicine? Cough, cough, cough!

_____ **6.** I love how this perfume smells. And it's only $40 an ounce!

_____ **7.** Shoot! This pen ran out of ink! I'll have to replace it.

_____ **8.** This is the ultimate stereo system. I don't care that I have to make many payments – it's worth it!

_____ **9.** I like this brand of toothpaste.

_____ **10.** How am I going to get to school if I don't have a car?

_____ **11.** Everyone in the class has a personal computer but me.

_____ **12.** My calculator stopped working. It needs new batteries.

# VII-7 Immediate Results vs. Waiting

**Objective:** Given a decision-making situation, the student will identify possible short- and long-term effects of a choice.

## Comments:

Sometimes students are tempted to make decisions that seem to be great for immediate satisfaction, but are not best in the long run. It might be hard to take the time to think through the consequences of making a decision, especially when a choice might yield something desirable right away. In this lesson, students are to consider situations that may yield better results if a choice is put off until a better time.

## Introductory Activities:

a. Ask students if they would rather have $1,000 right now or $1,000,000 in ten years. Tally their responses.

b. What would be the benefits of having money right away?

c. What would be the benefits of waiting and having a much larger sum?

d. What might be a drawback of waiting for the larger amount of money?

## Activity:

Explain to students that they are going to consider some situations on the worksheet "Immediate Results vs. Waiting" in which individuals must make a decision about some aspect of their life. They are to answer questions that direct them to consider short-term effects and long-term consequences.

**Answers:** *(examples)* **Situation 1-a.** whether or not he can join the truck driving program later or if it has to be right now, if he has any other sources of money, if he can work and go through training at the same time; **b.** he would have to do the training program later, he would have money to pay his rent, he could start saving money; **c.** he might have to borrow the money until he is finished with the training and can get another job; **d.** Students may suggest that Jeff work part-time and try to get into the program later. Since he doesn't have any money saved up, he may need to learn to budget his money and activities.

**Situation 2-a.** if Kari is going to work, how much money they have saved up, how much free time they want to spend with each other; **b.** yes; **c.** Kari thinks she would have something to take care of, maybe would not have to work, Sam would have to have a secure income to support the family, a lot of time might be spent at home instead of going out; **d.** they could save money, have time together, get to know each other, plan for children when they are more settled

**Situation 3-a.** how much she needs the job, if there is advancement in the job, how much of her day is spent directly involved with the boss, how much she enjoys her work; **b.** she would start all over, looking for work, might get a bad recommendation from her boss, but she might be directed towards a better job and better situation; **c.** learn patience, get respect from other employers who understand her situation, save money until she's in a better position to leave; **d.** talk to another supervisor, possibly talk to the boss, ask for a transfer within the company; **e.** Students may say that the stress is not worth the job. If Elinor is a good worker, she will probably be able to find another job.

**Discussion:** Students may have varied responses to the worksheet. Have them discuss how they arrived at their conclusions.

**Extension Activities:**

1. Waiting seems hard to do, especially for a teenager. Have students make personal lists of things they consider worth waiting for. Depending on the student, this may include a college degree, marriage, sex, buying a house, etc.

2. Have students write endings for the situations on the worksheet. There are ways for all of the decisions to end positively.

**Evaluation:**

Explain your feelings of the following well-known quotations:

"He who hesitates is lost."

"Fools rush in where angels dare to tread."

**Teacher Notes:**

_____

_____

_____

_____

_____

# Immediate Results vs. Waiting

**Directions:** Each individual below needs to make a decision about something in his or her life. The decision must be made right away; but help each individual figure out the consequences of doing something immediately or waiting.

**Situation 1:** Jeff can work at a hardware store for minimum wage right away or he can enroll in a technical program that will train him for truck driving, which is what he really wants to do. However, he does not have any money saved up and needs to pay rent.

**(a)** What factors does Jeff need to consider? _____

_____

**(b)** If Jeff decides to work at the store, what affect would that have on the factors in (a)?

_____

**(c)** If Jeff goes to truck driving school, how could he handle the factors in (a)?_____

_____

**(d)** What do you think Jeff should do?_____

_____

**Situation 2:** Sam and Kari have been married for a few months. Kari wants to have a baby right away and wants to stay home to take care of it. Sam has a pretty good job, but he's not sure he wants to be a father so soon.

**(a)** What factors do Sam and Kari have to consider?_____

_____

**(b)** Is it important that Sam and Kari agree on their decision? _____

_____

**(c)** What are some immediate results of having a baby right away? _____

_____

**(d)** What are some reasons for them to wait? _____

_____

**Situation 3:** Elinor works for a man whom she detests. He is often unfair with how much work he gives her to do, never compliments her on a good job, and has temper tantrums. Elinor likes her work, but she comes home stressed and edgy. Every day seems to get worse.

**(a)** What factors does Elinor have to consider?_____

_____

**(b)** What results would probably happen if Elinor quit?_____

_____

**(c)** What benefits might occur if she stayed on the job? _____

_____

**(d)** Is there anything Elinor can do to change her situation? _____

_____

**(e)** What do you think Elinor should do? _____

_____

# VII-8 Following Through

**Objective:** The student will state the importance of following through on a decision, particularly when it involves a commitment to others.

**Comments:**

Sometimes decisions can, and should, be reversed. If new information comes in, or something happens that changes original plans and goals, decisions may have to be adjusted. When one is in a position of making decisions that affect other people and require planning, however, it is a good idea to recognize when to stick with the decision. In this lesson, students are given situations to evaluate.

**Introductory Activities:**

Ask students to rate the following situations according to how important the decision is:

a. deciding to order pepperoni pizza and then changing your mind to sausage pizza

b. deciding to marry Tom and then changing your mind to marry Wayne

c. deciding to negotiate trade agreements with a European nation and then changing your mind to declare nuclear war instead

**Activity:**

This lesson involves following through on a decision. In the examples on the worksheet "Following Through," the decisions are from the point of view of a manager or person in a decision-making role; that is, others are subject to the effects of that decision. The decision is stated and the person is identified. The student must then decide which of the two responses indicates that the person is following through on the decision.

**Answers: 1.** b; **2.** a; **3.** a; **4.** b; **5.** a

**Discussion:** Each situation involves identifying a group of people who are affected by the decision. The decision itself may also be questioned. Use the following questions to discuss students' ideas about the importance of following through on a decision.

1. Would you say that the more people who are involved in a decision, the more important that decision is? **(possibly, but each individual decision that a person makes is very important to him or her)**

2. In example 1, do you think the decision is unfair? **(depends on whether or not employees were abusing the privilege)**

3. If some of the employees were spending half of their time talking on the phone, how would that affect the business?

4. Do you think the boss would allow exceptions?

5. In example 2, how many people are affected by the coach's decision? **(the players)**

6. If the situation changes, as it seemed to in the example, why shouldn't the coach change his mind? **(the other players are expecting a certain play or pattern)**

7. How would a last-minute change in plan affect the other players? **(they might be confused, caught off guard)**

8. In example 3, do you think the teacher changing a due date is unfair to students? **(probably, unless there was a lot of time)**

9. Do you know of examples of teachers changing assignment dates to make them later? How do you feel about that if you are one of the people who had planned to be finished on time?

10. How many people are affected by the bride's decision in example 4? **(the dressmaker)**

11. In the case of alterations, is it a fair policy to make someone purchase the dress if the person changes her mind? **(yes, since the alterations took time and involved work there's usually a policy stated up-front about this)**

12. In example 5, what types of decisions need to be made resulting from the decision to go to Florida? **(when to go, reservations, time off from work, etc.)**

13. Why would changing the geographical location of a vacation be an important decision? **(clothing, tickets, other plans)**

14. In this case, if everyone involved agreed they would rather go skiing, is anyone inconvenienced by the change in decision? **(not particularly)**

## Extension Activities:

1. Have students tell of examples of decisions that are important to follow-through on. They may have some anecdotes from personal experience about decisions that were not followed up on, leading to some interesting consequences.

2. People are constantly making decisions. Many daily decisions are seemingly of little consequence; for example, what to wear, what to eat, what route to take walking home, and so on. Yet in particular situations, these decisions could be crucial. **(dietary restrictions, social events, who might be waiting along a certain route home, etc.)** Others may involve a lot of people, time, or consequences. Have students make a list of 20 to 30 decisions that they have made in the past 24 hours. Have them rate the personal importance of each and describe the factors on their "rating scale."

3. Have students write and perform humorous role plays in which a character cannot make up his or her mind about a decision. ("I'll have a strawberry shake. No, wait, make that chocolate. Well, maybe peach sounds good. I'll have what she's having.")

## Evaluation:

Write a possible consequence of the person in each example below not following through on his or her decision:

a. I know my doctor tells me I need to have gall bladder surgery, but I've changed my mind. I don't want an operation.

b. I've decided not to sell the house after all.

c. No one in the company is going to get a raise this year.

# Following Through

**Directions:** In each set of cartoons below, one shows the person following through on a decision. Circle **A** or **B**.

**1. Decision:** There will be no more personal phone calls made on office time.

**A**
Maybe that was a bad decision – emergencies do happen from time to time.

**B**
People will plan their time better if they make phone calls during breaks.

**2. Decision:** Stretch Roberts will try for the last basket during this basketball game. He is the best shot on the team.

**A**
Give Stretch the ball!

**B**
Wait! Ace is in a better position – throw it to him.

**3. Decision:** The research paper will be due at the end of the semester.

**A**
Everyone knows the due date and should be finished.

**B**
I'm planning to go on vacation – I'll make the paper due in three weeks.

**4. Decision:** I'll take that wedding dress. It will need alterations, however, or it won't fit me just right.

**A**
Here's my deposit back – I decided I found another one I like better. I'm sure you can sell it again to someone who is my size.

**B**
There are so many things to plan; I will stick with this dress.

**5. Decision:** We're going to Florida over spring break.

**A**
Here are our plane tickets, hotel reservations, and new suitcases. I'm working on plans for what we'll do.

**B**
Let's go skiing instead. We'll need all new clothes.

## VII-9 Changing Bad Decisions

**Objective:** The student will offer at least one option available to a given individual who had made a bad decision.

**Comments:**

Unfortunately, not all of our decisions turn out to be the "right" ones. In retrospect, we can sometimes see that we should have asked more questions, thought a little longer, or maybe done a little more homework before making a decision. In this lesson, students are given situations in which an individual made a decision that turned out to be a mistake. They are to come up with a new decision to better the situation.

**Introductory Activities:**

a. Tell students: "I want everyone in the class to jump out of their seats and squawk like a chicken." Observe the chaos for a minute or two and then try to get the attention back!

b. Have students decide whether or not that was a good decision. **(probably not)** Why? **(loss of classroom control)**

c. Ask students to predict what would probably happen if you (the teacher) asked students to toss pencils around the room and scream at the top of their lungs. **(they would probably do it)** Why is it likely that you would not make the decision to ask them to do this, especially when your class was being observed? **(from the first episode, you were able to see that the class was willing to follow crazy orders; also it would make your discipline very questionable if the class were to be observed)**

**Activity:**

Students are to read the situations on the worksheet "Changing Bad Decisions" and decide what each person in the example could do to make the best of a bad decision. In each case, have students think about making a new decision, hopefully with new knowledge of the situation.

**Answers:** *(examples)* **1.** decide to take back the keys until further notice; **2.** decide to tell his parents that he doesn't know Amanda very well; **3.** decide to tie the puppy outside; **4.** decide to call home and get a ride with someone else; **5.** decide to take back the game and get a gift certificate instead; **6.** decide to be polite and inform them that they weren't expecting this number of people; **7.** decide to pick up her daughter and look for a new babysitter; **8.** decide to talk to the girl ahead of time about the problem and mention that there might be hard feelings

**Discussion:** Students may have various, creative ideas for the situations. Listen to them and try to come up with some good solutions.

1. In situation 1, Mr. Wu felt he had made a bad decision. Why? **(his daughter was not a careful driver)**

2. If he had thought about the situation more carefully ahead of time, would he have been able to figure this out before buying her a car? **(probably)**

3. What made this a bad decision? **(his daughter was not a good recipient of a car; it would only get her in trouble)**

4. Is a bad outcome the same thing as a bad decision? **(it could be thought of that way; the outcome would determine the value of the decision)**

5. In situation 2, at what point did Fred realize he had made a bad decision? (**when he saw the way she was dressed**)

6. Is there any way he could have foreseen that situation? (**possibly not, he didn't know her very well**)

7. Could the problems in situation 3 been thought of ahead of time? (**yes, puppies are somewhat predictable in that department**)

8. What was Debbie's bad decision? (**to get into the car**)

9. In situation 5, what could Peter have done ahead of time to pick a more appropriate present for his cousin? (**asked around to see what kind of games he liked**)

10. In situation 6, the Robertsons made an attempt to do something nice for their neighbors, and apparently were taken advantage of. How would this affect what they will do the next time they invite someone to dinner? (**probably specify how many are invited**)

11. What decision will Mrs. Greenberg make the next time she looks for a baby-sitter? (**decide to ask for references, observe the babysitter**)

12. In situation 8, do you think Paula will redo her next birthday list more carefully? (**probably**)

13. How could Paula still end up with a successful birthday party? (**make sure everyone will behave themselves, un-invite the key problem girl**)

## Extension Activities:

1. Have students look for examples of bad decisions. They may find examples from politics, in particular, political cartoons. Have them explain why the outcome was particularly bad for the individual who made the decision.

2. Have students share anecdotes of their own dealings with decisions they have regretted.

3. Have students talk to older adults who probably have some regrets about decisions they have made. If willing to share their ideas, have the adults talk about some of them in class.

## Evaluation:

Write a paragraph describing a decision in which you were involved that you would consider to be a "bad" decision. What was the outcome? Were there any clues that this decision would give this result? What would you do differently the next time, with this new knowledge?

Name _____ Date_____

# Changing Bad Decisions

**Directions:** What could each person below do to make a change in plans after realizing that he or she had made a bad decision? What new decision could be made?

1. Mr. Wu had decided to buy his daughter a new car. He soon realized that she was going to end up crashing it because she was not a careful driver.

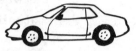

_____

_____

2. Fred realized he had made a mistake when he asked Amanda out for a date and she showed up at his parents' house wearing outrageous clothes and having purple-and-green striped hair.

_____

_____

3. Jill bought a new puppy and didn't think twice about taking it over to her girlfriend's apartment...until it had several "accidents" on the floor.

_____

_____

4. Debbie got into the car with Eddie and realized he had been drinking. She hoped he would get her home safely.

_____

_____

5. Peter bought a videogame for his cousin for a birthday present and then noticed that the cousin already had the game. The cousin made the comment that it was really a stupid game for only babies to play.

_____

_____

6. Mr. and Mrs. Robertson invited their new neighbors over for dinner and were surprised when they showed up with their seven children, eight in-laws, and three of their friends.

_____

_____

7. Mrs. Greenberg dropped her young daughter off at the new babysitter's and turned around to wave good-bye. The babysitter was already yelling at her daughter and threatening to spank her.

_____

_____

8. Paula sent out invitations to a birthday party at her house for Saturday night, when she realized that several of her friends were angry at one of the other girls she had invited because she was dating their boyfriends.

_____

_____

# VII-10 Using Resources

**Objective:** The student will identify at least ten different resources available to him or her.

**Comments:**

Many types of resources are available to most people if they will stop and think about them. Not only are people available to help, but there are other resources such as publications, institutions, possessions, and intangibles such as time, one's own skills and creativity. In this lesson, students are to think about types of resources available to them.

**Introductory Activities:**

Ask students what they could do if:

a. they needed $10 to buy something? **(write a check, go to the bank)**

b. a button came off of their shirt? **(sew it back on, take it to their mother)**

c. a friend asked if you would teach them how to play tennis? **(get them a book, go out on the court and spend time teaching)**

d. Define *resource*. **(something that is available to help relieve a situation or achieve a goal; examples are people, skills, tools, institutions, equipment, publications, etc.)**

e. What resources did you come up with for (a)? **(money, a bank)**

f. What resources did you come up with for (b)? **(a skill, a parent)**

g. What resources did you come up with for (c)? **(a skill, a book)**

**Activity:**

Make sure students have a fairly good idea of what is meant by a resource. Explain that they will now have some situations to consider which require the use of resources to solve. They are given one example of a possible resource on the worksheet "Using Resources" and are to think of two additional resources. They can discuss how the resources can be used to solve the problem.

**Answers:** *(examples)* **1.** realtor, neighbor; **2.** friend, brochure; **3.** tuxedo shop, other clothes; **4.** friend who just turned 18, post office; **5.** department of motor vehicles, police department; **6.** friend, phone book; **7.** teacher, computer tutorial; **8.** bus station attendant, phone call; **9.** community bulletin board, friends; **10.** doctor, information that came with the medicine

**Discussion:** Have students share their ideas of resources that would help solve the problems on the worksheet. You may want to keep a running list of what "type" of resource was selected; e.g., person, skill, institution, etc.

1. What personal resources – your talents, abilities, personality – do you have?

2. What kinds of problems or needs would someone who was new in town encounter? **(where to live, work, how to find places, etc.)**

3. What are some community resources that would help someone in this situation? **(maps, phone book, neighbors)**

4. What people are available as resources to you in situations where you need advice or someone to listen? **(friends, family, counselor)**

5. What people are resources for you if you needed help with physical tasks, such as moving, painting, or getting a ride? **(friends, neighbors)**

6. In what ways could these resources be helpful to someone: the local YMCA, library, a workshop, computer lab, newspaper, correspondence school classes, typewriter, ability to type, huge bank account?

## Extension Activities:

1. Have students take personal inventory of the resources available to them. Do they have a sister who can cut hair? a driver's license? a savings account? a car? Have them come up with at least 50 different items.

2. To help students remember the categories or types of resources, have them collectively or in small groups work on a wall poster with drawings, magazine pictures, photographs, etc., depicting resources. You may want to title categories such as: PEOPLE, SKILLS, PLACES, TOOLS, etc.

## Evaluation:

a. What is a definition for a *resource*?

b. Give an example of a person who is a resource for you, a tool that you have used, a building/institution, and a skill or talent that is a personal resource. Explain how each has helped you achieve a goal or relieve a problem situation.

Name _____  Date _____

# Using Resources

**Directions:** Read the following problems. Next to each one is listed a possible resource that could help solve the problem. Add two others to the list and then specify how you could use any of the resources to solve the problem.

**Problem**

**1.** You are unfamiliar with a city that you have just moved to. You want to find a place to live.

_____

**2.** You are responsible for planning a group trip to an amusement park. You think you heard something about a discount for more than ten people.

_____

**3.** You need to rent a tuxedo for a wedding that you will be in, but you are not sure of your size.

_____

**4.** You just turned 18 and want to register to vote.

_____

**5.** You have to renew your driver's license.

_____

**6.** Your car is making funny noises and you want to know who a good mechanic in town is.

_____

**Resources**

city map

_____

_____

phone book

_____

_____

friend who does alterations

_____

_____

city hall

_____

_____

parents

_____

_____

gas station manager

_____

_____

## Using Resources, continued

**7.** You are having trouble with your math and are afraid you aren't going to pass.

    tutor

_____

_____

**8.** You need to know what time the last bus leaves for the next town.

    bus schedule

_____

_____

**9.** You want someone to help you paint your house.

    newspaper

_____

_____

**10.** You have a high fever, stomach ache, and dizziness. The medicine you took is making you feel worse.

    pharmacist

_____

_____

## VII-11 Reliable Resources

**Objective:** Given examples, the student will identify reliable resources and explain why.

**Comments:**

"You can't believe everything you hear." Likewise, anyone can hang out a shingle but it is no guarantee that the person is a competent, trustworthy individual. Students need to learn to evaluate whether or not a resource is truly reliable. This might mean checking credentials, asking a friend for a recommendation, obtaining a written warranty, and considering the personal relationship of the person giving the comments. In this lesson, students are to evaluate resources and decide whether or not they are reliable.

**Introductory Activities:**

Give students the following choice to consider:

They are taking a trip and are going to fly. They can choose between – a flight on Airline A, which has a perfect flight record for the past 30 years, but is more expensive; or a flight on Airline B, which uses old planes with old parts and has the worst flight record of all major airlines but offers economy rates.

Which airline would students probably choose? **(Airline A)** Why? **(they value their life, has a better record, is more RELIABLE)**

**Activity:**

Have students complete the worksheet "Reliable Resources" which has examples of statements describing some resources. They must decide whether or not the resource sounds reliable or not.

**Answers:** *(suggested – students may be able to justify different responses!)* **1.** no; **2.** yes; **3.** yes; **4.** no; **5.** no; **6.** no; **7.** yes; **8.** yes; **9.** yes; **10.** no; **11.** yes; **12.** no; **13.** no; **14.** yes; **15.** yes; **16.** no

**Discussion:** Have students explain the reasoning for their answers on the worksheet. In some cases, more information about the situation would be helpful, but is not given.

1. What makes a resource seem reliable?

2. Why would you tend to doubt the reliability of a person who was trying to sell you a watch in a parking lot? **(don't know his reputation)**

3. How important is reputation in evaluating a resource? **(very important)**

4. How does a warranty or guarantee of a product or service protect your safety? **(can take it back if it's defective, it's like a promise that it will be acceptable)**

5. How important are credentials when checking out the services of a doctor, dentist, contractor, or other provider? **(very important)**

6. How could you go about checking on the credentials of such a person? **(ask friends, ask questions, check with the Better Business Bureau, etc.)**

7. Why might you trust the opinion of someone who was a family friend rather than someone with whom you did not get along personally? **(the family friend would probably have your best interests in mind, the other person may not care)**

**Extension Activities:**

1. Have students collect and display magazine ads of products that try to declare their reliability, e.g., watches that "keep on ticking."
2. Have students take note of television commercials that promise services, such as personal injury lawyers. Have them evaluate whether or not the ads seem reliable.
3. Have students examine warranties on items such as a car, pet, appliance, etc. What does the small print indicate?

**Evaluation:**

Give an example of:

(a) a reliable person

(b) a reliable product

(c) a reliable form of transportation

(d) a reliable piece of equipment

Explain your choices.

# Reliable Resources

**Directions:** Do these items sound like examples of reliable resources to you? Write YES or NO on the lines.

_____ 1. A doctor who got his license from a mail order magazine.

_____ 2. A builder who has built several houses in your neighborhood that appear to be very nice.

_____ 3. A phone number in the local phone book.

_____ 4. A salesperson for a used car dealership that is being investigated by the Internal Revenue Service for tax fraud.

_____ 5. A story about aliens coming to Earth to steal people.

_____ 6. An old car that is covered with rust, has a flat tire, and has a gas gauge on "empty."

_____ 7. The local weather report for tomorrow.

_____ 8. The number of calories in a candy bar as reported by the wrapper.

_____ 9. The warning label on a bottle of prescription medicine.

_____ 10. The personal habits of your neighbor as reported by the town gossip.

_____ 11. A 30-day warranty on game parts for a computer game you purchased at a department store.

_____ 12. A pair of jeans that is purchased from a rack marked "As is."

_____ 13. A watch from a man in a trench coat in a parking lot behind a bar.

_____ 14. A kitten purchased from a pet store with a two-month guarantee of good health.

_____ 15. The opinion of the wiring in your house from an engineer who is a good friend of your father.

_____ 16. The opinion of your piano-playing ability from someone who can't stand you.

# VII-12 Fact vs. Opinion

**Objective:** The student will correctly identify statements as being either fact or opinion.

**Comments:**

Part of making a judgment as to the reliability of a resource is considering whether the information is a person's opinion or if it is a fact. Some people can be very convincing and give seemingly logical arguments for statements that are not true. In this lesson, students are to examine statements and decide whether or not they are fact or opinion.

**Introductory Activities:**

  a. Define *fact.* (**something that is always true, based on evidence that no one can argue about**)

  b. Define *opinion.* (**an expression of how someone feels about something; may or may not be true**)

  c. Have students give an example of a fact about something in the classroom (e.g., the time, the color of the walls, etc.).

  d. Have students give an example of an opinion on how they feel about the school cafeteria food.

**Activity:**

Students are to examine the statements on the worksheet "Fact vs. Opinion" and decide whether or not it is an example of a fact or an opinion. Have them look for "clue words" or other subtleties that may indicate the comment is an opinion.

  **Answers: 1.** fact; **2.** fact; **3.** fact; **4.** opinion; **5.** opinion; **6.** opinion; **7.** fact; **8.** opinion; **9.** opinion; **10.** fact

  **Discussion:** Make sure students understand the reasoning behind the examples. Clarify any questions.

  1. Where is a good place to hear opinions expressed? (**cafeteria, pool hall, church socials, etc.**)

  2. When is a good time or during what events would you hear opinions expressed? (**political elections, debates, etc.**)

  3. Who or what would be a good, reliable resource to give you factual information about: investing your money? (**banker, investor**) buying a good car? (**consumer reports, friend in the business**) traveling to a foreign country? (**travel agent**)

  4. If someone appeared to be truly sincere, would that make him or her more believable? (**probably**)

  5. Why do we take into account the way a person acts and looks as much as the words they use? (**we tend to look at the whole person**)

  6. What were some clues on the worksheet that tipped you off that it was an opinion being expressed? (**"I think"; words like "always," "never," "everyone," etc.**)

**Extension Activities:**

1. Have students come up with a list of 20 facts and 20 opinions. Have them cite their sources for the facts.

2. Have students circulate quietly in populated areas and listen for opinions being expressed. Write the examples they hear (e.g., "I think the Bulls will win this year," "I like pizza," etc.) Compare findings.

3. Tape and discuss television commercials. How much of what is presented is factual? How much is opinion? Does it depend on the product?

**Evaluation:**

a. What is a fact?

b. What is an opinion?

c. Give three examples of facts.

d. Give three examples of opinions.

e. Take one of your opinions and turn it into a fact.

**Teacher Notes:**

_____

_____

_____

_____

_____

# Fact vs. Opinion

**Directions:** Are the following statements examples of facts or opinions? Write your answer on the lines.

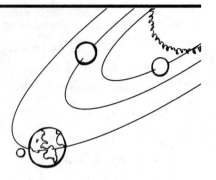

1. The owner's manual states that you should rotate the tires on a car and change the oil regularly to maintain it properly.

    _____

2. Earth is the third planet from the sun.

    _____

3. There are about 140 calories in a can of non-diet soda.

    _____

4. When buying an appliance, you should purchase the most expensive warranty possible.

    _____

5. Fish make better pets for people who live in apartments than cats or dogs.

    _____

6. It is easy to drive through Chicago in the middle of the day.

    _____

7. Thomas Jefferson was our third president.

    _____

8. I think First Bank and Trust will give you a good deal on a car loan.

    _____

9. No one in New York City is friendly to strangers.

    _____

10. Blood travels through the body through the circulatory system.

    _____

## VII-13 Time Management

**Objective:** The student will be familiar with several strategies for using time efficiently when given several tasks to complete.

**Comments:**

It seems as though there is never enough time to get everything done. Students may have their days filled with school, sports, working, friends, chores at home, and numerous other activities, all of which are important. Much can be accomplished if time is valued and used efficiently. Students are introduced to several time-saving strategies in this lesson.

**Introductory Activities:**

a. Ask students what they would do if they were given an extra hour in their day.

b. To have students experience at least one dimension of "time," select two or three volunteers and have them put their heads down on cue and have them raise their hands quietly when they think one minute is up. The rest of the class can observe. Did time seem to pass slowly for these students?

**Activity:**

on the worksheet "Time Management," students are to read the story of a girl who has mismanaged her time to an extreme. They are to note (this can be done by underlining specific passages in the story) instances in which the girl in the story got "off-track" or did not use her time efficiently.

**Answers:** overslept, had not done homework from night before, had not done laundry, slept through study hall, looked through magazine instead of studying, watched more TV than necessary, forgot soap at the store, shopped for nail polish

**Discussion:** Have students compare instances they selected as representative of mismanaged time.

1. At what point did this day begin to go off-track for Sandy? **(when she overslept, but it was set up for problems when she didn't do her work the night before)**

2. What could she have done the night before to be better prepared for this day? **(laundry, homework)**

3. What activities could have been shortened? **(length of time she slept, watched TV, or shopped)**

4. What activities could have been rearranged? **(prepare food for dinner before doing homework or talking with a friend)**

5. What activities could have been eliminated? **(shopping, talking with friend, watching TV)**

6. How could making a list have helped Sandy with shopping and other chores? **(could have helped her shorten her shopping time, keep reminding her of what she was supposed to be doing)**

7. Are there other shortcuts she could have taken to get everything done? **(ask friend to help with chores, shop on a different day)**

8. What is an example of activities that Sandy can and did do at the same time? **(walking dog and thinking about science project)**

9. What are some other activities that could be done simultaneously? (**doing laundry and thawing out frozen food, watching television and preparing food, walking the dog and practicing a speech, etc.**)

10. What do you think is Sandy's basic problem? Is she lazy, disorganized, or just too busy?

11. What would you suggest Sandy do to get ready for tomorrow? (**make sure she has clothes ready, homework done, sets the alarm, talks to mom about dinner plans, etc.**)

## Extension Activities:

1. Have students figure out approximately how many hours they spent on a typical school day involved in certain activities, such as: sleeping, studying, recreation and leisure, etc. Help them construct a circle graph depicting the different categories.

2. Have students design and maintain a daily time planner or schedule. Try it out for a week. Have them look for patterns of time that could be used in different ways.

3. List the various strategies for efficiently using time and have students make a conscious effort to try using them. You may want to make a colorful poster and put it in a conspicuous place. *Strategies:* shorten tasks, rearrange tasks, eliminate tasks, do tasks simultaneously, list tasks, prepare for tasks.

## Evaluation:

a. List and describe at least three time-management techniques.

b. List at least two activities you would like to spend more time doing. How could you plan to give yourself more time?

c. List at least two activities you could manage much more efficiently. Describe how you could do this.

# Time Management

**Directions:** Here is a day in Sandy's life. Look for examples of how she did not use her time wisely to accomplish everything she wanted or needed to do that day. Underline those examples.

The day started out when the alarm clock went off and Sandy rolled over and went back to sleep. When she woke up again, she realized she had overslept, missed the bus to school, and did not have time to do the homework she had left over from the night before. She got up, found the laundry basket, and took out some clothes to wear. She wished she had remembered to get the laundry done the night before. Her mother was busy working overtime and didn't do as many chores around the house as she used to.

After getting a late pass from the office, Sandy went to the first class of the day – study hall. Since there were only ten minutes left of class, she didn't feel she had time to start anything, so she put her head down and tried to catch up on some missed sleep.

Later in the day, she realized she had a test (which she put off studying for) and a paper that was due. She told herself she would get it done that night and turn it in the next day for at least partial credit.

After school, Sandy had basketball practice. She got a ride home with a friend who wanted to know if she could stay for a while and work on math together. Sandy thought that would be fine, but instead of working on math, they decided to look through a magazine and pick out new hair styles.

Soon, Sandy heard her mother's car pulling into the driveway and she panicked when she realized her mother had asked her to take out frozen chopmeat and let it thaw after school. She quickly ran into the kitchen and put it in the microwave, hoping it would begin to thaw.

Sandy, her friend, and her mother called for a pizza to be delivered and watched television for an hour to relax. Sandy's friend left and Sandy was about to get out her homework, but the TV movie sounded really interesting and she decided to watch it with her mother instead.

The dog scratching at the door reminded her that she needed to feed Bozo and take him for a walk. While walking, she thought about what she would choose to do for her science project. She thought that an experiment comparing two detergents would be good – and besides, she needed to catch up on the laundry so she would have something to wear to school tomorrow.

After the walk, Sandy's mom asked her if she would run to the store to get some soap. Sandy did, and stopped to look at the new nail polish and perfume that had just come in. She decided that these would be good birthday gifts to get for her friend. When she got home, she realized she had forgotten to get soap.

It was getting late, so she told her mother she would shop right after school tomorrow – if she had time!

## VII-14 Staying on Task

**Objective:** The student will identify several reasons why it is understandable to get off task and will identify several strategies for staying on task.

**Comments:**

Many problems would be solved if the task causing the problem was simply completed. Task completion is sometimes complicated by factors such as a student being distracted, tired, hyperactive, hungry, unfamiliar with the work, or just plain bored. Teachers can try to make material interesting, but at times there is work that simply must be done. The student needs to accept the importance of the task and stick with it until it is completed. In this lesson, students are to identify possible reasons why characters are off task.

**Introductory Activities:**

Inform students that you want them to take out a piece of paper and pencil and begin writing numbers counting by 3's (3, 6, 9, 12, 15, etc.). As they are writing, begin to tap a pencil on your desk, quietly and inconsistently at first, and then louder and more distracting. Look for signs of students coming off task. If necessary, run over to the window and cry, "Look at that!" Do you have any students who are still on task?

**Activity:**

Inform students that on the worksheet "Staying on Task" they are going to look over examples of people who are having trouble staying on task. They are to identify a reason why the person is off task.

**Answers: 1.** boring work; **2.** meaningless work; **3.** distracted by person; **4.** distracted by hunger; **5.** distracted by noise; **6.** basically hyperactive; **7.** not understanding what to do; **8.** work appears too hard; **9.** tools broke; **10.** work seems too long

**Discussion:** Have students share their ideas for being off task.

1. Why is it possible for someone to be unable to complete tasks at school but are able to watch television without blinking an eye for several hours? **(interest, motivation, time of day, etc.)**

2. What are some tasks people have to do that are not especially interesting, but are necessary? **(laundry, other chores, maybe schoolwork, etc.)**

3. How can you make dull tasks more interesting for yourself? **(think about something else that you will do when you are finished, time yourself, do it with a friend, etc.)**

4. What are some ways to tune out distractions, especially when you are doing homework or studying? **(find a quiet place, eat a snack, move around once in awhile)**

5. In each example on the worksheet, what could be done to help the person complete his or her task?

**Extension Activities:**

1. Have students come up with specific ideas for helping themselves stay on task. Ideas include:
    - reward self for completing a task, perhaps at the end, or perhaps when you reach a halfway point (allow yourself to get a snack, take a break)
    - work with a partner (agree to stay on task and help each other stay focused)
    - break the task down into smaller steps (make a checkmark after each smaller task has been completed)
    - be sure to ask questions if you don't understand what to do
    - allow yourself a certain amount of time to complete a task; set a timer and stick with it
    - if you're going to take a break, decide how many minutes long it will be

2. Have students select a task they find hard to stick with. Gradually increase the time spent on that task. Using a chart and a timer, set goals for how many minutes, laps, math problems, pages (or whatever unit is appropriate for the task) will be the ultimate goal.

**Evaluation:**

a. List three tasks that are hard for you to complete.

b. For each, give a reason why you find this task difficult to complete.

c. What suggestion could you give yourself for staying on task for each of the three tasks selected?

# Staying on Task

**Directions:** Each person below is experiencing difficulty in staying on task. What do you think is the problem in each case? Write your answer on the line.

| | |
|---|---|
| 1. This is soooo boring! | 2. What's the purpose of this? |
| 3. Wow! Is she pretty! | 4. I am so hungry! When is it lunch time? Where's the clock? |
| 5. Bang! Bang! Bang! Hey! Shut up!! | 6. I just can't sit still. What's going on over here? |
| 7. I have no idea what to do. I think I missed the directions. | 8. This looks like it's hard work. I don't think I can do it. |
| 9. Hey! My pencil broke again! | 10. We have to read 30 pages and answer 100 questions? Forget it! |

# VII-15 What Is a Goal?

**Objective:** The student will give at least one example of an appropriate goal for specific situations or events.

**Comments:**

A goal can be thought of as simply the endpoint of a quest. It could be an educational degree, the acquisition of a desired possession, or a feeling of personal satisfaction in having achieved something. It can be different things to different people. In this lesson, students are to think about goals and how they relate to different situations.

**Introductory Activities:**

a. Ask students to help define what a goal is. List their ideas on the board.

b. Define *goal* as the endpoint of a quest or target.

c. Have students give examples of some personal goals they have set for themselves.

d. Have students give examples of some goals that others have set for them.

**Activity:**

Students are to write at least two examples of goals that would be appropriate for the situations given on the worksheet "What Is a Goal?" At this point, the goals do not have to be extremely specific, but they should represent someone working towards the achievement of something. It may help them to think: "I would like to..."

**Answers:** *(examples)* **Family:** to get along better with my father, to write more often to my aunt; **Hobby:** to complete my art project, to get to the next level in karate; **School:** to have perfect attendance, to pass all of my classes; **Sports:** to get to all practices on time, to score 15 points in the next game

**Discussion:** Ask students to share their goals for the different areas represented on the worksheet.

1. Do you think most people have goals whether or not they are actually aware of them?

2. What are some goals that students contend with every day? **(classes, homework, passing tests, etc.)**

3. Do you think goals mean more if you set them yourself rather than having someone else decide them for you?

4. How does actually setting a goal (for example, putting it in writing) help you achieve it? **(it would be more specific, help you realize what it is that you need to do, etc.)**

5. What are some ways you can keep your goals in mind or stay aware of them? **(write them down, put the list on the refrigerator)**

6. How often do you think your goals change? **(probably pretty often)**

7. Do you think it is important to set goals for yourself?

**Extension Activities:**

1. Have students find interesting photos in popular magazines that indicate something or someone working towards a goal. It may be a monkey reaching for a banana, a secretary working on a computer, or any other type of picture. Have students share their ideas. (This may make a good bulletin board activity.)

2. Have students select a personal or educational goal that can be shared with the class. Write the goal in huge letters and put it up somewhere in the room. You may want to have students come up with class goals for themselves and/or a personal goal they want to work on for the next grading period.

**Evaluation:**

a. Define *goal*.

b. Give two examples of goals. For each, indicate whether it is a personal goal, educational goal, etc.

**Teacher Notes:**

_____

_____

_____

_____

_____

_____

# What Is a Goal?

**Directions:** For each situation below, identify at least two goals that would be appropriate.

**Example:**

Educational      – to get a high school degree

                   – to read five books about Russia

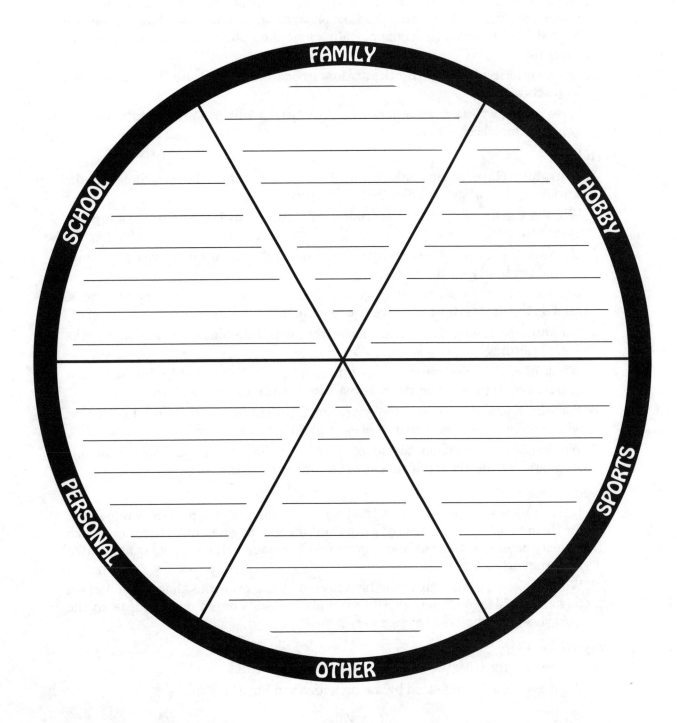

# VII-16 Setting Your Priorities

**Objective:** Given a situation and list of activities, the student will arrange them in a logical priority.

**Comments:**

It is important to have defined goals so that we know when we have reached them. Part of goal-setting is figuring out what is truly important to us or what is worthwhile of being a goal.

**Introductory Activities:**

a. Have students vote (by raising hands) on which activity they think is most important: math or science, reading or writing, playing baseball or playing football, voting for a politician or reading a book on philosophy, being a doctor or being a lawyer, etc.

b. Define *priority*. **(something that takes precedence, is done first or is most important)**

c. Have students write down at least one activity they will give priority to when they get home from school/work.

**Activity:**

**Discussion:** Have students talk about how they rated the activities on the worksheet and what variables they considered.

1. What is the limiting factor in situation 1? **(time – one week to accomplish everything)**

2. How would your priorities change if the fine on the library book was $10 a day? **(you'd probably do it sooner)**

3. Did most students put the 10-page paper as a high priority? Why might this be high on the list? **(might require more time, more planning)**

4. For situation 2, what is the main factor that would decide how you prioritize the items? **(money)**

5. What item did most students put first and why? **(probably house, most expensive item – or vacation, most interesting or important)**

6. For situation 3, if time and money are not the main factors to help set priorities, what do you think would be in this example? **(interest)**

7. Why would there probably be a lot of variance on the prioritizing of this list among students? **(students are interested in different things)**

**Extension Activities:**

1. Have students make a list of at least ten activities that are presently important for them to do or are things they are thinking about. Then have them rate each priority according to what main factor (time, money, interest, etc.) is associated with that activity.

2. What are some goals that would be reflected by the priorities that are important to someone? Have students write examples of goals based on the ideas on the worksheet and their own examples.

**Evaluation:**

a. Define *priority*. Give two examples of personal priorities.

b. What goal(s) is/are reflected by the priorities you have chosen?

# Setting Your Priorities

**Directions:** Read the following situations and prioritize the items by using numbers (1, 2, 3, and so on) to indicate what you would do first, second, third, etc. Your answers may be different than those of other people.

**Situation 1:** You have one week to get the following things done:

_____ return a library book that is overdue at 10 cents/day

_____ jog a mile

_____ write a 10-page paper

_____ get ice cream for a party tonight

_____ get your hair cut

**Situation 2:** You have $100,000 to spend.

_____ buy a toothbrush

_____ buy a dog

_____ buy a car

_____ buy a house

_____ plan for your vacation

**Situation 3:** You have some free time to do some things you normally may not have time to do. Money is not a problem. Don't feel rushed, either – you have all the time in the world to get everything done.

_____ cook a meal

_____ go to a movie with your best friend

_____ clean the toilet

_____ ski the slopes of Vail, Colorado

_____ learn to do ballroom dancing

## VII-17 Doing Things in Sequence

**Objective:** Given a specific goal as an example, the student will identify several steps that should be done in sequence to accomplish that goal.

**Comments:**

Once a goal is determined, the steps needed to reach that goal must be thoughtfully sequenced. Some goals, of course, may not require many steps – a short-term goal may simply be quickly accomplished. Other goals, however, such as completing a longer project, more intensive activity, or acquiring a skill may require more steps. In this lesson, students are to list steps that would be involved in working towards a goal.

**Introductory Activities:**

Have students list the steps that would most likely be involved in a major project, such as: building a house, planning a surprise anniversary party, making a yearbook for the school, painting a huge mural of the major events of the year, etc.

**Activity:**

Students are to consider the goals on the worksheet "Doing Things in Sequence" and list several steps that would lead to the attainment of the goal. The point of the lesson is to put the steps in order, not randomly just list activities. Students may need some clarification of this.

> **Answers:** *(examples)* **1.** study daily notes every day after class, review with a friend two days before the test, skim the notes the night before the test; **2.** start an exercise program cautiously, increase the intensity gradually, join a vigorous exercise program; **3.** clear off all food items, throw old papers into the trash, organize papers into files, put away all remaining loose items; **4.** take tennis lessons, practice often, play with a partner who is a good tennis player, try out for the team; **5.** set up a time to visit your grandmother, get the recipe, get the items on the recipe, have your grandmother show you any special tricks she uses

> **Discussion:** Have students compare their responses to the examples on the worksheet.

> 1. Some tasks are easier to organize sequentially. What are some examples of such tasks? **(making something that results in an end product, such as sewing, cooking, building, repairing, etc.)**

> 2. What are some examples of tasks or goals that don't necessarily have to be done in a particular order? **(any type of task that involves steps that can be done randomly and yet still complete the task)**

> 3. Why is it important to follow steps in order? **(some later steps may depend on getting the first ones done right)**

**Extension Activities:**

> 1. Have students write short plays (and then role-play them!) indicating what could happen if tasks were done with the steps in the wrong sequence. Skits might involve cooking, dressing, driving a car, etc.

> 2. Have students make a list of at least ten other important goals. What steps should be taken to complete the tasks necessary to reach the goal? Do they need to be done sequentially?

3. Students may enjoy making a short (4-panel) cartoon depicting someone doing the tasks involved in reaching a goal. Depending on the interest and ability of the students, they may enjoy making a sort of "puzzle" out of the sheet by cutting the panels apart and having other students put them in the correct sequential order.

**Evaluation:**

What are three important sequential steps that are necessary to complete the following goals:

a. to learn to write a report using the word processor

b. to teach my dog to come when he hears me ring a bell

c. to take orders and deliver chocolate bars to neighbors for a fund-raising project for the school

**Teacher Notes:**

_____

_____

_____

_____

_____

_____

# Doing Things in Sequence

**Directions:** Consider each goal below. List at least three steps that should be done in order to help accomplish that goal.

**Goal 1:** to get an A on the next science chapter test

_____

_____

_____

_____

**Goal 2:** to become more physically fit

_____

_____

_____

_____

**Goal 3:** to organize the mess all over my desk

_____

_____

_____

_____

**Goal 4:** to make the varsity tennis team

_____

_____

_____

_____

**Goal 5:** to learn how to cook lasagna the way my grandmother does

_____

_____

_____

_____

## VII-18 Realistic Goals

**Objective:** Given situations, the student will identify and give examples of realistic goals.

**Comments:**

Part of good goal-setting is making sure that the goals are reasonable and attainable. Not everyone can become a president, rock star, millionaire, or bank president. Factors such as education, luck, training, personality, physical ability, and lots of others can affect how realistic a goal is for someone. In this lesson, students are to identify whether or not suggested goals are realistic for the individuals in the examples.

**Introductory Activities:**

a. Hold up a huge book for students and inform them that your goal for them is to read the entire book by the next day and turn in a 50-page paper explaining your opinion of the book. After a pause, ask them how they feel about your goal for them.

b. Have students comment about why a goal may be attainable for one person but not another.

**Activity:**

Students are to read examples of individuals and their goals on the worksheet "Realistic Goals." They are to decide whether or not the goals seem realistic for the people involved.

**Answers: 1.** yes; **2.** yes; **3.** no; **4.** no; **5.** yes; **6.** no; **7.** no; **8.** yes

**Discussion:** Have students explain their responses. In some cases, students may have a difference of opinion as to whether or not the individual could attain the goal. Some may insist that with hard work or good luck, a goal could be attained. Try to keep students directed toward using only the information given on the worksheet.

1. Do you think any goal is attainable if someone tried hard enough or worked long enough towards that goal? (**no – sometimes other factors work against you, i.e., a physical disability, etc.**)

2. What if you don't have any ability in a certain area? Would you still experience some success if you worked towards a goal even if you didn't make the original goal? (**probably – and that is a good reason for adjusting the goal**)

3. Why is it important to consider your abilities and interests and other resources before making your goals? (**you want to set things up for success**)

4. What about people who "beat the odds" and do well even though others never thought they would reach their goals? How can you explain that? (**this happens, but not very often!**)

5. There are other factors you must consider when thinking about goals. What factor is important for Alvin in situation 1 if he is to reach his goal of working the night shift? (**he must perform well at night, he still has to get to work on time, etc.**)

6. What is required besides simply having artistic ability in situation 2 for Andi to be successful as a fashion designer? (**she may need some experience, further training, good luck**)

7. Why is situation 3 probably unrealistic for Pete? **(he just does not have the required ability)**

8. How likely is it that Pete will "beat the odds"? **(not likely)**

9. What could happen? **(he could grow, practice a lot, etc.)**

10. What might be a more attainable goal for Pete? **(become a good sports statistician!)**

11. Why would it be difficult for Alana in situation 4 to become a doctor in a foreign (for her) country? **(language barrier)**

12. What is the main reason this goal is probably unrealistic for Alana? **(she doesn't enjoy science, and there is a lot of science involved in training to become a doctor)**

13. How could the language problem be resolved for Alana? **(she could take English classes, get a tutor, train at a different medical center, etc.)**

14. What is the problem with Amanda's goal in situation 6? **(she hates to do the activity that would be the primary responsibility for the job)**

15. Could Amanda still be successful at being a chef even though she did not enjoy it? **(sure)**

16. Could someone be good at doing a job, even if he or she didn't enjoy the job? **(yes)**

17. How much is enjoyment a factor in being successful in reaching a goal? **(it is sometimes not even related at all)**

18. What do you see as David's problem in situation 7? **(he is not dedicated to following a plan that will reach his goal)**

**Extension Activities:**

1. Have students complete a "Goal Grid" containing examples of the following information:

| Goal | Realistic for | Realistic but unlikely for | Unrealistic for |
|------|---------------|----------------------------|-----------------|
| a. to become president | political families | a poor child from the ghetto | someone who is not a U.S. citizen |
| b. to play professional football | good athlete | someone with some ability and good attitude | legless person in a wheelchair |

\* Add other goals

2. Have students complete a personal "Goal Grid." Have them select at least three areas such as educational, social, personal, etc.

**Evaluation:**

a. Give an example of a goal that is realistic for you in the area of school.

b. Give an example of a goal that is desirable, but unrealistic for you in the area of sports.

# Realistic Goals

**Directions:** Read the examples below. Do you think the individuals have realistic goals for themselves? Write YES or NO.

_____ 1. Alvin doesn't like to get up early in the morning. He would like to find a job working the night shift at a factory. **Is this a realistic goal for Alvin?**

_____ 2. Andi is very artistic. She would like to go to art school to learn how to draw better and then become a fashion designer. **Is this a realistic goal for Andi?**

_____ 3. Pete is short and not very athletic. When he is older, he wants to play on a professional basketball team. **Is this a realistic goal for Pete?**

_____ 4. Alana is from a country where Spanish is spoken. She does not know very much English, although she is quick to learn. She is planning to stay in the new country and wants to become a doctor. She does not enjoy science classes. **Is this a realistic goal for Alana?**

_____ 5. Rich likes to work on cars. In fact, he is very good at fixing all kinds of machines. Some day he would like to open a repair shop for small engines. **Is this a realistic goal for Rich?**

_____ 6. Amanda hates to cook. When she tries, though, she can follow a recipe pretty well. She wants to open a restaurant and be the main chef. **Is this a realistic goal for Amanda?**

_____ 7. David wants to lose 10 pounds quickly. He has started jogging, eating salads for lunch, and limiting his other meals to having only three desserts. He followed this plan for two days. **Is this a realistic goal for David?**

_____ 8. Danielle is very pretty and outgoing. She likes to be the center of attention and is doing well in her modeling classes. She has decided to try out for a small part in a local movie. **Is this a realistic goal for Danielle?**

# VII-19 Adjusting Goals

**Objective:** The student will identify reasons why individuals may need to adjust their original goals.

**Comments:**

When it is evident to an individual that a particular goal is not realistic, attainable, or appropriate, it is important to recognize that a new goal is needed and to make those adjustments.

**Introductory Activities:**

a. Announce to students that you have decided to play professional hockey for a living. After comments have died down, ask students to explain why they think that goal may not be appropriate for you. **(probably unrealistic)**

b. Have students assist you in developing a new, but related goal. Perhaps you will play another sport, perhaps you will become a fabulous hockey fan, etc.

c. Have students list reasons why your original goal may be unrealistic for you. **(ability, interests, geographical location, etc.)**

**Activity:**

**Answers: 1.** c; **2.** b; **3.** a; **4.** e; **5.** d

**Discussion:** Go through the examples with students and have them select specific clues that indicated why the individual needed to adjust his or her goal.

1. How often do you think people change their goals? **(all the time)**

2. Are the reasons that people need to change goals periodically all bad or negative reasons? **(not at all – one may outgrow a goal that is too easy to achieve)**

3. When you adjust a goal "downward," isn't that lowering your standards or just giving up? **(not necessarily if it is more appropriate for the ability and interests of the individual)**

4. Can you think of some examples of when you changed goals because you became interested in something else?

5. What are some examples of changing a goal because you learned something new or obtained information that changed what you thought about something?

6. Have you had any unpleasant experiences that encouraged you to change your goals?

7. Why is it important to know when it is a good time to change your goals? **(so you don't waste a lot of time pursuing something that is not really what you want)**

**Extension Activities:**

1. Have students write short stories in which a character (perhaps based on a true experience) has a major change in goals. Have the other students identify the reason(s) why the change was necessary or beneficial.

2. Have students find cartoons (as in the Sunday paper) for examples of characters changing goals. Comics such as *Garfield* and *Peanuts* are good sources!

**Evaluation:**

a. List three reasons why someone might have to adjust an original goal.

b. Give an example of each of the three reasons you listed above.

# Adjusting Goals

**Directions:** The people below have to adjust their goals for various reasons. Match the reasons on the right with the situations on the left.

_____ 1. "Ace" couldn't make the varsity basketball team, so he decided to try out for the junior varsity team.

**a.** changing a goal because of a new interest

**b.** changing a goal because the original goal is off-track or won't bring you towards a larger goal

_____ 2. Jennifer realized that working a paper route was not going to get her enough money for her class trip in the spring, so she got several jobs cleaning houses which earns her more money.

**c.** changing a goal to match your ability

_____ 3. After going to a concert, Belinda decided that she no longer wants to be an actress – she wants to sing!

**d.** changing a goal because of new information

**e.** changing a goal because of an unpleasant experience

_____ 4. Fred wanted to become a surgeon until he took his first medical class and got poor grades, hated the thought of blood, and was told by his professors that he would never make it.

_____ 5. Carter didn't realize he could get a scholarship that would pay his way completely through college until he talked to his counselor. Then he decided he wanted to transfer to the state school that offered the scholarship.

## VII-20 What's a Risk?

**Objective:** The student will define a risk and give at least two examples.

**Comments:**

Life is filled with risks. Every time you cross a street, sign your name, or smoke a cigarette you are dabbling with some form of a risk. In this lesson students are given a simple definition of a risk – something associated with danger or loss – and consider several examples of risks.

**Introductory Activities:**

a. Ask students to raise their hands if they want to volunteer. Do not mention what they are volunteering for. Inform them that those with their hands up are risk-takers!

b. Ask students to consider the following situation: They have to pick Door 1 or Door 2 – behind one of them is a million dollars, and behind the other is something that will cause them great pain. Ask students to raise their hands if they would participate in this "experiment." Are these students risk-takers?

c. If possible, arrange some cookies in front of the room. Again ask for volunteers to try out your cookies. Before one takes a bite, teasingly tell him or her that you put a little arsenic in them – but you aren't sure which one. Who wants to take the risk now?

d. Define *risk*. (**something that potentially involves danger or loss**)

**Activity:**

Students are to consider the goals and situations on the worksheet "What's a Risk?" and decide which of the two risks that would help attain the goal is more costly, or is the greater risk. They are to put a check mark in front of that answer.

**Answers: 1.** second (you don't know the reputation of the person); **2.** first (assumption is made that you do not have a recommendation of the work of this facility); **3.** first (a signal is much safer); **4.** first (there are many dangers associated with hitchhiking); **5.** second (this doesn't really prove anything); **6.** second (young horses can have accidents and attitudes!); **7.** second (this is a definite commitment, perhaps one that could/should be tried later); **8.** second (it is putting off something that needs to be done soon)

**Discussion:** Have students discuss why the various responses are or are not risky towards achieving the goal.

1. What are some examples of risks that you take every day?

2. How dangerous are these risks? (**probably not very**)

3. Are there any activities that people do that do not have some element of risk?

4. Does every risk involve a goal? (**of some sort!**)

5. When you get in the habit of doing something often – for example, crossing a busy street in the middle, why does it seem to be less risky? (**becomes a habit, you get good at it**)

6. Are there things that are risky for one person but may not be for another? Explain. (**yes – skill is associated with how much risk is involved, e.g., sports, driving, etc.**)

**Extension Activities:**

    1. Have students cut out magazine or newspaper articles that show someone taking a risk. Try to decide what the goal is behind the risk being taken.

    2. Have students list 15 risks they will probably face during that day.

**Evaluation:**

    a. Define or explain what a risk is.

    b. Give two examples of risks you have taken recently.

    c. Explain what goal was behind each of the two risks.

**Teacher Notes:**

_____

_____

_____

_____

_____

_____

# What's a Risk?

**Directions:** Below are several goals and some risks that could be associated with achieving those goals. Decide which of the two is the greater risk. Put a check mark in front of your choice.

**1. Goal:** to make some money

_____  invest in a certificate of deposit

_____  withdraw some of your savings to give to a well-dressed stranger who says he knows of a good investment

**2. Goal:** to get your car fixed

_____  take your car to "Speedy-Fix"

_____  take your car to a reliable mechanic whom you have used before for repair

**3. Goal:** to cross a busy street

_____  look both ways, then run for it

_____  cross at the corner with a signal

**4. Goal:** to travel to another state

_____  hitchhike

_____  buy a ticket for a train

**5. Goal:** to make the football team

_____  give up other sports and practice as much as you can

_____  don't warm-up or wear any padding to prove how tough you are

**6. Goal:** to purchase a winning racehorse

_____  check the horse's track record

_____  buy something young so it will have time to be trained well

**7. Goal:** to free hostages

_____  negotiate with the hostage-takers

_____  storm the building with weapons

**8. Goal:** to maintain a healthy heart after you have had a diagnosis of clogged arteries

_____  arrange for recommended surgery

_____  hope that time will heal your heart

# VII-21 Why Take Risks?

**Objective:** The student will state three to five reasons why people take risks.

**Comments:**

People take risks for a variety of reasons. Some may include: excitement or the thrill of danger; desire to improve their situation in some way (e.g., gaining money); peer pressure; lack of knowledge; desire to push themselves to learn or become something different; or perhaps because there seem to be no other alternatives. In this lesson, these motives are examined.

**Introductory Activities:**

a. Pass out a $1 bill (can be counterfeit or play money!) to each student. Inform them that they can give you the dollar to get a ticket that reveals if they are the winner. The winner will get $100. Do they want to play? **(most will say yes)** Why? **(the odds are good, the consequences are good, the risk is small)**

b. Repeat the activity, but this time tell students that everyone will get a consequence including: $100, a slow painful death, an hour's detention, a candy bar, a free concert ticket of their choice, or 30 hours of community service. Do they want to play? **(some will probably have mixed emotions now – the risks are greater and not predictable)**

**Activity:**

Several reasons why people take risks are listed on the right-hand side of the worksheet "Why Take Risks?" Students are to match the risks on the left with a possible reason why someone would take that risk from the choices on the right. There are several possibilities for each risk; students should explain their thinking.

**Answers:** *(will vary – examples)* **1.** A,D; **2.** A,B; **3.** B; **4.** B,C,E; **5.** A,D,E,F; **6.** A,D; **7.** B,D; **8.** C,E; **9.** A,F; **10.** A,D; **11.** B,E; **12.** D,F; **13.** A,B,D; **14.** A,F; **15.** E; **16.** A, D,F; **17.** C,F; **18.** B,E

**Discussion:** The students' responses should generate quite a bit of discussion, as answers may be quite different.

1. What risks do you consider exciting?

2. Do you consider yourself a risk-taker or someone who is more conservative and likes to play it safe?

3. What situations on the worksheet involve danger?

4. What risks could you take in your life that would improve your situation, for example, change your job, gain you more possessions, etc.?

5. What is stopping you from taking those risks?

6. Have you ever been in a situation in which you felt there was only one alternative – and that was risky? **(perhaps involving disease or an accident)**

7. What risks are a result of peer pressure in your group?

8. What would happen if you resisted peer pressure from your group?

9. Why would it be a risk to break away from peer pressure?

10. What risks would you take to improve yourself? Do you desire to make self-improvement changes?

11. What are ways to combat ignorance? **(experience, education, ask people for advice, etc.)**

12. Why do you think some people are so hesitant to ask others for information that would prevent them from being in a risky situation? **(embarrassed)**

## Extension Activities:

1. Have students write a paragraph or short story about the most exciting risk they have taken. What was it like? Was the outcome good or bad? Would they do it again?

2. Have students do a book report on a famous risk-taker (e.g., a race car driver, stuntperson, aerialist, magician such as Harry Houdini, etc.). What motivation drives these people to take risks?

3. Have students make a personal list of at least five things they would like to do, but are afraid to try or are unwilling to take the risk.

## Evaluation:

Give one example of a risk that could be taken for the following reasons:

a. thrill

b. improve your life

c. last resort

d. peer pressure

e. self-improvement

f. ignorance

# Why Take Risks?

**Directions:** Match the risks on the left with the reasons or motives on the right. There may be more than one possible correct answer. Be able to justify or explain your responses.

**Risk**

_____ **1.** riding a roller coaster without holding onto the bar

_____ **2.** buying a lottery ticket

_____ **3.** investing money in the stock market

_____ **4.** having surgery

_____ **5.** taking drugs

_____ **6.** drinking more alcohol than you really want or intend

_____ **7.** joining a union

_____ **8.** giving a speech in front of people you don't know

_____ **9.** having sex without using protection

_____ **10.** getting a very different haircut

_____ **11.** going back to school after you had quit

_____ **12.** not wearing a seatbelt

_____ **13.** gambling with a small amount of money

_____ **14.** gambling with your life savings

_____ **15.** refusing to join in a group that is teasing someone else

_____ **16.** driving 100 miles an hour down a country road

_____ **17.** introducing your boyfriend/girlfriend to your very pretty cousin

_____ **18.** taking a class on how to sell real estate

**Reason**

**a.** desire for thrill, excitement, attention

**b.** wanting to improve your life or situation

**c.** no other alternatives

**d.** peer pressure

**e.** wanting to change yourself, improve self

**f.** ignorance

## **VII-22 Rate the Risk**

**Objective:** The student will give examples of low-, medium-, and high-risk situations.

**Comments:**

Not all risks involve the same amount of danger or potential loss. In this lesson, students are to rate various risks in terms of the degree of risk involved.

**Introductory Activities:**

Set up a table in front of the class and ask for three volunteers to assist you in the following experiments. Inform them that they will be blindfolded, seated in front of a plate, and will be given something to eat.

a. Ask for volunteers when the choices involve three candy bars.

b. Ask for volunteers when the choices involve two candy bars and one piece of moldy cheese (or something equally unappealing).

c. Ask for volunteers when the choices involve one candy bar and two unappealing items.

**Activity:**

Students are to rate many items on the worksheet "Rate the Risk" according to this rather subjective scale: 1 = low risk, 2 = moderate risk, 3 = severe risk. You may want to go over some examples with students so that they will differentiate among the different levels.

**Answers:** will vary

**Discussion:** As you go through the items, encourage students to talk about why the risk is or is not particularly dangerous in their own situation.

1. What are some examples of personal low-risk situations for you?

2. What are some examples of personal situations that you consider of moderate risk?

3. What are some high-risk situations for you?

4. Do you feel you have control over many of your risks?

5. Do you think some people are naturally high- or low-risk takers?

6. What do you think would tend to make someone a good risk-taker? **(experience, knowledge, successful personality)**

7. How would you rate yourself as a risk-taker?

**Extension Activities:**

1. Have students list at least five risk-taking occupations and research the training involved. What personality types or attributes seem to be common among risk-takers?

2. Locate an appropriate movie to show students, preferably one with cliff-hanging, thrilling moments. Enjoy!

**Evaluation:**

a. Give an example of a low-risk situation.

b. Give an example of a moderate-risk situation.

c. Give an example of a high-risk situation.

# Rate the Risk

**Directions:** Read the following list of risks and rate them according to the following scale: 1 = low or little risk; 2 = medium risk, some element of danger or loss; 3 = very risky!

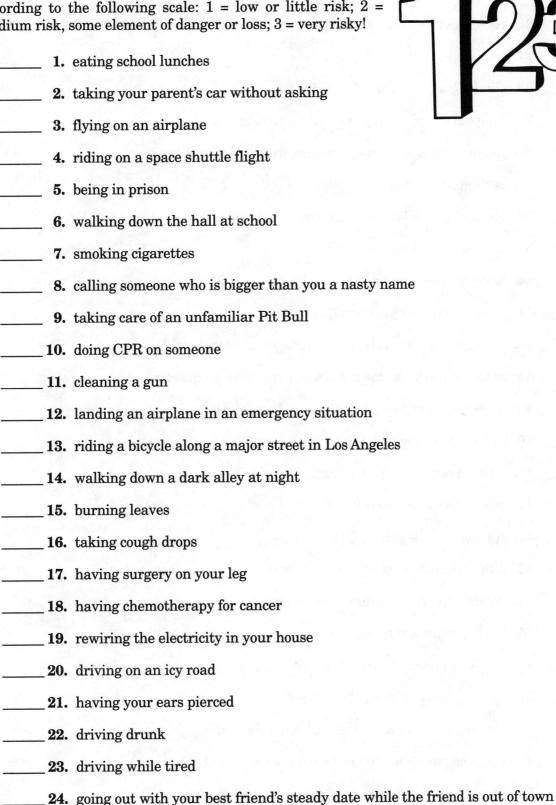

_____ 1. eating school lunches

_____ 2. taking your parent's car without asking

_____ 3. flying on an airplane

_____ 4. riding on a space shuttle flight

_____ 5. being in prison

_____ 6. walking down the hall at school

_____ 7. smoking cigarettes

_____ 8. calling someone who is bigger than you a nasty name

_____ 9. taking care of an unfamiliar Pit Bull

_____ 10. doing CPR on someone

_____ 11. cleaning a gun

_____ 12. landing an airplane in an emergency situation

_____ 13. riding a bicycle along a major street in Los Angeles

_____ 14. walking down a dark alley at night

_____ 15. burning leaves

_____ 16. taking cough drops

_____ 17. having surgery on your leg

_____ 18. having chemotherapy for cancer

_____ 19. rewiring the electricity in your house

_____ 20. driving on an icy road

_____ 21. having your ears pierced

_____ 22. driving drunk

_____ 23. driving while tired

_____ 24. going out with your best friend's steady date while the friend is out of town

## Rate the Risk, continued

_____ **25.** shoplifting small items

_____ **26.** robbing a convenience store

_____ **27.** hitchhiking

_____ **28.** climbing up a ladder to the third floor

_____ **29.** jumping out of an airplane (with a parachute)

_____ **30.** jumping out of a burning building from the third floor

_____ **31.** petting a tiger cub in a petting zoo

_____ **32.** swimming in a lake with snakes

_____ **33.** canoeing down rapids

_____ **34.** jumping from the top of one building to another

_____ **35.** cheating on your girlfriend/boyfriend

_____ **36.** eating pizza that has not been refrigerated for three days

_____ **37.** not going to the doctor if you know you have an infection

_____ **38.** investing all of your money in a real estate deal

_____ **39.** investing your money in a savings account

_____ **40.** riding a horse you have never seen before

_____ **41.** going to a tanning booth

_____ **42.** staring into the sun

_____ **43.** telling your parents a lie

_____ **44.** swearing at your teacher or principal

_____ **45.** lending your best friend some money

_____ **46.** standing under a tree during a lightning storm

_____ **47.** running away from a police officer

_____ **48.** playing "Russian Roulette" with a loaded gun

_____ **49.** skipping medication if you have epilepsy or diabetes

_____ **50.** eating food that you know will make you sick later

# VII-23 Risking Failure

**Objective:** The student will state reasons why people are afraid to risk failure.

**Comments:**

No one really wants to fail. Yet, at times, we all find ourselves in uncomfortable situations in which we must deal with the consequences of not succeeding. In this lesson students must decide what the characters on the worksheet might be facing in failure situations.

**Introductory Activities:**

Write a huge, complicated math problem on the board and invite three student volunteers to attempt it, one at a time. Inform them that if they get it right, the rest of the class will applaud them for 30 seconds. If they get it wrong, everyone will point at them and chant, "Dumb! Dumb! Dumb!" (Select your volunteers carefully!)

**Activity:**

Students are to read situations on the worksheet "Risking Failure" in which the characters are likely to fail. For each, they are to predict a "worst case" scenario or at least something embarrassing or dangerous that could be a likely result of the risk. Then they are to note a few precautions that could help the character handle the situation.

**Answers:** *(examples)* **1.** break leg/take some lessons, go slowly; **2.** she'll forget her lines/have a small part; **3.** he'll be involved in an accident/spend the night at the friend's house; **4.** the car will be a lemon/get advice from someone who knows something about cars; **5.** overdose/observe what happens to others, don't take it at all; **6.** they'll ignore her idea or laugh at it/prepare well, run it by one other person first for an opinion; **7.** shoddy work/use better materials; **8.** the niece will embarrass everyone/make sure an adult walks down the aisle with her; **9.** the two won't like each other at all/make it a quick date; **10.** the food will be awful/cook something simple, have it catered; **11.** he will fail the test/take some practice tests, have a tutor help him; **12.** the boss will be angry that she caught him in a mistake/ask if he would review her checking over of the work

**Discussion:** Some failures can be avoided, but others must simply be dealt with. There will be times when we are embarrassed, laughed at, excluded, or make mistakes. Encourage students to realize that taking a risk involves the potential to fail, but that how we handle that failure is likewise important.

1. How would you feel if you failed at something that was really hard for you to do?

2. How would you feel if you failed at something that you thought was really easy to do?

3. Do you admire people who have been successful at difficult things?

4. How many times can you fail at something before you personally give up? Do you think you give up easily when things get hard?

5. How do you feel if you fail at something you don't really care about? If someone else cares more about it than you do, does that change anything? (e.g., a teacher or parent wanting you to do well on something that doesn't matter to you)

6. How do you feel if you fail at something that means a lot to you?

7. How do you handle personal failure?

8. Are you satisfied with the way you handle failure?

9. Does it make you feel any better to realize that everyone has failures?

10. What do you think of the saying, "If at first you don't succeed, try, try again." Is there a time when you should quit trying?

## Extension Activities:

1. Have students research biographies of individuals (e.g., Helen Keller, Wilma Rudolph, inventors who have persisted with ideas, etc.) who have taken risks and have overcome failures or disabilities.

2. Show an appropriate inspirational movie about underdogs who have come out ahead (e.g., *Hoosiers, Breaking Away, Stand and Deliver*).

## Evaluation:

Give one example of a failure that could come from taking the following risks. Then state a way you could handle the failure in a positive way.

a. learning to ice skate

b. having an essay that you wrote displayed in the hall of your school

c. having a haircut that didn't turn out the way you intended

## Teacher Notes:

_____

_____

_____

_____

_____

# Risking Failure

**Directions:** Read the following situations. In each case, what is the worst possible thing that could happen if the person failed? What precautions could be taken to minimize the failure?

**1.** Joe thinks he is a pretty good skier, but he attempted a ski slope that is designated for "Experts Only."

Worst case: _____

Precautions: _____

_____

**2.** Ronda has stage fright, but she wants to try out for a part in the community theater.

Worst case: _____

Precautions: _____

_____

**3.** Jamal has had too much to drink, but he doesn't want to bother trying to find another ride home from his friend's house.

Worst case: _____

Precautions: _____

_____

**4.** April wants to buy her own car, but she refuses to listen to her father's advice to buy something sensible and safe. She decides to get an older car with a convertible top that seems to be running pretty well.

Worst case: _____

Precautions: _____

_____

**5.** Ted is at a party where the drugs and alcohol are flowing freely. Someone offers him a pill, but he isn't sure what it is.

Worst case: _____

Precautions: _____

_____

**6.** Dianne has an idea for advertising a product at her company, but she doesn't know if the other members of her team will like it.

Worst case: _____

Precautions: _____

_____

## Risking Failure, continued

**7.** Rick is building his own garage and plans to save a lot of money by doing the work himself and using the cheapest materials he can find.

Worst case: _____

Precautions: _____

_____

**8.** Alaina is getting married and wants her four-year-old niece to be a flower girl. The niece is cute, but is very unpredictable.

Worst case: _____

Precautions: _____

_____

**9.** Terry wants to set up his friend Joseph with an attractive girl he knows. Terry likes the girl a lot as a friend, but isn't sure if Joseph will like her.

Worst case: _____

Precautions: _____

_____

**10.** Amy is not the world's best cook, but she feels she should invite her co-workers over for supper since she has eaten with them so many times.

Worst case: _____

Precautions: _____

_____

**11.** Kevin gets nervous every time he has to take a test. It is very important that he does well on the college entrance exam.

Worst case: _____

Precautions: _____

_____

**12.** Sara knows her boss has made a huge mistake when he added up the orders for the day. She also knows that her boss is a perfectionist and never thinks he does anything wrong.

Worst case: _____

Precautions: _____

_____

# VII-24 Learning from Mistakes

**Objective:** The student will identify several ways to avoid repeating a mistake.

**Comments:**

It's bad enough to make a mistake, but even worse to keep repeating the mistake. In this lesson, students are introduced to several ways to get information about situations that hopefully can help them prevent making and repeating mistakes. These include: learning from a mistake; getting advice from others; knowledge from television/magazines, etc.; and using common sense.

**Introductory Activities:**

    a. Select a volunteer. Give the instructions "Write your name on the board." When the volunteer writes his or her name, insist that it is a mistake. Keep insisting until the volunteer realizes that you want him or her to put the words "your name" on the board.

    b. Select a second volunteer. Give the instructions: "Write your address on the board." This time, the volunteer will probably write the words "your address" quickly.

    c. Ask students how the second volunteer figured out so quickly what to do. **(learning from the first situation)**

**Activity:**

Go over the four examples of ways to learn from mistakes that are on the worksheet "Learning from Mistakes." Have students read the situations and select an appropriate answer that indicates how the character could avoid the mistake that concerns them. Inform students that there may be more than one correct answer.

    **Answers:** *(examples)* **1.** A, D; **2.** A, D; **3.** A, B, C; **4.** B; **5.** A, D; **6.** B; **7.** B; **8.** A, D; **9.** B, C; **10.** A, D

    **Discussion:** Have students share their ideas for how to avoid repeating mistakes. Emphasize that it is perfectly normal for people to make mistakes, but really unfortunate when people do not learn from them.

    1. What are some mistakes you have made that you have learned not to do again?

    2. What are some mistakes you can avoid by observing other people or seeing what they have gone through?

    3. What are some mistakes you can avoid by what you have learned in school or through other means of learning?

    4. What are some mistakes you can avoid by using common sense?

    5. What do you think of people who keep making the same mistakes over and over? Are they slow to learn or do you think they do not view these outcomes as mistakes?

    6. Are there some people whose advice you would not listen to just because you didn't care for the person?

    7. Would you take the advice of someone who had been through some similar problem as yours?

    8. What if you didn't like the advice they gave?

    9. Is it ever good to learn by making mistakes? Why or why not? **(sometimes yes – it can help drive home the point that something was an error or had an enormous consequence)**

**Extension Activities:**

1. Have students conduct an informal survey among their peers. What is the biggest mistake students have made recently?

2. Have students compile a list of 10 to 15 subjects or at least topics of information they think teenagers need to have extensive knowledge about.

3. Have students collect advice columns such as "Dear Abby." Evaluate her advice. Do students agree? disagree? Without looking at the columnist's advice, how would students handle the situations?

**Evaluation:**

Give an example of a mistake you could avoid based on the following experiences:

a. a mistake you have made

b. a mistake someone else has made

c. knowledge you have about a risky situation

d. common sense about life

**Teacher Notes:**

_____

_____

_____

_____

_____

_____

# Learning from Mistakes

**Directions:** How could these individuals avoid making the same mistake next time? Write the letter of your answer in the box. More than one answer may be appropriate.

**A.** Your own knowledge/experience

**B.** Other people's knowledge/experiences

**C.** Information from TV, magazines, other sources

**D.** Common sense

1. This is what Freda did to my hair!!!

2. I was under the sunlamp for an hour. I fell asleep.

3. That kind of car has a tendency to combust when you hit something. My buddy Stan has one and he read it in <u>Consumer Reports.</u>

4. My sister is having her fourth baby. I don't want that to happen to me.

5. I wish I had worn my seat belt.

6. My father got caught stealing money from his company.

7. My teacher showed me how to write a research paper. I won't get a D on the next one!

8. Hey – this plant is dead. Was I supposed to water it?

9. I'm not sure if I can get AIDS from drinking out of the same glass as someone with the disease.

10. Oh, no - I'm out of gas, I guess...

## VII-25 Risks and Their Payoffs

**Objective:** Given a goal and related risk, the student will evaluate how risky the activity is, consider what is invested in the risk, identify a probable payoff for taking the risk, and determine the likelihood of achieving the goal.

## Comments:

Some risks are worth taking, especially when the payoff is even more than you intended (for example, buying a winning lottery ticket). However, the investment and likelihood of achieving the goal must be considered as well. In this lesson, students are given several goals and activities involving various degrees of risk to attain the goal. They must weigh all factors and determine if the risk is worth the effort and payoff.

## Introductory Activity:

Present students with the following situation. They have an opportunity to win some money by choosing one of the following options: **Option 1** – It costs $100 to choose this option. They will be given $50,000 immediately if they can answer ten questions about states and capital cities; or **Option 2** – It costs $500 to choose this option. They have to recite the alphabet backwards. They will be given a penny on Day 1, two pennies on Day 2, four pennies on Day 3, and so on with the amount doubling each day for 30 days. They will have the amount of money earned on Day 30.

While students mull over their options, give them about ten seconds to make their decision.

Have students calculate how much money would be earned if they chose Option 2. (It actually comes out to over one billion dollars – $1,073,741,824.)

Have students state their opinions and ultimate findings about the risks involved for each option; the difficulty of the tasks; the investment; and the payoff. Which is now apparently the better risk?

## Activity:

Students are to complete information about given goals and risks on the worksheet "Risks and Their Payoffs." Information includes: (a) how risky the activity is – does it involve a lot of risk? (b) what is invested in going for the goal – a lot of time or money? additional work? (c) the payoff – prestige, money, fame, etc., and (d) the likelihood of reaching the goal.

> **Answers:** *(examples)* **Goal 2 (a)** moderate – there are a lot of safety features, **(b)** time for training, money for lessons, **(c)** excitement, thrill, **(d)** very likely; **Goal 3 (a)** not a lot of risk, the activities are all probably worthwhile, **(b)** time, money, **(c)** knowledge, experience, **(d)** low – not many people have the opportunity to become a president; **Goal 4 (a)** moderate social risk – you would be cutting off a lot of potential friends who aren't in the popular circle, **(b)** time, **(c)** you may become popular with the "right" people, **(d)** moderate – depends on if there are more popular or unpopular voters; **Goal 5 (a)** high risk, **(b)** money, moving hassles, time to move, etc., **(c)** to be "discovered," **(d)** unlikely – but sometimes it happens!

**Discussion:** Have students go over their various responses to the examples on the worksheet. There may be quite a bit of variety to their answers!

1. What are some examples of very secure risks? **(savings accounts, doing things you are already good at, trusting someone, etc.)**
2. What are some examples of very high risks? **(gambling for a lot of money, walking a tightrope without knowing what you're doing and having no net, etc.)**
3. Why do people take high risks? **(expect a high payoff)**
4. Why is education generally considered to be a good risk? **(most people find that a good education helps them in life later, either by getting a better job or leading to something else)**
5. Why do people buy lottery tickets? **(they hope they might win big!)**
6. Why is it a good risk to learn new skills? **(might pay off later)**
7. Do you think most successes in life come from taking big risks?
8. Do you think people like to take risks? **(to some extent)** Why/why not?
9. What is the biggest risk you have taken?
10. What is the biggest payoff you received from a risk?

## Extension Activities:

1. Have students participate in probability experiments such as flipping a coin 100 times (to get 50 heads, 50 tails), rolling a die (do you roll each number 1/6 of the time?), and other activities. How risky is an activity if you know the probability ahead of time?
2. Have students select a particular item or product, such as a television, car, or stereo. Use information from sources such as *Consumer Reports* to check out the "risk" involved in buying it.
3. Invite a banker or someone involved in investing to talk to the class about taking risks on money. What do they consider to be high-risk investments? What are the payoffs?
4. Have students research correlations between amount of education and average annual income. Is education a good risk?

## Evaluation:

a. Give an example of a high risk with a high payoff.
b. Give an example of a low risk with a high payoff.
c. Give an example of a high risk with a low payoff.
d. Give an example of a low risk with a low payoff.

# Risks and Their Payoffs

**Directions:** Below is a list of goals and some risks that could be taken to achieve that goal. For each example, consider (a) how risky the venture is, (b) what is invested in attaining the goal (money, time, training, etc.), (c) the payoff for taking the risk, and (d) how likely this would occur. Use the first example to help complete the chart.

**Goal 1:** to make a huge amount of money

  **Risk:** buying a lottery ticket

  (a) low risk                               (c) millions of dollars

  (b) small amount of money                  (d) very unlikely

**Goal 2:** to learn to sky dive

  **Risk:** jumping out of an airplane

  (a) _____    (c)_____

  (b) _____    (d) _____

**Goal 3:** to become president of the United States

  **Risk:** going to law school, spending summers working for politicians, taking government classes in school

  (a) _____    (c)_____

  (b) _____    (d) _____

**Goal 4:** to be voted the most popular student in class

  **Risk:** only socializing with other popular students

  (a) _____    (c)_____

  (b) _____    (d) _____

**Goal 5:** to become a famous actor on Broadway

  **Risk:** moving to New York City and working in a restaurant where talent agents have been said to "hang out" to discover new talent

  (a) _____    (c)_____

  (b) _____    (d) _____